P9-BIB-283

GEORGE F. KENNAN

CONTEMPORARY AMERICAN HISTORY SERIES

WILLIAM E. LEUCHTENBURG, GENERAL EDITOR

GEORGE F. KENNAN

COLD WAR ICONOCLAST

Walter L. Hixson

Columbia University Press
New York

A portion of chapter 11 was originally published, in slightly different form, in *Diplomatic History* (Spring 1988) 12:149–163. It is used here by permission of Scholarly Resources.

Columbia University Press
New York   Oxford
Copyright © 1989 Columbia University Press
All rights reserved

Casebound editions of Columbia University Press books are Smyth-sewn
and printed on permanent and durable acid-free paper

Printed in the United States of America
c 10 9 8 7 6 5 4 3 2 1
p 10 9 8 7 6 5 4 3 2 1

To Allie and Bill, for love and inspiration.

CONTENTS

PREFACE

George F. Kennan became the intellectual spokesman for the cold war consensus in the United States with the publication of the famous "X-Article" in the July 1947 issue of *Foreign Affairs*. Writing under the pseudonym "X" to protect his State Department identity, Kennan urged a policy of "long-term, patient but firm and vigilant containment" of the Soviet Union, which he depicted as a ruthlessly expansionist communist power.[1] However, despite his success in formulating and promoting the postwar containment policy, Kennan retired from the Foreign Service in frustration in 1950. Although he remained an establishment figure, from that time on he also developed a reputation as a critic of American diplomacy.

What had become of Mr. X? As both formulator and critic, insider and outsider, Kennan has proven more than elusive to those who have tried to answer this question and assess his importance in the history of American foreign policy. Kennan is, as Ronald Steel once put it, "the nearest thing to a diplomatic legend that this country's civil service has ever produced." He has been called "a mystic" by Dean G. Acheson; "an impressionist, a poet, not an earthling" by Eugene V. Rostow; an "architect of illusion" by Lloyd C. Gardner; a "consistent" global strategist by John L. Gaddis; and "one of the principal ambiguists among the American intelligentsia" by William F. Buckley.[2]

Preface

The collective interest in Kennan on the part of the foreign affairs establishment, as well as its critics, attests to his centrality to our understanding of cold war history. Long recognized as one of the West's "foremost experts" on Russia, Kennan is also well-known as a prize-winning historian and author of a compelling two-volume memoir. His writings and accomplishments have earned him the reputation as one of "the most brilliant and civilized of students of the public scene." In addition to his role as chief ideologist of containment, Kennan also helped formulate the "realist" paradigm which called for diplomacy to be based on calculations of power and national interest rather than ideals and "legalistic-moralistic" considerations.[3]

Although the realist, corporatist, and revisionist paradigms have provided useful models for the study of American diplomatic history, none of them offers an adequate framework in which to explain Kennan. He will not be best understood as a classical realist because his outlook on foreign affairs stemmed from his alienation from American culture and society rather than from an objective analysis of power and national interest. Similarly, corporatism, with its emphasis on political and economic collaboration by elites within the public and private sectors, does not tell us very much about Kennan, who was more often than not an outsider and critic of U.S. policy. This book does reflect the influence of revisionist historiography, which called attention to American economic motives and aggressive pursuit of self-interest while refuting the traditional argument that the Soviet Union had been solely responsible for the cold war. Despite these contributions, revisionism does not offer a framework that allows for a full understanding of Kennan, who can only be explained in the context of the linkage between his attitudes about American culture and the conduct of the nation's foreign policy.[4]

Kennan's reputation as the architect of containment has actually obscured a proper understanding of him as a congenital outsider and critic: as cold war iconoclast. Thus, Kennan's success in forging the cold war consensus—anomalous when viewed in the context of his entire career—has overshadowed his penchant for challenging consensus positions on foreign affairs. Kennan's standing as an outsider, rooted in his alienation from American culture and society, provided the framework for his dissent throughout the cold war. Although he called on the United States to assume world leadership in the postwar era, Kennan actually had little faith in the ability of the United States, as a democracy, to conduct an activist foreign policy. Throughout his career Kennan struggled to resolve the contradiction between his own desire to influence U.S. diplomacy and his belief that American society lacked the subtlety and sophistication to carry out an effective foreign policy. Kennan's attitudes about American culture and society prompted his resignation from the State Department and his transformation from advocate of global containment to cold war critic and neo-isolationist.

This assessment of Kennan differs fundamentally from previous studies which have depicted him as a realist in the classical tradition and one whose perceptions did not change in any fundamental way over the course of the cold war. In a survey of postwar national security policy, historian John L. Gaddis defended containment and implied that it was only when officials ignored or misunderstood Kennan's prescriptions that American diplomacy veered down the wrong path. More recently, political scientist David Mayers extended the study of Kennan beyond the early cold war, but failed to challenge the interpretive framework established by Gaddis. Mayers argued that Kennan's career reflected both the classical conservative's preoccupation with amelioration of society as well as the realist's quest to pursue the national interest and preserve a balance of power. Both authors echoed Kennan, whose own memoir asserts, contrary to my own interpretation, that the X-Article was a misleading depiction of his views. Moreover, both Gaddis and Mayers failed, in my judgment, to understand the extent to which Kennan's strategy embraced the concept of "liberation," or rollback, of Soviet power, nor did they adequately assess the global implications and contradictions of containment.[5]

Thus, *Cold War Iconoclast* offers a new and critical interpretation of containment and of Kennan's place in American diplomatic history. As Kennan himself came to understand, containment was a flawed strategy which expected too much of the United States and produced unfortunate consequences. The division of Europe, the nuclear arms race, the focus on Soviet capabilities rather than intentions, and virtual abandonment of negotiations were among the consequences that he deplored. Ironically, however, Kennan himself had been instrumental in creating the perceptions that underlay these policies through his own alarmist depiction of the communist threat in the early cold war period. Although Kennan emerged as a cold war critic after 1948, he remained a prisoner of his visceral anticommunist perceptions and periodically lapsed into his Mr. X persona. Thus, Kennan struggled, but with only limited success, to resolve the conflict between his enmity for the Soviet communism and his quest to forge a settlement of the cold war.

. . .

During the course of this project, I have learned that research and writing are not entirely the solitary labors that I once thought them to be. Indeed, many fine historians and good friends have improved my work and made the project much more rewarding than it otherwise might have been. This book began as a dissertation at the University of Colorado under the direction of Robert D. Schulzinger, without whose friendship, advice, editorial assistance, and breadth of knowledge it would not have been possible. I am also deeply grateful to Richard H. Immerman, who encouraged my work on Kennan from the outset and who saved me from scores of errors and ambiguities through his critical review of an early draft of the manuscript. Michael S. Sherry, good friend and colleague, reviewed the revised manuscript with great skill and sensitivity and offered both wise counsel and encouragement as I completed the final version. Robert H. Wiebe analyzed an early draft of the manuscript and made several suggestions that strengthened its clarity, cohesion and force of argument. Gary W. Hess also read an early version of the manuscript and offered sensible suggestions for revisions.

I also benefited from comments and suggestions from the following scholars and friends: Martin Beglinger, Bethann Berliner, Charles Bussey, Henry Binford, Joel Blatt, Patricia Cleary, J. Garry Clifford, Mark Colvin, Susan Constanzo, David Dalton, Carolyn Dean, Elizabeth Dennison, David DiLeo, Kurk Dorsey, Virginia B. Edwards, Judith Egerton, Barbara Engel, Aaron Epstein, Pamela G. Farnsley, Robert J. Ferry, John L. Gaddis, Lloyd C. Gardner, Petra Gödde, Karen Halttunen, Lowell Harrison, Laura Hein, George C. Herring, Clarence and Natalie Kearns Hixson, Maiza Hixson, Mary Emma Hixson, Tom Hogle, Andrew C. Isenberg, James Jankowski, David Joravsky, David D. Lee, Richard W. Leopold, William Leuchtenberg, Ralph Mann, David Mayers, Sarah Maza, Arthur F. McEvoy, Samuel McSeveney, Ron and Vickie Mitchell, William Myers, Suzanne Neuschatz, Bruce Orwin, Gary Ostrower, Michael Overstreet, John Pauly, Sally Pisani, Robert and Anne-Marie Pois, Lee Scamehorn, Michael Schaller, David Schmitz, James Whiteside, C. Ben Wright, and Mark D. Zellmer.

Preface

Books do not exist without publishers and it was my good fortune to work with skilled professionals at Columbia University Press. Executive Editor Kate Wittenberg offered both sage advice and the reassurance required to tame the anxieties of a first-time author. Leslie Bialler prevented many errors and improved the book's readability through his skilled copyediting.

Two vital resources—money and archival assistance—facilitated my research on Kennan. A generous grant from the Institute for the Study of World Politics allowed me to spend the Fall of 1984 at the Seeley G. Mudd Manuscript Library in Princeton. The Society for Historians of American Foreign Relations, through its Stuart L. Bernath Dissertation Fund, and the University of Colorado, through a graduate fellowship, also provided generous financial assistance.

While at Princeton Archivist Nancy Bressler, Jean Halliday and the rest of the Mudd Library staff offered professional assistance and tolerated my mood swings over several weeks in residence. The Harry S. Truman Library Institute supplied a summer research grant and Dennis Bilger guided me to the relevant documents. Sally Marks assisted me during a couple of visits to the National Archives, where I never quite found my way around. Also helpful were the archivists at the John F. Kennedy, George C. Marshall and Yale and Columbia University Libraries.

I also wish to thank George F. Kennan, whose marvelous career inspired this book and who graciously granted me a long interview in Princeton in October 1984. This book is by no means an official biography and I know from our limited correspondence that Professor Kennan does not approve of my interpretations of some of these issues. I sympathize, more than he might imagine, with anyone who must endure an outsider's intrusion into the realm of one's own life, thought, and personal history.

Finally, I wish to acknowledge the loving support of my parents, William F. and Dr. Allie C. Hixson, two wonderful people to whom this book is affectionately dedicated.

W.L.H.
Evanston, IL.
March 1989

xiii

GEORGE F. KENNAN

What could become of such a child of the seventeenth and eighteenth centuries when he should wake up and find himself required to play the game of the twentieth?

—THE EDUCATION OF HENRY ADAMS

There is nothing more difficult to carry out, nor more doubtful of success, nor more dangerous to handle than to initiate a new order of things.

—NICCOLÓ MACHIAVELLI

I

Worldly Prejudices, 1904–1944

GEORGE FROST KENNAN'S youth and early diplomatic experience provided the framework for his approach to world affairs. Bright
and introspective as a youth, Kennan became an ambitious intellectual
who coveted recognition by higher authority, yet worked in isolation
and adhered to his own set of standards. He shared the values and the
prejudices of his mentors in the U.S. Foreign Service, yet defined himself
as an outsider and experienced difficulty resolving personal and professional demands.

Emerging as a Russian expert within the Foreign Service, Kennan
became an advocate of isolating the Soviet Union and called for Germany to anchor the European balance of power. He thus opposed
President Franklin D. Roosevelt's efforts to cooperate with the USSR
against the Axis powers in World War II. Elitism, romantic nostalgia,
contempt for democracy, alienation from urban-industrial society, and
visceral anticommunism—these were the dominant features of Kennan's
worldview as he strove to gain recognition as America's preeminent
expert on Russia.

Born in Milwaukee on February 16, 1904, Kennan was raised in a
comfortable middle-class home, but the death of his mother a few weeks
after his birth and the emotional distance maintained by his father made

for a difficult childhood. Kossuth "Kent" Kennan, a railroad attorney and income tax specialist of Scotch-Irish ancestry, fifty-two years old at his son's birth, acted "more like a grandfather" than a father to the boy and charged Kennan's three older sisters with the primary responsibility of raising him. Kent Kennan's second wife, whom he married when George was five, showed little affection for the child.[1]

Kennan was both introverted and intellectual as a child. As he recalled in his memoir, he spent his childhood in "a world that was peculiarly and intimately my own, scarcely to be shared with others or even to be made plausible to them." He was a pensive youngster and often sat for hours gazing into the distance, consumed with his own thoughts. An aunt once found this habit of his so exasperating that she exclaimed, "George, stop thinking!"[2]

In both his childhood and adult life Kennan found that his ideas and ruminations were often so intensely personal that he despaired of making them clear to others. He was not at his best in a group setting and would never be able to sustain himself in the role of a "team player"— not least because he nearly always believed his teammates were his intellectual inferiors. Early on, these inclinations led Kennan to view himself as an outsider, one who was convinced of his own intellectual superiority and yet did not really expect that his views would receive confirmation from others.

Young Kennan's penchant for solitude laid the foundations of a career as a scholar-diplomat and critic. As a boy he liked to withdraw into the attic of his home, where he would spend hours reading, writing, and reflecting on his world. This practice would carry over into his adult life, as Kennan isolated himself to write in his diary and draft essays, policy statements, and books on world affairs. In addition to his voracious reading, he showed an ability to master foreign languages at an early age, having become virtually fluent in German after a six-month period of family residence in Kassel, in central Germany, in 1912.[3]

When Kennan was twelve his father sent him to St. John's Military Academy in nearby Delafield, Wisconsin, where he learned discipline, patriotism, and respect for national service. He achieved the rank of lieutenant, played tennis and football, displayed a natural inclination for music with the guitar, and was class poet in his senior year. Despite these activities he complained of loneliness and spoke of no close friends at the school. At St. John's and later in college at Princeton, he showed himself to be shy and ill at ease in social settings.[4]

Kennan's decision to attend Princeton reflected both ambition and romanticism—two of his strongest personality traits. He selected Princeton not only because he recognized that a diploma from the elite East Coast university would enhance his career prospects but also as a result of the inspiration he derived from F. Scott Fitzgerald's *This Side of Paradise,* whose youthful protagonist, Amory Blaine, had left the Midwest to attend that school. After first failing and then having to retake portions of his entrance examinations, Kennan was the last student admitted in 1921 and found accommodations in a rooming house far off campus. The pattern was thus set from the outset: he was a loner at Princeton; "hopelessly and crudely Midwestern"; an "oddball on campus" who suffered a "cruel" ostracism from the social clubs that dominated student life. He weathered a serious bout with scarlet fever during his first year, which only compounded his isolation and unhappiness.[5]

Kennan never recovered from this bad start at Princeton. He compiled an academic record notable for its lack of distinction, given his intellectual abilities. He absented himself "heroically and self-consciously" from graduation ceremonies and "hurried off" after receiving his diploma in 1925. The unhappy performance reinforced Kennan's standing as an outsider, and he resolved to "make [his] own standards" in life, "not just accept those of other people."[6]

Having abandoned earlier plans to study law, Kennan decided to pursue a career in professional diplomacy after hearing a pitch from a Foreign Service recruiter. He had little interest in accumulating great wealth, though it was all the rage in the 1920s, and feared that he would fall into an "occupational rut" if he was not careful. A career in diplomacy responded to these concerns and would allow Kennan to pursue his interest in international politics, one of the few areas in which he had excelled in his coursework at Princeton.[7]

With these thoughts in mind he took private tutoring and passed the written and oral examinations required for entry into the U.S. Foreign Service, and at a propitious time. The 1924 Rogers Act—named for a Massachusetts congressman but pioneered by a small group of career servants—combined the once independent and feuding Diplomatic and Consular services. Reflecting a drive for efficiency and professionalism that characterized twentieth-century progressive reform, the Rogers Act established uniform salaries and procedures for recruitment, training, promotion, and pensions of foreign affairs bureaucrats. In 1926, much to his own surprise, Kennan became one of only eighteen new recruits out of several hundred original applicants to be accepted into the newly amalgamated Foreign Service.[8]

Acceptance into the Foreign Service, itself a "pretty good club," helped make up for the snubs Kennan had endured at Princeton. Diplomatic service enabled him to establish his own elite credentials, and because he shared many of the values of his colleagues in the State Department, he would not have to change his outlook to conform to group norms. Indeed, the palpable sense of snobbery, disdain for the opinions and preoccupations of the masses, and racial and ethnic discrimination of the early Foreign Service were congenial to his own way of thinking. Kennan modeled himself on elite diplomats such as Joseph C. Grew and William Phillips, veterans of America's early diplomatic service who "expected the politicians and the public to form their overseas policies in accordance with the professional diplomats' interpretation of world events." Kennan's Midwestern roots and lack of great family wealth distinguished him from many of his pampered East Coast colleagues, but he, like most of them, was a white, Anglo-Saxon Protestant with an Ivy League education.[9]

During his indoctrination into the Foreign Service Kennan mastered the techniques of political reporting, learned proper deportment, and began to develop the elegant prose style that distinguished his writings throughout his career. "The appropriate and graceful use of language," he explained in his memoir, "is one of the prime requirements of the diplomatic profession."[10] Kennan embraced all the trappings of the Western diplomatic tradition early in his career and strove to embody the good form, civility, tact, and discretion that characterize the venerable art of diplomacy. In many respects, as Kennan himself often declared over the years, style was more important than substance, means more revealing than ends.

Not content with mastering the mundane practices of everyday diplomacy, Kennan prepared himself to serve as a scholar as well as a diplomat. In recruiting his friend Charles Thayer into the Foreign Service in 1935, he explained that he would be joining a "corps of younger officers who will be scholars as well as gentlemen, who will be able to wield the

4

pen as skillfully as the tea cup."[11] Even before he began his service in Russia, Kennan had published articles on European history, geography, and literature, read all thirty volumes of Anton Chekhov's work plus six volumes of his letters, and contemplated writing the great Russian dramatist's biography. He had pored over the dispatches of nineteenth-century Western diplomats in Russia, whose observations he found pertinent to understanding contemporary Soviet society. Kennan amused Ambassador William C. Bullitt and others in the Moscow embassy by toting about a well-worn unabridged copy of Sir Edward Gibbon's classic, *The Decline and Fall of the Roman Empire,* from which he was in the habit of quoting aloud. Kennan's colleagues respected his intellect but found, as diplomat Loy Henderson put it, that "he was so engrossed in his own ideas that he never learned how to go along or get along."[12]

Although Kennan shared many of the values of his Foreign Service colleagues, the conflict between the solitary intellectual absorbed in his own thoughts and the professional diplomat charged with carrying out government policy provided a source of recurring tension throughout his diplomatic career. Early on he expressed "disgust with Uncle Sam's foreign service" and complained that diplomacy was "not a profession but a way of life . . . which must certainly stifle every real initiative, atrophy every talent, sap any strength a man might have." As a result of the tension between personal and professional demands, he became something of a chronic resigner, either submitting his resignation or threatening to do so on myriad occasions throughout his diplomatic career.[13]

Both a romantic attachment to the Russian past and the circumstances of his own birth impelled Kennan toward a career as a Soviet expert within the Foreign Service. On February 16, 1845—exactly fifty-nine years before his own birth—the first George Kennan, a cousin to George F. Kennan's grandfather, had been born. A journalist, the elder George Kennan became famous for writing an exposé on life in the frozen Siberian tundra, where the Russian tsars exiled their political prisoners. A bitter opponent of the 1917 Bolshevik Revolution, he had urged President Woodrow Wilson to undertake the 1918 Allied intervention in Russia. To honor the fame of the elder Kennan, as well as the coincidence of birthdates, the newborn's parents christened another George Kennan on that cold Milwaukee day in February 1904. For his middle name they chose Frost, not after the weather but in remembrance of the elder Kennan's traveling companion, George Frost, whose sketches of Siberian scenes complemented George Kennan's prose. Decades later, after he had matured and become famous in his own right, George Frost Kennan admitted that he had long felt that he had been "in some strange way destined to carry forward as best I could the work of my distinguished and respected namesake." [14]

Noting that a focus on Russia was in the family tradition, Kennan became the first American diplomat to receive specialized training in Russian affairs. After completing his initial seven-month Foreign Service training program, he refined his knowledge of French and German while serving in consular posts at Geneva and Hamburg before removing to Berlin to study Russian language and culture under the direction of Robert F. Kelley, head of the State Department's European Affairs division, and a corps of anti-Soviet émigrés. Kennan's mentors stressed that the Bolsheviks were a "pariah regime" bent on world conquest, and Kelley himself oozed "unremitting hostility toward the USSR." The United States had, of course, declined to recognize the Bolshevik regime and sought to isolate it behind a "cordon sanitaire" of anti-Soviet states at the Allied peacemaking councils at Versailles in 1919. [15]

Washington's official contempt for the Soviet experiment scarcely compared with that of the White Russian émigrés under whom Kennan studied at the University of Berlin's Seminar für Orientalische Sprachen, an institution created by Otto von Bismarck to prepare diplomats for foreign, and especially Oriental, assignment. The two years of training in Berlin had a "profound influence" on Kennan and shaped the attitudes he adopted toward the Soviet Union. The young diplomat identified with his émigré instructors, who romanticized the authoritarian regime of imperial Russia and insisted that the Bolsheviks "had destroyed all that was of value in Russian life." Kennan showed "extraordinary progress" in his Russian language studies but received little training in the history and theory of Marxism, except for its emphasis on atheism and world revolution. [16]

Kennan and the other young Russian specialists apprenticed in Riga, Latvia, one of the three Baltic republics that had gained independence as a result of the fall of the Russian empire in the Great War. Riga, the "window to the East," was as close as Kennan could get to Russia, as the State Department denied his request to travel inside the USSR. Ever nostalgic, he imagined that Riga itself was "in many respects a minor edition of Petersburg," populated by figures "right out of Tolstoy," and scenes "right out of Chekhov stories." He blamed the Soviets for having denied him the opportunity, enjoyed by his namesake, to experience life in tsarist Russia. While serving in Riga Kennan studied Soviet economic geography, monitored the Communist Party newspaper *Pravda*, and forwarded the names of visiting Americans who made the mistake of showing their sympathy for Bolshevism.[17]

By the time Kennan completed his service in Riga, his elitism, romantic nostalgia, and anticommunism had begun to cohere into a consistent —and in many respects reactionary—worldview. His Ivy League education and Foreign Service training had convinced Kennan that it was the duty of elites to govern society and that in a democratic society the untutored masses would prove unable to exercise effective authority over domestic and foreign affairs. Fitzgerald novels and Chekhov stories encouraged his penchant for romanticizing the past and strengthened his identification with the upper classes of both American and European societies. He could not abide communist ideology, which targeted for destruction the elite classes that Kennan himself apotheosized. The Marxist-Leninist emphasis on historical determinism, renunciation of traditional diplomacy for class struggle, and sanction of virtually any means to achieve the end of proletarian revolution were in opposition to all that Kennan held dear.[18]

Ironically, the man who became famous for his desire to contain Soviet communism actually had a greater affinity for the Russian authoritarian tradition than for the American egalitarian one. Kennan, who adhered to antidemocratic values throughout his career, declared as a young diplomat that he preferred authoritarian rule to democracy and held "no brief for the rule of the majority" in the United States. "The mass of our population [was not] sufficiently enlightened, sufficiently homogeneous in its political thought to be capable of taking responsibility for government," he asserted in a private manuscript written in 1938. Kennan called for the country to travel "along the road which leads through constitutional change to the authoritarian state" and advocated government by "an intelligent, determined ruling minority, responsible in a general sense to the people at large rather than in a direct sense to groups of politicians and lobbyists or to voters of individual districts."[19]

Kennan had nurtured his authoritarian inclinations during a stint in an Austrian sanitarium where he recovered from an attack of duodenal ulcers in 1935. He cited an Austrian social insurance law as a model of the exercise of effective central government authority that was made possible by the absence of lobbyists, "demagoguery," "public wrangling," and appeals to "the emotions and greed of the public" for which "democratic politicians" were famous. Democracy, in his view, gave release to the baser instincts of humanity and prevented cultured elites from shepherding society toward progress and enlightenment.[20]

Kennan's authoritarianism encompassed traditional attitudes on both race and gender, but the wielding of political power by women seemed to threaten him most. He proposed to restore the lost "strength and dignity" of American women by revoking their suffrage, explaining that loss of the vote would not constitute a serious blow because America would remain essentially "a matriarchy" in which women dominated social and economic affairs. "They control in large part the family [and] the nation's purse," their tastes dominated cultural life, and their lobbies made "the politicians tremble at their approach." Kennan, who had married a Norwegian woman, Annelise Sorenson, in 1931, insisted that American women had failed to live up to their responsibilities and had "ruined in large part some of the greatest aspects of [their] own sex." In comparison with women of other countries, he charged, American women were "high-strung, unsatisfied, flat-chested and flat-voiced."[21]

In addition to his sexism, Kennan shared the racial and nativist prejudices that prevailed in the Foreign Service and throughout much of American society in the first half of the twentieth century. Just as the Foreign Service elites prevented Southern and Eastern European immigrants, African-Americans, women, and Jews from joining their ranks,[22] many of these same groups (although not Jews) would constitute the nonvoting masses under Kennan's scheme of elite governance. Invoking a sense of noblesse oblige, he pledged that the ruling elite in his authoritarian society would respect the rights and needs of African-Americans and immigrants rather than abandoning them as "fodder for the rent sharks, ward heelers and confidence men of the big cities."[23]

Kennan's antidemocratic values, advocacy of elite governance, and Victorian racial and sexual mores reflected his romantic attachment to the bygone eras of European and early American history in which an aristocracy had governed, established popular tastes, and maintained a balance of power among nations. He shared the suspicions of democracy and the cultivated aristocractic bearing that seeped through the pages of

8

Gibbon's *Decline and Fall of the Roman Empire* and Alexis de Tocqueville's *Democracy in America,* two epic classics that left a deep imprint on his thinking. "For years," he observed in 1968, "Gibbon's dictum 'Under a democratical government the citizens exercise the powers of sovereignty; and those powers will be first abused, and afterwards lost, if they are committed to an unwieldy multitude' has lain at the heart of my political philosophy."[24] He was equally accepting of Tocqueville's assertion that

> a democracy finds it difficult to coordinate the details of a great undertaking and to fix on some plan and carry it through with determination in spite of obstacles. It has little capacity for combining measures in secret and waiting patiently for the result. Such qualities are more likely to belong to a single man or to an aristocracy.[25]

Throughout Kennan's career the lessons of Gibbon and Tocqueville underlay his pessimistic assessments of democratic foreign policy. Although he would summon America to world power in the postwar era, Kennan shared Tocqueville's conclusion that the United States as a great democracy lacked the patience and freedom of action to conduct an effective diplomacy. Even more compelling was Gibbon's majestic study with its tragic perspective on the decline of a great civilization. Late in his career Kennan would apply the lessons of Rome as perceived by Gibbon to pronounce his own verdict on the "decline of the West." Like Gibbon, who saw the barbarian invasion across Rome's frontiers as the logical culmination to a civilization suffering from internal decline, Kennan would attribute the decline of the West to internal decay and moral corruption.[26]

Just as Gibbon assumed the bearing of a Roman senator, Kennan identified with the national gentry of early America. He was delighted to find through his reading of the classic history *The Rise of American Civilization,* by progressive historians Charles and Mary Beard, that the founders of the American republic had also nurtured undemocratic tendencies. He declared with obvious approval that the founding fathers would

> turn over in their graves at the mere thought of the democratic principle being applied to a population containing over ten million negroes, and many more millions of southern Europeans, to whom the democratic principle is completely strange and incomprehensible.[27]

9

Worldly Prejudices

In addition to his contempt for the egalitarian tradition, Kennan was more than a little uneasy about the rapid transformation of the physical landscape and the changes in American culture and society as a result of industrialization. Confessing his "nostalgia for America's past and an uneasiness about her future," the young diplomat adjusted himself to the realities of twentieth-century urban-industrial society with great "hesitation and reluctance." Returning from service in the Soviet Union in 1938, he deplored the "aching newness and shallowness" as well as the proliferating "artificialities of urban life" that he encountered in Washington, D.C. Automobiles and commercial advertisements were the symbols of industrial society that disturbed him most. He sought the solace of a long bicycle tour in his native Wisconsin after returning that summer, but complained that the cars "whirred past me in monotonous profusion . . . hurtling gadgets, with their loads of cramped, motion-drugged humanity." As for the advertisements, it was as impossible to escape from them "as from the air itself." Their words "poured out like bullets and sought their marks on the consciousness of the individual." How could the false and misleading messages "pass off without serious social consequences?"[28]

Kennan's Old World elitism and his attitudes on race, gender, and urban-industrial society make up a portrait of a reactionary. His devotion to the past made him, in his own words, "a guest of one's time and not a member of its household."[29] Convinced that the decline of aristocratic authority had unleashed a historic epoch in which the unrefined masses would prove unable to control the forces of modernization and the changing patterns of international relations, Kennan embraced a tragic outlook on human affairs that distinguished him from his colleagues in the State Department.

The linkage he made between the nation's society and its foreign policy would play a critical role in Kennan's perceptions about postwar American internationalism. His antidemocratic values and alienation from industrial society in the United States clashed with his personal quest for influence and with his call for Washington to assume the mantle of world leadership in the postwar era. A patriotic public servant as well as an expatriate critic of American society, Kennan struggled to resolve the conflicts in his own thinking throughout the cold war.

· · ·

Nothing better illustrated the dangers of democratic foreign policy, as Kennan saw it, than the unrealistic policies adopted toward the Soviet Union during the presidency of Franklin D. Roosevelt. After sixteen years of nonrecognition of the Moscow regime, Washington normalized relations under the new president in 1933. Even before FDR took office, however, Kennan asserted that he himself had "more background and general acumen" than the "journalistic and academic experts" and "American liberals who now find the Soviets so pleasant." He was convinced that U.S.-Soviet relations should be left in the hands of experts such as himself rather than being subjected to the vagaries of the democratic political process.[30]

Roosevelt was all for elite diplomacy but his distrust of State Department professionals led him to centralize American foreign policy under his own direct authority. After first assuring himself that a majority of Americans were receptive to the idea, FDR accorded the USSR formal diplomatic recognition after a series of meetings with Soviet Foreign Minister Maxim Litvinov in Washington. Roosevelt endeared himself to the Russians by naming William Bullitt, who had urged Woodrow Wilson to grant recognition in 1919, as the first American ambassador to Moscow. With the United States mired in the Great Depression, business leaders, academics, journalists, and other leaders whose views Kennan disdained hoped to gain new Russian markets and to see the USSR balance the growing power of Germany and Japan in Europe and Asia. The Soviets shared Washington's concern about their two powerful neighbors and also coveted the legitimacy in the international community that U.S. recognition would afford.[31]

Kennan's enmity for Soviety communism outweighed realistic concerns about the belligerence emanating from Tokyo and Berlin, and he opposed recognition in a meeting of State Department Russian experts. Two years earlier he had declared that the communist and capitalist systems were "unalterably opposed," that there was "no middle ground" between them, and that "within twenty or thirty years either Russia will be capitalist or we shall be communist."[32] He argued that recognition would assist Soviet economic development and allow Moscow unfair advantage over Western businessmen because of the Kremlin's state monopoly over trade relations. Unrepentant in his memoir thirty-four years later, Kennan declared that "never—neither then nor at any other date—did I consider the Soviet Union a fit ally or associate, actual or potential, for this country." [33]

Opposition to recognition presented Kennan with a dilemma, however, as his training and expertise made him a logical choice to fill a post at the new American mission in Moscow. While on leave from Riga in Washington in 1933, he conferred with Ambassador Bullitt, who was more impressed by the young diplomat's knowledge of Russian language, culture, and economics that by his opposition to normal relations. Declaring that he was "essential" to the new mission, Bullitt arranged for Kennan, not yet thirty, to accompany him to Moscow where he extended his credentials to Soviet President Mikhail Kalinin in a Kremlin ballroom ceremony in December 1933. Although they would become bitter foes by the mid-1950s, on December 12, 1933, Bullitt was "impressed by the ability and character of a man his age" and expected Kennan to be "the wheelhorse of the embassy here." Although Kennan's initial assignment to Moscow was temporary, Bullitt and, ironically, the Soviets themselves urged that he be assigned as a permanent member of the embassy staff. Kremlin officials cited the need to retain a man who was fluent in Russian, and they also expected that Kennan would be sympathetic to their cause in view of his elder namesake's exposé of the tsarist regime. [34]

The Russians misjudged Kennan, of course, but his views on the Soviet Union were not uncomplicated. He nurtured an emotional attachment to Russia's language, culture, and people even as he denied the legitimacy of the Soviet regime, a dichotomy that was apparent throughout his career and which contributed to his frequent swings of opinion about Russia.

During the honeymoon period in Soviet-American relations in the first months after recognition, the young diplomat and his colleagues roamed the Soviet capital with relative freedom, and he, his wife, and fellow "third secretary" of the embassy, Charles "Chip" Bohlen, enjoyed "Russian-American parties in shabby Moscow apartments," dinners, operas, skiing, and ice-skating along the Moscow River. Kennan and Bohlen once assisted some young Russian thespians in a production of *The Front Page,* a fellowship they enjoyed immensely. Kennan performed well in a variety of routine diplomatic tasks and expressed pride that the Moscow embassy was one of the first "to take a primarily

intellectual and scholarly attitude" toward research and political reporting.[35]

Kennan traveled as widely as possible—to Leningrad, the Caucasus,
and elsewhere—and enjoyed the company of "ordinary Russians" even
as he lamented the passing of the imperial aristocracy and expressed
contempt for notions of proletarian progress. After touring resorts along
the Black Sea coast in 1936, he asserted that common Russians would
"make pig-sties" of the hotels and villas because of their absence of
"esthetic resources and imagination. . . . Had the fathers of the Revolution really imagined that once the upper and middle classes had been
kicked out of these watering places, the members of the proletariat
would move in and proceed to amuse themselves gracefully and with
taste?"[36]

Given his attitudes toward the Soviet regime, the "honeymoon" in
Soviet-American relations had never existed for Kennan, but it existed
for no one within a year of U.S. recognition. Disputes over the debt and
loan agreements, which had been part of the Roosevelt-Litvinov recognition process, and Soviet dictator Joseph Stalin's failure to deliver on a
promise of a new embassy site destroyed the amicable beginning to
formal diplomatic relations. Then on December 1, 1934, the assassination of Leningrad Communist Party chief Sergei Kirov signaled Stalin's
"great purge" in which 1,108 of 1,966 delegates of the 1934 Party
Congress were arrested and 98 of 139 of the congress's Central Committee members executed. Three days after Kirov's murder, as fear gripped
the Soviet capital, Kennan suffered an attack of duodenal ulcers, which
often afflicted him at stressful times, and spent most of the next year
convalescing in Vienna. By the time Stalin culminated the "revolution
from above" with a bizarre series of show trials in 1937–38, the diplomat had returned as second secretary to Bullitt's replacement, Joseph
Davies.[37]

The appointment of Davies, a wealthy attorney and contributor to
Roosevelt's campaigns, angered Kennan and the other professional diplomats who considered the new ambassador a naïve political appointee.
Davies was more charitable in his assessment of Kennan, whom he
judged "an exceptionally able man, thoroughly familiar with Russian
conditions here." Davies had Kennan translate, as well as "fetch his
sandwiches," at the 1937 purge trial of seventeen alleged "anti-Soviet

Trokskyite" conspirators, former Bolsheviks whose forced confessions to treason convinced Kennan that "the Russian mind . . . carried both truth and falsehood to such infinite extremes that they eventually meet in space, like parallel lines, and it is no longer possible to distinguish between them." But the lawyer Davies, mesmerized by the Soviet legal system and the "terrific . . . human drama," found credence in the conspiracy charges.[38]

To Kennan's mind, Davies reflected the naïveté and unprofessionalism that not only characterized Roosevelt's diplomacy toward Russia but also raised serious doubts about the ability of a democracy to conduct a realistic foreign policy. Preoccupied with domestic political constituencies, the administration had failed to understand that the barbaric and imperialistic Stalin regime was engaged in a "battle for power pure and simple" and cared nothing for "principles, ideals [and] human lives." Instead of confronting these realities, as Kennan saw it, the administration had sacrificed its best source of information on Russia by abolishing the Eastern European Affairs division in 1937 and exiling his former mentor, Robert Kelley, to a post in Turkey. Kennan refused to accept the bureaucratic rationale for the State Department reorganization and later offered the baseless charge in his memoir that it reflected "the smell of Soviet influence" inside the U.S. government.[39]

Kennan drew on a simplistic reading of Russian history to bolster his contention that the Soviet regime was not one with which the West could expect to conduct normal diplomatic relations. Whereas the West had inherited a superior religious and cultural tradition from Rome, according to Kennan's Gibbonesque perspective, the Russian mentality had been shaped by the dogmatism, cruelty, backwardness, and "utter lack of the chivalrous spirit" of Byzantium. Centuries of invasion by "Asiatic hordes" contributed to Moscow's congenital suspicion of foreigners and to its "acute and abnormal sense of 'face' and dignity." These characteristics gave Russia all the traits of "a typical oriental despotism," which meant that it could not be trusted nor expected to respect Western ways and traditions.[40]

Disgusted with American naïveté toward Russia, Kennan requested a reassignment in 1937, which Davies granted with the observation that the young diplomat had been in Moscow "too long for his own good." Assigned to occupy the "Russian desk" in the European Affairs division, Kennan returned to Washington and, when Davies himself resigned in

1938, recommended that no successor be named as a means of protesting the harassment of Western diplomats in Moscow. Before he departed, Kennan and some of his colleagues had apprehended an embassy doorman planting a bugging device, one of many such provocations they were forced to endure. He argued that the Soviets had demeaned the "dignity of the ambassadorial title" through their actions and Washington should deliver a signal of its refusal to bow to such byzantine intrigues. Assistant Secretary of State George Messersmith considered Kennan "one of the finest of our younger officers" but rejected the advice to leave the ambassadorship unfilled, and Roosevelt appointed Laurence Steinhardt to replace Davies in 1939.[41]

As events in Europe cascaded toward a second world war, the combination of Kennan's anti-Sovietism and his Germanophilism led to a dramatic underestimation of Hitler and the Nazis. Kennan was no fascist, but he respected authoritarianism and thought the Germans could anchor a stable, anticommunist order in East-Central Europe—a position to which he was to cling until well after World War II. Kennan had mastered the German language and resided for extended periods in Berlin, where he had met his wife, and in Hamburg, a vantage point that had allowed him in 1927–28 to witness "the immense moral and intellectual agony of the Weimar Republic [which] was enacted daily, like a drama, before one's eyes." In 1931 he declared that the Germans were "the final hope . . . [and] now the final despair of western European civilization."[42]

Kennan's emotional ties to Germany blinded him to the reality of Nazi fanaticism. In 1935 he declared that Hitler's territorial ambitions reflected a legitimate desire to unite the German-speaking regions of Europe, and that it would take "the wildest stretch of the imagination" to suppose that Hitler sought expansion into Russia. While imputing rational aims to the Führer, he asserted that the Soviets, as "revolutionary communists," were "the most unalterable opponent of any effective peace in the West" and predicted that Moscow would avoid direct involvement in war in order to serve "in the capacity of a vulture" in the aftermath of conflict.[43]

Unable to convince officials in Washington that Russia, not Germany, posed the greatest threat to American national interests, Kennan requested another reassignment and became second secretary of the American legation in Czechoslovakia. He arrived in Prague on September 29,

1938, the very day that the Munich conference compromised Czech independence. Kennan's dispatches from the Czech capital reflected a remarkable insensitivity to the brutal Nazi occupation and the ensuing pogrom against Jews. The removal of Jews from government posts did not concern him because, he explained in February 1939, the action applied only to a "small" number of "full-blooded Jews." By contrast, Soviet harassment of a small number of American businessmen and diplomats had elicited an outraged response. Kennan and his wife tried to dissuade a Czechoslovakian Jew, "a pitiful figure of horror and despair," from suicide, "not because she or I had any great optimism with respect to his chances for future happiness but partly on general Anglo-Saxon principles and partly to preserve our home from this sort of an unpleasantness."[44] Kennan's strong sense of nostalgia found him lamenting the demise of "the limited degree of unity which the Hapsburg empire represented" before World War I, and he was not averse to great-power domination of Czechoslovakia, as long as it was German and not Russian.[45]

Kennan's theoretical "realism" on foreign affairs, for which he would become famous in the 1950s, depended on the establishment of a calculated balance of power and avoided such "idealistic" preoccupations as democracy, self-determination and world government. The diplomat wanted Germany to anchor the European balance of power, however, and he would experience enormous difficulty accommodating himself to the decline of German power and the extension of Soviet influence in the postwar period. Thus emotional preoccupations often structured Kennan's "realistic" approach.

Even though the outbreak of war in Europe brought him to the belated realization that "the Nazi system is built on the assumption that war, not peace, represents the normal condition of mankind," Kennan still rejected cooperation with Moscow. In the aftermath of Operation Barbarossa, Hitler's June 22, 1941, invasion of Russia, he opposed following the British lead by offering "moral support" to the Russians, whose signing of the Nazi-Soviet Pact dividing Eastern Europe into spheres of influence in 1939 had aided Hitler's belligerent course. Association with Stalin, he argued, "would lend to the German war effort a gratuitous and sorely needed aura of morality" and would link the United States with "a regime which is widely feared and detested," even by its own people.[46]

By the time of Pearl Harbor, Kennan had been reassigned to Berlin to report on Nazi aggression. Germany declared war on the United States four days after Pearl Harbor, and the Gestapo interned Kennan and 130 other Americans at Bad Nauheim, near Frankfurt. Second in command to Chargé d'Affaires Leland Morris, Kennan displayed leadership under pressure as he supervised the internees in their dank hotel, fielded complaints about the cold and the food, organized a band ("Kennan's Kats"), church services, and recreational events. After it was over, detainees declared that he had shown "unfailing understanding in handling troublesome day-to-day problems" and indeed had been "the strongest man" during more than five months of their captivity at Bad Nauheim.[47]

Upon his release in May 1942, Kennan grew bitter over his status in the Foreign Service, particularly when he learned that the government had refused to pay his salary for the time in confinement on the ludicrous grounds that he had not been "working." Although he was eager for advancement, Kennan was out of step with the Roosevelt administration's diplomacy and thus frustrated in his desire to influence policy. Upon hearing of his assignment as counsellor of the legation at Lisbon, the ambitious diplomat complained of the "waste" of his talent "plugging away at administrative jobs" while others "achieved public prominence." He probably had in mind his friend and fellow Soviet expert Charles Bohlen, who had been selected as Roosevelt's interpreter at the wartime conferences. Kennan longed to gain the kind of recognition that Bohlen had achieved and to put himself in a position to voice his opposition to the wartime collaboration with Moscow.[48]

Kennan, after reluctantly assuming his post in Portugal, still managed to make his presence felt at the White House. He familiarized himself with Portuguese history and politics and concluded that America's desire for air bases in the Azores (an island group 900 miles west of Portugal) might compromise Portuguese president Antonio Salazar's neutrality in the war. In direct violation of his instructions from Washington, Kennan assured Salazar—a dictator whose authoritarianism he respected—that the United States would turn over possession of the air bases to Portugal after the war. He was willing to "take full personal responsibility" for his insubordination but asked to return to Washington "to explain, if necessary personally to the president." Recalled in October 1943, Kennan weathered a tongue-lashing from Secretary of War Henry Stimson but won Roosevelt's support for his position after a brief meeting with the President. His assertive diplomacy reduced the risk of conflict with Salazar, which might have upset planning for the 1944 Normandy invasion. His handling of the incident showed both Kennan's faith in his own convictions and his willingness to go to considerable lengths to make himself heard and see his positions vindicated by the ultimate authority.[49]

Following the appointment of a new ambassador to Portugal in 1943, the State Department assigned Kennan to London to serve as a political adviser to John G. Winant, the ambassador to Britain and the American delegate on the European Advisory Commission, which was to coordinate surrender terms and Allied occupation policy. After a brief hospital stay caused by a flare-up of his ulcers, Kennan began looking into the proposed occupation zones in Germany and found that those claimed by the U.S. Joint Chiefs of Staff conflicted with an Anglo-Soviet boundary agreement. He returned to Washington and, in a remarkable accomplishment for a junior Foreign Service officer, arranged a second meeting with the President. Informed of the snafu over the occupation zones during their April 3 meeting, Roosevelt chuckled at the young diplomat's anxiety and confessed that the proposed occupation zones were "just something I once drew on the back of an envelope." FDR redefined the zones in a letter to Winant, but the State Department, appalled at Kennan's effrontery, sent the "physically exhausted" diplomat on a long vacation.[50]

By this time Kennan had lost all faith in the Roosevelt administration's handling of the war and was openly critical of the Grand Alliance that united Washington, London, and Moscow against the Axis powers. The Soviet expert did support the extension of lend-lease to the USSR, noting that "the maximum military support of the Russians is inexorably dictated by circumstances and cannot be questioned," but he sharply opposed the Allied war aim of "unconditional surrender." Kennan feared that the policy would prolong the war, destroy the German state, and render all of Europe vulnerable to Soviet influence and a succession of communist dictatorships. He said nothing about the possibility of a separate peace between Russia and Germany, an event which had occurred in the midst of World War I and which FDR sought to avoid through the devices of the Grand Alliance and unconditional surrender. Kennan had no faith in Roosevelt's plans for a postwar order based on cooperation among the great powers—the "four policemen" (including

China)—and he was convinced that FDR's approach to the war merely played into Stalin's plans for the extension of Soviet influence in the postwar era.[51]

Thus, by the time he was sent on his long vacation in 1944, Kennan had served with ability and distinction in a variety of diplomatic posts, but his elitism, nostalgia, antidemocratic values, and faith in his own perceptions about Russian and foreign affairs frequently found him out of step with U.S. government policy. He had been frustrated in his efforts to shape policy toward Moscow and to gain the recognition and advancement that he thought he deserved. Kennan would continue to chafe over what he considered Washington's naïve policies toward Russia, but he never stopped striving to make himself heard. In time his persistence would pay off. Kennan would seize the opportunity to become the intellectual spokesman for an epoch of confrontation with the Soviet Union and world communism.

II

Forging the Consensus

KENNAN DEVOTED his twenty-two months in the American embassy in Moscow between 1944 and 1946 to opposing the wartime *mariage de convenance* with the Kremlin. Alarmed by the threat of postwar Soviet expansion, he charged that Stalin was exploiting the Grand Alliance to extend Kremlin influence and called for an open declaration of separate spheres of influence. Within months of the Allied victory, officials in Washington embraced Kennan's perceptions. His famous Long Telegram from Moscow, which advocated containment of the Soviet Union, assumed the aura of official policy while elevating him to prominence in the foreign affairs establishment.

Kennan played a critical role in forging a consensus for containment through his series of essays and lectures from 1944–1947. He called on the Western powers to employ a variety of means to contain the Soviet ideological-political threat. Kennan argued that such a policy would not only halt Kremlin expansionism but also set in motion a process that would either force Moscow to capitulate or lead to the destruction of the Soviet regime. Kennan made this point in the famous "X-Article," whose publication in the July 1947 issue of *Foreign Affairs* culminated his effort to refocus American diplomacy toward containment of the putative Soviet threat. Ironically, Kennan—a perennial outsider—would become the chief ideologist for postwar American internationalism.

In the summer of 1944, Kennan returned to Moscow, this time as minister-counsellor of the American embassy. W. Averell Harriman, the U.S. ambassador since the previous October, had first wanted Charles Bohlen assigned to the post, but failed because he was needed in Washington. Himself a businessman untrained in the Russian language or culture, Harriman explained to Roosevelt at the Teheran Conference that it was "of real importance" that he get Kennan as number two, to oversee the everyday operations of the embassy. FDR's envoy even promised to make arrangements for an "ulcer diet" in order to persuade Kennan to return to Moscow. He accepted the assignment and made his way to the Soviet capital via Teheran and Stalingrad, where the ruins of the pivotal battle of the war revived his dichotomous image of the proud Russian people struggling under the tyranny of a cynical regime.[1]

Although the Russians and the Americans had collaborated successfully against the Nazis, the strains within the Grand Alliance were all too evident to the diplomats in Moscow. Harriman and Kennan received little cooperation from Soviet officials on such problems as the denial of requests to use American aircraft in Russia and to obtain exit visas for Russian women who had married Americans, the detention of embassy pouches by Soviet officials, the censorship of American press reports from the USSR, the transfer of lend-lease materials to third parties, the myriad disputes over deportations and defections, and the difficulties over provision and repatriation of the prisoners of war of both countries. According to his autobiography, Harriman persisted in pressing American demands on these issues "long after George Kennan had given way to these frustrations" and abandoned all hope of negotiating with the Kremlin.[2]

If the Soviet bureaucracy frustrated Kennan, Stalin's territorial ambitions along Russia's vast borders were positively alarming. As Soviet political power followed in the wake of the Red Army in Eastern Europe in the summer of 1944, Kennan declared that "the jealous eye of the Kremlin can distinguish, in the end, only vassals and enemies; and the neighbors of Russia, if they do not wish to be the one, must reconcile themselves to being the other."[3]

In one of a series of essays he wrote in opposition to the Grand

Alliance, Kennan asserted that Stalin's refusal "to pursue a decent, humane and cooperative policy in Europe" left the "Anglo-Saxon powers" no choice but to secure "the division of Western Europe into spheres of influence." He argued (in something of an understatement) that the Nazi invasion had touched a "sensitive nerve" that now prevented the Russians from being "entirely reasonable" in their quest for a "fairly extensive sphere of influence in certain neighboring areas of Europe and Asia." He doubted that the Kremlin leaders had decided "exactly how far this sphere will extend, and are waiting partly to see how we will react to their efforts toward expansion."[4]

Kennan's recommendations in this essay went to the heart of the postwar containment strategy. He urged American leaders to act in concert with the British and other allies to draw a line "beyond which we cannot afford to permit the Russians to exercise unchallenged power," and warned that the Western powers "must be prepared to use all means at our disposal to maintain our position." With victory in Europe and Asia only a matter of time by the fall of 1944, Kennan had begun to formulate a strategy to contain Soviet power in the postwar period. He had been frustrated in his efforts to influence American policy toward Russia throughout the war, however, and had little confidence that his message would find a receptive audience in Washington.[5]

The smashing of the Warsaw uprising by the Nazis in the late summer of 1944 angered U.S. embassy personnel in Moscow and prompted Kennan to take up his pen for another assault on the wartime alliance with the Kremlin, which had offered no assistance to the Polish rebels.[6] In "Russia—Seven Years Later"—the title reflecting his personal odyssey to and from his posts in Moscow—Kennan railed against the simplistic perceptions of the USSR that prevailed in America. Stressing the continuities of Russian foreign policy over the centuries, he depicted Stalin as a "shrewd and pitilessly realistic" despot who sought the same "territorial and political expansion which had once commended itself so strongly to Tsarist diplomatists." Now that Russia had survived the Nazi onslaught, Stalin intended to restore the historic Russian empire, including the Baltic states, Poland, and all of Slavic Europe, and to control the Dardanelles. Power carried more weight than ideology with the Russians, who did not care "whether a given area is 'communistic' or not" so long as it was under Soviet control. Simple-minded Americans spoke of the need to "understand Russia," but had no place for the

American who was "really willing to undertake this disturbing task." Kennan felt that he stood alone "on a chilly and inhospitable mountaintop where few have been before, where few can follow, and where few will consent to believe that he has been."[7]

Ironically, despite the strong sense of alienation he expressed in "Russia—Seven Years Later," the essay marked the point at which Kennan began to make in imprint on American policy. Heretofore, his anti-Sovietism had been "very definitely discouraged by Harriman, who derived considerable amusement from Kennan's earnestness in the matter," but the Warsaw uprising had shaken the ambassador's faith in cooperation with Russia. Although he still opposed Kennan's call for dispensing with the Grand Alliance, Harriman forwarded the diplomat's essay to Washington and urged the administration to curb Moscow's expansionism with American economic power. Under the influence of Kennan's anti-Soviet reports, Harriman—who was to exert a strong influence on Harry S. Truman after Roosevelt's death—would adopt a *quid pro quo* approach to Russia as the war came to an end.[8]

Roosevelt and British Prime Minister Winston Churchill still preferred collaboration over confrontation, at least until the war's end. Concerned over the surrender to Russia of Romania, Finland, and Bulgaria and the impending liberation of Greece, Yugoslavia, and Hungary, Churchill agreed with Stalin to divide southeastern Europe into spheres of influence. Roosevelt embraced the October 1944 Balkan "percentages agreement" and remained hopeful about postwar cooperation with Stalin.[9] Hence the Allied leaders essentially followed the spheres-of-influence approach advocated by Kennan while maintaining the façade of self-determination. Such distinctions were important, however, as the American public continued to nurture naïve perceptions of the Soviet Union and "Uncle Joe" Stalin.[10]

As the war ground toward its conclusion, Kennan continued to point out instances of Soviet unilateralism to support his call for an open break in East-West relations. He warned that Russia was encouraging Communist and sympathetic parties and pursuing land reform while manipulating the internal affairs of occupied nations through its domination of the Allied control commissions.[11] Moscow would make Romania "pay through the nose" for the participation of its troops in the Ukraine invasion, for "its non-Slavic racial origin and Latin Catholic cultural traditions," and for the lack of "affection" shown to the liberating Red Army. The Russians would loot the country, undermining its independence and making it amenable to Soviet influence. After conversations with Russian officials in November, Kennan hoped that Allied protests would result in a more reasonable and cooperative Soviet attitude, but this flash of optimism disappeared when Kremlin officials removed property belonging to a Romano-American oil company in Bucharest, thus displaying their "complete disrespect for the views that our government has expressed." Kennan's protest to Soviet Foreign Minister Vyacheslav Molotov elicited the response that the oil company had been German-owned since 1940 and was thus subject to Soviet plunder.[12]

Yearning for a policy of "manly" confrontation, Kennan recommended that Washington withdraw from Allied control commissions in which it had no real voice in Czechoslovakia, Bulgaria, and Hungary and cease cooperation in China, where Stalin sought "a minimum of foreign influence other than Russian." Instead of pursuing tripartite agreement in Austria, the United States should occupy its zones as a display of resolve. The Soviets "could hardly be successful for long" in their own occupation zone, he explained, "if the remainder of the country were to turn out to be more orderly and prosperous."[13] This comment reflected Kennan's belief that exposure to a superior Western model would arouse opposition to communism within occupied areas and lead to the "liberation"[14] of states under Soviet influence.

In Washington, as Charles Bohlen prepared to accompany Roosevelt to the Yalta summit, Kennan tried to convince his colleague of the inevitability of East-West confrontation in the postwar period. Kennan sounded like an "Open Door" revisionist historian as he argued that the United States and Britain, as commercial Atlantic powers, required the maintenance of "a stable, adjusted, forward-looking Central Europe," interests that were in "basic conflict" with those of Russia, a "jealous Eurasian land power, which must always seek to extend itself to the West and will never find a place, short of the Atlantic Ocean, where it can from its own standpoint safely stop." Rejecting Kennan's "naïve" advice, Bohlen countered that Soviet intentions were "not yet clear" and admonished that "quarreling with them would be so easy, but we can always come to that."[15]

The accession of Harry Truman to the presidency on April 12, 1945, did not change American policy overnight, but the new President meant to be "firm in his dealings with the Soviet Government."[16] Truman adopted a more confrontational style than Roosevelt and challenged Stalin's plans to install pro-Soviet puppets in Eastern Europe. Although Truman, bumptious and inexperienced in foreign affairs, was hardly the sort of cultivated elite that Kennan envisioned in executive leadership, before the end of his first year the new President would adopt the approach toward the Soviet Union that Kennan had long advocated.

When the war in Europe came to an end, Kennan appeared on May 9, 1945, in Harriman's absence, on the embassy balcony to salute a crowd of cheering Muscovites that had assembled below. Moved by the display of emotion on the part of ordinary Russians, he ordered a Soviet flag draped next to the American flag and shouted, "congratulations on the day of victory. All honor to the Soviet allies." However, according to American reporter Ralph Parker—who later renounced the West to write Soviet propaganda—Kennan muttered during the celebration that while the war against Germany was over, the real war was only beginning. Although in his memoir Kennan describes the reporter's claim as a "dreamlike distortion," such a statement would have been consistent with his views at the time.[17]

To Kennan the end of the war marked an almost apocalyptic turning point and the arguments he expressed at the time presaged those he would make in the 1947 X-Article. The West had within its power, Kennan declared in May 1945, the ability to compel a retreat culminating in the overthrow of the Kremlin's "antiquated system of government," but if it failed to act, Moscow would seize the initiative in world affairs.[18] The Soviet Union depended on constant expansion for its survival, but the areas that Stalin sought to incorporate had once "proved indigestible to Tsardom," and the "shades of Nicholas I" were now present once again. Citing Gibbon's discussion of the struggles of the Roman emperors to maintain authority over their distant provinces, Kennan predicted that within "five or ten years" Russia would be "overshadowed . . . by clouds of civil disintegration."

He argued that Moscow could not hope to maintain its empire unless it continued to receive both "moral and material assistance from the West," which meant that the Western democracies represented "the greatest and most powerful auxiliary instrument" of Russian expansionism. The United Nations Organization sanctioned Soviet hegemony; extensive material support from the West allowed the Kremlin to recover and consolidate its power; and the Western powers had shown that they could "always be depended upon to collaborate enthusiastically in this appeasement." However, if, "contrary to all normal expectations," the West mustered the "political manliness" to withdraw its support, Russia would "probably not be able to maintain its hold successfully for any length of time over all the territory over which it has today staked out a claim." Reduced to a "baring of the fangs," the Soviet regime, lacking air and naval power, would be contained and ripe for liberation.[19]

While Kennan envisioned nothing less than the demise of the Soviet regime, officials in Washington initiated a clumsy policy designed to capitalize on America's preponderant economic power. Kennan advocated economic pressure even though, unlike Harriman, he doubted that such measures alone could redirect Soviet foreign policy. He approved of Truman's decision to terminate lend-lease aid and to deny credits and assistance to Russia through the American-dominated United Nations Relief and Recovery Agency, the International Monetary Fund and the World Bank. Creation of the IMF and the World Bank at the 1944 Bretton Woods Conference afforded Washington unparalleled influence over the world economy.[20]

Kennan categorically opposed all of the wartime summits, which he viewed as forums for the appeasement of Stalin. While the Yalta Conference in February 1945 marked the apogee of the Grand Alliance, in Kennan's view the summit merely sanctioned Russian domination of postwar Europe and he wondered whether a "compromise peace" with Nazi Germany might represent a more favorable prospect.[21] Kennan displayed equal contempt for efforts to reach agreement on a reunited Germany at the Potsdam Conference in July and August 1945. He insisted that "the idea of a Germany run jointly with the Russians is a chimera" and recommended that the Western allies denounce Soviet unilateralism in eastern Germany while making it clear "that we now consider ourselves free to dispose of German territory in the west . . . without reference to the views of the Soviet Government." Although Truman, British Prime Minister Clement Atlee and Stalin agreed to treat Germany as a single economic unit, the creation of separate occupation zones actually set in motion the process of dividing the Reich. The Potsdam decisions on the German boundary, including Polish annexation of East Prussia and Russia's absorption of the Baltic port city of Königsberg, fueled Kennan's contempt for the Grand Alliance.[22]

Instead of sanctioning Soviet ambitions at summit conferences, the United States had an opportunity, as Kennan saw it, to bury the legacy of prewar isolationism for a policy of active world leadership, if only it would seize the initiative. He decried American "appeasement" and asserted that the nation was losing "the moral leadership of Europe which was ours for the taking, which everyone wanted us to assume, which our national interests demanded we should assume." Collaboration and material assistance were helping the Russians establish a European hegemony "no less hostile to our interests than would have been the hegemony of Germany." The diplomat called for an "active" policy of opposing Soviet expansionism and demanded that his prescriptions "receive something more than the polite admixture of resignation and pity with which the opinions of experts on matters of foreign policy are customarily consigned to the Department's files." The United States, he declared, must "teach the Russians to respect us," not by attempts to "act chummy with them" or through "fatuous gestures of goodwill" but through assertions of power. "It may be bad practice to take a sledge hammer to swat a fly," he allowed, but "with the Russians it is sometimes necessary."[23]

Angry over his nation's refusal to break with Russia even after the surrender of Japan, Kennan submitted his resignation in August 1945. "Anyone who sees the problems of our diplomacy as I do," he explained to Bohlen, "can do more to achieve their solution outside the framework of the Foreign Service than inside it." To H. Freeman ("Doc") Matthews, director of State's European Affairs Division, Kennan expressed his frustration over the "squandering of the political assets won at such cost by our recent war effort, our failure to follow up our victories politically and over the obvious helplessness of our career diplomacy to exert any appreciable influence on American policy." Officials in Washington held in abeyance the letter of resignation from the talented but temperamental Russian expert.[24]

The failure in London of the Big Three foreign ministers to resolve their differences over European questions in September 1945 foreshadowed the undoing of the Grand Alliance and thus raised Kennan's spirits. The absence of accord had come as a "distinct shock" and produced a "definite staleness" in the Kremlin, declared Kennan, who hoped that the combination of the stalled negotiations and the loss of material assistance from the West would prompt the unraveling of the

Stalin regime that he had forecast in May. "If anything could test [the] unity of [the] Kremlin," he explained, "this would be it."[25] Kennan opposed Secretary of State James F. Byrnes' attempts to salvage the Grand Alliance, suspecting with some justification that his "main purpose is to achieve some sort of an agreement, he doesn't much care what," and he was delighted when Byrnes failed to achieve accord.[26]

In the Truman White House, Chief of Staff Admiral William D. Leahy and Navy Secretary James V. Forrestal shared the perceptions of the Soviet Union that had long governed Kennan's outlook. Republican Senator Arthur S. Vandenberg of Michigan, a critical player in the nation's bipartisan foreign policy, stepped up his criticisms of Russia and State Department experts on the Near East issued almost daily warnings about Soviet designs on Turkey and Iran, pinpointing the next front in the emerging cold war.[27] When Truman himself declared in January 1946 that he was "tired of babying the Soviets" and rejected further compromise, the Grand Alliance was history.[28]

State Department officials recognized that the nation was now adopting the policy toward Russia long advocated by Kennan and they responded favorably to a January 29 telegram in which he had called for a reappraisal of the "basic thinking which lies behind [the] present Soviet approach to overall questions of international affairs."[29] After Stalin trumpeted Russian military power in a speech in February and declared that future conflict with capitalist powers were inevitable, those who had forgotten about such Marxist-Leninist verities during the wartime alliance expressed shock. At the same time the Treasury Department wanted to know why the USSR had declined to participate in the IMF and the World Bank. Concluding that Kennan was the man to answer these questions, "Doc" Matthews invited the diplomat to assess the motives behind Soviet foreign policy and later claimed credit for having "engineered" the stunning impact of Kennan's "Long Telegram" from Moscow.[30]

The Long Telegram reflected no intellectual departures for Kennan, whose basic perceptions had been formed and articulated in his wartime essays and dispatches. However, for the first time the diplomat, accustomed to being ignored, had been *asked* to submit an analysis and "now, by God, they would have it."[31] Bedridden with one of his frequent illnesses, Kennan dictated the 8,000-word telegram to his secretary on February 22 and designated it "Eyes Only, President and Secretary of

State." Nevertheless, it would soon be read by thousands. The message depicted an unstable, xenophobic Soviet regime whose very survival depended on expansion, particularly along its own borders. He argued that throughout history Russian rulers—"neurotic," "insecure," and fearful of comparison with the West—had sought to insulate Russia from Western influence by establishing buffer zones along its borders. Marxist ideology, "a dogma which pictures the outside world as evil, hostile, and menacing" yet carrying the seeds of its own destruction, merely served as a "fig leaf" that justified the naked despotism of the regime. Soviet leaders employed communist ideology to justify the exercise of "military and police power in [the] Russian state, for that isolation of [the] Russian population from the outside world, and for that fluid and constant pressure to extend [the] limits of Russian police power which are together the natural and instinctive urges of Russian rulers."

Given these "realities," Soviet behavior in the future would be characterized by intensive military industrialization; constant pressure for expansion; manipulation of the UN; assaults on Western colonialism; and economic autarchy in the Soviet Union and its satellite states.

On the "subterranean plane," Stalin directed "an underground operating directorate of world communism, a concealed Comintern" that sought to expand Soviet influence through association with Communist parties, front organizations, labor unions, national associations, racial organizations, cultural groups, women's clubs, and liberal magazines in nations across the globe. In its unceasing drive to undermine order and stability in the West, the Kremlin would seek "to disrupt national self-confidence, to hamstring measures of national defense, to increase social and industrial unrest, to stimulate all forms of disunity." Moscow would deny all responsibility for its subversion, allowing the Soviet Union to pursue an outward façade of cooperation while its agents fomented international revolution. The Kremlin, he explained, "desires that its power should be felt but not seen."[32]

The Long Telegram depicted a manichean world pitting the West against "a political force committed fanatically to the belief that with us there can be no permanent *modus vivendi*," but Kennan held out the promise of victory. Containing the Soviet threat posed "undoubtedly [the] greatest task our diplomacy has ever faced and probably the greatest it will ever have to face," but the Western powers needed only to muster their political will in order to compel a Soviet retreat and the eventual liberation of Russia itself from communism. Although impervious to reason, the Kremlin was "highly sensitive to [the] logic of force" and remained "by far the weaker force." As realists, the Russians could be expected to withdraw when confronted by superior power. Moreover, Kennan argued, picking up the theme of previous essays, once contained the Soviet regime would find its internal weaknesses exposed in sharp contrast to the superior Western model. As he had done before and would do so again in the 1947 "X-Article," Kennan argued in the Long Telegram that containment of Soviet expansion was the first step toward liberation—the destruction of the Communist regime. The "success of [the] Soviet system as form of internal power is not yet finally proven," he declared.[33]

"Doc" Matthews circulated Kennan's "magnificent" telegram to officials throughout the State Department, where the document met with universal acclaim. Such was its revelatory power that one State Department official advised that Kennan's telegram was "not subject to condensation" and had to be "read in full." "There was a universal feeling that 'this was it,' " recalled diplomat Louis Halle, that "this was the appreciation of the situation that had been needed." Diplomat Loy Henderson declared that Kennan's argument "hits the nail on the head," Byrnes praised its "splendid analysis," and Forrestal made it "required reading" for hundreds of military officers. Kennan had put into words and authoritative tones an interpretation of Soviet behavior that a consensus of decision makers in Washington had come to share.[34]

The Long Telegram elevated Kennan from obscurity to influence in the foreign affairs bureaucracy of the United States. The outsider at his boyhood military academy, at Princeton, and in his campaign against the Grand Alliance suddenly found himself forging the containment consensus. The State Department sent copies of his telegram to diplomatic missions around the world, lending his interpretations of Russian history and his call for confronting Soviet expansionism the aura of official policy. The Long Telegram provided the first of several lifelong demonstrations that Kennan was a man who could command influence through the force of his arguments and the power of his prose.

Even as the State Department circulated telegram number 711 from Moscow to its embassies overseas, Kennan's perceptions of Russia appeared vindicated by events in the Near East and by Winston Churchill's historic declaration on March 5, 1946, that an "iron curtain" had descended across the European continent. The USSR violated an Allied agreement requiring the departure of foreign troops from Iran by March 2 and agreed to leave only after receiving promises of an oil concession, which were later rejected by the Iranian parliament. Washington condemned the Soviet Union for its actions in Iran before the UN Security Council and Truman approved of Churchill's public advocacy of Western military preparedness and the "fraternal association of the English speaking peoples," calls which Stalin not unreasonably interpreted as the basis for an anti-Soviet alliance.[35] The Communist Party newspaper *Pravda* called Churchill a "convinced reactionary" while castigating his proposal for a new "cordon sanitaire" and Kennan reported that the Soviet response to Churchill's address "represents [the] most violent Soviet reaction I can recall to any foreign statement."[36]

Kennan took advantage of his sudden popularity in the wake of the Long Telegram to press for reassignment under the threat of resignation. He complained of suffering from the "grippe" in the "sunless, vitamin-less environment" of Moscow, where the "demands of work leave no time for leisure or relaxation." He importuned State Department officials to reassign him to London or to make him the head of a Foreign Service training center in the United States, declaring that if action was not soon taken "I am afraid I will have to submit [a] telegraphic resignation and ask to be relieved by May 1."[37] State Department officials decided that Kennan was uniquely qualified to educate Americans on the need to confront Soviet ambitions. "There isn't anyone anywhere, connected with the Foreign Service, who is today in such a key position to be of assistance on certain vital problems we are now facing," Assistant Secretary of State William Benton declared. He offered Kennan "any kind of responsibility or position we could open up for you here in the State Department."[38]

The Truman administration decided to make Kennan the point man in a campaign to sell both official and public audiences on the need to contain the Soviet Union. Returning to Washington in April 1946, the diplomat assumed the post of "deputy for foreign affairs" at the new National War College in Washington D.C. Vice Admiral Harry Hill, the War College commandant, had asked Byrnes to provide the college with an experienced Foreign Service officer to instruct its 100 students (thirty from each of the three military services and ten from the State Department) and was "delighted" to get Kennan. The War College assignment provided Kennan an opportunity to study and lecture before official audiences and to travel across the nation to promote containment.[39]

The driving force behind the War College was Navy Secretary Forrestal, a fervent anti-communist, advocate of military preparedness, and benefactor to Kennan. A Roman Catholic and former investment banker, Forrestal asserted that Soviet communism was "as incompatible with democracy as Nazism or fascism." Indeed, he was so obsessed with the Russian menace that it contributed to his mental illness and suicide in 1949. Impressed by the Long Telegram, Forrestal attended many of Kennan's War College lectures and circulated the diplomat's interpretations of Soviet behavior.[40]

The War College appointment satisfied Kennan's desire to serve in a pedagogical role and he put aside his anti-democratic values in an effort to help shape public perceptions of the Soviet threat. On a speaking tour across the nation in the summer of 1946, he brought the message of the Long Telegram before public officials, politicians, newspaper editors, academic groups, and business executives whose support of containment was deemed essential. Kennan reported that "stag" audiences of "keen and vigorous" businessmen were most amenable to his "realism" on relations with the Soviet Union, but he perceived "an intellectual snobbery and pretense . . . jealousies and inhibitions" among academic audiences during the month-long speaking tour. The diplomat observed "real Communist activity" and identified "Soviet agents" within "intellectual circles" on the West Coast.[41]

Kennan's tour was successful judging by the responses of some of the groups with whom he met. A spokesman for the Portland Committee on Foreign Relations told the State Department that his group "spent a very pleasant and unusually worthwhile evening with Mr. Kennan" and a *Milwaukee Journal* editor declared that the diplomat had provided the newspaper's editorial board with "a very sound estimate of the Russian situation."[42]

The Truman administration borrowed extensively from Kennan's perceptions in drawing up its own 100,000-word assessment of the Soviet threat. Presidential aides Clark Clifford and George Elsey quoted from the Long Telegram to bolster their conclusion that Soviet foreign policy posed "a direct threat to American security" and they called on the United States to hold the line in Europe and Asia until Moscow could be compelled to abandon its expansionism. Reviewing Clifford's report before its submission to the President in September, Kennan suggested only minor changes, declaring that "the general tone is excellent and I have no fault to find with it."[43]

It was a heady time for Kennan. In only a few months he had emerged from isolation and obscurity in Moscow to help forge the cold war consensus in the United States. From September 1946 to May 1947, in "a veritable outpouring of literary and forensic effort," he lectured regularly not only at the War College but also at other military institutions and East Coast colleges and universities. He worked with "stimulating thinkers and teachers" such as Yale's Bernard Brodie and developed "a closer and wider acquaintance among top military and naval figures in this country than any other civilian in the Foreign Service or the [State] Department." Because he had had "both the prestige and the guts to talk up successfully to the military leaders," Kennan credited himself with helping to coordinate the nation's political and military policies.[44] Forrestal maintained "the keenest interest" in the War College lectures and sometimes invited Kennan and Bohlen to dinner at his Georgetown home, where the intense Navy Secretary probed the experts for information about Russia.[45]

In addition to Forrestal, Kennan worked closely with Undersecretary of State Dean G. Acheson. On October 8 Kennan sent Acheson a copy of a lecture he had delivered the previous week attacking Henry Wallace, whom Truman had fired from his Cabinet for publicly questioning containment. Kennan scored the former Commerce Secretary for naïveté and "the warmth of his sympathy for the cause of Russian communism" and told Acheson that in place of Wallace's "fatuous gestures of appeasement," he would continue to inform the public of the "correct interpretation of our Russian policy." The diplomat regretted having to reject "nine-tenths" of the requests he received for speaking engagements in deference to "my duties here in the War College and to limitations of personal time and strength." Acheson urged Kennan to "accept as many of the invitations to speak as you can" in the interest of promoting "public understanding" of the hard line on Russia.[46]

As he wrote, lectured, and gained admirers in the Truman administration, Kennan refined his thinking about containment. He believed that world events had outpaced strategic thought and that the United States needed "a grand strategy no less concrete and no less consistent than that which governs our actions in war." Immersing himself in the classical works on diplomacy and warfare of Niccoló Machiavelli and Karl von Clausewitz, Kennan took it upon himself to formulate a comprehensive strategy for postwar American internationalism.[47]

He offered containment as a "constructive" alternative to the "two main aberrations" of the early postwar period: the Wallace-left call for cooperation with the Soviet Union on the one hand, and right-wing demands for war with Russia on the other. In an October 1946 War College lecture, Kennan advocated a quiet and flexible diplomacy designed to "contain the Russians indefinitely by confronting them firmly but politely with superior strength at every turn of the game." By this means the Western powers "ought to be able to maneuver them back into the limits within which we would like them to stay." This lecture marked the first time Kennan employed the word "contain" to describe American strategy.[48]

Impressed by Machiavelli's praise of power politics as well as Clausewitz's dictum that "war is nothing else than the continuation of state policy by different means," Kennan concluded that the Soviet threat was primarily ideological-political. Devastated by two world wars in a single generation, the USSR did not have the means nor intent to spread communist power by military aggression, but would be unstinting in its support of communist parties and front organizations throughout the world. Because Moscow employed unlimited "varieties of skulduggery" —including not only the everyday tactics of intimidation and subversion but also "seduction, blackmail, theft, fraud, rape, battle, murder, and sudden death"—the United States had to pursue containment through a variety of means.

The weapons of containment included a powerful military establishment; a monopoly on atomic weapons; effective propaganda; covert operations; economic assistance; and a healthy society at home to serve as a model for others. Kennan admitted that the implementation of containment carried the risk of war but concluded that there was "no real security and . . . no alternative to living dangerously" in view of the Soviet threat. Scoring "liberals who want us to go easy on the Russians," he warned that "the price of peace has become the willingness to sacrifice it to a good cause."[49]

Despite the warning, Kennan expected Russia to capitulate short of a major war because of the weakness inherent in "totalitarian states." He and others who linked Nazi Germany and the Soviet Union in a totalitarian model believed that such states were vulnerable despite their military and police power. "Totalitarianism is a device of despair, arising from specific and particularly painful problems of adjustment," he explained. Only a "temporary phenomenon," the totalitarian state was fundamentally unstable in its dependence on maintaining an "upper crust of centralized power. Let anything enter in which breaks that upper crust, and underneath you have absolutely nothing but chaos."[50]

The United States could contribute to the disintegrative forces inherent in Soviet totalitarianism by halting Russian expansionism and then reversing its flow. The first step was to contain the immediate threat of ideological-political subversion in Western Europe. Only then, reasoned Kennan, could the West win back the eastern half of Europe which had been sacrificed to Soviet power. "Today we must recognize," he explained in January 1948, "that we tacitly acquiesced, as part of the whole conclusion of the war, in the Red Army advance into those countries and in the establishment of Soviet political control." It was now the task of the United States "to create conditions unfavorable to the maintenance of Soviet power in Eastern Europe." Liberation in Eastern Europe was a *sine qua non* of containment: "We must get them out," Kennan declared. "We cannot settle for their remaining there indefinitely."[51]

After successful containment in the West and rollback in Eastern Europe, one of two things would happen: either the USSR would be compelled to negotiate from a weakened position to resolve the outstanding issues of World War II, or—should Kennan's fondest hopes be realized—the regime would collapse from its own internal weaknesses. By implementing containment the West could begin "rolling back" international communism, a process that would culminate in "a general crumbling of Russian influence and prestige which would carry beyond . . . the satellite countries, and into the heart of the Soviet Union itself." Because "we and our friends have a preponderance of strength right now," he explained, containment would achieve either "a mellowing of Russian policy, or there will be internal changes in Russia which will relieve us of some of the pressure."[52]

Although Kennan seemed confident that the West held the upper hand in the struggle with the Soviet regime, he was uncertain as to the timing of the anticipated changes in Moscow. If the United States were to assert itself, he told a group of Chicago businessmen early in 1948, "I predict to you confidently that within six months we will be able to do business over the table with our Russian friends, about the future of Germany, and about a number of other matters. A balance will then have been restored on the European continent." Only six days later, however, he warned that Americans might be in for the long haul. "I don't think we should become too defeatist about this or that we should quail at the prospect that it may be a long and wearisome process," he advised. "You sometimes have to muster up the same sort of determination in political warfare, which is what this is, as you do in military warfare." In the 1947 "X-Article" Kennan declared that if the West could "contain Soviet power over a period of ten to fifteen years," the internal weaknesses of the totalitarian regime would take hold.[53]

As he had done in his essay marking the end of the war in Europe and in the Long Telegram, Kennan suggested that once Soviet expansionism had been contained the regime would disintegrate as a result of being exposed to an "invidious comparison with the West." He cited the observations of a nineteenth-century French aristocrat, the Marquis de Custine, author of *Russia in 1839,* as an authority on Russia's fear of comparison with the West, but as Kennan himself later admitted, Custine was a flawed observer. In his 1971 book, *The Marquis de Custine and His Russia in 1839,* Kennan concluded that Custine's work was "dreadfully and almost shamefully inaccurate" and "was not a very good book about Russia in 1839." He insisted, however, that the Marquis's 1839 work was "an excellent book, probably in fact the best of books, about the Russia of Joseph Stalin." Uncomfortable with Custine's condemnation of imperial Russia, Kennan simply applied his arguments to the Soviet state.[54]

Kennan, while not ruling out negotiations with Russia, believed that talks could occur only after Soviet expansion had been arrested and communist power had begun to recede. Initially his wartime recommendation—a clearcut division of Europe into spheres of influence—would result; but he did not expect such a division to be permanent. Once the West had displayed its resolve to the Soviets, Moscow would either negotiate to settle postwar disputes or, better still, the example of a prosperous Western Europe would set in motion the forces that would destroy the regime.

Although Kennan designed his strategy as a response to the Soviet ideological-political threat, he advocated a powerful American military

37

establishment. The country required "alert, modern and effective" ground and naval forces, including a rapid deployment force able to respond "on any limited theater of operations, even if far from our shores." He favored universal military training, bolstering of the reserves, additional strategic bases, and declared that the United States "must maintain its position of preeminence in the air."[55] Kennan's call for rearmament reflected what historian Michael Sherry has called the "dogma of deterrence" that arose in strategic, military and scientific circles as a result of World War II. The shocks of appeasement, blitzkrieg, and Pearl Harbor prompted American planners, including Kennan, to advocate measures that would deter attack or allow for a rapid response in the event of war. They focused on the Soviet Union, which alone had emerged from the war with the military-industrial power and geographic position that could pose a threat to American security.[56]

But even more significant in Kennan's thinking, a powerful military establishment would demonstrate American credibility to oppose the extension of communist influence. "The American shadow is bound to fall on all those countries where the issue of communism vs. national independence is being fought out," he explained. If the United States failed to develop and show a readiness to deploy its military power, "we would never know . . . whether or not we could have won the cold war." Kennan advocated outright American military superiority for five to ten years, after which the country should maintain "a permanent state of adequate military preparation."[57]

In sharp contrast to what would become his views after 1950, Kennan declared in January 1948 that he was not "excited or alarmed" about the existence of atomic weapons. The bomb was "a relative, not an absolute, quantity in the pattern of warfare," although "serious thought" had to be given to the "suicidal nature of atomic warfare in a world in which more than one country has bombs."[58] For the time being he advised maintaining the American monopoly on atomic weapons and considered discussion of arms control "useless and misleading" until "a general and adequate relaxation of tensions between the Soviet Union and the Western world" had been effected.

Kennan endorsed a policy of atomic deterrence and the ability to respond with "instant retaliation," although he would criticize John Foster Dulles for emphasizing the same position in 1954. In 1947, however, Kennan advised Acheson that the Kremlin leaders would not hesitate to use the bomb as a means of extortion if they had the exclusive possession of it and Washington should therefore "quietly and vigorously proceed to develop the U.S. capacity to absorb atomic attack and to effect instant retaliation." Kennan supported cooperation with Great Britain and Canada on the development of atomic energy in order to convince the Kremlin that its efforts to gain atomic superiority constituted a "dangerous pipedream" and to 'maneuver Moscow into a grudging acceptance of the main points of our program" for international control of atomic weapons.[59]

Kennan's position on atomic weapons reflected a consensus on the subject within the Truman administration. In presenting the nation's policy before the UN Atomic Energy Commission in June 1946, Bernard Baruch called for an international authority that would monopolize all atomic energy operations, punish violators, and preclude the Soviet Union from exercising its UN veto on atomic energy questions. Effective international control would have been difficult to achieve under any circumstances in 1946, with both nations committed to developing atomic arsenals, but by wielding the "winning weapon" to secure Soviet adherence to America's terms, the Baruch Plan foreclosed any possibility of agreement. Kennan endorsed Baruch's proposal and urged the United States to fulfill its "sad duty of retaining its preeminence in the production and maintenance of such weapons and of the auxilary equipment which serves them."[60]

The success or failure of containment ultimately depended more on the quality of American society than the extent of the nation's atomic stockpiles, Kennan argued. Indeed, the most effective weapon against communist subversion was "the pitiless glare of truthful and factual publicity" that would convince peoples of the world of Moscow's duplicity in contrast to a superior Western model. Kennan invariably concluded his lectures and essays in the late war and early cold war years by warning that containment hinged on the development of a strong domestic society to serve as an example for other societies to emulate. "This is the point at which domestic and foreign policies meet," he explained. The United States needed to "keep at all times a preponderance of strength in the world," as he put it in one lecture, but it was "by no means a question of military strength alone. It is a question of political, economic, and moral strength. Above all it is a question of our internal strength, of the health and sanity of our own society." In the Long

Telegram Kennan compared communism to a "malignant parasite which feeds only on diseased tissue" and declared that if the United States strengthened its own society, that action would constitute a "victory over Moscow worth a thousand diplomatic notes and joint communiqués. If we cannot abandon fatalism and indifference in the face of deficiencies of our own society, Moscow will profit."[61]

These allusions to American domestic society point to a fundamental contradiction in Kennan's thinking and explain in part his later disenchantment with containment. Ironically, even as he called for the United States, the world's preeminent industrial democracy, to serve as a model for other nations to emulate, he had already condemned representative government and had expressed his own profound alienation from modern industrial society. Kennan tried to resolve this conflict by calling for the United States to adopt "far-reaching reforms in our public life and in our basic concepts of American society" in place of the "reactionary belief that we have a form of government so superior that it needs no further development or improvement." He argued that America could correct its internal deficiencies and serve as a model for others only through stronger central government authority and greater collectivism. "We need have no fear of developments in the direction of collectivism . . . when they are dictated by national interest, and when they do not detract from civil liberties," he declared. Government by a collective elite was central to Kennan's thinking on containment and the failure of such a "reform" to occur contributed to his later disillusionment with American internationalism.[62]

Officials paid little attention to Kennan's views on American society, although they were more than willing to embrace his perceptions of the Soviet Union. Forrestal in particular remained in close contact with Kennan and in December 1946 asked the diplomat to revise a paper on dialectical materialism and Soviet policy by former Smith College professor Edward F. Willett. Kennan declined that request but did agree, somewhat reluctantly, to write an essay of his own. At first, as Forrestal's aide John T. Connor recalled, Kennan "said he didn't have time to start from scratch himself, but when the Secretary's burning interest was emphasized, he finally agreed to undertake the job."[63]

Kennan drafted an essay entitled "The Soviet Way of Thought and Its Effect on Foreign Policy," which he presented at a Council on Foreign Relations discussion meeting at the Pratt House in New York on January

7, 1947. This essay, which Kennan also delivered at the War College on January 24, was the first draft of the famous "X-Article." As in previous essays he argued that the Kremlin's actions stemmed from impulses buried deep in the Russian tradition while Marxist ideology, with its emphasis on a menacing capitalist world, served to justify the Soviet police state. The requirements of American policy boiled down to this: the Kremlin's "inherent expansive tendencies must be firmly contained at all times by counter-pressure which makes it constantly evident that attempts to break through this containment would be detrimental to Soviet interests."[64]

Forrestal found Kennan's first draft "disappointing" and sent Connor to ask the diplomat to "take another crack at it." Connor found that Kennan, "displeased with his own efforts," was eager to revise the essay and this time Connor and Forrestal agreed that "the results were astonishingly good."[65] "I am most grateful for your final paper," Forrestal wrote on February 17 after receiving Kennan's second draft, entitled "Psychological Background of Soviet Foreign Policy." "It is extremely well-done and I am going to suggest to the Secretary [of State] that he read it." As Connor recalled the situation, Forrestal "thought that the paper deserved wide circulation, particularly on the [Capitol] Hill," but Kennan declared that it would be "inadvisable" in view of his position in the government to have his name on the article. "We finally worked out a plan whereby the Secretary distributed copies with the simple statement that it was prepared at his request, without any identification of the author," Connor explained. "In due course, the clamor for its wider circulation was so great that it was published."[66]

Indeed, Kennan's analysis of the psychological origins of Soviet behavior intrigued Hamilton Fish Armstrong, the editor of *Foreign Affairs,* an establishment publication with a circulation of 19,000. After Kennan spoke before the Council of Foreign Relations (publisher of *Foreign Affairs*) in January, Armstrong asked to publish his paper. In his memoir Kennan explained that he offered Armstrong the paper on the condition that it would be published anonymously so as not to compromise his official standing, but Louis Halle, a close associate of Kennan's, later explained that "since this article represented the newly formulated position of the United States Government, it would have been self-defeating to put it forward simply as the thought of one man."[67] The State Department cleared Kennan's piece for publication on April 8 and in its

July issue, *Foreign Affairs* carried the article, now entitled "The Sources of Soviet Conduct," and authored by "X." The journal paid Kennan $100 for his effort.[68]

In its perceptions of the Soviet Union and advocacy of containment, the X-Article reflected continuity with Kennan's wartime essays and the Long Telegram. In virtually all of his essays and lectures from 1944 to 1947, he emphasized the traditional rather than ideological motives behind the Kremlin's expansionist foreign policy and its inveterate antagonism toward the West. He consistently advocated an assertive American international diplomacy backed by a strong military and argued that containment could lead to liberation extending into Russia itself. Like the Long Telegram and his other essays, the X-Article placed no faith in negotiations "until the internal nature of Soviet power is changed."[69]

Like the previous essays, the X-Article depicted Marxism as a "convenient rationalization" and "pseudo-scientific justification" for the Soviet dictatorship. As products of the "Russian-Asiatic world," men with "Oriental mind[s]" whose attitudes were "unmodified by any of the Anglo-Saxon traditions of compromise," Stalin and his deputies would oppose any accommodation with the West in order to pursue the expansionist foreign policy on which the very existence of the USSR depended. Soviet foreign policy was like "a fluid stream which moves constantly . . . to make sure that it has filled every nook and cranny available to it in the basin of world power." The Kremlin would be patient, even cautious, but like a "persistent toy automobile wound up and headed in a given direction," it would exert "constant pressure toward the desired goal" and could be stopped only when it encountered "unanswerable force." Thus, the Western powers must adopt a policy of "long-term, patient but firm and vigilant containment of Russian expansive tendencies . . . by the adroit and vigilant application of counter-force at a series of constantly shifting geographical and political points, corresponding to the shifts and maneuvers of Soviet policy."[70]

Once again Kennan asserted in the X-Article—as he had done since the end of the war in Europe—that containment was a first step toward the destruction of the Soviet regime. With the Russian people exhausted from their recent history of collectivization and war, the USSR was "economically a vulnerable, and in a certain sense an impotent, nation." If the "disunity . . . chaos and weakness" beneath the crust of state power were to explode, "Soviet Russia might be changed overnight from one of the strongest to one of the weakest and most pitiable of national societies." There was a "strong" possibility, in Kennan's judgment, "that Soviet power, like the capitalist world of its conception, bears within it the seeds of its own decay, and that the sprouting of these seeds is well advanced." By "holding the line" with a policy of "firm containment" backed by "unalterable counter-force," the United States could "increase enormously the strains under which Soviet policy must operate, to force upon the Kremlin a far greater degree of moderation and circumspection than it has had to observe in recent years, and in this way to promote tendencies which must eventually find their outlet in either the break-up or the gradual mellowing of Soviet power." [71]

The anonymous dissection of the Soviet adversary in *Foreign Affairs* aroused widespread speculation about who its author might be. On July 8 newspaperman Arthur Krock called the X-Article a "guide to official thinking about Russia" and Kennan's authorship soon leaked to the press. When *Life* and *Reader's Digest* received permission to publish excerpts and reprints, "containment" of Soviet communism entered the American vocabulary and Kennan became a public figure. [72]

The X-Article marked the apogee of Kennan's influence on American national security policy. The once alienated diplomat had become the intellectual spokesman for postwar American internationalism and had contributed in no small degree to the Truman administration's decision to bury the wartime legacy of cooperation with Moscow. Yet Kennan has spent more than four decades since the publication of the X-article attempting to depict it as unrepresentative of his views at the time. The article, he wrote in his memoir, "suffered, unquestionably, from serious deficiencies" which included his omission of discussion about Eastern Europe as well as his failure to make clear the ideological-political rather than military nature of the Soviet threat. Kennan's "third great deficiency" was his failure to mention that containment applied only to the five industrial regions of the world—the United States, Great Britain, the Rhine valley, the Soviet Union, and Japan. [73]

Elsewhere, in his War College lectures and planning for European economic recovery, Kennan did indeed emphasize the ideological-political character of the Soviet threat and the omission from the X-Article of this element of his thought was no doubt influenced by his efforts to accommodate "Mr. Forrestal's needs." Forrestal was, after all, an administrator of a branch of the *military* services and Secretary of Defense from 1947 to 49. Kennan's contention that he meant to limit containment to the five industrial regions of the world was inconsistent with his later actions, however. Although he did warn against offering military and economic aid "on a grand scale" and often referred to the primacy of containment in industrial regions, when it came time to make decisions on the implementation of containment in areas beyond the five major industrial regions—in the Near East, in Korea, in Southeast Asia, and in Latin America—he advocated the assertion of American power. Containment, as it evolved in Kennan's own thinking, was, as we shall see, global in scope.[74]

Despite Kennan's belated apologies and a spirited defense of his position by historian John L. Gaddis and political scientist David Mayers, the X-Article was not a misleading depiction of his views in the early cold war. Alarmed by the potential for the spread of Soviet influence in the postwar era, Kennan clearly wished to contain the Kremlin and he shared Forrestal's desire to heighten public and governmental awareness of the perceived threat. In this respect, the X-Article was nothing if not a tremendous success and Kennan saw no reason to apologize for it at the time.[75]

Like his essay marking V-E Day and the Long Telegram before it, the X-Article reflected amateur historical scholarship on Russia and a naïve faith in liberation, both of which characterized Kennan's thinking in the early postwar period. He was justified in expressing his concern about the extension of Soviet influence at the war's end but unlike Roosevelt Kennan proved unable to temper those concerns with a realistic recognition of the inevitability of Moscow's emergence as a world power in the wake of its victory in Europe. Instead of accommodating himself to this change in the global balance of power, Kennan embraced a host of specious assumptions and historical parallels between Stalin and the tsars and even underestimated in his emphasis on traditional Russian despotism the extent to which Stalin and his comrades were true believers in Marxist ideology. As subsequent events proved, Kennan's faith in liberation, or a dramatic "mellowing" that included Soviet withdrawal from Eastern Europe, were the products of wishful, rather than realistic, thinking.

At the time, however, Kennan could only be gratified as the X-Article crowned his efforts to forge a consensus for containment of the Soviet

Union and world communism. After serving for years as an outsider and critic, he had been summoned to Washington to play a prominent, perhaps even indispensable, role in establishing the intellectual framework for postwar national security policy. Kennan soon saw containment implemented in a manner of which he did not approve and came to realize that he had been guilty of exaggerating the weaknesses and vulnerability of the Soviet regime. But by the time Kennan understood the implications of containment, he had lost all influence over American diplomacy.

III

The Global Planner

AFTER PLAYING a critical role in forging the cold war consensus, Kennan rose to the inner circle of the American foreign policy establishment as the State Department's Policy Planning Staff (PPS) director. With his days outside the foreign policy consensus seemingly behind him, Kennan was a key aide to Secretary of State George C. Marshall as the Truman administration implemented an international diplomacy aimed at securing the integration of Western Europe and Japan into a multilateral economic order centered in Washington. He helped shape the European Recovery Program, encouraged a reverse course in occupied Japan, and advocated containment of communist insurgencies across the globe.

Kennan's thinking on international affairs established him as one of the leading "realists" of the postwar era, but in some respects his realism was purely theoretical. The "balance of power" he advocated actually envisioned domination by the United States as it sought to undermine the Soviet regime. Along the same lines Kennan's commitment to maintaining American credibility in the struggle against world communism overshadowed his theoretical desire to limit containment to certain vital regions and found him advocating a policy of global intervention on the part of the United States. In addition to the contradictions inherent in Kennan's own thought, American cultural values and domestic politics prevented the United States from implementing a "realistic" foreign policy in the early cold war period.

The publication in 1951 of *American Diplomacy, 1900–1950*—one of the most influential books in the history of U.S. diplomacy—established Kennan's reputation as a leading theorist of "political realism." Like political scientist Hans J. Morgenthau, theologian Reinhold Niebuhr, and other postwar realists, Kennan rejected universal principles—"one world-ism"—in favor of a pragmatic foreign policy based on power realities. Realists tended toward the Calvinistic and warned that conflict among nations was inevitable owing to the innate fallibility of human beings. They argued that international conflict could best be accommodated through the establishment of a balance of power among competing states and a diplomacy aimed at preserving such a balance. Employing lessons of the past as a guide to practical diplomacy, realists advised that choices be made on the basis of national interest rather than "fictional arrangements or ideal blueprints for peace."[1]

Kennan and the other postwar realists drew their inspiration from classical figures—Thucydides, Hobbes and Machiavelli—but it was the violence of their own times that convinced them of the need to revive an old paradigm to restore order in the postwar world. As they surveyed the scarred landscape of the recent past—over the corpses of Wilsonian idealism, isolationism, appeasement and total war—classical realism appeared as salvation. Like the European statesmen who had gathered in Vienna to restore a world torn apart by the Napoleonic wars, the post-World War II realists perceived the world as an arena of bitter conflict and perpetual rivalry. While placing themselves in the context of classical international relations theory, Kennan, Morgenthau, Niebuhr, and other realists condemned the liberal internationalist tradition that they claimed had dominated Western diplomacy for most of the twentieth century. As they apotheosized power and national interest, the postwar realists decried Wilsonian idealism and the "legalistic-moralistic" approach to world affairs which, as Kennan complained, had run "like a red skein" through the history of American diplomacy.[2]

The realist paradigm provided a source of legitimization for Kennan's approach to the cold war. Realism reinforced his anti-democratic values through its sanction of elite authority over foreign policy and its warnings about the dangers of succumbing to mass emotional compulsions.

Kennan and other realists deemphasized ethical and moral considerations and justified containment on the basis of national interest and the balance of power. Despite their efforts to distance themselves from ideology and morality, however, Kennan, Morgenthau, Niebuhr, and other postwar realists were inveterate anti-communists who sought to isolate and weaken the Soviet Union.[3]

Kennan, like most realists, rejected international forums and universal agreements and called on the United States to act unilaterally to restore order and capitalist stability in the vital centers of Europe and Japan, thereby containing putative Soviet expansionist thrusts. The United Nations Organization—largely a forum for toothless resolutions and the striking of postures—was more likely to impede American objectives than enhance them. Indulgence in such idealism would limit the nation's freedom of disposal over its strength and resources at a time when the ongoing "political war" with Moscow represented "the decisive turning point in our civilization." Moreover, a UN in which each country held equal voting strength bore no relation to the realities of world power and Anglo-American influence eventually would be undermined because a "colored bloc" controlled 60 percent of General Assembly voting strength, making the UN "a backward-area dominated body."[4] Kennan anticipated the decline of American influence over the UN when he warned that Washington and its allies could not count on support from developing nations, whose representatives he characterized as "neurotic products of exotic backgrounds and tentative western educational experiences, racially and socially embittered against the West."[5]

A *sine qua non* for realists such as Kennan was the establishment of a calculated balance of power. Only a pragmatic balance of forces—as opposed to world government, or "high sounding phrases about democratic ideals"—could prevent the conflict among states from spilling over into global war. "International society," he explained in 1948, "is not advancing toward peace and enlightenment and prosperity"; rather, it was "still an arena of deadly contest and rivalry . . . hatred and fanaticism." Only through the establishment and maintenance of a balance of power could the United States "absorb and contain those hostile or unruly forces in the world with which we ourselves cannot deal by direct action." Realists accepted as inevitable the subordination of weak to powerful states in the quest for a balance of power.[6]

Critical to the establishment of a balance of power, Kennan argued, were five industrial regions of the world "where the sinews of modern military strength could be produced in quantity." Liberal capitalism prevailed in the United States and Great Britain while the Soviet Union controlled only its own battered industrial region. As a result of the war, power vacuums remained to be filled in Germany and Japan, the fourth and fifth of Kennan's vital centers. The burden of postwar American diplomacy was to fight off the threat of communist subversion while reconstructing Germany and Japan "to a point where they could play their part in the Eurasian balance of power, and yet to a point not so advanced as to permit them again to threaten the interests of the maritime world of the West."[7]

Although the USSR controlled only one of the five power centers—its own—Kennan remained preoccupied with the threat posed by the communist "international conspiracy" emanating from Moscow. If Stalin successfully exploited war-weariness and his ties with foreign communist parties to extend Soviet influence into Central and Western Europe while the United States remained idle, Great Britain would be alone and vulnerable. Japan, too, would succumb to internal communist subversion unless Washington implemented an assertive program of economic and political recovery. Containment was the only viable strategy to combat Stalin's bid for the "political capture" of Europe and Asia and to establish a balance of power amenable to Western interests.[8]

Armed with the realist worldview and elevated to a position of influence in the Truman administration, Kennan charted a course of global containment from 1947 to 1950. Although he called on the United States to lead, Kennan warned that "the present 'bi-polarity' will, in the long run, be beyond our resources" and thus it was "urgently necessary for us to restore something of the balance of power in Europe and Asia by strengthening local forces of independence and by getting them to assume part of our burden." After Secretary of State Marshall read portions of this report—Kennan's "Resumé of the World Situation"—before the Cabinet on November 7, 1947, Truman requested and received his own copy of Kennan's assessment.[9]

Before American allies could assume their share of the burdens of containment, Washington had to establish an economic recovery program to head off the communist threat to the security of Western Europe. In Britain, the global empire was disintegrating while the domestic economy was nearing collapse as a result of food and resource shortages and a mounting debt. Wartime devastation was also impeding economic recovery in France and Italy, where communist parties loyal to Stalin shared power in the postwar governments. One of the most severe winters in memory darkened the recovery efforts and the spirits of West Europeans in early 1947. In the midst of this crisis, Marshall and Stalin deadlocked in mid-April discussions in Moscow over a German peace treaty, and when the Soviet dictator counseled patience, Marshall concluded that he was stalling in hopes that communist parties would sweep to power across Europe. Declaring upon his return that "the patient is dying while the doctors deliberate," Marshall mobilized the government for a European aid program.[10]

As the nation's leading expert on Russia, Kennan played a critical role in the formulation of the Marshall Plan, the centerpiece of American strategic planning for economic recovery and ideological-political containment in Western Europe. Marshall had perceived the need for long range planning during his service as Army Chief of Staff and told Undersecretary of State Dean Acheson to set up a planning group in the State Department in early 1947. Marshall, who had been "favorably impressed" by Kennan after the two held discussions in Washington in 1944, concluded that he was "by far the best qualified man" to head the new State Department "planning unit" that would oversee the implementation of containment, a conclusion shared by Acheson and Forrestal.[11]

Kennan's appointment as director of the new Policy Planning Staff (PPS) in May 1947 made him a top policy maker in the Truman administration and a close confidant of Marshall. The two men had adjoining offices and Kennan did not merely admire but "in a sense loved" the sixty-seven year-old American hero, who embodied the gentlemanly code of honor and national service that Kennan revered and who served as something of a father figure to him. The relationship with Marshall helped smooth Kennan's transition from temperamental outsider to consensus policy planner. Marshall left no doubt that he was in charge but also made it clear that he respected Kennan's judgment. In January 1948, for example, the general commended Kennan for his "splendid work" as PPS director and declared that "your calm and analytical approach to our problems is most comforting and your judgment is a source of great confidence to me."[12]

Formally established on May 5, 1947, the PPS actually began work on a European recovery program under Kennan's direction several days earlier. Acting with the haste that Marshall had ordered, Kennan assembled economic forecasts for the nations of Western Europe and organized a staff that included Carleton Savage (the executive secretary); Asian expert John Paton Davies; Williams College international law professor Joseph Johnson; and diplomats George Butler and Ware Adams. Acheson vetoed Kennan's appointment of Paul Nitze as an economic specialist, explaining that he was "a Wall Street operator." The PPS eventually added Jacques Reinstein as its economic expert; Henry S. Villard, Africa and Near East specialist; and attorney Isaac Stokes, in addition to outside consultants. The press soon began to refer to the PPS as "the new 'brain trust' on foreign policy." [13]

The National Security Act of 1947, proposed by Truman in February and approved by Congress in July, shaped the role of the PPS. The legislation coordinated the military service branches under a Cabinet-level Secretary of Defense and created both the Central Intelligence Agency and the National Security Council. The PPS forwarded recommendations to the NSC, whose numbered papers became American policy when approved by the President. In October 1947 the State Department designated Kennan as its representative on the NSC. [14]

Reporting directly to Marshall and Undersecretary Robert A. Lovett, the PPS was to develop long-range policy and establish "a framework for program-planning as a guide for current policy decisions and operations." Kennan and his staff drew on a wide range of resources to coordinate State Department planning. "For us in the Policy Planning Staff," he recalled years later, "the world was our oyster; there was no problem of American foreign policy to which we could not address ourselves." An advisory body, the PPS had "no operational responsibility" and could not issue directives. [15]

Kennan dominated the PPS. He solicited reports from the staff and frequently employed consultants on policy questions but personally wrote most of the PPS reports and advised his charges that "the opinion of this staff is what you fellows can make me understand and believe." If a majority diverged from the director's view, Kennan on rare occasions forwarded a separate dissent along with his own recommendations. [16]

Kennan and his PPS colleagues were convinced that the success or failure of the Marshall Plan, or European Recovery Program (ERP), would determine whether or not containment was a viable strategy. The loss of Western Europe would constitute "the single greatest deterioration in our own international position that our history has ever known," Kennan declared. If they subverted Europe, the Russians could "continue to dream their dreams of the smashing of our society and the domination of the world," but if the United States held the line, European recovery would provide the first step toward Western integration leading to the isolation and defeat of Soviet communism.[17]

Kennan echoed earlier statements by Marshall when he declared that the Kremlin was stalling negotiations in anticipation of the collapse of the Western economies and in hopes that the United States would withdraw into isolationism. A program for European recovery was thus "of urgent and primary importance" to combat the Soviet strategy. In the short term, the United States would seek to purge communists and invigorate the economies of Britain, France, and Italy, but Germany was the key to a lasting European recovery. Kennan still opposed negotiating with Moscow over Germany and favored integrating the merged American and British occupation zones (Bizonia), arguing that it was "imperatively urgent" that economic recovery and the revival of a productive capacity in western Germany receive "top priority in all our occupation policies."[18]

Still a strong Germanophile, Kennan rejected the wartime proposal of "pastoralization" and sought to reestablish Germany at the center of a trans-national European federation. Washington's postwar policy centered on plans to rebuild the Western German economy as a means of thwarting communist subversion while attempting to lure eastern Germany out of the Soviet orbit. Kennan urged "the maximum interweaving of German economy with the remainder of Europe" and the creation of a supra-national federation of anti-communist states across West-Central Europe in order to bolster economic integration. The goal was to bring western Germany "into a European federation, but to do it in such a way as not to permit her to dominate that federation or jeopardize the security interests of the other western European countries," he explained.

The unilateral approach to postwar Germany reflected Kennan's opposition to negotiations with Moscow until containment had thwarted Kremlin efforts to extend its influence. If the Russians succeeded in their efforts to gain "political control of the key countries outside the iron curtain," he explained, ". . . they will see no reason to settle with us at this time over Germany when they hope that their bargaining position will soon be improved." But once the ERP had restored stability and confidence in Western Europe, the Russians would "be prepared, for the first time since the surrender, to do business seriously with us about Germany and about Europe in general."[19]

As a special committee of the State, War and Navy Coordinating Committee (SWNCC) drew up specific plans for European recovery, the PPS focused on submitting a set of principles to be used in framing a master plan for U.S. assistance to Western Europe. "The American effort in aid to Europe," argued the first paper issued by the PPS, "should be directed not to the combating of communism as such but to the restoration of the economic health and vigor to European society." The United States would bypass the UN—specifically its Economic Commission for Europe, in which the Soviet Union participated—unless it adhered to American economic principles. Kennan stressed that American aid should be contingent on anti-communism and urged Marshall to call on the Europeans to draw up their own plans for economic recovery, primarily to inspire confidence among them but also to shield Washington from absorbing all of the blame in the event of a failure that could be exploited by communists. As Kennan had hoped, the decision to have the Europeans devise their own aid program inspired confidence and prompted a purge of communists from the governments of France and Italy.[20]

The formal recommendations of the PPS became the basis of the ERP. Acting as speechwriter, Charles Bohlen combined Kennan's draft of PPS 1 with the recommendations of Will Clayton, assistant secretary of state for economic affairs, to produce Marshall's program for European recovery. The Secretary used the occasion of his June 5 commencement address at Harvard to announce the American intention to assist Europe.[21]

The Marshall Plan reflected the Cold War ethos long espoused by Kennan in that it envisioned no cooperation with the USSR and sought to drive a wedge between Moscow and its client regimes in Eastern Europe. Kennan—like Forrestal, Acheson, Marshall, and Truman—had abandoned negotiations with Stalin on grounds that the Soviet dictator was "very deeply committed to the principles of a final showdown between capitalism and socialism." Offers of cooperation were insincere, only "dialectics" promoted by Stalin and "apologists in this country . . . people like Mr. [Henry] Wallace."[22] If Marshall Plan monies had, for appearance's sake, to be offered to the continent as a whole, Kennan argued, then it was "essential" that the Soviet satellites either "exclude themselves" or "agree to abandon the exclusive orientation of their economies."[23]

Marshall took Kennan's advice to "play it straight" by inviting Soviet participation in an all-European recovery program, but the offer was disingenuous. If the offer were accepted, the United States would insist that Russia, itself devastated by the war, nevertheless contribute to the aid to Europe rather than receive it. Truman Administration policy makers counted on the Russians to balk at requirements that they divulge closely guarded information about the Soviet economy nor was the Kremlin expected to accommodate itself to the American dominated World Bank and International Monetary Fund. As Bohlen later observed, the Marshall Plan was offered in such a way as to "make it quite impossible for the Soviet Union to accept." Having abandoned efforts to achieve agreement with Moscow, American officials intended to establish friendly governments and a dollar-centered multilateral economy in as much of Europe as possible, but were careful to avoid assuming the onus for the division of the continent.[24]

Kennan's strategy to exclude the Soviet Union from the ERP succeeded on July 2 when Soviet Foreign Minister Vyacheslav Molotov strode out of the Paris conference called to consider recovery plans. Under pressure from Moscow, the nations of Eastern Europe also withdrew from the ERP deliberations. The American initiative prompted Stalin to extend Soviet authority into Czechoslovakia, which withdrew from the ERP conference on orders from Moscow.[25]

As the talks continued among representatives of the Western nations throughout the summer in Paris, Kennan asserted that the momentum toward cooperation in Western Europe had delivered the "greatest blow to European communism since [the] termination of hostilities." An effective program to rebuild the European economies could "transform lassitude and futility into enthusiasm and purpose," he declared. Raw materials—particularly coal and steel—would be furnished, agricultural production increased, multilateral trade established, currency stabilized, transportation rebuilt, recovery achieved.[26]

Kennan's optimism had soured by late August following a trip to Paris, where the conferees had created a Committee on European Economic Cooperation, but had achieved little else. Their deliberations revealed "all the weakness, the escapism, the paralysis of a region caught by war . . . and sadly torn by hardship, confusion and outside pressure," he observed. Concluding that the representatives of the sixteen nations meeting in Paris were incapable of devising their own recovery program, Kennan urged an approach in which "we would listen to all that the Europeans had to say, but in the end we would not *ask* them, we would just *tell* them" what sort of assistance program to implement.[27]

Contemptuous of the role of representative institutions in the making of foreign policy, Kennan complained about delays in the U.S. Congress over the administration's request for ERP appropriations and suggested that State Department elites, unencumbered by public debate, could have acted with skill and alacrity.[28] However, Congress did pass a $597 million interim aid bill for Austria, France, Italy and—to appease "Asia-first" Republicans—China, in December 1947. By that time the Council of Foreign Ministers had disintegrated and Russia had responded to the Marshall Plan with its own "Molotov Plan" for Eastern Europe. The Soviets had also created the Cominform to advertise the blessings of socialism across the globe.[29]

The Marshall Plan succeeded in promoting Western European integration and recovery along multilateral capitalist lines, but it hardened Soviet attitudes and cemented the division of Europe. As a program that achieved the "elusive quest" of the interwar period by integrating the French and German economies into a privatized "free world" system oriented around the U.S. dollar, the ERP has been judged "one of the most successful peacetime foreign policies launched by the United States in this century."[30] Yet to the Russians—excluded from the ERP on the advice of Kennan, among others—the Marshall Plan signaled a capitalist offensive aimed at eroding the Soviet sphere of influence as a prelude to challenging communist authority inside Russia itself.[31]

Even after approval of the ERP set in motion the momentum toward recovery and anti-communism in Western Europe, Kennan remained fearful that communists would seize power in Europe before recovery funds could arrive from Washington. Mindful that Bolshevism had triumphed after Russia had been ravaged by war in 1917, he warned that radicals would seek "to disrupt progress under the existing regimes, to throw life into chaos, and eventually to effect the actual overthrow of existing authority and the establishment of workers' governments."[32] The Soviet drive for "the political conquest of Europe" included infiltration of labor unions and political organizations as well as a propaganda drive aimed at persuading the Europeans "that the Anglo-Saxon powers were imperialistic and thirsty for power and had evil designs on people in other countries."[33] Already a series of labor strikes and left-wing demonstrations had led him to urge European leaders to exercise arbitrary authority even as he advised officials in Washington of the need to "manipulate our aid program dexterously for political purposes," advice that Marshall accepted.

Concerned about the immediate threat of Soviet-sponsored internal subversion, Kennan urged development of "a covert political action capability" as a tool of American policy in the cold war. The diplomat supported the creation of the CIA to replace the wartime Office of Strategic Services and served as a "special consultant" to CIA director Hoyt S. Vandenberg during the agency's formative months. Kennan advocated "the maximum development of the propaganda and political warfare techniques," explaining in December 1947 that the political weapons needed to combat Moscow's "non-direct aggression" were "pathetically weak and rudimentary." Moreover, because of "pitiful" American propaganda, Western Europeans had "the damnedest ideas you can imagine of what the United States is after."[34] On May 16, 1948, he implored Lovett to get "some funds right away" for covert operations in Europe, warning that "if this is not done now it will mean that this Government has given up hope of conducting effective political warfare activities for the duration of this administration." Kennan offered to personally supervise a covert operations "directorate."[35]

Kennan's recommendations won approval in June 1948 under NSC 10/2, which created an Office of Special Projects within the CIA to conduct "espionage and counter-espionage activities." Citing the "vicious covert activities of the USSR," the national security paper authorized "propaganda; economic warfare; preventive direct action, including sabatoge, anti-sabatoge, demolition, and evacuation measures; subversion against hostile states . . . and support of indigenous anti-communist elements in threatened countries of the free world."[36]

Years later, in 1975, in testimony before the Church Committee of the U.S. Senate, which was investigating intelligence abuses, Kennan would explain that he and other policy makers had urged covert operations in response to communist subversion in Western Europe. According to the Church Committee's final report, United States "political action meant direct intervention in the electoral processes of foreign governments rather than attempts to influence public opinion through media activities."[37]

CIA covert operations, an integral component of postwar American national security policy, could be used to undermine indigenous communists in Western Europe, thus contributing to containment in the "free world." But Kennan had also said that American strategy should "encourage in every way the spirit of independence and freedom among the Eastern European peoples" and espionage, subversion, and propaganda were means to this end as well. Kennan hoped that through the judicious use of covert operations and the other ideological-political components of containment the United States could promote liberation in the communist bloc by means short of war.[38]

While the CIA initiated covert operations and Congress debated long-term ERP funding, Kennan and the PPS turned their attention to the Mediterranean, where they asserted that "the international Communist movement" was "engaged in a resolute and energetic effort" to establish a Stalinist dictatorship in Greece. The PPS also worried about a communist takeover in Italy, where Washington desired "a friendly, democratic regime" but had to contend with a powerful communist party. To ward off a communist threat to the Iberian peninsula, the PPS recommended support of the dictatorship of Francisco Franco through "normalization of U.S.-Spanish relations, both political and economic."[39]

The way in which the Truman administration built public support for the extension of American power into the Mediterranean brought to the surface many of Kennan's doubts about the ability of a democratic society to conduct a mature foreign policy and prompted his first dissent over the implementation of containment. On February 21, 1947, the British Foreign Office informed the State Department that because of financial instability and war-weariness, Britain could no longer assume its traditional role as the preeminent power along the southern coast of Europe. The message, not unexpected, carried serious implications, particularly for Greece, where a leftist insurgency sought to overthrow the monarchy that Britain had returned to power at the war's end.[40]

Called in to chair an impromptu State Department meeting on the day the British note arrived, Kennan declared that London's withdrawal would leave the Mediterranean open to Soviet ideological-political penetration and he therefore urged that a recommendation in favor of the United States assuming the British position be forwarded to the President. Few officials disagreed and in his Truman Doctrine speech of March 12, 1947, the President, depicting a world divided between the "alternative ways of life" of freedom and totalitarianism, declared that it "must be the policy of the United States to support free peoples who are resisting attempted subjugation by armed minorities or by outside pressures." From Kennan's realist perspective, the presidential address, with its universal pretensions and manichean imagery, aroused memories of idealistic crusades to make the world safe for democracy. He argued that American assistance should be confined exclusively to combating communism in Greece and that no aid be extended to Turkey, where no communist insurgency existed. He raised these objections with Acheson, who declined to order revisions in Truman's text on the basis of Kennan's critique.[41]

As was often the case, Kennan had ignored the domestic political context of U.S. diplomacy in formulating his critique of the Truman Doctrine. In the real world of domestic politics, an unelected President confronted an opposition-controlled Congress and considerable hostility among the press to his call for $400 million in economic and military aid for Greece and Turkey. The Republican Chairman of the Senate Foreign Relations Committee, Arthur Vandenberg, had advised the President that he would have to "scare the hell out of the country" to obtain congressional approval and thus Truman exaggerated the communist threat and, nine days after his address, issued an executive order creating a Federal Employee Loyalty Program. The enunciation of the Truman Doctrine followed by the creation of a program designed to extirpate radicals from government encouraged public fear of Communism and thus built support for the President's policy. Congress approved the aid package and Truman signed it into law on May 22, 1947.[42]

The Truman Doctrine reflected a fundamental misperception about the conflict in the Mediterranean and set a precedent for American intervention in other nation's civil wars. Although Bulgaria, Yugoslavia, and perhaps Albania supported the Greek left, Stalin had conceded Greece to Churchill in the 1944 spheres agreement and the Kremlin had remained indifferent, if not in fact hostile, to the indigenous leftist insurgency in Greece. In 1948 Yugoslav leader Josip Broz Tito would demonstrate the limitations of Soviet influence and explode the myth of monolithic communism, but in the wake of the fears fostered by the Truman Doctrine such lessons were not easily mastered.[43]

Kennan's response to the Truman Doctrine reflected his inability to resolve a conflict between his commitment to opposing communist insurgencies and his desire to limit containment to certain vital regions of the world. Although the southern Mediterranean was not one of the five regions he had identified as crucial to preserving a balance of power, Kennan viewed the Greek civil war as potentially decisive in the struggle with the Soviet Union and stood ready to expand the American military presence in the Mediterranean. Direct U.S. military intervention in the region had already been publicly ruled out and he agreed that such involvement "must generally be considered as a risky and profitless undertaking, apt to do more harm than good." However, if communists began to gain ground, Kennan declared that Washington should bolster an existing naval presence in the Mediterranean and threaten to construct permanent air bases to encourage Moscow to apply "a restraining hand . . . on the Greek and Italian communists." The policy, then, would be to reduce the American military presence only if the communist activities ceased, whereas "further communist pressure will only have the effect of involving us more deeply in a military sense." Kennan's carrot and stick diplomacy hinged on the false assumption that Moscow controlled the leftist insurgency in Greece.[44]

Underlying Kennan's advocacy of containment in Greece—and indeed throughout the world—was his commitment to establishing American credibility and his fears of a communist "bandwagon" effect. The diplomat feared that the "fall" of Greece would "set in motion such a process of panic and defeatism among those resisting communism that communist parties would be able to take over in other countries besides Greece on the strength of this reaction."[45] Kennan thus considered containment vital throughout West-Central Europe and the Mediterranean on the assumption that a single communist victory would inspire communist parties in other countries to attempt to seize power—to jump on the bandwagon. "To deliver up the Near East to Russian political penetration," he explained, ". . . might well be sufficient to push both Italy and France across the fateful line . . . of communist dictatorship" and North Africa and the Iberian peninsula would be next. The loss of Greece could thus represent only the first step toward the eventual loss of Europe, leaving the United States "a lonely country, culturally and politically." Isolated, America would be vulnerable, for "the fact of the matter is that there is a little totalitarian buried somewhere, way down deep, in each and every one of us." On the other hand, if the United States could deliver "a resounding setback to international communism" in Greece, the event could "turn a critical tide and set in motion counter-currents which could change the entire political atmosphere of Europe to our advantage."[46]

Kennan's observations on containment in Greece reveal the extent to which he viewed the cold war as a psychological struggle. Like others in the Truman Administration, he feared that the triumph of communism in any country would have a disastrous bandwagon effect throughout the world. Conversely, successful containment of communism would reassure non-communist regimes of American credibility to come to their defense and would inspire them to fight off communist insurgencies inside their own borders. Because the outcome of conflicts in individual nations carried implications beyond the significance of a single country, *no insurgency* could be allowed to triumph out of fear of the psychological repercussions of a communist victory. This perception of the communist threat virtually ensured that containment would become a global policy despite Kennan's theoretical quest to limit the strategy to vital military-industrial regions.

Kennan recognized that American efforts to defeat Communist insurgencies carried the risk of direct American military intervention in the struggles of individual nations and he warned against the United States becoming involved "in a series of civil wars." Interventions of this nature would "put us in a false position, and into a series of commitments we can probably never get out of. I don't see how any great nation can make itself the arbiter of civil wars of other countries and come out with a clean pattern."[47] Although he warned about the dangers of U.S. intervention, Kennan's fear of a bandwagon effect, determination to uphold the nation's credibility, and efforts to isolate the USSR overshadowed these concerns and led to his advocacy of global containment.

Although the PPS considered Europe its top priority during the early days of the cold war, containment evolved into a global strategy when Kennan and his staff applied it to Asia, Africa, and Latin America. In August 1948 Kennan identified the "vital" areas of containment as all "territories of the Atlantic" from Canada to the Iberian peninsula; Morocco and much of West Africa; "South America from the bulge north"; the Middle East, including Iran; and Japan and the Philippines.[48]

Second only to Western Europe in the minds of America's global planners was securing a noncommunist Japan as the focal point of ideological-political containment across the "great crescent" of Asia, an area south of the Soviet Union, stretching from the Kurile Islands to Pakistan. Japan was to be restored as the political and economic center of a vast, noncommunist region in Asia. Kennan had few illusions about America's ability to shape events in Asia, where U.S. culture and politics had "very little applicability." In order to be successful, the realist planner advised, Americans had to "dispense with all sentimentality and day-dreaming . . . of unreal objectives such as human rights, the raising of living standards, and democratization."[49]

General of the Army Douglas MacArthur, World War II hero and Supreme Commander for the Allied Powers (SCAP) in the Pacific, posed a formidable obstacle to the implementation of containment in Japan. Policy reversals and political opportunism characterized MacArthur's command, which he hoped to ride to the Republican nomination for President in 1948. Kennan and other administration officials feared that MacArthur's reform agenda, which included dissolving the large Japanese economic cartels (the Zaibatsu), instituting purges and war crimes trials, and concluding a hasty peace treaty would impede economic recovery and throw the islands open to Soviet subversion.[50]

Kennan's top adviser on Asia, diplomat John Paton Davies, warned in August 1947 that MacArthur's draft peace treaty would leave Japan vulnerable to "Sovietized totalitarianism." A month later Kennan concurred, telling Undersecretary Lovett that the draft treaty "does not seem to be related to any realistic pattern of objectives" and should be delayed until occupation policy "can be systematically thrashed out." As part of a broad administration offensive against SCAP authority, in late February 1948 Marshall sent Kennan to Tokyo, advising him to be wary of MacArthur's mammoth ego and blustering. To avoid offending the Supreme Commander, Kennan "very much wished to avoid giving the impression of this being a high-powered mission," though it was the first of several that the administration launched in pursuit of a "reverse course" in Occupied Japan.[51]

MacArthur displayed his disdain for State Department interference by subjecting Kennan to a thundering monologue on the Asian mentality and the wisdom of his own efforts to bring democracy and Christianity to Japan. The diplomat weathered this storm and after conducting a series of interviews concluded that the root of MacArthur's maladministration was his underestimation of the threat of communist subversion in Japan. The Supreme Commander was "not worried about indirect aggression by political penetration" because of his conviction that "the Japanese people are strongly averse to communism and will not accept it." Declaring that he was "unable to agree with a portion of this pattern of thought," Kennan argued that policy should be redirected toward "the achievement of maximum stability of Japanese society, in order that Japan may best be able to stand on her own feet when the protecting hand is withdrawn." Occupation administration had to be brought into line with the broader national security policy of containment, which entailed securing Japan from outside "military pressures"; initiating "an intensive program of economic recovery"; and "a relaxation in occupational control, designed to stimulate a greater sense of direct responsibility on the part of the Japanese Government." Kennan had little interest in promoting democratic reform, which he insisted would be exploited by communists, but instead sought to promote economic recovery and political stability by empowering Japanese elites.[52]

The atmosphere of sycophancy around MacArthur and evidence of a parasitic "American brand of Philistinism" among the occupation forces disturbed Kennan during his Far Eastern tour. While the Japanese struggled to recover from the wartime devastation, he complained that the Americans in Tokyo "monopolized . . . everything that smacks of comfort or elegance or luxury" and he found them typical of the "monotony of contemporary American social life, its unbending drinking rituals, the obvious paucity of its purposes, and its unimaginative devotion to outward convention in the absence of inner content and even enjoyment." Disgusted by the shallowness of American culture, Kennan had no desire to see it transplanted on to Asian shores.[53]

Anxious to maintain a smooth working relationship at the highest levels of the Truman administration, Kennan kept these explosive thoughts off the record while shepherding through the national security bureaucracy the broad outlines of the reverse course in occupied Japan. Following his return to Washington, he submitted PPS 28/2, which emphasized ideological-political containment and attacked SCAP policies that were seen as undermining that goal. Deconcentration, the taking of repara-tions in the form of industrial capacity, the ousting of strong national-ists, war industry leaders, and senior police officials undermined eco-nomic recovery and political stability, leaving Japan vulnerable to communist subversion.

"Heretofore," Kennan observed, "the trend of the occupation has been quite agreeable to the Russians—many of the occupational policies being almost indistinguishable from the 'softening up' policies which Russian has pursued in Soviet occupied countries in Europe." He argued that a modern Japanese security force was best equipped to maintain order and purge suspected communists, a principal goal of the reverse course. An internal security force would allow for reducing the size of the American occupation that he found so offensive as well as undermin-ing the appeal of communist propaganda which focused on an imperial Western presence in Japan.[54]

The implementation of the reverse course required "a further period of occupational control" before the conclusion of a Japanese peace treaty with Russia and the other allied powers, Kennan advised. As with ideological-political containment in Europe, economic recovery and the show of resolve in Japan would convince Moscow to abandon subver-sion for negotiation on Western terms. "If we were to embark on a program of recovery as opposed to reform, of stability as opposed to uncertainty, nothing," he insisted, "could be better calculated to bring the Soviets to the peace table more swiftly and at our terms." After receiving the endorsement and minor alterations of Army and State Department planners, the recommendations embodied in PPS 28 went to Truman as NSC-13 and received the President's approval.[55]

Kennan's mission succeeded in reorienting occupation policy toward a program aimed at reducing the risks of internal communist subversion in Japan. The changes in the American approach to Occupied Japan illustrated that military victory alone counted for very little "unless it is followed up with a political program no less determined, no less re-sourceful, no less energetic and realistic than the military effort" itself, the diplomat told a War College audience in May 1948. Without the follow-up program of ideological-political containment, the "gains of the battlefield can be lost in a shorter time than it took to win them. It is here, if anywhere, I think that we have been dangerously weak in the post-hostility period."[56]

64

By the fall of 1949, Kennan had concluded that the pace of stabilization of the Japanese economy and society were sufficient to terminate the American occupation and effect a peace treaty with Tokyo. The State Department selected him as its spokesman in opposing the Joint Chiefs of Staff, who argued that a peace treaty would remain premature until Japanese democracy and "western orientation" were "established beyond all question." Uninterested in establishing democracy in Japan, Kennan argued that the absence of a peace treaty fueled resentment among the Japanese and offered an issue around which to rally anti-Western sentiment that might be exploited by Russia. At the same time, the continued presence of a large contingent of American troops remained, in his judgment, "an irritating and not a stabilizing influence on the Japanese population."[57]

Kennan's recommendations brought him into conflict with the leading Republican internationalist, John Foster Dulles, to whom, in an act of bipartisanship, the new Secretary of State, Dean Acheson, had given responsibility for concluding the Japanese peace treaty. A prominent attorney who aspired to be Secretary of State himself, Dulles was a man of distinction but Kennan viewed him as a political intruder into the realm of professional diplomacy. Dulles's draft treaty envisioned the retention of Western conventional forces in Japan and Okinawa in contrast to Kennan's proposal to provide an indigenous "strong, mobile central police force, with a powerful maritime branch, capable of acting anywhere in Japan under orders of the central government."[58]

After reviewing drafts of the proposed treaty in the summer of 1950, Kennan expressed "dismay" over Dulles's legalistic-moralistic approach and the "school-masterish and smug attitude" conveyed toward Japan. He argued that the peace treaty would undermine "our future political relations with the Japanese people" and would "obscure for them a correct view of their own national interest."[59] Fearful that American occupation policy would play into the hands of Soviet-sponsored internal subversion, Kennan underestimated the ability of the United States to convert its World War II enemies into lasting allies. This was true of his views about western Germany no less than Japan.

In China, on the other hand, the imminent threat of communism posed only "a minor security concern" to Kennan because the Kremlin's ability to control events on the mainland was "severely qualified." Showing a sharp appreciation of Chinese realities—for which he credited

John Paton Davies—Kennan wrote that "the salvation or destruction of China lies essentially with the Chinese—not with foreigners." This approach played poorly in Congress, however, as the "China lobby" argued in behalf of Jiang Jieshi's regime and a "China bloc" of senators and representatives proved receptive to their blandishments. Kennan opposed intervention in the Chinese civil war, arguing that it was the "normal practice" of the United States not to interfere in another country's domestic contests. Characterizing calls for military and economic aid to Jiang as "frivolous and irresponsible," he declared that Americans should reconcile themselves to the possibility of "further deterioration of the situation [that] we may be powerless to prevent."[60]

As Jiang's regime collapsed in the fall of 1949, Kennan reversed himself, overrode the opposition of his staff, abandoned pretenses about America's "normal practice" of nonintervention, and called for a U.S. military takeover of Taiwan and the Pescadore islands off China's coast. Unlike Jiang's vocal supporters, Kennan had no intention of *saving* the regime but called, instead, for "the *removal* of the present Nationalist administrators from the islands and the establishment of a provisional international or U.S. regime which would invoke the principle of self-determination for the islanders." Acting on his own "instinct," Kennan asserted that if the action was "adopted and carried through with sufficient resolution, speed, ruthlessness, and self-assurance, the way Theodore Roosevelt might have done it, it would not only be successful but have an electrifying effect in this country and throughout the Far East."[61]

Kennan hoped to prevent the spread of Chinese communism from the mainland to Taiwan and the offshore islands and had no faith in the ability of Jiang's regime to anchor ideological-political containment, believing instead that it was an inviting target for communist subversion. While he doubted that Moscow could exercise direct authority over China, Kennan still feared the psychological repercussions, or bandwagon effect, of any communist success and he hoped, once again, that bold American action would serve as a demonstration of American resolve. The Truman administration, under heavy domestic pressure, committed itself to containment of the islands, but was in no position to consider Kennan's ill-conceived proposal to effect Jiang's ouster.

The Generalissimo's supporters in Washington blamed the destruction of his regime on incompetence and even treason within the Truman administration. Vocal Republicans, languishing in a seventeen-year absence from the White House, attempted to discredit Truman and Acheson by blaming them for the fall of China in October 1949 and by spreading the charge of disloyalty against the Democrats. In such a climate Washington could not recognize the new regime in Beijing, even had the administration been so inclined.[62]

Although he condemned the Chinese communists for overthrowing "the legitimate and recognized government of China"—the same government he proposed that the United States itself overthrow on Taiwan —Kennan called on the administration to "aggressively assume the offensive in what is rapidly developing into a major issue between it and the legislature." The administration had a good record in the Far East, he advised Acheson in June 1949, but had failed to make its case with the public to avoid open criticism of Jiang. Kennan encouraged the decision to publish the State Department White Paper that explained America's inability to control events in China. Recalling the impact of his own X-Article, Kennan also recommended publication of "an anonymous interpretive article on the Chinese situation." The President should then culminate the public relations offensive with a major speech sounding "a ringing and confident assertion of the correctness of our policy."[63]

Despite its efforts to provide a realistic assessment of events in the Far East, the Truman administration reeled from the blows delivered by its critics and redoubled its commitment to containment in the rest of Asia. In addition to Japan, the PPS called for the Philippines to serve "as a bulwark of U.S. security" and to "assume an active and constructive role in developing a counter-force to communism" in Asia.[64] Equally significant was the Southeast Asian mainland, a region which had "become the target of a coordinated offensive plainly directed by the Kremlin."

World War II had unleashed powerful nationalist movements committed to overcoming legacies of European and Japanese colonialism in Southeast Asia, changes that confronted American planners with a dilemma. The PPS realized that "colonialism in an advancing world is an unnatural social relationship" and that any attempt to oppose nationalism constituted "an anti-historical act likely in the long run to create more problems than it solves and cause more damage than benefit." The problem, however, was that the Soviet Union, posing as a liberator, "appears recently to have begun to introduce its own direct agents" into Southeast Asia. The Kremlin sought "ultimate control" in order to use the region as " a pawn in the struggle between the Soviet world and the Free World." The primary objective in Southeast Asia, Kennan explained, was "to contain and steadily reduce Kremlin influence," thus allowing the region "to develop in harmony with the Atlantic community and the rest of the Free World."

The first step toward containment in Southeast Asia was to convince France and the Netherlands to abandon "irrational" colonial regimes that offered "an ideal culture for the breeding of the communist virus." Kennan called for "the sympathetic encouragement of Asiatic nationalism" as the only alternative "between polarization and Stalinization." The Dutch attempt to reassert authority in Indonesia, for example, constituted "a disruptive element" and the PPS recommended empowering republican leaders who would oppose international communism in the islands. Only in Malaysia, where the British presence provided the sole alternative to communism, should colonial control be maintained.[65]

Kennan and his Truman Administration colleagues thus struggled to reconcile the quest for containment with the dangers of Western intervention in a region dominated by a highly charged atmosphere of anticolonialism. But because Southeast Asia was "an integral part of that great crescent formed by the Indian Peninsula, Australia and Japan," the stakes were too high for Washington to remain aloof. The success of the entire containment program in Asia depended, Kennan explained, on developing "economic interdependence between [Southeast Asia], as supplier of raw materials, and Japan, western Europe and India, as suppliers of finished goods, with due recognition, however, of the legitimate aspirations of SEA countries for some diversification of their economies."

As in the case of Greece, Kennan overestimated Soviet influence over indigenous national communists such as Vietnam's Ho Chi Minh and feared that a bandwagon effect would ensue in the event of a communist triumph in Southeast Asia. Although only of "secondary strategic importance" by itself, he explained, the region nevertheless represented "a vital segment on the line of containment" and should be made to serve as "an interdependent and integrated counterforce to Stalinism in this quarter of the world." Loss of Southeast Asia in the wake of the "grievous political defeat" suffered in China would constitute "a major political rout the repercussions of which will be felt throughout the rest of the world, especially in the Middle East and in a then critically exposed

Australia." Such reasoning transformed peripheral regions into vital proving grounds of American credibility and eventually underscored the call for U.S. military intervention in Indochina.[66]

Literally no area of the world escaped the attention of Kennan and his staff during the early cold war. In January 1948 the PPS studied the thorny issue of the partition of Palestine, an event that ushered in an epoch of Arab-Israeli conflict in the Mideast. Washington had endorsed the UN-mandated partition in 1946 but persistent Arab-Jewish clashes boded poorly for the chances of a peaceful solution. Reflecting the prevailing State Department outlook, Kennan showed more concern for access to Mideast oil and the prospects of Soviet political penetration than for Zionism. The PPS concluded that "U.S. prestige in the Moslem world has suffered a severe blow and U.S. strategic interest in those areas will continue to be adversely affected to the extent that we continue to support partition." He declared that the best policy would be to "extricate ourselves . . . as rapidly as possible" from a "confused and tragic situation" which he blamed primarily on "the Jewish leaders and organizations who have pushed so persistently for the pursuit of objectives which could scarcely fail to lead to violent results." Fears that Moscow would exploit unrest in the Middle East, not anti-Semitism, underlay Kennan's recommendations, which Marshall embraced. However, mindful of the Jewish vote in a longshot election bid and sensitive to the plight of Jews in the wake of the Holocaust, Truman overrode Marshall and the PPS in favor of partition and the recognition of Israel.[67]

In North Africa, Kennan supported maintaining French colonialism in an effort to appease an important European ally and bolster containment. Washington should assure leaders in Paris that "we are not seeking to disrupt their empire" and that "in our opinion the people of Morocco can best advance under French tutelege." The focus of the American approach to this region was to "stress the fact that we are prepared to cooperate in every feasible way with the object of combating communism in the area." The best Kennan could offer North African nationalists was the "gradual evolution of dependent peoples toward self-government."[68]

Kennan's PPS recommended that the United States tap the support of the Catholic Church, labor, landowners, and liberals to oppose the spread of communism in Latin America. The diplomat warned, however, that cooperation with "reactionary forces" in the region might in the long term undermine American interests and thus "should be very carefully considered in the light of our long-range national interests." He recommended bolstering police forces, refusing passports to known communists and, above all, economic development as means of effecting ideological-political containment in the region.[69] Although Kennan endorsed the 1947 Treaty of Rio de Janiero and wrote a speech in favor of collective defense which Truman delivered in Latin America, he later criticized NSC 56, which emphasized military defense in the region under the auspices of the Rio Treaty. Kennan strove to maintain the focus on ideological-political, as opposed to military, containment and argued that "substantial increases in armed forces and armaments could result in a weakening of solidarity through the aggravation of national fears and rivalries."[70]

In the winter of 1950 Kennan visited Mexico City, Caracas, Rio de Janiero, São Paulo, Montevideo, Buenos Aires, Lima, and Panama City in a tour coinciding with a meeting of U.S. ambassadors to the region. Protestors greeted the diplomat in Rio and São Paulo, denouncing U.S. imperialism and burning Kennan in effigy. Police recorded 100 arrests in San Paulo alone on March 6. Assuming that only communists would protest U.S. policies in Latin America, Kennan asserted that the region was "honeycombed" with Stalin's agents.[71]

Victorian racism and Eurocentrism underlay Kennan's approach to Latin America and the developing world. Contemptuous of Latin culture, he doubted that there existed "any other region of the earth in which nature and human behavior could have combined to produce a more unhappy and hopeless background for the conduct of human life." For this he blamed the "merciless cruelty" and "religious fanaticism" of the Spanish invasion which had left a legacy of poverty and shattered ideals. Latin Americans attempted to hide "the wretchedness and squalor of the hinterlands" behind "the inordinate splendor and pretense" of their cities, while their "subconscious recognition of the failure of the group" manifested itself in a "pathetic urge to create an illusion of desperate courage, supreme cleverness, and a limitless virility where the more constructive virtues are so conspicuously lacking."

After psychoanalyzing the Latin character, Kennan warned the United States against adopting "an indulgent and complacent view of Communist activities in the New World," an attitude that would represent "historical turning-away from traditional United States policy in the hemisphere." The planning chief endorsed the courting of authoritarian regimes opposed to communism even if they employed "harsh governmental measures of repression," thus anticipating an argument popularized by diplomat Jeane Kirkpatrick in 1979. Authoritarian regimes provided "preferable alternatives, and indeed the only alternatives, to further communist successes," Kennan explained. Concern over communist penetration thus compelled his support of the type of authoritarian regimes he had condemned in Russia and Eastern Europe even though he acknowledged the relative weakness of communist parties in the region. Latin American desk officers in the State Department resented Kennan's intrusion into their domain, but shared his anti-communist perceptions.[72]

From the inception of the Marshall Plan in the spring of 1947 to his departure as PPS director in 1950, Kennan had charted an aggressive course designed to contain communism and isolate and weaken the USSR. The diplomat promoted a successful program to foster economic recovery and political stabilization in western Europe and Japan while relations with Moscow continued to deteriorate. Obsessed with the threat of communist subversion, Kennan had little sympathy with proponents of democratic reform and self-determination and denied the legitimacy of indigenous communist parties.

Despite Kennan's theoretical desire to limit containment to the five regions in which military strength could be produced in quantity, the record of the PPS reveals that he urged the extension of containment into the Mideast, North Africa, Latin America, Taiwan, across the "great crescent," and the Pacific Ocean. When the NSC and the President embraced these recommendations, Kennan saw containment implemented on a global scale.

Despite his theoretical realism, Kennan's pursuit of America's national interests entailed establishing a "balance" of power weighted heavily against the Soviet Union and determined to crush communist movements across the globe. He was as guilty as anyone in the Truman administration of assuming that Moscow controlled virtually all communist activity in the world. Fearful of a bandwagon effect, Kennan asserted the need to establish U.S. credibility to oppose communist movements on all fronts, with the exception of mainland China, which he recognized was beyond America's grasp. The diplomat viewed the cold war as a deadly struggle in which the United States had to spearhead containment of communist insurgencies across the globe or face the erosion of its own economic and political independence.

Although he recognized the power of revolutionary nationalism and foresaw the dangers of American intervention in third world conflicts, Kennan's intense fear of the psychological repercussions of communist victories made him willing to take risks in the assertion of American power. Unfortunately, he did not have the luxury of hindsight to draw upon during his formulation of containment. The perception of monolithic communism emanating from Moscow today seems naïve in the wake of the Sino-Soviet conflict and the full flowering of polycentrism, but such realities were not apparent to those who witnessed the shocks of Munich, blitzkrieg, Pearl Harbor, the "loss" of China and the outbreak of war in Korea. Kennan's perceptions may well have been different had he contemplated the results of a recent study which suggests that nations are far more likely to "balance"—to unite against a menacing power—than to bandwagon by acquiescing to a threatening power's demands. Political scientist Stephen Walt found in his analysis of the sweep of postwar international relations that balancing was "far more common than bandwagoning" and only the weakest and most isolated states tended to succumb to great-power pressure.[73]

Kennan's strident anti-communism and his willingness to support intervention undermined his efforts to implement a realistic program of ideological-political containment. The American public, responding to the simplistic perceptions embodied in the Truman Doctrine and the X-Article, virtually ruled out accommodation between the Kremlin and the "Free World." Even before he resigned as PPS director and resumed his accustomed role as an outsider and critic of the foreign policy consensus, Kennan realized that such perceptions lay at the root of an alarming trend toward the militarization of containment. In attempting to reverse this development, however, he would enjoy considerably less success than in his effort to summon the nation into the global confrontation with the USSR.

IV

The Militarization of Containment

Successful at helping to forge the cold war consensus and implement containment on a global scale, Kennan began to lose influence over American foreign policy in 1948. By the end of that year the Truman administration had agreed to American participation in the North Atlantic Treaty Organization over his objections and rejected his call for German reunification within a supranational European federation. Citing NATO, the refusal to negotiate with Russia over the division of Europe, the decision to build a hydrogen bomb, and NSC-68 as deviations from ideological-political containment, Kennan became the State Department's leading advocate of disengagement in Europe. The militarization of containment prompted Kennan's resignation as PPS director, eroded his faith in postwar American internationalism, and found him reassuming his accustomed role as outsider and critic.

An indirect dialogue between Kennan and journalist Walter Lippmann in 1948 underscored the changes in the diplomat's thinking on containment. While recovering in Bethesda Naval Hospital from an attack of duodenal ulcers, Kennan drafted a belated reply to Lippmann's critique of containment. Believing that the X-Article was "a dangerous statement of policy," Lippmann—an expert on foreign affairs since World War I —had subjected Kennan's essays to a penetrating analysis that was published in 1947 as *The Cold War*. He argued that X's strategy hinged on the "unproved assumption" that Soviet power was weak and impermanent and labled containment "a strategic monstrosity" that could "be implemented only by recruiting, subsidizing and supporting a heterogeneous array of satellites, clients, dependents and puppets." Lippmann urged a negotiated withdrawal of both Russian and Western forces from Europe, arguing that Washington and its allies should pay the necessary "ransom" to Russia in the form of trade agreements, concessions, and reparations to obtain peace treaties pertaining to Germany and Austria. "For a diplomat to think that rival and unfriendly powers cannot be brought to a settlement," Lippmann advised, "is to forget what diplomacy is about."[1]

"What is wrong in fact with the whole policy of containment?" Kennan shot back in a reply that he drafted but never sent to Lippmann. Declaring that containment "has worked better than I would dared to have hoped a year ago," the diplomat argued that American actions had saved several nations from communist subversion and could still defeat Soviet power. "When I say that they have their own internal contradictions which will eventually trip them up," he wrote, "I speak with greater confidence, and I am willing to let time be the judge." Doubting that the cold war could be resolved by an agreement "to let bygones be bygones," Kennan declared that

> the saddest part of this year's experience with the high affairs of state is not the realization of how hard it is for a democracy to conduct a successful foreign policy—although that is sad. It is the realization that if it did conduct a successful foreign policy, so few people would recognize it for what it was.[2]

Despite the spirited defense from his hospital bed in April, by the end of 1948 Kennan was in substantial agreement with Lippmann's critique of containment.

Although the unavailability of Soviet diplomatic records continues to limit cold war scholarship, it is generally believed that the USSR viewed the Truman Doctrine, the Marshall Plan, and the revitalization of western Germany as aggressive programs designed to undermine Moscow's sphere of influence in Europe.[3] As Kennan himself noted in November 1947, the implementation of containment in Western Europe had prompted "a consolidation of communist power throughout Eastern

Europe" and was at the root Stalin's intention to "clamp down completely on Czechoslovakia."[4] Presumably Stalin's fears of a renascent Germany and "capitalist encirclement" prompted the February 1948 coup in which communists began to oust noncommunist Cabinet members from the Czech coalition government in a series of events that stirred memories of Hitler and prompted warnings against appeasement in the West. Truman declared that "moral God fearing peoples . . . must save the world from Atheism and totalitarianism."[5]

Western observers blamed Moscow for the death in Prague of the Czech liberal leader Jan Masaryk—who either committed suicide or was thrown to his death on March 10—and reacted with plans to bolster Western defenses. Meeting in Brussels one week after Masaryk's death, leaders from Britain, France, Belgium, the Netherlands, and Luxembourg signed a fifty-year collective defense treaty in which they declared that an attack on one nation would be considered an attack on all. In a speech before the full Congress that same March 17, Truman applauded the move and called for swift passage of the European Recovery Program, resumption of the draft, and universal military training. Congress approved the first two, but not the last.[6]

Although Kennan had anticipated the possibility of a Soviet-inspired coup in Czechoslovakia, the news of the events in Prague still proved shocking and prompted him to advocate extreme measures in response. Fearing that the Czech coup might have been the first of a series of adventuristic Kremlin actions, he called for a prompt display of American credibility to defend Europe and head off a possible bandwagon effect. The PPS director suggested that the Italian Communist Party be outlawed before its popularity could be tested in upcoming elections and advocated direct American military intervention in the likely event of an ensuing civil war in Italy. "This would admittedly result in much violence and probably a military division of Italy," he cabled from Manila, but "it might well be preferable to a bloodless election victory, unopposed by ourselves, which would give the Communists the entire peninsula at one coup and send waves of panic to all surrounding areas." The Truman administration rejected this panicky advice, but authorized covert intervention in Italian politics.[7]

By the time Kennan returned from Asia and recovered from a flareup of his ulcers, American officials had approved British Foreign Minister Ernest Bevin's proposal to include the United States in the Brussels collective defense treaty based on Articles 51 and 52 of the UN Charter, which authorized regional collective security pacts. Secretary of State George Marshall approved the recommendation and informed London that Washington would "proceed at once in the joint discussions on the establishment of an Atlantic security system." At the same time, the Western powers took unilateral action toward the creation of a western German state in the spring of 1948, which prompted Moscow to break off Allied Control Council discussions, thus terminating efforts at great power cooperation in Germany.[8]

The momentum toward a Western military alliance represented a deviation from ideological-political containment and left Kennan alarmed. He favored providing assurances of American military backing in the event of Soviet aggression in Western Europe, but opposed a formal military alliance that would detract from combating the central threat, which was internal communist subversion. He advocated "realistic staff talks" about the military defense of Western Europe in the event of war rather than "a public political and military alliance" and opposed plans to seek the support of Republican leaders Arthur Vandenberg and John Foster Dulles for a Congressional resolution on coordinating defense plans with Western Europe.[9]

American involvement in Europe's defense strengthened containment, as Kennan saw it, only insofar as it bolstered the confidence of Europeans to resist Soviet-sponsored ideological-political subversion. The diplomat accepted the need for discussions "to keep the ball rolling and keep up the hopes of peoples in Europe"[10] but argued that economic recovery and political stability were more important than "intensive rearmament," which would bring "an uneconomic and regrettable diversion of effort." A collective security pact was "not the main answer to the present Soviet effort to dominate the European continent."[11]

Kennan argued that "the West could win this cold war," but only if it focused on combating the ideological-political threat rather than devoting its attention to the unlikely prospect of a Soviet blitzkrieg. After reluctantly endorsing the concept of an Atlantic alliance, he tried to limit its geographic scope by excluding Italy, Greece, Turkey, Norway, and Sweden, suggesting instead that they serve as "stepping stone" countries that could allow their territory to be used by NATO members in the event of war with Russia. Thinking of Turkey and Scandinavia, Kennan warned that "there was a certain danger in incorporating states which lay so close to the Soviet orbit," adding that there was "no logical stopping point in the development of a system of anti-Russian alliances until that system has circled the globe and has embraced all the non-communist countries of Europe, Asia and Africa."[12]

Kennan's chief concern was that NATO would cement the division of Germany and of Europe and undermine efforts to liberate Eastern Europe from Soviet hegemony. The Western alliance would destroy the prospects for Austrian and German settlements and make it impossible for the satellite nations "to contemplate anything in the nature of a gradual withdrawal from Russian domination, since any move in that direction would take on the aspect of a provocative military move." He declared that the United States "should not do things which tend to fix, and make unchangeable by peaceful means, the present line of east-west division."[13]

Rejecting Kennan's advice, the Truman administration mobilized public support for an unprecedented American commitment to the defense of Europe. The Vandenberg Resolution, which sailed through the Senate by a vote of 64–4 on June 11, crowned these efforts and paved the way for American participation in NATO in 1949. Despite his reservations, Kennan met his obligation as one of the Truman administration's top diplomats and helped draft NSC-9, the leading policy paper on the issue of American involvement in the European security pact. NSC-9 drew on several State Department policy studies, including Kennan's own PPS 27/2, which called on Western Europeans to draw up their own defense plans, just as they had been asked to plan their own program for European recovery. Approved by Truman on July 2, NSC-9 recommended that the Brussels Pact be broadened into a collective defense agreement for the "North Atlantic area," which encompassed most of Western Europe, the United States, and Canada.[14]

Kennan's was a lonely voice in opposition to NATO. West Europeans craved reassurance against invasion in the wake of two world wars and most American officials viewed NATO as a necessary corollary to the ERP and ideological-political containment. The combination of European pressure and the support of Forrestal, Marshall, Robert Lovett, and John D. Hickerson, head of the State Department's European Affairs division, overwhelmed Kennan's objections. In addition to disagreeing with Kennan over the alliance, Hickerson and the other heads of the geographic desks resented the very existence of the PPS, which had direct access to the Secretary of State and the authority to propose policy for "their" regions. "There was bound to be resentment and disquiet about the ability we had initially to go to the Secretary and hand him recommendations which the heads of the geographic areas had not really agreed to," Kennan observed in 1950. The geographic experts "were bound to feel that this was undercutting their authority."[15]

To Kennan, the creation of NATO was a seminal event which changed his thinking on the cold war and his own place in the foreign affairs bureaucracy. By late 1948 he had become more willing to look at events from the Soviet perspective and had grown as concerned about what he perceived as American overzealousness as he had been in previous years with the threat of Soviet-sponsored communist subversion. NATO cemented the division of Europe into military blocs just as the Marshall Plan had divided the continent into economic spheres and neither promised to lead to German reunification, liberation in Eastern Europe, nor to place maximum pressure on Moscow. Kennan, who was becoming increasingly disenchanted over the unfolding of the cold war, grew distant from his colleagues in government and by 1950 had made an almost complete reversion to his accustomed role as outsider and critic of the foreign policy consensus.

In Kennan's judgment NATO reflected a preoccupation with militarism and a disturbing tendency to base American diplomacy on worst-case scenarios. He warned Marshall against making the assumption "that because the Soviets, according to our calculations, have the *capability* to do a certain thing, this is necessarily what they would do" and advised that the threat of subversion in contrast with outright military aggression was "the difference between Stalin and Hitler." Western statesmen, he complained, had become so preoccupied with the military vulnerability of western Europe that they could think of little else than military defense and this caused them "to take their eye off the real ball, which is economic recovery and the liquidation of the internal communist menace." The preoccupation with military affairs threatened to "close the doors to any eventual peaceful solution" and "leave the Russians no way out even if they wanted to get out," thus making the division of Europe "insoluble by any other than military means."[16]

The Berlin Blockade in the summer of 1948 carried the threat of just such a war and encouraged the militarization of Western policy. In early June the Western powers attempted to calm French concerns over the revival of western Germany by creating an international authority to oversee the Ruhr industrial region and through a pledge that American troops would remain in Germany indefinitely. Following an agreement to coordinate economic policies in the three occupation zones of western Germany, the Allies announced plans to circulate a new currency in Berlin. As the Western powers moved to unify their sphere, Moscow responded on June 24 with a blockade of overland routes to Berlin in an effort to shut off and incorporate the German capital into Russia's eastern sphere. Washington responded with a massive airlift to supply West Berlin and cold war tensions were at a peak.[17]

Resolute in his advocacy of maintaining Western credibility through the defense of Berlin, Kennan declared in a speech written for Marshall that "we cannot let down the people of Berlin without letting down the people of the world." He also criticized the Joint Chiefs of Staff for considering withdrawal from Berlin, arguing that its "symbolic significance" justified the risk of war in Central Europe and that abandonment of Berlin would create a "general impression of western weakness" that would encourage further adventurism by Stalin. In October Russian experts Kennan and Charles Bohlen declared that the Kremlin was "solely" responsible for the threat to peace and opposed negotiations as long as the Berlin Blockade continued.[18]

Responding to a request from Defense Secretary James V. Forrestal for a comprehensive statement on the Soviet Union in the wake of the Berlin Blockade, Kennan declared that Russia remained "the outstanding problem of U.S. foreign policy." American diplomacy still sought to reduce the Kremlin's power and influence and to force a reversal of Moscow's foreign policy by means short of war. The USSR must be made to eschew conflict as the basis of international life, to grant the right of independence throughout Europe, and to allow noncommunist nationalism and freedom of association across international borders. The Marshall Plan had laid the foundations for a revived Western Europe and had forced Moscow to reveal its "crude and ugly" domination of Eastern Europe, a process that had served "to discredit the satellite governments with their own peoples and to heighten the discontent of those peoples and their desire for free association with other nations." Kennan still advocated an aggressive program of ideological-political containment, backed by a strong military, to effect the gradual erosion of Moscow's sphere of influence and argued that "the long-term danger of war will inevitably be greater if Europe remains split along the present lines than it will be if Russian power is peacefully withdrawn in good time and a normal balance restored to the European community."[19]

Truman and the NSC accepted the broad outlines of Kennan's paper on Russia with the adoption of NSC 20/4 on November 24, 1948. The policy statement added the assertion, however, that "Communist ideology and Soviet behavior clearly demonstrate that the ultimate objective of the leaders of the USSR is the domination of the world." Such statements, combined with the events in Czechoslovakia and Berlin, contributed to the tendency, deplored by Kennan, to perceive the Soviet threat as predominantly a military one.[20]

The fears fostered by the Czechoslovakian coup and the Berlin blockade ensured the approval of NATO, the militarization of containment, and Kennan's growing disenchantment with his nation's approach to the cold war. From his wartime essays through the X-Article, Kennan had argued that ideological-political containment would compel a Soviet retreat, but he now recognized that Russia would cling to its sphere of influence in Europe. Writing early in 1950, he explained that NATO

> must have appeared to the Russians as, of course, an alliance against them. They must have realized that from then on, in giving up any influence anywhere in eastern or central Europe they ran the enormous prestige risk of abandoning territory to a military alliance in which their outstanding adversary in the eyes of the world played a dominant part. From then on it must have appeared to the Kremlin leaders that there were only two possibilities conceivable from the standpoint of their interests: either the firm retention of their hold on eastern and central Europe, or a military conflict.[21]

The cementing of the division of the continent meant that Kennan's postwar strategy was coming unglued. The West had displayed its credibility and had begun to rebuild a multilateral capitalist economic system while warding off communist subversion in Western Europe, yet the Soviet Union had neither collapsed nor receded, as Kennan had repeatedly predicted it would do, but instead held to its positions. He now recognized that the increasingly militarized conflict and the division of Germany promised to perpetuate a stalemate in the cold war rather than the victory over the Kremlin he had been forecasting since the end of the war in Europe.

The failure of liberation and the militarization of containment prompted Kennan to reverse course and advocate immediate negotiations with the Soviet Union. In his essays and lectures on containment since his return to Moscow in 1944, the diplomat had sanctioned negotiations only if Soviet power began to recede and communist subversion had ceased. However, the realization that immediate negotiations offered the only means to avoid the permanent division of Europe now prompted his advocacy of German reunification and the withdrawal of foreign troops from Central Europe. With Russia still struggling to recover from the war and now plagued by Yugoslavia's dissidence, he thought Stalin might be willing to negotiate on these questions. Kennan discovered, however, that his own country was not.

Germany was the key to any hopes for a successful negotiated settlement in Europe and the inability of the USSR and the Western powers to reach such an agreement ensured a lasting cold war. Since Potsdam both powers had been unable to resolve the conflicting goals of Russia's demand for reparations and America's desire to preserve German industry as a bulwark for rebuilding multilateral capitalism in Europe. "The guts of the problem of peace with Russia is Germany and Austria," Kennan declared. "If a settlement can be reached there, the face of Europe will change overnight" but in the absence of agreement on unification, both the Western powers and the Soviets would continue to pursue unilateral policies in their respective occupation zones leading to the permanent division of Germany.[22]

Kennan advocated a negotiated settlement in which the major powers would agree to "disengage" their troops from Germany, which would then be unified and put at the center of a nonaligned Western Europe. On August 12, 1948, he forwarded PPS 37, which called for a "broad settlement" with the Soviet Union over Germany, Austria, and the disputed Adriatic port city of Trieste. Such a settlement, he declared, could resolve the Berlin crisis, save both powers from costly occupation programs, and assuage Western European security fears as the Soviets withdrew to the East. "The strongest arguments against the course which I favor," Kennan noted, "are those which related to the danger of the reestablishment of a unified Germany." He admitted that the West faced "a painfully difficult decision" but doubted there would ever be a more propitious time to seek "disengagement" in Europe. He explained that if the division of Europe cannot be overcome peacefully at this juncture, when the lines of cleavage have not yet hardened completely across the continent, when the Soviet Union (as I believe) is not yet ready for another war, when the anti-communist sentiment in Germany is momentarily stronger than usual, and when the Soviet satellite area is troubled with serious dissension, uncertainty and disaffection, then it is not likely that prospects for a peaceful resolution of Europe's problems will be better after a further period of waiting.[23]

Kennan's call for a negotiated settlement received virtually no support in the State Department. Hickerson concluded that "the dangers of the proposed approach outweigh its advantages and it would not be in the interests of the United States to make this proposal." Hickerson argued that the Soviet Union respected armed strength, not international agreements, and that since containment had not been fully implemented "it would be highly dangerous to agree to unite Germany along the lines you propose until Western Europe is stronger, both economically and militarily." Responses from State's Occupied Areas and Economic Affairs divisions concurred with Hickerson and on September 8 Kennan forwarded the negative responses to Marshall and Lovett, adding only a terse, "I disagree with them all."[24]

Persistent in his efforts to encourage disengagement from Germany, Kennan solicited the views of outside consultants for a new PPS study. The consultants included Dean Acheson, who had resigned as Undersecretary on June 30, 1947; *Foreign Affairs* editor Hamilton Fish Armstrong; Edmund Walsh, director of the Georgetown Foreign Service school; the presidents of B.F. Goodrich and Vassar College; and prominent East Coast attorneys. Under Kennan's direction, the "special consultative group" endorsed his PPS 37/1, or "Program A," which attempted to establish the American negotiating position on Germany in the event of a renewed meeting of the Council of Foreign Ministers.[25]

The essence of Program A was the establishment of a provisional German government and the simultaneous termination of military authority throughout Germany. Both sides' occupation forces would withdraw to garrison areas while a new control machinery would supervise "free elections" of a government to preside over a disarmed, demilitarized, and no longer divided Germany. No power would control German police forces, economic arrangements, nor have the right to exercise a veto. Kennan asserted that Program A could be implemented "to the overall benefit of U.S. interests" while satisfying "legitimate Russian interests and requirements to a reasonable degree." He admitted that the proposal represented "a starting point for what will probably be long and difficult negotiations."

Program A laid a foundation for a settlement of the war on a basis highly favorable to the United States. It envisioned a German government in which an anti-communist coalition could be expected to "win a working majority in any reasonably free national election" and called for the German economy to be integrated into the Western multilateral system through the ERP. Soviet demands for excessive reparations would be rejected although the Russians deserved some assurances "that German trade will not be oriented exclusively to the west."[26] Predicting that Russia would not accept the program as offered, Kennan—in striking contrast to his advice on the Marshall Plan—advised the United States to "respect reasonable Soviet interests" and "not play for a disagreement." In the wake of the militarization of containment Kennan now cast doubt on the prevalent State Department view, of which he had once been the principal advocate, that Russia could be compelled in time to negotiate from a weakened position.[27]

In attempting to build support for Program A, Kennan stressed that it applied only in the event of a new CFM meeting and only if the proposals received the support of Britain and France. He urged that German demilitarization and the withdrawal of Russian forces eastward be stressed as benefits in order to combat sure opposition from the French, who after two wars in a single generation desired anything but German reunification. By offering Program A as a negotiating position, Washington would at the very least put itself in position to "offset charges that we do not really want any settlement with Russia." Kennan emphasized that a negotiated settlement provided the only means to resolve the Berlin blockade and declared that there was "no alternative other than a completely negative position."[28]

What is most striking about Program A was not that Kennan offered a settlement weighted toward Western interests, but that such a program received virtually no support. Again, the State Department's offices of European Affairs, Economic Affairs and Occupied Areas opposed Kennan's proposals and when the substance of Program A leaked to the *New York Times* in May, it raised "a good deal of hell in Europe." Robert Murphy, the State Department representative in Germany, observed that the plan was "a very worthwhile document" but added that "the trouble with our good blueprints often seems to be that they get bloody noses bumping into Russian, French, and at times, British stone walls."[29] The National Military Establishment opposed the withdrawal of troops to garrison areas and portrayed the action as a menace to European security. Responding to General Lucius D. Clay's criticism of his plan, Kennan declared that "if our troops remain, Russian troops remain. If Russian troops remain, zonal boundaries remain. If zonal boundaries remain, there can be no serious talk of a solution of the German problem *as a whole*" and thus the cold war would continue.[30]

In the type of irony that stalks Kennan's career, the widespread acceptance of the logic of his own Long Telegram and X-Article ensured the failure of his efforts to forge a political solution of the division of Europe. Opponents of Kennan's plan—in Western Europe and in the United States—regarded negotiations with the Soviet regime as futile, as Mr. X himself had advised. Kennan now lamented that he had been unable "to find anyone in the Department who agrees with me" on the need for disengagement and on December 1 Lovett returned Program A to Kennan, advising that it "should be reconsidered in light of non-concurrences."[31] The chasm between Soviet-American interests in Germany may have been too deep to bridge in any case, but in the wake of the Czech coup, the Berlin blockade, and the creation of NATO, the United States and its allies had embraced worst case scenarios and abandoned the option of negotiating with Moscow.

Kennan regretted that the militarization of containment diverted attention from the opportunities offered by a breach in Soviet-Yugoslav relations. Under Josip Broz Tito, Belgrade had stubbornly resisted Stalin's authority until the angry Soviet dictator expelled Yugoslavia from the Cominform. Coinciding with the great power crisis in Germany, Yugoslavia's dissidence may have contributed to Stalin's decision to institute the Berlin blockade. Kennan believed that Tito's disaffection and the independence displayed by Polish communist leader Wladyslaw Gomulka had hardened Moscow's diplomacy. "The more the satellite area disintegrates, the more fellows like Tito there are and the more fellows like Gomulka," he explained in September 1948, "the more the Russians see the writing on the wall and the more they tend to hold on to this and to that."[32] He recognized that the Soviet-Yugoslav rift struck "at the heart of the Stalinist concept of Russian expansion through the instrumentality of complete Kremlin control of world communism" and that Tito had successfully "defied the Kremlin myth" of the infallibility of Stalin.[33]

The existence of a polycentric communist world offered the possibility "that you can get an evolution of those Communist regimes back into the direction of regular nationalist regimes with whom you could do business," the diplomat advised in November 1948. Citing several lingering geographical and political disputes between China and the Soviet Union, he suspected that Mao Zedong "might already be infected with the Tito virus." Stalin would exercise great caution in his relations with China, because "a Communist state which defies the Kremlin's authority is a more horrible prospect in Moscow's eyes than the most incorrigible capitalist state."[34]

Kennan urged covert American support of Yugoslavia and advised Washington to increase economic and even military aid in the event of a Soviet-Yugoslav war. The United States extended financial aid in the summer of 1949, including an Export-Import Bank loan, but Stalin—in no position to conduct a shooting war in the Balkans—settled for a war of vituperation with the dissident Yugoslavs.[35]

Excited by the prospect that Tito's might be the first link in a chain of defections undermining Kremlin influence, Kennan attempted to apply the lessons of Yugoslavia to the satellite countries. He recognized the fundamental distinction between Yugoslavia and Moscow's satellites, namely that Tito's regime had achieved power on its own whereas Stalin had created most of the other regimes. Still, Washington should seek by "covert and overt" means to "foster a heretical, drifting away process" in Eastern Europe and prepare to accommodate itself to schismatic Communist regimes that would replace the Stalinist governments. Still committed to liberation in the East bloc, Kennan insisted that "these regimes must be replaced by nontotalitarian governments desirous of participating with good faith in the free world community."[36]

Kennan employed Yugoslavia's defection to bolster his argument for disengagement, explaining that a settlement in Germany and Austria would remove Soviet justification for the presence of the Red Army in Eastern Europe. A negotiated settlement in Europe would "go a long way toward loosening the Kremlin's hold not only on [Germany and Austria] but also on adjoining satellites," he explained. By adhering to a model of monolithic communism and confronting the Soviet Union with an American military alliance in central Europe, the West only played into Stalin's hands. Kennan explained that the Western military presence in central Europe compelled Eastern European communist regimes "to become or remain a part of the monolith, since they would otherwise be helpless outlaws between the two all-inclusive camps of communists and anti-communists."[37]

Following Truman's defeat of Thomas Dewey in 1948, Kennan's efforts to head off the militarization of containment depended on winning the support of the new Secretary of State, Dean Acheson. Even before Acheson received Truman's nomination, Kennan, frustrated over the militarization of American diplomacy and his own loss of influence, had threatened to resign from the State Department. He told Acheson that his view had long been that "our main problem was a political one and that we had a good chance of coping with it by political means" but "today I am skeptical." Weary of the bureaucratic infighting with the geographic desks, Kennan called for the designation of a single division to be responsible for the policy and left little doubt that the ideal form of elite diplomacy would be one which left him in charge of making the important decisions. He scored the "inexcusable" lack of respect accorded to the Foreign Service and charged that the State Department had done a poor job of propagandizing American views both at home and abroad. The diplomat threatened to take an academic position unless Acheson addressed some of his complaints. "I'd rather be at Yale, or where you will—any place where I could sound off and talk freely to people—rather than in the confines of a department in which you can neither do anything about it nor tell people what you think ought to be done."[38]

Although experienced in foreign affairs Acheson, upon taking office, lacked the strategic vision with which he is often credited. He had no fixed policy on Germany and confessed that he did not know how the United States had come to favor the creation of a western German state. As Acheson assumed his post in late January, Kennan chaired an NSC subcommittee in which he blamed the narrowness of Army negotiators and the recalcitrance of Britain and France for the failure to achieve a negotiating posture on Germany. Just before Kennan left on a tour of Germany on March 10, Acheson declared that he would defer a policy statement until the planning chief returned, but his decision to replace Kennan with Robert Murphy as head of the NSC steering committee on

German policy reflected the diplomat's waning influence. As head of the Office of German and Austrian affairs, Murphy was "to have authority and responsibility to settle the immediate operating problems," Acheson declared.[39]

A tour of Germany and conferences with Western officials in Paris strengthened Kennan's desire to see the United States withdraw from the center of Europe. In advice reminiscent of his recommendations on Occupied Japan, he warned that the "inelastic and insensitive" military occupation would breed resentment and defiant nationalism injurious to Washington's interests and advocated "the virtual abolition of Military Government" in favor of a smaller allied control commission. As one who viewed American culture as boorish, Kennan could not abide the prospect of its making a lasting imprint on Germany. "I can think of nothing which would be more helpful and refreshing," he declared, "than the departure of these bloated staffs of allied officials and their dependents which still camp upon the German cities and in part upon the German economy."[40]

Seeing no answer to the German problem within the sovereign-national framework, Kennan proposed a European federation wherein individual states would relinquish their sovereignty to a new central authority. Striving to create a balance of power that would be different from the bilateral one taking shape in Europe, he envisioned a three-tiered grouping of forces stretching from Washington to Moscow. The United States, Britain, and Canada would anchor one axis, the Soviet Union another, while in the middle a federation of West, Central, and—so far as possible—East European states would balance the two great powers. Kennan's scheme offered the possibility of German reunification under a supranational authority and would, he argued, enhance opportunities for securing the independence of the Eastern satellites.

Kennan justified the United States-Britain-Canada union on historic and racial ties, but the middle tier of his three-power scheme hinged on the unlikely union of Germany and France under a single authority. "Everything possible should be done to promote at this time closer Franco-German understanding and association," he explained, "so that some day Germany could conceivably be absorbed into [the] larger European family without dominating or demoralizing others." Kennan's call for a European federation leaked to the press in September and became the target of bitter opposition in France. Opposed to union with

87

Germany and the "desolidarization" of Britain from Europe, the French argued that they would then be vulnerable to a renewal of German aggression. The Paris leadership also doubted that Europe would be secure from a Russian invasion without formal American and British participation in the European union.[41]

Unmoved by the French concerns, Kennan sought to reestablish Germany as a dominant power in Europe as part of his quest to lure the East European satellites away from Russia's grasp. The participation of the United States and Britain had been vital in containing the Soviet ideological-political threat immediately after the war, but he now called for Germany to replace Russia on the one hand and the United States and Britain on the other as the leading power in Central Europe. As he explained to Acheson in October,

> western Europe today is not really a politically viable entity in the long run without full U.S. and U.K. participation, but a European union which left out U.K. and ourselves would have much more drawing power as an organizer of Europe in the future than would be one of the Atlantic Pact group. It would be an entity in which the Germans had far more leadership. The Germans know more about how to handle such problems—in Czechoslovakia, Yugoslavia and Poland—than we do. I want to make clear the horrifying significance of this, which is that the Germans again get a place in Western Europe which is going to be very important. But it often seemed to me, during the war living over there, that what was wrong with Hitler's new order was that it was Hitler's.[42]

While diplomacy is supposed to be the art of the possible, Kennan's proposal to remake European politics represented a naïve attempt to undo the consequences of World War II. A strong partisan of German culture since his childhood and residence in Berlin in the early 1930s, Kennan had been reluctant to condemn even Nazi aggression and had insisted until American belligerence in the war that Russia rather than Germany posed the central threat to Western security. Showing that his views had undergone little revision, Kennan once again proposed to restore Germany as a great power in Europe, as if World War II had been a great misunderstanding which the Americans, Europeans, and Russians should now simply put behind them in the interests of a realistic balance of power.

Acheson rejected Kennan's scheme to reunify Germany as part of a larger European union and refused to consider any form of negotiated disengagement from the continent. He declared that the withdrawal of British and American troops from occupied Germany was "too high a price" to pay for obtaining Soviet withdrawal from eastern Germany. When Truman approved Acheson's approach, the United States had effectively accepted the division of Europe.[43] Bitter, Kennan now understood "that we do not really want to see Germany unified at this time, and that there are *no* conditions on which we would find such a solution satisfactory." He predicted that "some day we may pay bitterly for our present unconcern with the possibility of getting the Russians out of the Eastern Zone."[44]

Kennan thought there had been a propitious opportunity to forge a European settlement with Russia in early 1949 when Stalin, suffering from a propaganda defeat over the ineffective Berlin Blockade, had signaled his willingness to renew negotiations in response to inquiries from journalist Kingsbury Smith. The Soviet dictator dropped his demand that the allies eliminate the new currency in Berlin—a significant concession—but did insist that the creation of a new West German state be postponed pending another meeting of the Council of Foreign Ministers. Kennan declared that the offer represented "a very major change in the situation" and that Stalin had abandoned his plans for the ideological-political conquest of Western Europe. However, the Western allies, uninterested in negotiations with the USSR, refused to delay the establishment of a West German government and the "basic law" of the future Federal Republic of Germany was signed on May 8 in Bonn.[45]

Although the major powers terminated the Berlin blockade and airlift on May 12, the subsequent CFM summit produced no agreement over Germany. Russia proposed a return to the Potsdam approach of German unification under four-power supervision, but Acheson brooked no compromise that stopped short of a united Germany oriented toward the West, a position fully as unrealistic as Kennan's call for a European federation in view of the Russian occupation of eastern Germany.[46]

The movement toward separate German states and the signing of the NATO treaty confirmed that the major powers had failed to achieve a political settlement and paved the way for Kennan's resignation as PPS director. Soon after taking office, Acheson had discouraged the diplomat from resigning and, with Charles Bohlen, urged Kennan to consider a long leave of absence instead. Having already stepped down as the State Department representative on the NSC, Kennan in May 1949 replaced

Bohlen as the State Department counselor, a purely advisory position he was to hold simultaneously with the titular leadership of the PPS until taking a sabbatical leave.[47]

Paul Nitze, whom Kennan had added to the PPS and whom Acheson no longer considered a mere "Wall Street operator," began to assume the actual leadership of the PPS and replaced Kennan as the regular attendant of the State Department's Combined Policy Committee meetings. Nitze tried to remain loyal to Kennan throughout the year, but his sympathies lay with Acheson's approach to containment.[48] If there had been any doubts that Kennan would resign as PPS director, they vanished in September when Webb ordered Kennan's paper on Yugoslavia (PPS 60) funneled through the area desks and sent back for revision; previously, the planning staff papers had gone directly to the Secretary of State. Kennan correctly interpreted the change in procedure as a diminution of his ability to shape policy.

Kennan spent his waning months as PPS director opposing the militarization of containment. Following Congressional approval of American participation in NATO in July 1949, Truman and Acheson presented a $1.4 billion military assistance program to Congress, another reflection to Kennan's mind of the Pentagon's "dangerously oversimplified" interpretation of Soviet behavior. The military based its planning on worst-case scenarios without considering "the possibility that the Russians might not be planning a war against the West and [with] no concern for the handling of our military matters in such a way as to enable us to defeat Soviet purposes without another major conflict." Wary of what Dwight D. Eisenhower would later label the "military-industrial complex," Kennan called for greater coordination between the Pentagon and the State Department, explaining that "it does little good for us to think these things here when an entirely different intellectual world is evolving its own process across the river."[49]

The successful Soviet test of an atomic weapon in September "must inevitably lead to an intensification of the tendency to view European problems in a military light," he mused. The atomic blast shocked American policy makers, most of whom had not expected the event for a few more years. Still the State Department's most effective propagandist, Kennan published an officially sanctioned essay in *Reader's Digest* to soothe public fears of a possible atomic war with Russia,[50] but the forces of dispassionate analysis suffered another setback in October as

Mao's Red Army chased Jiang Jieshi off the mainland and installed a communist government in Beijing.

As a result of the Soviet test and the triumph of Chinese communism, American officials undertook a reexamination of atomic policy at a time when the threat of international communism had never seemed greater. Throughout 1949 Kennan had conducted a series of meetings with American, British, and Canadian officials on coordinating resource allocation and information sharing on atomic energy matters.[51] After the Soviet test, he advocated a program of international control and the stockpiling of only a few atomic bombs to deter attack. In this case, as in most substantive policy matters, the State Department and the Truman Administration rejected Kennan's advice. Instead of settling for minimal deterrence, Washington elected to speed work on a new "super" bomb, thus launching a new phase in the American-Soviet arms race.

In the wake of the successful Soviet test, Truman ordered increased production of atomic bombs in the United States and appointed a special NSC committee comprising Acheson, AEC chairman David Lilienthal, and Defense Secretary Louis Johnson to make recommendations on whether to produce a new hydrogen bomb. After meetings with consultants, Kennan argued that a decision to go ahead with development of the hydrogen bomb would add another impediment to any sort of negotiated settlement with Moscow. "Wouldn't we be pushing the Russians against a closed door and demanding that they go through it?" he asked. "What door can we leave open for them to go through with a certain degree of grace?"[52]

The decision to develop thermonuclear weapons was the ultimate manifestation of the militarization of containment. Kennan rejected the notion that nuclear weapons served any rational purpose, pointing out that in the event of war the bombing of Russian cities would only stiffen popular resistance, and yet "the military have been basing all their plans on the use of the bomb." If the use of the atomic weapon served no purpose, "then there might be some advantage in agreeing with the Russians that neither of us would use it at all." In a convoluted, if revealing, response to Kennan's argument, Acheson observed that "if for a variety of reasons we wish to agree with the Russians not to use the bomb such a decision would make rather awkward a request of Congress for additional appropriations to make more bombs which we weren't going to use."[53]

J. Robert Oppenheimer, the "father" of the atomic bomb program, had developed his own gnawing doubts about the ability of human beings to control the technology of mass destruction. In November, Oppenheimer—head of the AEC's General Advisory Committee—complimented the "sympathetic and nondoctrinaire framework" of Kennan's views on international control of atomic weapons and soon opposed the development of the hydrogen bomb. "You probably do not know to what extent you have become my intellectual conscience," Kennan told Oppenheimer after Truman's special committee had overruled him and approved the H-bomb.[54]

While Paul Nitze was Acheson's closet advisor in deliberations over the super bomb, Kennan formulated a critique of American nuclear strategy that would provide the basis of his dissent for the next forty years. He urged a policy renouncing "first use" of atomic weapons and in favor of pursuing arms-control negotiations with Moscow. Kennan noted, in an understatement, that Nitze and the PPS staff "were not entirely in agreement with the substance" of his views and therefore, he explained the Acheson, "since I was afraid that this report might be an embarrassing one to have on the record as a formal Staff report, I have redone this as a personal paper."

In contrast with the Long Telegram and X-Article, Kennan now opposed efforts to compel a change in the Soviet system and considered arms control a top priority. He called for the United States "to move as rapidly as possible toward the removal of [atomic weapons] from national armaments *without insisting on a deep-seated change in the Soviet system.*" Kennan argued that American officials needed to decide either that they were willing to employ atomic weapons in a military conflict with the Soviet Union, or to regard them "as something superfluous to our basic military posture—as something which we are compelled to hold against the possibility that they might be used by our opponents." In that case, the nation would hold only a minimum of bombs to ensure credible deterrence and would "make it our objective to divest ourselves of this minimum at the earliest moment by achieving a scheme of international control."

Kennan believed that as a result of the militarization of Western policy, the United States had adopted the first option without having understood its strategic implications. He realized that effective international control probably required curbing civilian use of atomic energy—

in both Russia and the United States—and raised the thorny issue of inspection of each country's atomic facilities. Despite the difficulties, Kennan insisted that "an imperfect system of international control seems to me less dangerous, and more considerate of those things in international life which are still hopeful" than a policy of first use and strategic superiority. Having renounced nuclear weapons, the West could match Russia's conventional military superiority in Europe, he added.[55]

Although he had not been "excited or alarmed" over the arms race during his early formulation of containment,[56] Kennan now concluded in the wake of the militarization of containment and his own loss of influence that the weapons of mass destruction were far too dangerous to be cultivated by fallible human beings, especially in a democratic society. The "peculiar psychological overtones" of atomic weapons would "tend to give them a certain top-heaviness" as instruments of national policy in a democracy and they would "inevitably impart a certain eccentricity to our military planning," he explained. In reality atomic weapons could not achieve any end other than destruction but in the absence of international control their continued cultivation would "encourage the belief that somehow or other results decisive for the purposes of democracy can be expected to flow from the question of who obtains the ultimate superiority in the atomic weapons race."

Kennan drew a strong distinction between atomic and conventional armaments. Conventional weapons could be employed as a means to an end "other than warfare, an end connected with the beliefs and the feelings and the attitudes of people, an end marked by a submission to a new political will and perhaps to a new regime of life, but an end which at least did not negate the principle of life itself." Nuclear weapons, on the other hand, reached "back beyond the frontiers of western civilization, to the concepts of warfare which were once familiar to the Asiatic hordes" and could not "be reconciled with a political purpose directed to shaping, rather than destroying, the lives of the adversary." Weapons of mass destruction failed "to take account of the ultimate responsibility of men for one another" and implied "that man not only can be but is his own worst and most terrible enemy."[57]

Once again, the Truman Administration rejected Kennan's advice. R. Gordon Arneson, the President's atomic energy consultant, criticized Kennan's "fundamentally incorrect assumption; namely that it is possible to achieve prohibition of atomic weapons and international control of atomic energy that has any meaning, without a basic change in Soviet attitudes and intentions, and, in fact, in the Soviet system itself." John Hickerson condemned Kennan's reliance on "the good faith of the USSR, whose record in matters of good faith is 'well known'" and asserted that "we can maintain a wide superiority in atomic weapons over the Soviet Union, probably for an indefinite period of time."[58]

Displaying no enthusiasm for Kennan's approach, Nitze advocated going ahead with the super bomb out of fear that Russia would develop it first. Only Deputy Undersecretary of State Dean Rusk commented favorably on Kennan's ideas, noting that American strategy needed to be reassessed. Persuaded by the critics, Acheson joined Johnson and Lilienthal in urging development of thermonuclear weapons and withheld Kennan's paper from Truman, who on January 31 ordered the go-ahead for the new bomb. To Kennan the retention of first use, construction of the super bomb, and failure to achieve international control of atomic weapons placed further impediments in the way of a negotiated settlement with Russia. However, Moscow already had initiated its own hydrogen bomb program and it is doubtful that it would have been willing to abandon that research for any scheme of international control.[59]

In conjunction with the approval of the super bomb program, Truman on January 31, 1950, ordered a general "reexamination of our objectives and . . . strategic plans," a review that culminated in NSC-68. Nitze assembled a committee of the PPS and defense planners to draft the new policy statement with which Kennan, preparing for his trip to Latin America, had no involvement. "With the preparation of NSC-68," he told a historian in 1959, "I had nothing to do. I was disgusted about the assumptions concerning Soviet intentions which underlay this and other manifestations of American policy at that time."[60]

Thus the drafting of the sweeping new statement of American Soviet policy punctuated Kennan's fall from power. The essence of NSC-68 — one of the most significant policy papers in the history of American diplomacy—was its call for massive rearmament. Depicting the Soviet Union as bent on world conquest, NSC-68 authorized "a rapid and sustained build-up of the political, economic, and military strength of the free world." In the wake of the Soviet atomic blast and the fall of China, the trend of world events promised "a serious decline in the strength of the free world relative to the Soviet Union and its satellites." The United States confronted its "deepest peril"; its military strength was "dangerously inadequate"; the continued growth of Soviet power would produce a "disastrous situation" by 1954. The State and Defense Department collaborators agreed informally that the Defense budget should increase more than 300 percent—from $13 billion to $40 billion annually—to counter the communist bid for world domination.

The call for rearmament outpaced anything Kennan had ever recommended, but in its tone NSC-68 was reminiscent of his essays and policy papers from 1944 to 47. NSC-68 endorsed Kennan's plea for ideological-political containment and drew heavily on the ousted planning chief's NSC 20/4 (formerly PPS 38), but the national security paper stressed Soviet military capabilities rather than Russia's intentions. NSC-68 emphasized "the Kremlin's design for world domination" whereas Kennan had long downplayed the prospect of a Soviet invasion of Western Europe and insisted that Stalin had no grand design but simply sought to expand Soviet influence and undermine the West whenever and wherever opportunities existed.

NSC-68 was thus a reflection of the militarization of containment. Its authors argued that the Soviet Union, now equipped with the atomic bomb and devoting 40 percent of its resources to the military, held such an advantage that negotiations would be fruitless until the West had completed a massive military build-up of its own. This point of view, if not the precise recommendations, would have met the approval of Kennan in 1946–47, but by late 1948 he favored broad-scale negotiations over Germany and nuclear weapons. NSC-68 failed to acknowledge the significance of Tito's defection and the possibilities offered by a polycentric communist world, whereas Kennan emphasized these developments as a means of promoting instability in the satellite countries. Perhaps most significantly, while Kennan had intended containment to be *temporary* strategy which would either lead to the dissolution of the Soviet Union or force it to negotiate on terms favorable to the West, NSC-68 accepted the existence of the cold war as a permanent feature of life. "The cold war is in fact a real war," admonished the paper, "in which the survival of the free world is at stake."[61]

Following Truman's approval of NSC-68 on September 30, 1950, the Defense budget leaped from $13 billion in 1950 to $48.7 in 1953. The United States poured billions of dollars into its foreign military assistance program, authorized the production of tactical and strategic nuclear weapons and a chain of overseas air bases that virtually encircled the Soviet Union and China, and strengthened its capacity to conduct covert operations and psychological warfare.[62]

The decision to construct the super bomb and the passage of NSC-68 confirmed the militarization of containment while eroding Kennan's faith in American postwar internationalism. He declared that Washington and its allies had "unconsciously embrace[d] the assumption that a war so much prepared for cannot fail to be eventually fought" and in their "preoccupation with a military contest which we are constantly forced to conduct in our imaginations" had forgotten "to do those things which might still keep such a contest from becoming a living reality."[63] In less than three years Kennan had been transformed from a confident and influential policy planner into an outcast who had become deeply troubled by the prospect of nuclear war.

Personality conflicts, as well as policy disagreements—especially with Acheson—underlay Kennan's loss of influence in cold war policy-making. He had developed mutual respect between himself and Marshall, whose office adjoined his own, but failed to win Acheson's support. In 1959 Kennan recalled that although he and Acheson did respect one another, they rarely agreed on substantive issues, particularly on Germany. Kennan attributed the rejection of his recommendations "to the influence of our military authorities and the European division of the Department, whose contrary views found Mr. Acheson's support." In his own memoir Acheson recalled that he found Kennan's memoranda "beautifully expressed, sometimes contradictory" and noted that the diplomat mixed "flashes of prophetic insight" with suggestions of "total unpracticality." The replacement of Robert Lovett with James Webb and the resignation of Forrestal because of mental illness also deprived Kennan of longtime associates in the bureaucracy, yet none of these men had supported his call for German reunification as part of a supranational European federation.[64]

Kennan's arrogance also irritated his colleagues as his viewpoints diverged from the foreign policy consensus. "Oh, God, what has George been up to now," Acheson moaned on one occasion when an admiral complained about comments made by Kennan that were critical of the military. In reporting the diplomat's intention to take a sabbatical leave, *Time* cited his "impatience at the demands of domestic politics" but also noted that Kennan, "a virtuoso, worked poorly on a team [and] often irked his colleagues with his ivory towerishness." The diplomat's ulcers flared as his influence waned, prompting the *New York Times* to observe that he had "pushed himself beyond the point where it is in the long range interests of himself or the Foreign Service that he should continue."[65]

Ironically, Kennan saw his positions rejected, at least in part, because so many officials had embraced the perceptions of the Long Telegram and the X-Article. Acheson, Hickerson, Nitze and others equated negotiations with appeasement, as Kennan himself had done until 1948. Many officials also continued to believe that American pressure would compel Moscow to accept Western terms in any settlement. This view, once a cardinal tenet of containment, had been abandoned by Kennan.

The timing and force of the Long Telegram and X-Article were such that virtually the entire foreign affairs bureaucracy responded to Kennan's message, but he could not always command influence through his finely crafted essays. Yet Kennan eschewed the normal gambits of bureaucratic gamesmanship and persisted in drafting his positions and refusing to alter them. "Once he got on paper, George couldn't be moved then," Bohlen recalled. Another diplomat recalled that Kennan "was a little inclined to think that once he writes his elegant prose, that's the way it's going to be, everybody's going to be convinced by that. It didn't always work that way, of course."[66] Nitze recalled that Kennan "felt like his job was done" when he submitted his planning papers, allowing the Secretary of State to accept or reject the advice. Nitze, on the other hand, "would get into the bureaucratic infighting to give life to the ideas." Kennan, the congenital outsider, was a poor bureaucrat.[67]

To Kennan's credit he had shown the flexibility of mind to alter his perceptions and policy recommendations in 1948–49 to accommodate a fluid international environment. He was no less committed to containment and liberation extending into Russia itself, but he now argued that negotiations were a means to this end. He became frustrated and diverged from the foreign policy consensus as his colleagues in the national security bureaucracy and much of the public rejected his advice and clung to an extreme perception of the Soviet Union which justified massive rearmament and the creation of a military-industrial complex. NATO, NSC-68, and the hydrogen bomb were the symbols of Kennan's loss of influence and the militarization of containment.

The Militarization of Containment

No longer able to influence the foreign affairs bureaucracy, Kennan weighed offers from Dartmouth, Harvard, MIT, and the Carnegie and Rockefeller foundations before announcing on March 7, 1950, that he was taking a year's leave of absence to accept Robert Oppenheimer's offer to contemplate foreign affairs at the Institute for Advanced Study at Princeton.[68] Barring an unforeseen crisis, he would begin the sabbatical on July 1. But the unforeseen usually occurs in international affairs and the events of June 25 not only delayed Kennan's leave, but also ensured the lasting militarization of containment.

V

Korea: Containment
on the Perimeter, I

T HE OUTBREAK of war in Korea on June 25, 1950, came at a time when Kennan was reassessing the global diplomacy he had advocated since the beginning of the cold war. The diplomat who had summoned the United States to world leadership from 1944 to 47 now doubted that the nation possessed the maturity required to fulfill that role. Despite these doubts and his opposition to the militarization of containment, Kennan advocated U.S. military intervention in response to the outbreak of fighting in Korea, which he blamed on the Soviet Union. Kennan's support for intervention in Korea showed that his fear of a communist bandwagon effect and his preoccupation with preserving U.S. credibility overshadowed his doubts about America's ability to conduct an effective foreign policy as well as his theoretical desire to limit containment to "strongpoint" regions.

Containment dominated American foreign policy as Kennan prepared to take his leave of absence in 1950, but the man who had introduced the term now opposed the means by which the United States sought to implement the anti-communist strategy. He had been unable to dampen enthusiasm for the United Nations; the NATO alliance had been approved over his objections, cementing the division of Germany as well as of Europe; the United States had deemphasized ideological-political for military containment; and, according to Kennan at least, the Congress and public opinion continued to undermine the ability of realist diplomats to conduct the nation's foreign policy.[1]

Stung by his defeats on these issues, Kennan asserted in a private essay that American diplomacy since World War I constituted "a vast and historic failure." The essential objective of international relations was national security, but in the absence of a reunified but pacified Germany to balance Russian power in Europe, the nation's security had not been enhanced by the outcome of the two great twentieth century wars. America's mass democracy lacked the maturity required to keep international affairs in realistic perspective and thus even in victory war had the effect of "a sort of an emotional or alcoholic debauch" in which "we may think we know what we are doing when we enter in to it . . . but by the time we come out of it we do not know this anymore." The product of the great twentieth-century "debauches" was the cold war, a seemingly permanent state of conflict that carried the constant risk of escalation into nuclear holocaust. "Either we both hang on doggedly to the grips we have with our teeth on our respective spheres of Europe, . . . and see whose internal contradictions catch up first with whom," Kennan wrote, "or this thing goes on into the military phase." One difference between this assessment and his views in the early cold war was the uncertainty Kennan now expressed over whose contradictions —Soviet or American—would materialize first.[2]

As a longtime critic of American culture and society, Kennan rejected idealistic claims of U.S. "exceptionalism," a faith in which had prompted *Time-Life* publisher Henry Luce to proclaim the birth of the "American century" on the eve of U.S. involvement in World War II. The militarization of containment had reinforced Kennan's doubts about the nation's ability to conduct a subtle diplomacy. Although the United States was a great power, the diplomat called on Americans to "act with due consciousness of our own deficiencies and our own lack of answers in many fields which foreign peoples require." The nation should play only a "modest" role in world affairs, mainly by serving as a model for others to emulate, and should abandon any claims to "universal ambitions and pretensions" which reflected "arrogance and even intolerance based on a terrifying smugness and lack of historical perspective."[3]

Kennan's doubts about America's ability to measure up to the obligations of postwar internationalism reflected his own anti-democratic values as well as his alienation from post-industrial society. In Kennan's thinking, American domestic problems of rapid population growth, depleting natural resources, urban decay, technological change, and disintegration of family and community represented "a very deep crisis," the amelioration of which required "greater modesty and humility" in foreign affairs. Recognition of the domestic malaise "ought really to give a jolt to people who talk about this being the American century," he declared. "We are not yet ready to lead the world to salvation. We have got to save ourselves first; and we have got to gain immensely in understanding."[4]

The outbreak of fighting in Korea came in the midst of Kennan's reassessment of postwar American internationalism and forced him to come to terms with conflicts in his thinking. As in Vietnam (see chapter 11), war on the Asian perimeter forced Kennan to weigh his opposition to the advance of communism against his doubts about America's ability to conduct a policy of global containment. In both cases Kennan's preoccupation with preserving American credibility overshadowed his doubts about the nation's ability to function effectively as a great power and prompted his support for U.S. intervention. Kennan still feared that any communist victory—especially one accomplished by direct military action—would undermine Western credibility and precipitate a bandwagon effect injurious to U.S. interests.

Perilously wedged between China, Japan, and the Soviet Union, Korea emerged from World War II as a divided and occupied nation, and one that Kennan wished to preserve from Soviet influence. As the Grand Alliance collapsed in January 1946 he urged the State Department to abandon negotiations with Russia over Korea and to bolster the southern regime headed by the American-educated septuagenarian, Syngman Rhee, whose lack of popular support mirrored Jiang Jieshi's position on the Chinese mainland.[5] Political instability in southern Korea had undermined Kennan's faith in containment by the fall of 1947, however, and the Policy Planning Staff advised that the United States could "not count on native Korean forces to help us hold the line against Soviet expansion" and should therefore withdraw from the peninsula. Attempting to restrict the application of containment to vital regions, Kennan concluded that Korea was not of decisive strategic importance and therefore "our main task is to extricate ourselves without too great a loss of prestige." He admitted that there was a "real likelihood" that Korea would become a Soviet satellite, but concurred with military officials who did not consider Korea an essential theater in the cold war. On September 24, 1947, the PPS recommended "that our policy should be to cut our losses and get out of there as gracefully but promptly as possible."[6]

By the time he appeared before a House committee in defense of the Truman administration's request for economic assistance to southern Korea in June 1949, however, Kennan once again advocated containment on the peninsula. Both the United States and the Soviet Union had withdrawn their occupation forces by that time, but neither had abandoned plans to gain an ally in a unified Korea. Kennan argued that Washington should hold the line in Korea in order to bolster Japan and the nations across the "great crescent" of Asia against communism, particularly as Jiang's forces were being driven into the sea by the Chinese communists. He now asserted that Rhee would stand "a pretty good chance to hold" in the event of a civil war with the North Korean communists led by Kim Il-sung, as long as the regime in the south received U.S. economic and political support. He warned that the failure of containment in Korea would upset the "delicate state of balance" in the world and cause "waves of panic and trouble which can be extremely serious in their effects."[7]

Kennan's testimony underscored the Truman Administration's commitment to ideological-political containment in Korea. Much has been made of Secretary of State Dean Acheson's omission of Korea from the nation's "defense perimeter" in a public speech in January 1950, but his comments merely reflected the administration's faith that containment could be achieved short of military means and did not constitute an abandonment of the peninsula.[8] Kennan was a staunch advocate of ideological-political containment but warned that in the event of any U.S. *military* involvement in Korea "we might make fools of ourselves and give the Korean Communists and the Russians a perfectly gratuitous little triumph. . . . I do not think that our forces should be mixed up in that," he told the House committee. "The Russians would love to see that situation come about and they would sit back there and laugh their heads off if we got our forces engaged with any Koreans at all."[9]

The precise origins of the Korean War remain unknown, but the Truman Administration, and the Soviet expert Kennan most especially, appear to have been wrong in placing blame for the North Korean invasion squarely on the Soviet Union. Although documentation remains insufficient to provide a definitive explanation of the origins of the attack, it is clear that by attributing the conflict to orders received from Moscow the administration dramatically underestimated the domestic context of what was essentially a Korean civil war. As historian James I. Matray argues, "those who stress Soviet responsibility for the Korean War assign far too little importance to the domestic origins of the conflict. Both Koreas were obsessed with ending the partition and merely were waiting for the first opportunity to stage a 'war of liberation.' " Political scientist Bruce M. Cumings also stresses the domestic origins of the conflict, arguing that the North Koreans "moved in June 1950 not at Stalin's order, but to unify their country, revolutionize the South, and thereby provide the basis for a self-contained national communism that could resist great power pressure from any source, including China and the Soviet Union." Historian Burton I. Kaufman also believes that "the North apparently attacked the South unilaterally" without the knowledge of Stalin or Mao. In his memoir Nikita S. Khrushchev recalled that Kim Il-sung "was the initiator" and that Stalin, although worried about the prospect of U.S. intervention, "didn't try to dissuade him" from attacking southern Korea. As had been in the case of the Greek insurgency in 1947, however, the Truman administration and Kennan himself dismissed the possibility that the North Koreans had acted on their own or were imbued with Titoist tendencies.[10]

Although Kennan had warned the previous year of dire consequences in the event of U.S. military involvement in Korea, he advocated a prompt and unilateral military response to the North Korean attack and later claimed to have exerted "significant influence" on the administration's decision to send U.S. combat troops into Korea. Truman declined to seek a congressional declaration of war for the "police action," but the United States committed its own forces and used its influence to gain UN sanction for intervention. On the advice of Kennan and other planners, the administration interposed the Seventh Fleet in the Formosa Strait to ward off a Chinese invasion of Tawain, an action that placed the United States in the middle of the Chinese civil war and created a lasting roadblock to normal relations with Beijing.[11]

In the days following the outbreak of the war, Kennan deferred his planned leave of absence from the government at Acheson's request in order to participate in deliberations over the implications of the fighting.

The resultant policy paper, NSC 73, adopted language from a draft prepared by Kennan, which advocated containment by military means in Korea and vigilance over the possible outbreak of additional peripheral conflicts. While sure that Stalin had ordered the North Korean assault, Kennan declared that Russia meant "to avoid open involvement and did not intend to launch a general war." He called for a U.S. declaration of war against Russia, however, in the event that communist insurgents attacked in either Iran or East Germany and he joined with NSC consultants in declaring that a Soviet invasion of Yugoslavia would warrant American aid to Tito but not a declaration of war. Kennan's paper argued that the United States "would have adequate grounds for air and sea attacks on targets in Communist China" should Mao's forces intervene in Korea, although such action would have to be considered "in the light of circumstances prevailing at the time." [12]

Of utmost concern to Kennan and other officials was the possibility that the assault in Korea might be followed by an attempt to destabilize Japan. The United States should anticipate "the establishment at any time of a rival Japanese government in North Korea, and attempts at infiltration and subversion on a serious scale in Japan," he warned. Kennan also expected "intensified hostilities" in Vietnam, where the national communist Ho Chi Minh opposed a French puppet regime supported by the United States. Kennan still downplayed any military threat to Western Europe, but expected the Kremlin to "continue to conduct against us in the coming period the most intensive and savage type of political warfare, interspersing political, psychological, covert-subversive, and limited military means as may seem to them suitable and advisable." [13]

Underlying Kennan's endorsement of military containment in Korea was his fear that a rash of communist subversion would follow if the North Korean assault were to pass unchallenged by the West. He shared the view held by top officials in the Truman Administration that Washington had to establish its credibility to respond to communist aggression. "The testing of our firmness in other areas may take every form known to Communist ingenuity," he warned the day after the invasion. "If any weakness or hesitation is encountered on our part, anywhere, it will be instantaneously exploited by the Communists to undermine confidence in us in Europe and elsewhere and to start a turn of political sentiment against us." The absence of a display of American resolve in

Korea would "encourage the international communist movement to take every conceivable action to embarrass us at this time, particularly in Asia."

The bandwagon effect that Kennan meant to head off would "not be the result of any new orders received from Moscow but would stem from the encouragement which the communist elements had received [from a North Korean victory] and from the corresponding discouragement of their opponents." A successful North Korean offensive, he explained, would encourage communists in such diverse areas as Taiwan, Vietnam, Iran, and Berlin. "An outcome of the Korean hostilities which would be seriously damaging to western prestige would presumably advance the hopes and plans for . . . these operations, and quite possibly for others the outlines of which are less clear to us today." [14]

Considerations over prestige, credibility, and cold war psychology dominated Kennan's thinking in response to the war in Korea. He expressed no second thoughts about the U.S. decision to intervene in Korea , which was "unquestionably the correct one," but warned that

> we will be on very dangerous terrain if we fail to recognize the following subtle but wholly valid and vital distinction. It was not tolerable to us that communist control should be extended to South Korea *in the way in which this was attempted* on June 24, since the psychological radiations from an acquiesence in this development on our part would have been wholly disruptive of our prestige in Asia. Nevertheless, it is not essential to us to see an anti-Soviet Korean regime extended to all of Korea for all time; we could even eventually tolerate for a certain period of time a Korea nominally independent but actually amenable to Soviet influence, provided this state of affairs were to be brought about gradually and not too conspicuously, and were accompanied by a stable and secure situation in Japan and a quieting down of the existing tensions and fears in that general area. [emphasis added] [15]

Although Korea, like Southeast Asia, was of secondary strategic importance in and of itself, it was transformed overnight into a vital perimeter of containment as a result of the communist attempt to seize power by overt military means. Under these circumstances, Kennan argued, Washington had to respond with force in order to establish its credibility to allies and enemies alike and head off the anticipated bandwagon effect. He believed the objective of the United States should be limited to a policy of containment that would make it clear that Washington would not appease communist aggression. This limited objective would check communist expansion short of a major war, discourage additional Communist attempts to seize power in other countries, and reinforce the perception among America's allies that the country could be counted upon for assistance in the struggle against Communism.

In a "Round-Up of Communist Intentions" prepared for Acheson on August 8, Kennan insisted that the communist threat remained primarily ideological-political, despite the putative Soviet-ordered invasion of southern Korea. Not seeking a wider war, the Russians had "simply wanted control of South Korea; saw what looked to them like a favorable set of circumstances in which to achieve it; [and] feared that if they did not achieve it now, time might run out on them." The Kremlin had not expected a U.S. military response "and thought that if we did try to intervene we would get there too late." Neither Mao nor Stalin intended to intervene directly as long as North Korea held the advantage, Kennan advised, but he and Charles Bohlen agreed that

> when the tide of battle begins to change, the Kremlin will not wait for us to reach the 38th parallel before taking action. When we begin to have military successes, that will be the time to watch out. Anything may then happen—entry of Soviet forces, entry of Chinese Communist forces, new strike for a UN settlement, or all three together.

Worried by the bombing of the North Korean port city of Rashin, near Vladisvostok, Kennan warned that "we must be prepared at any time for extreme Soviet reactions."[16]

While Kennan advocated a limited war to preserve an independent regime in southern Korea while demonstrating U.S. credibility, the Truman administration embraced a disastrous policy aimed at liberating the entire peninsula. America's Asian policy was "so little promising and so fraught with danger that I could not honestly urge you to continue to take responsibility for it," Kennan advised Acheson on August 23. Instead of pursuing limited war aims in Korea, "sectors of our public opinion and our official establishment are indulging themselves in emotional, moralistic attitudes which, unless corrected, can easily carry us toward real conflict with the Russians and inhibit us from making a realistic agreement about that area." Kennan was one of few officials willing to challenge openly the authority of General Douglas MacArthur, who dominated the American campaign in Korea and who pressed Truman to take the war north of the 38th parallel. "A military commander in a foreign territory is never a suitable vehicle of political policy," Kennan declared. "We are tolerating a state of affairs in which we do not really have full control over the statements that are being made—and the actions taken—in our name."

Kennan advised Acheson not to seek liberation in Korea, but instead to press for a negotiated settlement linking the positions of Japan and Korea between the two world powers. Under his plan, the United States would consent to the neutralization and demilitarization of Japan (except for strong internal police forces) in return for a Soviet agreement to end the Korean War and seek a UN settlement on the fate of the peninsula. Washington would agree to a neutralization of Taiwan, abstain from voting on China's admission to the UN, and encourage France to seek as graceful as possible withdrawal from a "basically hopeless" situation in Indochina. Four months earlier Kennan had urged support of the French position in Vietnam.[17]

Japan was the key to Kennan's proposed settlement with Moscow. He believed that the unilateral American occupation of Japan had prompted Stalin to order the North Korean invasion and therefore argued that the maintenance of U.S. military forces in Japan under sanction of the proposed Japanese Peace Treaty was not only a bad idea for the restructuring of Japanese society but also made achieving "an agreement with the Russians over Korea far more difficult than it would otherwise be." Despite Kennan's plea, the North Korean invasion only reinforced the American decision to determine unilaterally the conditions of the Japanese Peace Treaty, which was signed in September 1951.[18]

Including the terms of the Japanese occupation in discussions may well have proven useful, but Kennan's negotiating strategy ignored the internal dynamics of the Korean civil war. It was by no means clear that Moscow could have compelled the type of settlement he envisioned even if Stalin had been so inclined. Moreover, Kennan's proposals would have required dramatic adjustments in American Far Eastern policy— adjustments that would have been sharply opposed by the China lobby, prominent officials such as John Foster Dulles, and much of public opinion. Despite the obstacles, however, the history of conflict in Korea, Taiwan, and Vietnam suggest that no effort should have been spared in seeking a negotiated settlement of the cold war in Asia.

After blunting the initial North Korean offensive, however, American officials sought to deliver the kind of psychological blow to international communism that Kennan himself had long espoused. His and Bohlen's warnings of the likelihood of Soviet or Chinese intervention following a turn in the war proved prescient in the fall of 1950. After MacArthur's successful September 15 landing at Inchon, over the next several weeks the American and UN forces cut off several North Korean contingents from their supply lines and reversed the course of the war by crossing the 38th Parallel and proceeding toward the Manchurian border. Eager for a victory to quiet its domestic critics, the Truman administration ignored China's warnings that the military advance would not be tolerated and on November 24, as MacArthur's forces approached the Yalu River flowing between Korea and China, 200,000 Chinese "volunteers" intervened and in weeks had retaken the North and renewed the southern offensive.[19]

As a Eurocentric realist and one who had long employed the word "oriental" as a pejorative term, Kennan shared the anger most Americans experienced toward China in the wake of the massive intervention that caused thousands of American casualties. The United States had "bent over backwards" to accommodate China, he declared, citing no examples, and Beijing now deserved "nothing but a lesson." For the moment, however, it was "much too late today to do anything but pick up the pieces," Kennan lamented in a letter to Bohlen. "We are the victims mainly of an absolutely unbelieveable and stupendous military blunder."[20]

The Chinese intervention confronted American policy makers with their most difficult days of the war and Kennan reflected that mood in the contradictory advice that he offered in subsequent weeks. The diplomat had taken his leave of absence from the State Department by the time of the Chinese intervention, but found little tranquility at Princeton with the threat of all-out war looming in Asia. He let it be known that his expertise was again available to the beleaguered diplomats in Washington who had seen their dreams of liberation replaced by the specter of defeat. Summoned to the State Department in early December, Kennan sharply opposed the option of withdrawal that CIA Director Walter Bedell Smith had recommended to preserve limited American resources for Europe and Japan. Kennan argued that a complete withdrawal from the peninsula "would be mercilessly exploited by [Moscow] to our disadvantage."

Considerations of prestige and credibility also prompted Kennan to drop his earlier recommendation that negotiations be opened with Moscow. He argued that if the United States consented to talks under the pressure of the Chinese counterattack, communists throughout the world would receive encouragement from what would be perceived as an American capitulation to aggression. "If there was any soundness at all to the principle of negotiation from strength," he observed, "then this was the worst time for us to attempt negotiation."[21] Kennan was willing to allow American troops to pay a high price for the preservation of U.S. credibility in Korea. If efforts to "attempt to hold a beachhead would mean the loss of our entire forces or any other exorbitant consequence, that was that, and we had to accept it," he declared on December 5.[22]

Kennan reversed himself in the wake of another Chinese offensive which pushed the U.S./UN forces south of the 38th parallel in early January 1951. Now, for the first time since the outbreak of the war, he recommended that the United States consider the option of unilateral withdrawal from Korea. Washington had two choices, as he saw it. One was to stabilize the front and then apply "real pressure" against China through "harassing their lines of communication and making their position thoroughly awkward and uncomfortable" in an effort to achieve an agreement on a joint U.S. and Chinese withdrawal from the peninsula. "If we cannot do that," he advised Paul Nitze, "then I think our best course is to leave voluntarily." Washington would justify its unilateral withdrawal on grounds that continuing the war in Korea would only result in useless destruction on such a scale as to deprive South Korean political independence of any real meaning. He predicted that once America left, Korea would become "a bone of contention" between China and the Soviet Union and that opportunities would arise for the United States to "settl[e] our score" with Beijing and in the process "redress this damage to our prestige and to the cause of stability in Asia."[23]

The Truman administration chose neither to strike at China nor to withdraw from the peninsula in the winter of 1951. Rejection of the first option prompted General MacArthur's public attack against the administration and forced Truman to relieve him of his command in April. The strong public reaction to this event reflected growing impatience with limited war, but the restraining influence of America's allies, limitations on U.S. military resources, and concern over the possibility of

Soviet intervention forged a consensus to settle for containment based on the prewar status quo in Korea.[24]

By the time the Korean War assumed the characteristics of a stalemate in the winter of 1951, Kennan once again advised a negotiated settlement with Moscow. He told Acheson that only Russia, as the great land power in the region, could compel an end to the war. Washington should exploit "informal channels and with the obligation of complete secrecy" make known its willingness to settle for a "return to the *status quo ante* the North Korean invasion." Once a secret agreement had been achieved, both parties could make a joint announcement of the settlement in the UN. Kennan expressed optimism over the chances for a settlement because "the present situation in Korea is unsatisfactory to both the Soviet Union and the United States. There would appear to be a mutuality of interest sufficient to make possible such an arrangement."[25]

This time the State Department took Kennan's advice to pursue negotiations with Russia. Longtime allies H. Freeman Matthews and John Paton Davies proposed allowing Kennan to take advantage of his formal leave from the government to open secret discussions with Jacob Malik, the Soviet UN delegate, and Acheson agreed. When American officials approached the Soviet diplomat in early May, however, he was less than enthusiastic. Malik declared that Kennan "has had a great and unfortunate influence on United States policy toward Russia" and he had no doubt that "Kennan's voice is still heard in American policy circles." Despite this initial negative response, on May 26 Kennan wrote to Semen Tsarapkin, a deputy at the Soviet UN mission whom Kennan had known in Moscow, asking for a "quiet talk some time in the near future" with Malik.[26]

The Soviet envoy accepted and on May 31 received Kennan at his home in New York. The two and one-half hour meeting began awkwardly when Malik spilled a tray of fruit and wine on himself, but soon the two diplomats, conversing in Russian, addressed the question of a ceasefire in Korea. Kennan floated the notion of a "termination of hostilities approximately in the region where they are now taking place," near the 38th Parallel. Malik countered that a ceasefire could be arranged only on the basis of the withdrawal of all foreign troops and an American willingness to discuss recognition of Mao's regime. When Kennan replied that his government intended to keep the question of

China separate from the Korean War, Malik doubted whether a settlement could be achieved on such a basis. American officials had previously endorsed Kennan's proposal to "play the role of the offended party" if Malik insisted on giving the Chinese a role in the negotiations. The United States would insist that the Chinese were "hysterical and childlike and that it was impossible to do business with them" in contrast to the "responsible, businesslike" Russians. The two envoys adjourned the meeting without coming to terms but agreed to meet again.[27]

The second Kennan-Malik discussion of June 5 was more productive. Kennan got the impression that this time Malik's statements reflected instructions from the Politburo which opened the door to negotiations in Korea. Malik insisted that the Soviet Union, as a party not directly involved in the war, could not issue terms for halting the conflict. He suggested that Washington take up the issue with North Korea and China, but no longer insisted on China's recognition in the UN. These proposals convinced Kennan that Stalin would pressure Mao and Kim Il-sung "to show themselves amenable to proposals for a cease-fire." After concluding the cordial talk, Kennan thought it "likely" that cease-fire arrangements could "be obtained from them with firmness and persistence on our part and at a cost in nerves and temper no greater than that which was involved in the final settlement of the Berlin blockade." He claimed that "a high degree of Kremlin influence will be reflected" in discussions with representatives of the governments in Beijing and Pyongyang.[28]

A prompt settlement of the war near the 38th Parallel would mean that containment had worked in Korea, Kennan declared. He insisted that the Chinese communists had already "been taught a terrific lesson" by America's refusal to back down in the wake of the Chinese offensive. "Our action in Korea, so often denounced as futile, may prove to have been the thing that saved Southeast Asia and laid the foundation for the renewal of some sort of stability in the Far East." But all of this depended on concluding a negotiated settlement.

In the absence of a settlement, however, a prolonged military struggle in Korea carried the risk of escalation into a general war, particularly as the Russians felt a "mortal apprehension" over the use of American military power near their borders and were "congenitally suspicious of our motives and inclined to regard us as unfathomable and unreliable opponents." Kennan feared that Moscow's "silence and scrupulous non-interference in the Korean fighting" concealed "the most exteme turmoil" inside the Kremlin and "the hour of Soviet action, in the absence of a cessation of hostilities in Korea, may be much closer than we think," he told Acheson. "My antennae tell me that if the Korean fighting does not stop soon, we should watch out for trouble."[29]

Three days later, however, Malik announced in a UN radio address that the USSR favored a negotiated settlement of the war in Korea and as a first step proposed that "discussions should be started between the belligerents for a ceasefire and an armistice providing for the mutual withdrawal of forces from the 38th Parallel." On July 2 North Korea agreed to the offer of General Matthew B. Ridgway, MacArthur's successor, to open negotiations. Talks began inconclusively at Kaesong and later were shifted to Panmunjom. A long and frustrating process had begun unaccompanied by a ceasefire, as both sides attempted to improve their negotiating positions on the battlefield.[30]

Kennan's nomination as the new U.S. ambassador to the Soviet Union in December 1951 placed in Moscow a man eminently qualified to conduct direct negotiations with Soviet authorities. As the war in Korea continued throughout 1952, State Department officials considered the possibility of achieving a settlement in Korea through direct negotiations between Kennan and Stalin. They hoped that such talks, or the simultaneous initiatives being made to China through the Indian government, could achieve a breakthrough in the talks, which became stalemated over the issue of voluntary repatriation of prisoners of war. By the summer of 1952, however, Kennan had concluded that an anti-American propaganda campaign then under way in the Soviet capital reflected Moscow's opposition to achieving a settlement in Korea. He therefore rejected making overtures to the Soviet government, declaring that such an approach "would not be useful," and might even be "unfortunate and dangerous" unless it was "backed up by some real means of pressure." U.S. Ambassador to Japan Robert Murphy, U.S. military commanders in Korea, and the Joint Chiefs of Staff concurred with his assessment.[31]

In an effort to enhance Soviet interest in promoting a ceasefire, Kennan recommended a carefully calibrated program of military escalation directed against China. While warning against "overt military steps on our part," he explained that the pressures which might compel Moscow to agree to a settlement in Korea were "in [the] nature of blockading and harassing operations along [the] China coast, hit-and-run raids, gradual introduction of selective strategic bombing in central and southern areas, etc." Such measures were to be "carefully coordinated, designed to weary China, to throw them off balance, over-strain their economy and transport." Kennan rejected any further political commitments to Jiang and opposed action against the Chinese civilian population as well as "any unwise attempts at penetration on land which could result in getting [America's] finger caught in door."

Leading officials in the Truman administration shared Kennan's desire to escalate American military pressures in an effort to break the stalemate in Korea. As a result, the United States increased the number and intensity of bombing sorties over North Korea and initiated the type of hit-and-run campaigns along the Chinese coast that Kennan and others had recommended. The administration and the UN command in Tokyo also adopted the diplomat's argument that the harassment would force China to increase its demands for supplies from Russia, thus sowing divisions within the communist bloc and encouraging Moscow's support for a negotiated settlement.[32]

By the time the Eisenhower administration inherited the Korean entanglement, Kennan had left his post in Moscow. Eisenhower and his Secretary of State, John Foster Dulles, drew up plans to take the war directly to China and expressed their willingness to use atomic weapons to bring about a resolution of the conflict. At this point Kennan had abandoned the view that Moscow alone was capable of compelling an end to the hostilities and in April 1953 he advised the Policy Planning Staff that recent Soviet editorials made it clear that the men who had inherited power following Stalin's death in March were "definitely interested" in arranging a ceasefire but that no progress could be made as long as Washington insisted on "acting as though the Chinese were [Moscow's] helpless puppets." It was, after all, Chinese and not Soviet forces which had to cease firing, Kennan explained. The conflict no longer served the interests of any of the major powers (if indeed it ever had) by the spring of 1953 and the very real threat of escalation subsided with an agreement over prisoner repatriation. Despite Rhee's attempt to sabotage the arrangement by releasing thousands of North Korean prisoners, the armistice was signed on July 27 and the war ended in a stalemate at the 38th parallel.[33]

Kennan—like Acheson, other State Department and Pentagon officials, and Truman himself—had advocated military intervention in Korea to check a putative Soviet advance and to head off a feared bandwagon effect in other parts of the world. Kennan and his colleagues thus dramatically underestimated the internal dynamics of the Korean conflict even as they exaggerated the importance of U.S. prestige and credibility in the course of international politics. Kennan offered much advice on how to respond to the events in Korea, but his views changed so often that he failed to advocate a consistent position on such critical issues as Korea's strategic significance and whether or not to negotiate with Moscow in an effort to end the war. He did oppose the effort to achieve liberation in Korea and thus displayed a more sober appreciation than did his colleagues of the dangers of taking the war to the north in the fall of 1950.

Kennan's advocacy of U.S. military intervention in Korea undermines the argument that he favored "strongpoint" over "perimeter" containment.[34] Perimeter areas such as Greece, Korea, Taiwan, and Vietnam were not among the five military-industrial centers that Kennan himself had identified as crucial to the world balance of power, yet he advocated U.S. intervention on grounds that the absence of such a response would encourage communists to strike again elsewhere in the world. The psychological perception of a bandwagon effect turned peripheral areas of the world into vital proving grounds and permitted no room for subtle distinctions between strongpoint and perimeter containment.

Kennan's extreme fear of communism, his preoccupation with cold war psychology, and his influence in effecting the global containment policy all contributed to the decision to engage in a fruitless military contest in Korea. The conflict ensured the approval of NSC-68 and the militarization of containment, both of which Kennan had opposed before resigning as PPS director. The first shooting war with communism resulted in a huge increase in the U.S. military budget and produced several far-ranging commitments, including the establishment of U.S. military bases in Japan and South Korea, a stronger commitment to containment in Southeast Asia, lasting involvement in the dispute between Taiwan and mainland China, the assignment of U.S. troops to Europe on a permanent basis, West German rearmament, and the establishment of an integrated NATO command. Not the least of the effects of the war were the 140,000 American casualties and the fuel poured upon the wave of anti-communist hysteria that came in its wake.[35] Kennan opposed virtually all of these developments but he had supported U.S. intervention in the conflict that brought them about.

VI

An Appointment with Evil

K ENNAN'S APPOINTMENT as America's eighth ambassador to the Soviet Union in April 1952 placed him in a position for which he was eminently qualified but utterly unable to play a useful role. His estrangement from the Truman administration's approach to the cold war and inability to bear the strain of life in Moscow undermined Kennan's hope that he might exercise a favorable influence on Soviet-American relations. The abortive ambassadorship brought flooding back the emotional responses that had characterized his prewar and wartime experiences in Moscow, thus illustrating Kennan's struggle to resolve the conflict between his realistic and emotional attitudes toward the Soviet Union.

Kennan spent the first few weeks of his leave of absence from the State Department in the fall of 1950 resting and working outdoors on his East Berlin (!), Pennsylvania farm, but only when he removed to Princeton did he realize "the preposterous fact of my liberation" from professional diplomacy. Located in a bucolic setting, the Institute for Advanced Study, which Kennan joined at the invitation of J. Robert Oppenheimer, provided its elite corps of scholars time for contemplation and intellectual interchange. This "decompression chamber for scholars," as Oppenheimer once described it, offered a welcome respite in the wake of Kennan's bureaucratic struggles in the State Deparment and the wrenching events in Korea. While working at the Institute he maintained close contact with Oppenheimer and historian Edward Meade Earle and exchanged notes with another IAS fellow, Albert Einstein, who once complimented Kennan's "fine remarks about basic moral issues . . . in this time of widespread madness."[1]

Previously unable to indulge his scholarly bent because of everyday demands in the State Department, Kennan seized the opportunity to launch a study that culminated in the publication of *American Diplomacy, 1900–1950,* a slender but popular volume that scores of college professors adopted as a primer on foreign affairs.[2] The book stemmed from a series of lectures delivered in Chicago in the spring of 1951 which focused on the Spanish-American War, U.S. Far Eastern policy, and the two world wars—incidents of twentieth-century diplomacy that Kennan employed to buttress his thesis that the nation had indulged in idealism and ignored power realities in its preoccupation with establishing a "legalistic-moralistic" framework for the conduct of foreign affairs. He condemned the United States for failing to make its influence felt in the early stages of World War I and for obscuring its real national interests through a crusade to make the world "safe for democracy" when it did enter the conflict. In the interwar period, Washington should have made a greater effort to support Weimar Germany, a policy that might have prevented the rise of Hitler and the agony of a second world war. Like Hanson Baldwin, Kennan argued that unconditional surrender had been a "great mistake" in World War II and that American interests would have been better served had some remnant of the defeated states been preserved in order to provide for a stable postwar balance of power. He took the nation to task for its penchant for molding romantic illusions —as in the quest for a special relationship with China and friendship with Stalin. Kennan's realism thus condemned prewar isolationism as well as interventions cloaked in the rhetoric of great international crusades, but called into question the ability of a mass democracy to maintain its equilibrium in the conduct of foreign affairs.[3]

Despite his call for realism in *American Diplomacy,* Kennan's experience as the American ambassador to Russia in 1952 showed that he had by no means overcome his own penchant for moralistic responses to Soviet behavior. Kennan's appointment came after the outbreak of fighting in Korea, the Chinese intervention, and the opening of discussions with the Soviet envoy Jacob Malik had already interrupted his leave of absence. In September 1951 he requested a second year's leave after which he asked to receive a foreign assignment rather than a State Department post in which the "divergence between my own views and those that have been, and are, current in the shaping of policy" would create conflict.[4] Despite Kennan's opposition to the militarization of containment and the division of Germany, Acheson and Truman decided that he was the best candidate to replace Alan G. Kirk, who was drained after two and half years in the Soviet capital. Truman first hinted that Kennan might be appointed in late November, telling the press that he "would make a good ambassador. He certainly knows his way around there."[5]

Although the Moscow ambassadorship was a prestigious post for which he was uniquely qualified, Kennan was reluctant to accept. A year earlier he had asked Acheson to consider him as the next ambassador to London, suggesting that he had seen enough of Moscow for one lifetime, and he was rightfully concerned about his disagreements with the administration. But Kennan had already conducted secret talks with Malik over Korea and Acheson wanted him in position to meet directly with Stalin in the event of a potential breakthrough in negotiations. Acheson solicited Charles Bohlen's assistance in persuading Kennan to take the post and a sense of duty ultimately prevailed. "Of all the jobs in the world," he recalled, "this was the one which I had the least right to refuse."[6]

The announcement of Kennan's nomination on December 27, 1951, was "not the result of any suggestion on my part," he told the Senate Foreign Relations Committee. "It was the idea of the President and the Secretary of State." The nomination received widespread support in the American press. Even *Time,* critical of containment, offered lukewarm praise and the convoluted argument that Kennan's "possible defects as a top planner of U.S. policy would not be defects in a U.S. Ambassador to Russia" since that job was "primarily one of analyzing Russian policies and motives at which Kennan is one of the best living practitioners."[7]

The Soviet Communist Party newspaper *Pravda* displayed even less enthusiasm for Kennan by assailing his record of "hatred" toward Russia and falsely accusing the diplomat of viewing a Soviet-American war as inevitable. Radio Moscow declared that "it is not by chance that the State Department appoints as diplomats . . . shady persons who are usually spies of long standing." The Soviet press pointed out that Kennan's presidency of the "Free Russia Fund," a Ford Foundation-sponsored program for Soviet and East European emigrés, constituted a conflict of interest and accepted his appointment only after Kennan resigned the post.[8]

The Foreign Relations Committee heard only two hours of testimony from Kennan before confirming his nomination on April 1, 1952. He kept an appointment later that day with Truman, who merely wished him good luck in Moscow. The Ambassador emerged from the meeting to tell reporters that he looked forward to the "opportunity to contribute to a relaxation of tensions and to an improvement of the international atmosphere" and declared that both objectives were "obviously and urgently desirable and I see no reason why they should not be within the realm of possibility if the desire is shared on the other side." Privately, Kennan assured reporters that if anyone could warm the frigid climate of Soviet-American relations, it was he.[9]

In actuality Kennan had little opportunity to ameliorate East-West relations as long as his strategic conception diverged from that which governed the Truman-Acheson approach to the Cold War. The divergence of views continued to center on Germany and the militarization of containment. In the weeks before he left for Moscow Kennan secured an appointment with Acheson, who advised him to take no initiatives that might upset the administration's continuing program of European integration, both economic and military. Feeling "extremely lonely," Kennan set out "with a very heavy heart . . . empty-handed, uninstructed, and uncertain, to what [was] surely the most important and delicate of the world's diplomatic tasks at this particular juncture."[10]

While Kennan insisted that a preoccupation with military preparedness obscured the ideological-political threat and increased the chances of an eventual war with Russia, the administration was committed to bolstering the Western military alliance. Acheson precipitated a "great debate" in the United States in 1951 with his decision to reinforce NATO with American troops, something that he had once publicly told a senator the administration "absolute[ly]" would not do. Working closely with Chancellor Konrad Adenauer, Washington sought to add West German military power to the "free world" arsenal in Europe, a proposal that made France nervous but whose dangers were to be checked through the creation of an all-European army within a new European Defense Community (EDC), which was to be a corollary of NATO.[11]

More willing than he had been from 1944 to 47 to look at events from the Soviet perspective, Kennan argued that Stalin had his own vivid memories of Hitler, saw no justification for Western European rearmament, and rejected the argument that NATO sprang from benign defensive considerations. "The Soviet leaders," he explained, "found it easy to conclude that the Atlantic Pact project concealed intentions not revealed to the public" and that the United States and its allies intended "to bring to a head a military conflict with the Soviet Union as soon as the requisite strength had been created on the Western side." Moscow ordered the Korean invasion to counter Western militarization in Europe and Japan—according to Kennan—but the action only served to confirm the Western perception of a Soviet grand design and thus prompted U.S. military intervention.

Kennan supported West German rearmament only in the context of an EDC that would allow for a U.S. military withdrawal from the continent as a prelude to a new détente with Russia. "Neither western Germany nor EDC, nor indeed any unit in which the western Germans are a part, should enter in to any sort of relationship of alliance with us," he declared. "Under no circumstances should western Germany be permitted to join NATO." Kennan preferred the all-European EDC to direct American involvement in the continent's military defense, but even EDC left "nothing for discussions with the Russians about the future of Germany and . . . overcoming of the split in Europe generally."

Having grown pessimistic over the prospects that containment might lead to the disintegration of the Soviet regime, Kennan continued as he had done since 1948 to advocate a negotiated settlement based on German reunification and the neutralization of most of Europe. Even if negotiations proved fruitless, he advised, the opening of talks might serve to overcome the perception that prevailed in Moscow that "we have already hinged our policy exclusively to the destruction of their power and have excluded the possibility of accommodation or compromise with them."[12]

Kennan failed to shape the views of American and West European leaders, few of whom shared his burning desire to reunify Germany as the centerpiece of a neutral central Europe, but most of whom did cling to the perceptions of Soviet behavior that characterized the Long Tele-gram and X-Article. While most Western leaders, and perhaps the Sovi-ets as well, saw security in a divided Germany, Kennan was convinced that such a course would become "increasingly dangerous and onerous both to ourselves and to our allies." Despite his own history of advocat-ing liberation extending to Russia itself, Kennan now criticized Ameri-can diplomatists for embarking "upon a path the logic of which would eventually bring us squarely to the view of John Foster Dulles: that the accent of our policy should lie on an attempt to subvert and overthrow Communist power." Kennan saw "no end to such a policy but failure or war." [13]

Despite the divergence of views between Kennan and the administra-tion, he expressed the hope upon his arrival in Moscow on May 6 that his mission would spark a fresh start in U.S.-Soviet relations. "I want to assume that everything I've thought up to now is wrong, and see whether I come out at the same place this time," he explained. Kennan reasoned that Stalin may have abandoned hopes of world conquest as a result of America's displays of credibility around he world and might be ready to come to terms in Europe and Asia. [14]

Kennan's flash of optimism and his prestige impressed the young Foreign Service Officers who served under him in Moscow. "We were terribly excited to hear that he was coming," one of them, Richard Davies, recalled in 1979. "He was the person on whom most of the younger officers—certainly in Soviet studies—modeled themselves." "Morale picked up immediately," Frank Rounds, another of Kennan's subordinates, recalled. "His enthusiasm, his energy, his curiosity; all of us sort of caught a bit of this." Working long hours, Kennan revitalized the operations of the largest foreign embassy in Moscow, which encom-passed all or part of eight buildings, but the effort left him "pale and tired after only a few days." [15]

As the author of containment and one of the Wests top experts on Russia, Kennan became "the acknowledged leader of the entire Western community in Moscow" and received good press at home. Richard Rovere and Harrison Salisbury wrote complimentary pieces in the *New Yorker* and the *New York Times,* respectively. "Not only does [Kennan] look with trained eyes," Salisbury gushed, "but he has the trained mind to interpret what goes on before his eyes." [16]

During his first weeks in Moscow Kennan strove in the face of Soviet provocations to gain the respect of the Kremlin in order to encourage the regime to conduct diplomacy with him. "Their first inclination, I've always felt, is to look upon you as they look upon their own representatives—as someone who has been told what to say and can be counted on to say it at every opportunity," he explained. "One reason they have you followed everywhere is to learn what sort of person you are, and I think that when they find character, they respect it."[17]

This cheerful approach soon wore thin, however, largely as a result of Kennan's anger over the daily barrage of anti-American propaganda in the Soviet press. While hardly novel in Moscow since the demise of the Grand Alliance, anti-American diatribes had intensified as a result of the Korean War. "Day after day the American military are openly committing atrocities and acts of brigandage," read one *Pravda* account. Under the headline "Cannibalistic American Imperialism," another *Pravda* writer declared that "all peace loving nations are deeply indignant over the monstrous atrocities of the U.S. soldiery" in Korea. Americans were "the bloodiest beasts, the worst enemies of humanity" the operators of prison camps reminiscent of Dachau. The Soviet press accused Acheson and Truman of "slander" and "hackneyed, trite lies," charging that "not one of their speeches is without anti-Soviet attack."[18]

Perceiving "special motives" in the anti-American campaign, Kennan asserted that Moscow wanted to bolster low morale among world communists by stepping up attacks on U.S. imperialism, and also meant to discredit him personally. On June 19 Soviet Foreign Minister Andrei Vyshinsky assured Kennan that he was not the target of Moscow's propaganda, which, he explained, merely counterbalanced anti-Soviet rhetoric in the United States. The U.S. envoy told Vyshinsky that he wanted to improve Soviet-American relations "but what I had seen here since my arrival really caused me to question whether there was any point in such effort, since it could not be entirely a one-way street."[19]

Angry that anti-American statements continued to pour out even after his meeting with Vyshinsky, Kennan decided to make an issue of Soviet propaganda. "I think we must be careful, precisely in this semi-oriental country," he advised the State Department, "not to permit our presence and silence to be exploited as an exhibit to others of our weakness, our lack of pride and dignity, and our helplessness in the face of insult." "The thing that strikes me hardest," he wrote directly to Truman on August 11, "is the extent to which the Soviet Government has lost contact with the West. There is simply no real channel for exchange of views." Kennan told the President that the United States should insist upon a cease-fire in Korea and a termination of the "violent and dirty" anti-American propaganda as prerequisites for any amelioration of U.S.-Soviet relations. As a result of Kennan's reports, Acheson formally complained about the "virulence of the present anti-American campaign" to the Soviet ambassador to the United States, Alexander Panyushkin.[20]

To Kennan the propaganda campaign violated the traditions of proper form and civility in diplomatic exchanges between nations and he could not abide the Soviet behavior. "It is no easy thing to take this outrageous and provocative propaganda material, permeated as it is with the smell of a vicious and shameless mentality, and subject it to a calm and dispassionate analysis," he told the State Department's H. Freeman Matthews in June. "I do not particularly mind the life here," he wrote to another colleague, "but I find it impossible to adjust comfortably to the incredible volume and hatefulness of lies these people manage to put out about us and themselves and everyone." "The anti-American propaganda of course got to him very much," Richard Davies recalled. "He took it very personally."[21]

While they endured the propaganda barrage, Kennan and his embassy charges were also the targets of Soviet surveillance and petty harassment. The Russians proscribed travel more than twenty-five miles outside of Moscow; forbade the Americans to speak with Soviet citizens; and required them to purchase common Soviet publications through the Foreign Ministry. Whereas in the 1930s and 40s Kennan had counted friends among the Soviet employees at his residence, in 1952 stone-faced servants at Spaso House shunned communication; groundskeepers refused to work; and security agents followed Kennan wherever he went, depriving him of relaxing strolls among the Russian people. "I came gradually to think of myself as a species of disembodied spirit," he recalled, "capable, like the invisible character of the fairy tales, of seeing others and of moving among them but not of being seen, or at least not of being identified by them." He attended the Moscow theater weekly but on every occasion four security officers muscled patrons from the seats behind the Ambassador in order to take their posts. "This made for a very morbid kind of evening," Richard Davies recalled.[22]

Kennan found some peace during weekend visits to his dacha in the countryside, but could hardly relax in Spaso House, which had become a target of Soviet espionage. In September he assisted electronic technicians as they uncovered a bugging device planted in the wall behind the Great Seal of the United States. Despite his own lack of enthusiasm for such projects, American armed service attachés in the embassy conducted their own espionage activities and often assumed posts on the roof to photograph overflying Soviet planes. "So dense was the atmosphere of anger and hostility," Kennan recalled, "that one could have cut it with a knife."[23]

The intensity of the Kremlin's anti-American campaign and the zeal for espionage found Kennan distraught after only a month in Moscow. In June 1952 he refused a request by Peer de Silva, chief of operations of the CIA's Soviet bloc division, to station a U.S. espionage agent in the Moscow embassy. After turning down the request as contrary to the spirit of diplomacy, Kennan asked de Silva to provide him with two lethal cyanide capsules that he proposed to swallow in the event that relations deteriorated to the point that the Soviets arrested him and attempted to force him "to make statements that would be damaging to American policy."[24]

Kennan concluded that the propaganda, surveillance and harassment signalled Moscow's opposition to negotiations over the Korean War and other issues. The U.S. Ambassador discouraged the administration from opening a direct line of communication between himself and Stalin in response to the Kremlin's "totally arrogant and defiant policy." Kennan adopted a stance of "manful reserve, dignity, and independence of U.S. policy" in order to "strain [the] nerves of people committed to [the] thesis [that] we are slipping, and encourage critics of their policy." He asserted that his refusal to approach representatives of the regime, except for the one meeting with Vyshinsky, was "having beneficial effects here and should by all means be continued." The United States had taken the initiative too many times and an "empty-handed appeal" for help in Korea would only be exploited by the ruling clique as a "vindication [of] their policy in general, and of [the] violently anti-American line in particular."

In addition to abandoning his earlier call for negotiations with Russia, Kennan urged a reduction in East-West trade to "an absolute minimum." Washington and its allies should resolve to live with the political and economic consequences of such action. Kennan had no desire to see the United States "expedite [the] tempo of Communist military industrialization" and he had misgivings about the involvement of Western businessmen with Communist trade monopolies. Kennan's recommendations ran counter to his desire for a new détente, but he blamed the actions of the Soviet regime for the deterioration of relations.[25]

While Kennan spent much of his time venting his anger at the Russians, he also complained about changes that undermined his ability to shape policy and fueled his inclination to resign from the Foreign Service. American ambassadors had lost influence and prestige over the course of the cold war as officials in new agencies such as the Policy Planning Staff, National Security Council, Joint Chiefs of Staff, Department of Defense, and the CIA assumed many of their former responsibilities. "The good old despatch form—that of the personal address by a chief of mission to a theoretically interested Secretary of State—now seems to have passed away with many of the other older features of diplomacy," Kennan lamented in a nostalgic reverie. "Why the Government wants an Ambassador here is still difficult for me to fathom."[26]

Complaining that he had no voice in personnel decisions, Kennan charged that the embassy was "absurdly overstaffed . . . in order that people in Washington can feel happy about the organization tables and training schedules." Asserting that "nobody is going to do any real thinking about Russia," Kennan advised a fellow diplomat that the State Department

> must not be thought of as a wise and informed analyst, capable of putting two and two together or of remembering today what you said last week. Think of it rather as a multitude of well-meaning, mildly interested, but harried and distraught people, whose memories go back, with luck, something like forty-eight hours and who, though they might be capable of rational process, are scarcely apt to be found indulging in it with respect to your particular field of interest.[27]

Weary and pessimistic after only a few months in Moscow, Kennan longed to return to Princeton. As long as the war in Korea continued, with Soviet weapons killing American GIs, with Stalin irresolute and with the American foreign affairs establishment committed to military containment in Europe and Asia, he felt that little could be accomplished in Moscow. Estranged from the administration he served and sickened by the paranoid atmosphere that enveloped Moscow as Stalin prepared to launch yet another purge in 1952, Kennan acted to liberate himself from a predicament that had grown intolerable.

Upon arriving in Berlin on September 19, 1952—his first stop en route to a meeting of American ambassadors in London—Kennan condemned the Soviet regime in terms that virtually ensured his removal as Ambassador to Russia. Fully aware that he would be questioned by reporters when his plane touched down at Tempelhof Airport, Kennan prepared the usual diplomatic responses during the flight. When a Paris reporter asked about everyday life in the Soviet capital, however, he lashed out.

"Don't you know how foreign diplomats live in Moscow?" Kennan exploded. As the reporters scrawled in their notebooks, he compared life in Russia to conditions which had prevailed under the Nazis. "Had the Nazis permitted us to walk the streets without having the right to talk to any Germans," Kennan declared, recalling his months of internment during the war, "that would be exactly how we have to live in Moscow today." Alluding to the "icy-cold" atmosphere in the Soviet capital, he declared that as long as the Soviets permitted the anti-American campaign and the Korean war to continue, it was clear that they had "no intention of improving relations with us." [28]

The repercussions set in on September 26 when *Pravda*, taking the usual week to report the news, attacked Kennan under the headline "American Slanderer in a Diplomat's Mask." The page-three story asserted that "Kennan lied ecstatically" and declared that his "crude anti-Soviet sally leaves no doubt that such a statement could only be made by a person unable to restrain his malevolent hostility to the Soviet Union, who not only desires no improvement in American-Soviet relations, but uses every opportunity to make them worse." The article charged that the Ambassador had violated the "elementary rules obligatory for a diplomat." [29]

On October 3, while Kennan was visiting his daughter in Geneva, the Soviet government delivered a diplomatic note declaring him *persona non grata* and demanding his recall as ambassador for his "slanderous attacks hostile to the Soviet Union in rude violation of generally recognized norms of international law." On the same day Acheson said the United States "does not accept as valid the charges made by the Soviet Government," but the perturbed Secretary told Kennan to stay in Europe until after the November presidential election. Kennan won widespread support in the Congress, especially from the Republican right-wing. Senator William Knowland of California, for example, demanded the removal of the Soviet ambassador, Georgi Zarubin, and the withdrawal of diplomatic recognition from the "uncivilized Communist regime," advice which Acheson rejected.[30]

Richard Davies, the diplomat who served under Kennan in Moscow, concluded that the Ambassador had provoked his own expulsion rather than simply resigning from the post. Unable to achieve a breakthrough in the cold war, Kennan believed that "he had, both in terms of his own self-image and of the image he felt he had in the eyes of others, somehow failed, which of course he hadn't," Davies explained. "He couldn't go back to President Truman and say, 'I have to resign.' That would have been a kind of admission of failure. So how to get out of this?' Kennan found himself "under enormous psychological pressure, surrounded by suspicion and provocations and the kind of treatment which he being I would say a pretty sensitive person was particularly impressed by—and depressed by—finally there was no other way out for him although he knew he shouldn't say what he did, than to say something which would result in [his expulsion]."[31]

Kennan did not admit to having attempted to provoke his removal from Moscow, but he offered no apologies for his remarks and could barely contain his relief at not having to return to the Soviet capital. As he had put it to Bohlen one day after the *Pravda* attack: "I do not favor keeping an Ambassador in Moscow at all in present circumstances. If there must be an Ambassador, I do not favor its being me."[32] The diplomat wrote Robert Oppenheimer that he was leaving Moscow for "complex" reasons which the public would be unable to understand. "I have therefore had to be content to permit a greatly oversimplified but not too unfortunate impression to become established, and must ride it out on that basis."[33]

Most, but not all, of the American press rallied around Kennan. The *Baltimore Sun* argued that the diplomat's removal had little to do with his Berlin commentary, explaining that "the Russians are afraid of him. The man is too good, he knows too much for the Kremlin's comfort." The *San Francisco Chronicle* agreed: "They fear his acute powers of observation and analysis being brought to bear on the forbidding Russian system." But Cyrus L. Sulzberger criticized Kennan in the *New York Times*: "Things are definitely worse than before the brilliant author of the containment policy presented his credentials at the Kremlin. They are likely to remain so for some time as a result of his perhaps unnecessary Berlin press conference." There was other criticism, too: "With all due respect to Mr. Acheson's righteous indignation over the Russian note," declared the *Nation,* "we can hardly imagine a less diplomatic public utterance than the American Ambassador's."[34]

Refusing to shoulder the blame, Kennan wrote from Germany to a friend that the Soviet regime "would not have expelled me unless they had felt that I was coming too close to the exposure of some of their frauds and outrages, which it seems to me it was my job to do." He sounded more contrite over the Berlin statements in his memoir, however, calling the comparison of Soviet and Nazi practices "an extremely foolish thing for me to have said."[35] After Acheson cleared Kennan to come home, the diplomat admitted that he "blew my top," but found "a certain comic opera quality" in the train of events. "The upshot was one which was to the eminent satisfaction of almost everyone concerned. The Soviet Government wanted to get rid of me, and did. I desperately wanted to leave, and succeeded in doing so." In a reference to the Republican right, Kennan observed that his removal had "earned me the praises of a great many people in this country whose admiration I did not particularly covet." Only the United States government was unhappy, he added, but "it could not reproach anyone for an anti-Soviet remark four weeks before the election. So outwardly, everyone was happy."

The Moscow experience reflected Kennan's ongoing struggle to resolve the conflict between his emotional and realistic attitudes toward the Soviet Union, a conflict that was exacerbated by his physical presence inside Russia. He had opposed the Truman Administration policies which, he had argued, left the Soviets little choice but to cling to a sphere of influence in Eastern Europe and to prepare to defend themselves in the event of war with the United States. Kennan had blamed Washington and the Western allies for placing a roadblock in the path of a negotiated settlement of the cold war and argued that under such circumstances little but intransigence could be expected from the Stalin regime.

After only four months in Moscow, however, Kennan's enmity for Soviet communism had roared to the surface and overwhelmed his pragmatic analysis of East-West relations. Repulsed by Soviet cynicism and propaganda, he ceased complaining about the militarization of containment in the West and blamed Russia for the war in Korea, the division of Europe, and other international problems. Although he had called for a negotiated settlement to end the division of Europe since 1948, shortly after returning to Washington Kennan declared that he still believed the United States "should never have established *de jure* diplomatic relations at all with the Soviet government" because of its communist ideology, a posture that would have left the West "free to conduct whatever political warfare we wished against the Soviet regime."[36] The Moscow ambassadorship thus prompted Kennan to reassert reactionary positions which would have precluded the opening of a new ear of détente that he himself had only recently advocated.

Kennan's abortive tenure as U.S. Ambassador to Russia showed that he had outlived his usefulness as a professional diplomat. Convinced that he knew more than his superiors in Washington, Kennan lacked the deference to authority and the circumspection which professional diplomacy requires. In retrospect it is clear that the appointment never should have been made, nor accepted, and that Kennan could make his best contribution as a historian and outsider and critic of American diplomacy. But Kennan experienced difficulty in balancing his reluctance to bring to an end a distinguished career in the Foreign Service with the realization that he could accomplish little by remaining in professional diplomacy. John Foster Dulles soon took care of this problem for him by declining to offer Kennan a post in the new administration. With his ouster from both Washington and Moscow, Kennan would achieve the rare distinction of becoming *persona non grata* in both capitals.

VII

The Politics of Liberation

F OLLOWING HIS abortive ambassadorship to the Soviet Union, Kennan retired from the Foreign Service amid public controversy with John Foster Dulles in 1953. He remained for a time as a consultant to the government and tried unsuccessfully to head off West Germany's integration into NATO. Kennan emerged as an active Democrat and a close adviser to Adlai E. Stevenson in 1956, but the retired diplomat's controversial positions on European diplomacy undermined his influence. Despite his call for negotiations with Moscow, Kennan remained torn between his realistic and emotional responses. The 1956 Hungarian revolt reignited his dream that liberation would extend into the Soviet Union itself, this in spite of his own criticism of the Republican rollback policy.

While Kennan remained in Europe after the Soviets had declared him *persona non grata* in the in the fall of 1952, the Republican Party culminated a successful campaign to take the White House for the first time in twenty years. John Foster Dulles, a New York attorney and prominent internationalist who would be Secretary of State, spearheaded the Republican attack on the Truman Administrations's foreign policy amid a climate of anti-communist hysteria. While Dwight D. Eisenhower promised to end the war in Korea, the Republican Party platform castigated the "negative, futile and immoral" policy of containment which had consigned the peoples of Eastern Europe to remain the "captive nations" of the Soviet Union. If elected the new administration pledged to foster "contagious, liberating influences which are inherent in freedom" and create "strains and stresses within the captive world which will make the rulers impotent to continue their monstrous ways."[1]

Although liberation had been an integral component of Kennan's original strategy, he sought to distance himself from the Republican Party rhetoric. It might be justifiable, even "enjoyable," to "go at it hammer and tongs" with Russia, but the costs of all-out war were simply too great. Kennan found no fault with the desire to overthrow the Soviet regime and liberate Eastern Europe—asserting that the thinking behind it was "sound"—but argued that the only chance to achieve this aim was through a long process of ideological-political containment and negotiation.[2]

The Republican attack on containment put Kennan on the defensive and found him simultaneously defending his strategy even as he claimed that he had been "incorrectly charged with being the author of the containment policy." Despite that disclaimer Kennan still argued that containment could eventually "weaken" Soviet power through "the continued systematic frustration of its designs in the non-Communist world, and partly by creating difficulties . . . in its satellite area." Noting that many Americans were frustrated by restraints on American diplomacy, he conceded that it "may be a subjective necessity for us as a democracy to have in our policy elements of something more aggressive and positive than we have been able to have in the past" while leaving the door open for negotiations.[3]

Aside from occasional public talks, Kennan retired to his Pennsylvania farm to await a summons from the administration following Eisenhower's defeat of Illinois governor Adlai Stevenson in November. Kennan was acquainted with Eisenhower, who as President of Columbia University in 1950 had offered him the post, which Kennan declined, as head of a new Russian institute on campus. Kennan was better acquainted but not friendly with Dulles, a fellow Princeton man with whom he had contended over the Japanese peace treaty in 1950 and who had "shouted down" his proposal that Washington remain neutral on the question of Communist China's admission into the UN. Kennan's position on China and his support for limited war aims in Korea, while

Dulles advocated liberation of the entire peninsula, made the Soviet expert a "dangerous man," Dulles allegedly told a news reporter in 1950.[4]

Kennan and Dulles also clashed on the role of morality in foreign policy. Dulles declaimed in the Republican campaign that containment was an immoral policy because it consigned the peoples of Eastern Europe to permanent domination by Moscow.[5] He insisted that "certain basic moral concepts" should be observed in international life and "some sort of international canon law" developed. Kennan considered such proposals idealistic and regarded the attorney Dulles as a proponent of the futile legalistic-moralistic approach to world order. Even if international legal codes could be agreed upon, Kennan argued, they would almost certainly be ignored, like the Kellogg-Briand Pact, at the moment when it served some nation's interest to overlook them. Kennan's realism called for basing foreign policy on national interests rather than moral precepts and years later he asserted that Dulles's invocation of morality was hypocritical. "Foster Dulles, in my deep conviction . . . did not have an ounce of real piety in his system; the hypocrisy was pure, as was the ambition. Both were unadulterated by any tinges of genuine Christian charity or obligation."[6]

Kennan and Dulles thus frequently disagreed and, quite simply, did not like one another, yet in some respects there was little difference in their approach toward the Soviet Union. While Dulles trumpeted rollback as an alternative to containment, Kennan himself had long envisioned liberation as part of his strategy toward Eastern Europe and Russia itself. Both Kennan and Dulles were visceral opponents of communism and both advocated a global foreign policy employing means short of war. However, Dulles did reject Kennan's call for German reunification and disengagement in Europe and Kennan could not abide the Eisenhower Administration's reliance on nuclear weapons as a key component of its diplomacy.

In view of their disagreements and his attacks on containment, Dulles probably had no intention of offering Kennan a new Foreign Service assignment, but Kennan assured his own ouster by delivering a broadside against liberation in a speech before the Pennsylvania Bar Association in January 1953. Having toned down his own predictions of the demise of the Soviet regime, Kennan warned of the need "to be extremely careful of doing anything at the governmental level that purports to affect directly the governmental system in another country, no matter what the provocation may seem." He explained that a policy of liberation actually implied a renunciation of formal diplomatic relations—a position that Kennan himself advocated privately that same month—and was "replete with possibilities for misunderstanding and bitterness. To the extent it might be successful, it would involve us in heavy responsibilities." In sharp contrast to the arguments he had put forward in the early cold war period, Kennan now argued that the prospects for a successful liberation policy were "very small indeed" because "the problem of civil disobedience is not a great problem to the modern police dictatorship."[7]

Although Kennan made no mention of the new administration in his speech, his argument clearly targeted Dulles, who had trumpeted liberation throughout the campaign and as recently as the previous day in testimony before the Senate Foreign Relations Committee. The press delighted in the debate between two prominent internationalists representing the competing political parties. "Dulles Policy 'Dangerous,' Kennan Says" screamed the page one headline of the *Washington Post*. While Dulles offered no public response to the speech, the Republican right wing excoriated Kennan. Senator Joseph McCarthy, whose charges of communist infiltration in the State Department commanded popular attention, called the speech "a typical Acheson-type tirade against those who have been exposing traitors."[8]

Kennan professed shock at the publicity highlighting his differences with Dulles, but as with the Berlin press conference several months earlier, it seems quite likely that Kennan expected events to develop much as they did in response to his statements. He was, after all, no stranger to the media's penchant for controversy and had been closely associated with reporters since the X-Article. He cultivated relationships with several prominent writers, including James Reston, Harrison Salisbury, and Joseph and Stewart Alsop, and corresponded regularly with Walter Lippmann. Kennan intended the bar association speech as a major statement on Soviet policy and he knew that it would be reported. Kennan's speech reflected his desire to reassert his standing as a member of the foreign policy elite even as he anticipated his return to private life.

Kennan played the role of the innocent once the controversy with Dulles appeared on the nation's front pages. Unable to locate Dulles in Washington, he wrote to H. Freeman ("Doc") Matthews, head of the

State Department's European Affairs office, stressing that the speech had been written weeks before Dulles's Senate testimony and that it "did not have him in mind, but other certain editors, legislators and professional propagandists for minority groups interested in Russia who would like to see us commit ourselves to a policy of intervention." But since Dulles also publicly threatened a more aggressive strategy, such a distinction made little difference. Kennan concluded the January 18 letter, which he asked Matthews to forward to Dulles, with an offer to resign in a year when he would be fifty years old and eligible for additional retirement benefits.[9]

After Kennan met briefly with Dulles on January 22, the State Department attempted to defuse the controversy by releasing a statement explaining that the bar association speech had not been intended as an attack on Dulles and that both men now "considered the episode closed." On the same day, however, Dulles sent letters to 16,500 State Department employees calling for their "positive loyalty" and hinted that there might be shakeups within the State Department. Asked whether Kennan would receive a new assignment in the Foreign Service, Dulles said he had "not gone into" the matter.[10]

Despite this claim by Dulles, Kennan and Dulles may well have agreed in their meeting that the diplomat would resign rather than receive another assignment. In a letter dated January 23—the day after their State Department meeting—Kennan wrote to Dulles that "in view of the fuss stirred up about my recent speech and in the light of other considerations . . . I have come to the conclusion that it would be better if I were to retire voluntarily at this time from government service and retire to private life." Apparently Dulles decided to accept Kennan's resignation, but chose not to respond directly to the letter, perhaps because of an aide's warning several weeks later that "Kennan would probably release to the press" any response from Dulles, thus fueling controversy.[11]

Indeed, the press continued to pay close attention to Kennan's fate with respect to the new administration and most accounts were sympathetic to him. Even before the bar association speech, the *New York Times* had asserted that America's European allies hoped that Kennan, rather than Harvard president James B. Conant, would receive appointment as High Commissioner to West Germany and throughout January and February Kennan was variously mentioned as a candidate to become ambassador to Egypt, Switzerland, Italy, or Yugoslavia. Within the administration, Dulles adviser George V. Allen recommended that Kennan replace him as ambassador to Yugoslavia, noting that Kennan might be able to formulate a definitive analysis of the reasons for Tito's break with Stalin. "Well, I'll think about it," Dulles responded.[12]

While the press speculated about Kennan's future, the diplomat himself learned that Dulles simply planned to take no action on the matter, which under departmental procedures designed to phase out political appointees meant that he would be automatically retired ninety days after the end of his previous assignment. On March 13 the *New York Times* cited "high administration sources" in a story announcing that Kennan would be retired in such a manner and Dulles summoned Kennan to his office that same day to make it official. Two days later Kennan told Robert Oppenheimer that Dulles had said "he knew of 'no niche' for me in government at this time, and that I would have difficulty getting confirmation by the Senate for any representative position, tainted as I am with 'containment.' We parted in what was apparently a hearty agreement that I should now retire, although our reasons for this were not identical."[13]

Kennan received more sympathy from Foster's brother, Allen Dulles, the new CIA director, who offered Kennan a position with the agency in a meeting at Charles Bohlen's Washington home soon after Kennan learned that he would be retired. Kennan received written notice of his termination on April 6, when Foster Dulles wrote, in an apparent reference to the January 23 letter from Kennan, that since Kennan had decided to retire he had "no alternative but to comply with your wishes." On April 7, after conferring once again with Foster Dulles, who encouraged him to accept a position with the CIA, Kennan declined that offer and the next day the State Department announced that he would retire to academic life by mutual agreement with Dulles, although he would remain a "regular consultant to the government."[14]

The nation's press sided with Kennan in the controversy with Dulles. Typical was the reaction of the *Boston Globe,* which declared that Dulles had wasted Kennan's taxpayer-financed expertise on Russia. "His exit from the diplomatic scene is a severe and costly loss for the country," the paper declared. Drew Pearson's "Washington Merry-Go-Round" syndicated political column castigated Dulles for giving "the deep-freeze treatment" to Kennan even though he had proven to be an "amazingly accurate" forecaster of Russian behavior in the past. Among the other papers which defended Kennan at Dulles's expense were the *New York Times*, the *New York Herald-Tribune*, the *Milwaukee Journal*, the *Chicago Sun-Times*, and the *Christian Science Monitor*.[15]

Dulles paid the price of a few days' press criticism to be rid of Kennan and avoid the ordeal of a confirmation hearing that would have followed the diplomat's nomination to a new ambassadorial post. Debate on Charles Bohlen's nomination to replace Kennan as the Ambassador to Moscow had dragged on in March as several senators hostile to the former Roosevelt interpreter questioned his loyalty and involvement in the "Yalta sellout" before the Republican-dominated Senate Foreign Relations Committee consented to his appointment. Having one hold-over Soviet expert from the Democratic administration was enough for Dulles, who in spite of the Yalta connection had little trouble choosing Bohlen, a "cautious diplomat" who was far less outspoken and not directly identified with containment.[16]

Eisenhower speechwriter Emmett John Hughes made an attempt in the summer of 1953 to relieve some of the embarrassment of Kennan's departure, arguing that "it would be gratuitously rude to allow an officer who has served as long as Mr. Kennan to 'retire' by the crude—and silent—expedient of simply failing to offer him a diplomatic post." Hughes said that he was "quite aware of [Dulles's] personal distaste for some of Mr. Kennan's theorizing and philosophizing about foreign policy," but suggested that Eisenhower pay a courtesy call on Kennan to thank him for his government service. Dulles refused to arrange such a meeting but did draft a letter, which the President signed, accepting Kennan's retirement and thanking him for his government service.[17]

Despite the public controversy over his retirement as well as his ongoing opposition to the militarization of containment, Kennan served as a consultant to the new Republican administration and even assisted in the drafting of a new statement of national security policy. When Bohlen finally departed for Moscow to replace him as ambassador, Kennan found that "senior people seem to want me to remain somewhere near government and available to it for consultation on a regular basis." He analyzed speeches and articles from the Soviet press for CIA director Allen Dulles[18] and even put aside his disagreements with Foster

Dulles long enough to draft a speech on the dangers of Latin American communism, which the Secretary of State delivered before an Organization of American States meeting in Caracas.[19]

In May 1953 Eisenhower named the retired diplomat to head one of three teams in a "highly classified and urgent project"—code-named "Operation Solarium" for the small penthouse on the White House roof —which was to produce a "new basic concept" for the administration's national security policy. Eisenhower and Dulles planned to go beyond containment to effect "a more dynamic and aggressive strategy aimed at creating a climate of victory and reducing Soviet power," but the President wanted to analyze the prospects for success and most especially the costs of the new approach.[20] Kennan headed "Task Force A," whose mission was to make recommendations based on the "broad gauge political, military, economic and psychological planning for the future." The recommendations of his nine-member team reflected his own influence as well as that of Paul Nitze, who once again found himself serving under Kennan in the Solarium Project. Task Force A advocated a program of ideological-political containment centered on Japan and Western Europe, warned against "blanket policies," and recommended "a better U.S. stance on the unification of Germany issue"—all pet issues of Kennan. But the team's report also called for "a higher level of defense expenditures," explaining that if such spending was "possible politically, it is possible economically"—arguments previously offered by Nitze in NSC-68. Task Force A also called for reduced East-West trade and stressed that China was "an enemy" as long as the Korean and Indochinese conflicts continued.[21]

Eisenhower, Dulles, and their advisers evaluated the report of Kennan's team along the recommendations forwarded by two separate Solarium task forces before establishing the administration's security policy in September 1953 with the approval of NSC 162/2. The document called for the continuation of global containment but emphasized the utility of anti-communist alliances, expressed a willingness to use nuclear weapons, deemphasized negotiations, and argued that the death of Stalin in March 1953 would not result in fundamental changes in Soviet foreign policy. Kennan exaggerated his influence on the Solarium Project in his memoir—in which he claimed to have "had my revenge" against Dulles by "saddling him, inescapably, with my policy"—when in fact NSC 162/2 was an amalgam of all three task force reports and Kennan actually disagreed with the administration's emphasis on anti-communist alliances and nuclear weapons and thought that Stalin's death *would* make a difference in Russia's approach to world affairs.[22]

Asked by Allen Dulles for his assessment of the impact of the death of Stalin, Kennan argued that the new collective Soviet leadership, more moderate than Stalin, was "definitely interested in pursuing with us the effort to solve some of the present international difficulties." He warned against accepting Moscow's "maximum asking price," but urged a flexible negotiating posture on disputes over Germany, Austria, Korea, and Southeast Asia. The Soviet expert advised the CIA director that the succession process remained "in a highly unsettled state [and] it should be our endeavor, as it seems to me, to keep it so." Allen Dulles circulated Kennan's interpretations within the CIA, to his brother, and throughout the executive branch.[23]

Kennan correctly predicted that Georgi Malenkov—apparently Stalin's chosen successor—would be unable to retain power and speculated that the troika of Lavrenti Beria, Vyacheslav Molotov, and Nikolai Bulganin would replace him and be more receptive to accommodation with the West. Here Kennan overestimated Beria's prospects—the murderous former secret police director was soon arrested, tried, and executed by his comrades. Nikita S. Khrushchev, whose ascendance Kennan, like most Western experts, failed to note at the time, engineered Beria's arrest.[24]

Kennan believed that Stalin's death offered a propitious opportunity to open talks with the new Kremlin leaders over Germany and the division of Europe, but as in 1948 Washington showed little interest in negotiating with Moscow. Unlike most officials, Kennan was not inclined "to deprecate the seriousness of Soviet intimations that negotiation would become impossible" once West Germany entered NATO and he deplored the tendency in the West to "make light of these Soviet warnings." He admitted that negotiations would be tedious in any event, but insisted that "the Russians would pay a larger price to get our forces out of western Germany than was generally supposed in the West."[25] Kennan argued that the Soviets did not originally intend to create an East German satellite—otherwise Stalin would not have demanded German territory for Poland at the end of World War II in order to weaken German power and increase the size of the Polish buffer zone between Russia and Germany.[26]

The Politics of Liberation

The rhetoric of liberation, appeasement of the domestic right wing, and the insistence of the Eisenhower Administration on German rearmament all worked against the negotiated settlement in Europe advocated by Kennan. At the same time French fears of German rearmament and exhaustion from defeat in the colonial war in Vietnam prompted the National Assembly's rejection of the European Defense Community in August 1954, an action which paved the way for West Germany's inclusion in NATO.[27]

Returning from a lecture tour in the Federal Republic of Germany in 1954, Kennan responded to France's rejection of EDC by offering an alternative to militarization and the perpetuation of a divided Europe. He proposed that the United States issue a "simple declaration" stating that "we consider the independence and integrity of the present West German territory, including Berlin, to be vital to the interests of this country." Citing the Monroe Doctrine as a precedent, he called for the United States to issue a warning that it would respond with force to any violation of West German sovereignty. Such an approach would achieve Western security requirements but would not confront the Russians, as would Western Germany's inclusion into NATO, with the choice between "clinging indefinitely to their position in Eastern Germany or of abandoning the area to be automatically included in what they regard as a military alliance hostile to them."[28]

Dulles had threatened an "agonizing reappraisal" in the event that France rejected EDC, but the Eisenhower administration had no intention of abandoning the European military alliance. Indeed, through his military command in Europe during the war and his service as NATO's supreme commander, Eisenhower had built a strong commitment to the Western alliance. "A German army was crucial to his vision of what NATO would become," Eisenhower biographer Stephen Ambrose explained, "and NATO was, as always, his first concern." Hence, in the fall of 1954, Eisenhower sent Dulles to London, where he and British Foreign Secretary Anthony Eden and West German Chancellor Konrad Adenauer agreed on German rearmament under NATO auspices. The West German army would be limited to twelve divisions and Germany would not be allowed to cultivate its own nuclear weapons. These provisions assuaged fears in France, which narrowly approved the program. In April 1955 the U.S. Senate approved West German entry into NATO, delivering another crippling blow to Kennan's hopes for German reunification as the basis of a broad settlement with Moscow. Russia responded by creating its own East European military alliance, the Warsaw Pact.[29]

West Germany's inclusion in NATO, the logical culmination of Western policy since the end of the war, left Kennan discouraged. European integration was "as dead as a doornail" as a result of the decision to bring "a rump Germany into a formal military alliance" with Western Europe and the United States. "When I reflect that two great wars were fought in vain and at frightful cost to prevent Germany from occupying the place to which the logic of history has been impelling her and that the only gainers from this have been the Russians," he mused, "it seems to me an awful shame that we are still plugging away at this unprofitable effort."[30]

By refusing to negotiate a settlement in East-Central Europe, the United States gave the impression that it desired war, Kennan asserted in March 1955. "We are a self-centered nation and in recent years we have been more concerned to prove to other Americans that we were not soft on communism than to prove to [the] outside world we really desired peaceful solutions." In the notes he scrawled for the talk, Kennan declared that an outbreak of war was now "probable," in which case "anything can happen—except one thing—victory."[31]

Kennan's emotional attachment to a unified Germany partially explained his despair over inclusion of the Bonn government in NATO but as significant was his conviction that without a reunified Germany at the center of a nonaligned continent, East-Central Europe would remain Soviet-dominated and the nuclear arms race would continue. Whereas Kennan hoped to secure a loosening of Russian hegemony in Eastern Europe through ideological-political containment and negotiations with Moscow, the Eisenhower administration—following the path of Truman and Acheson—chose to confront Russia with a permanent military alliance, an approach which made any real liberation impossible. In the absence of a negotiated settlement in Europe, talk of liberation and disarmament was "a complete phony," Kennan declared. Arms control "could come, conceivably, only after restoration of a balance of power on the Eurasian land mass."[32]

Kennan's opposition to the Eisenhower Administration's diplomacy and his dislike of Dulles encouraged the politicization of the retired professional diplomat. Although he nurtured anti-democratic values and had avoided active involvement in politics throughout his Foreign Service career, Kennan had become associated with top Democrats while serving in the Truman administration. Conflict with Dulles and admiration for Adlai Stevenson now encouraged his active involvement in Democratic Party politics—indeed, there was perhaps more truth than flippancy to his quip that "it took Foster to make me a Democrat."[33]

In the wake of his retirement from the Foreign Service, Kennan considered launching a career of his own as a Democratic politician. As he explained to his friend Charles Thayer, he was struggling to decide "whether to go on becoming a 'public figure' here at home (people are now coming at me with suggestions that I run for various public offices) or to be a scholar and recluse and free thinker and to say the various unconventional things I actually believe." Although his "instincts incline[d] to the latter," Kennan decided to launch a bid for Congress in 1954.[34]

Democratic leaders in Pennsylvania's nineteenth district encouraged his run for Congress in hopes that the nationally known diplomat whose farm reposed in the district could unseat the incumbent Republican. Declaring in a reference to McCarthyism that there was "a real evil abroad in this land" and scoring the "demagoguery of individual politicians," Kennan filed papers for office in early March but abruptly withdrew his candidacy several days later. In his memoir he explained that he belatedly learned that the nonpartisan Institute for Advanced Study and the Rockefeller Foundation would not maintain their financial support of his academic research in the event that he mounted a campaign for public office. While this no doubt was a consideration, the abortive campaign also reflected Kennan's naïveté about American democracy. Believing that elites should govern society, he expected the other Democratic candidates in Pennsylvania to step aside for the famous architect of containment. "I think he had the idea that everybody would stand up and cheer" his decision to enter the campaign, Kennan's State Department associate, "Doc" Matthews, recalled, but to his dismay three other Democrats remained in the race. Kennan "didn't know what getting his neck into Pennsylvania politics would do to him, so, after about three weeks he dropped that," Matthews recalled. Having received a quick education in the "realities" of Pennsylvania politics, Kennan pulled out of the race and abandoned plans for a political career.[35]

While thinking better of a campaign of his own, Kennan emerged as one of the Democratic Party's leading foreign policy analysts and a close adviser to Stevenson. On January 12, 1954, Dulles announced the Republican administration's "New Look" policy which relied on the threat of "massive retaliation" over defensive perimeter wars to deter communist aggression, in what amounted to an open declaration of atomic diplomacy. Already pointing to another campaign against Eisenhower, Stevenson requested opinions on the New Look from Kennan, Nitze, Chester Bowles, and Tom Finletter—the top Democratic "wise men" on foreign affairs.[36]

Kennan declared that the New Look was "simply 180 degrees wrong" and increased the chances of a devastating nuclear war. The communist threat remained "a political and psychological one" and while Soviet support of communist movements was "an irritating international impropriety," it was not a sufficient cause for war with Russia. Moreover, the threat to employ nuclear weapons made "even less sense" with Moscow in possession of its own atomic arsenal and Kennan therefore urged Stevenson to adopt the position that the nation cultivated nuclear weapons reluctantly and only for purposes of retaliation, declined to base its defense on them, and would seek agreement on international control at the earliest possible moment.[37]

As the 1956 presidential campaign approached, the Eisenhower administration responded to mounting public pressure for negotiations by meeting with the Soviet leadership in Geneva in July 1955. Under the direction of General Secretary Khrushchev, Moscow had signaled its willingness to negotiate in May by announcing that it would sign the Austrian State Treaty. The Russians had long linked disengagement from Austria with resolution of the German occupation and had declined to withdraw Soviet troops in protest of American and allied policies toward Germany. However, Khrushchev now ended the impasse over Austria in order to promote détente, and the four occupying powers signed the treaty which made Austria neutral and armed with its own defense forces.[38]

Through their very presence at the Geneva summit the two world powers relaxed international tensions, but achieved little real accord on vital issues. Eisenhower angered Khrushchev and USSR Premier Nikolai Bulganin with his insistence that a reunified Germany be free to join NATO, something the Russians would never allow, and the American President failed to impress Khrushchev with his "Open Skies" initiative, which called for free and mutual spying on each country's military establishments (the United States had already begun its own secret overflights of Russia with the new U-2 spyplane). Both powers concurred on the possible benefits of increased trade and the dangers of thermonuclear weapons, yet returned from the summit and promptly resumed stockpiling hydrogen bombs.[39]

Kennan failed to share in the upbeat "spirit of Geneva" which both parties pledged to maintain after the summit. He blamed the West for the failure to pursue détente, declaring that the absence of meaningful accord was the result of the United States being "rigidly committed to a program for [German] unification which took little account of Soviet interests." He mused that it might already be too late to redeem East Germany after twenty-two years of "totalitarian rule." Kennan leaked his dissent to Joseph and Stewart Alsop, who printed his views in their November 14 column.[40]

Members of the press respected Kennan's knowledge, frequently solicited his responses to international events, and referred to him in such complimentary terms as America's "foremost expert" on Russia. *New York Times* political writer James Reston paid close attention to Kennan, whom he described as "probably the shrewdest observer of Soviet policy, not only in this country but in the entire Western world." Liberal journals applauded Kennan's call for a moderate policy toward post-Stalinist Russia in contrast to the inflammatory rhetoric upon which Dulles relied in an effort to keep his communist adversaries off balance. "Let us not," Kennan wrote in *Harper's*, "after having criticized the Russian communists all these years for being too totalitarian, pour scorn and ridicule upon them the moment they show signs of being anything else."[41]

Kennan's attacks on Eisenhower-Dulles diplomacy mounted as the 1956 presidential campaign got under way. On January 24 Dulles told the Senate Foreign Relations Committee that the Soviet Union was "in a very bad way" and that the administration's diplomacy had forced the Russians "to revamp their whole creed from A to Z." The most publicized response came from Kennan, who declared that the Soviet threat was "more serious today than at any time since 1947" and that he did "not recognize the world Mr. Dulles is talking about."[42]

Kennan campaigned in behalf of Stevenson in 1956 and positioned himself for consideration as Secretary of State in the event of a new

Democratic administration. Stevenson, an articulate fellow Princeton man, exemplified the elite intellectual leadership that Kennan believed the nation required. The former Illinois Governor's much-publicized ambivalence about entering the presidential campaign and his cultured style of leadership were qualities with which Kennan could readily identify. As he emerged as one of Stevenson's principal advisers on foreign affairs, reporters singled out Kennan as "one of the few men to be mentioned as candidates for Secretary of State, should the Democrats win the 1956 election." In a 1984 interview, Kennan did not recall whether he anticipated an opportunity to direct the nation's foreign policy in the event of a Democratic victory in 1956, but declared that if he had "had the backing of the President and the Congress, I could have done a good job." He added that it was "unlikely that I could have had that backing."[43]

As the campaign unfolded Stevenson concluded that his hopes of reversing the outcome of 1952 depended on a successful assault on Eisenhower's diplomacy and he asked Kennan to prepare "a sharp digest of our situation which I hope won't sound more like Kennan than Stevenson." On March 31 Stevenson massaged Kennan's ego after receiving his "splendid" advice. "How I wish I could write with the facility and perception that you do! I may be uttering some of your own words in a speech one of these days, and I hope you will forgive me if you detect no by-line." Because of his hectic campaign schedule, the candidate explained, he found it "difficult to keep up with what's going on, let alone saying anything sensibly and promptly which could be useful politically. Help! Help! And thanks for the magnificent help!"[44] The close association with Stevenson gratified Kennan but he could muster little respect for the primary system, about which he complained privately, and added that "statesmanship will not be what it should be in this country until people write their own speeches; and I wish [Stevenson] would stop having his written for him."[45]

Proposing a sharp attack on the administration's diplomacy, Kennan advised Stevenson to abandon "the whole concept of 'bi-partisan foreign policy,'" explaining that he personally "wouldn't want to sponsor, or share responsibility, for anything that Foster did, even if I were able to write the ticket." The retired diplomat advised Stevenson to stress the "serious signs of disintegration" in the country's international position on grounds that Washington was losing the ideological-political struggle with the Kremlin. The administration not only had failed to counter charges that it was responsible for the stalemate in the cold war but also, by shutting off international exchanges and reducing East-West trade (a position Kennan himself had advocated during Stalin's reign), had placed itself in a position in which "communist propagandists [could] argue, quite plausibly, that the iron curtain is today generally on the American rather than on the Soviet side." Eisenhower and Dulles had "done nothing" to develop a coherent policy on colonialism, "obviously one of the two or three greatest world issues at this time." Instead, the United States had "floundered around" and suffered "a deplorable loss of dignity" by attempting "to earn popularity instead of respect among other people, and we have succeeded in earning neither."[46]

Turning to the Mideast, Kennan advised Stevenson to reject positions which tended to make Israel "a permanent ward and military liability of the United States." He approved of allowing Israel to purchase American arms but warned against "getting in deeper and deeper" as it had been "perfectly clear from the beginning that a Jewish state could be maintained in that area only by force of arms." Kennan argued—months before the Suez crisis—that it might "be better that [a Mideast] conflict come now, while it can still be isolated, than to have it come several years hence, when our responsibility will have been increased and the chance of isolating it reduced."[47]

Stevenson and his other advisers rejected Kennan's positions on Israel, but he did influence Stevenson's decision to urge a test ban of nuclear weapons in the atmosphere. Such tests had spurred widespread fears throughout the world since March 1954, when fallout from an American blast had contaminated several Pacific islands and killed a Japanese fisherman.[48] Kennan called for "a readiness to abandon further tests of nuclear weapons, on a basis of complete reciprocity and some reasonable arrangement for inspection" and added that he could "think of almost nothing that would go farther to alter in our favor the atmosphere in which our diplomacy has to operate abroad."[49]

Stevenson marshaled the recommendations of Kennan, Arthur Schlesinger Jr., and Thomas Murray of the Atomic Energy Commission in the preparation of a major address of nuclear weapons before the American Society of Newspaper Editors. On April 21, 1956, he endorsed a unilateral test ban, warning that testing could be resumed after an interim period if Russia did not reciprocate. Stevenson's proposal elevated the debate on American foreign policy and advanced a position that both nations—after scores of additional above-ground tests—would eventually accept in the 1963 Limited Test Ban Treaty.[50]

While Stevenson made use of some of Kennan's views, the candidate's other advisers—especially Kennan's longtime associates Paul Nitze and Averell Harriman—opposed his call for the neutralization of Germany.[51] Kennan had no choice but to bow to the opposition: "I have my ideas about specific problems of foreign policy," he explained to Stevenson's policy coordinator, Tom Finletter, "but I am not at all sure that they would be ones which Adlai ought to put forward publicly at this time; nor do I think they would meet with general agreement among those of us to whom he looks for help and advice in these foreign policy questions."[52]

Although Kennan did not push his views on East-Central Europe before Stevenson, he expressed them publicly in another lecture that attracted national attention. Speaking before the Pittsburgh Foreign Policy Association on May 3, Kennan asserted that the failure to negotiate a political settlement outside the two armed alliances ensured continued Soviet domination of Eastern Europe. "Where regimes of this nature have been in power for more than a decade," he observed,

> there can be no question of putting Humpty Dumpty together again and restoring the *status quo ante*. . . . There is a finality, for better or for worse, about what has now occurred in Eastern Europe; and it is no form of service to these people to encourage [them] to believe that they could return and pick up again where they left off ten or twenty years ago. Whether we like it or not, the gradual evolution of these communist regimes to a position of greater independence and greater responsiveness to domestic opinion is the best we can hope for as the next phase of development in that area.[53]

To proponents of liberation, realistic statements such as this one by Kennan constituted "appeasement" as well as "abandonment" of Eastern Europe, and they attacked him accordingly. Typical was the response offered by his former superior in Moscow, William C. Bullitt, now a rabid anti-communist. *U.S. News and World Report* reprinted Kennan's address with a rejoinder in which Bullitt condemned Kennan for his "readiness permanently to abandon the enslaved peoples of Eastern Europe to the Kremlin criminals." Kennan responded that "liberationists" actually "want and hope for a third world war, but are unwilling to say so. Any attempt to suggest lines of approach to the Soviet problem designed to avoid such a war arouses their fury. This is why they are so annoyed with me" and "will continue, therefore, to attack me." Despite his public statement and comments offered to distance himself from "liberationists," Kennan had by no means abandoned his own hopes for the disintegration of Soviet power.[54]

Representative Thaddeus Machrowicz, a Michigan Democrat, took note of Kennan's position as an adviser and demanded to know whether Stevenson endorsed the ex-diplomat's views on Eastern Europe. Unwilling to risk a charge of appeasement, Stevenson responded that he "emphatically reject[ed]" Kennan's position. Admitting to having received advice from Kennan, Stevenson declared, however, that Kennan was "in no way connected with my staff and never has been. . . . Although I hold Mr. Kennan and his views in great respect, I disagree strongly with some of the positions he has taken."[55]

Even as proponents of liberation condemned Kennan for his public recognition of the reality of Soviet hegemony in Eastern Europe, the Kremlin's position in the region was growing increasingly tenuous. The death of Stalin had prompted unrest in the satellites followed by a Kremlin "New Course" in East Central Europe in the summer of 1953. A revolt in East Germany led the regime of Walter Ulbricht to enact reforms; communist reformer Imre Nagy replaced Matyas Rakosi in Hungary; and economic reforms were also initiated in Czechoslovakia. In response, the Eisenhower administration encouraged liberation propaganda by the Assembly of Captive European Nations, an American-based emigré association, and Radio Free Europe, but Eisenhower and Dulles did not mount a direct challenge in the Soviet sphere, realizing that such action risked war with Russia.[56]

After a period of relative calm, Khrushchev gave new impetus to East European nationalists who desired to repudiate Soviet hegemony. On February 24–25, 1956, the Soviet leader attacked Stalin's legacy of "brutal violence" and his "capricious and despotic character" before the Twentieth Congress of the Communist Party Central Committee. For hours Khrushchev condemned Stalin for violations of Soviet legality, anti-Leninism, and a "clear debasing and belittling of the role of the party."[57]

The speech established Khrushchev's authority in the Kremlin, but fueled rebelliousness in the satellites. If Khrushchev could denounce Stalin, reasoned millions of Poles, Czechs and Hungarians, why should they not challenge the puppet governments that Stalin had installed in their countries? In September protests in Poland led to the rehabilitation of Wladyslaw Gomulka, the communist leader whom Stalin had deposed in 1949. To avoid an open breach with Warsaw, the Politburo agreed to reduce Soviet interference in Polish religious affairs and to curb collectivization and secret police repression.

The Polish dissent spurred demonstrations in Hungary, where on October 23 students at the Technical University in Budapest demanded Soviet troop withdrawal, decentralization of the country's planned economy, and a democratic government. As the Voice of America stepped up encouragement of dissent behind the Iron Curtain, Dulles proclaimed that "the great monolith of communism is crumbling." Russian troops stationed in the country clashed with student demonstrators, but Hungarian leader Imre Nagy pleaded to continue the reforms and secure the withdrawal of Soviet troops.[58]

Despite Kennan's recent pronouncements on the "finality" of the satellite arrangement, the events in Poland and Hungary inspired a stunning reversal in his thinking. The satellite unrest revived his dream of liberation in East-Central Europe, just as it had done for Dulles and, in an interview with Joseph Alsop, Kennan declared that the events in Hungary meant that "the end of Moscow's abnormal power and domination throughout all of Eastern Europe" was in sight. The demonstrations had given "an enormous impetus" to the "disintegration of Moscow's authority" and the Kremlin's "period of ascendancy is already at an end. After this," Kennan declared, "there will be no central communist leadership."

In arguments reminiscent of the Long Telegram and X-Article, the retired diplomat asserted that the decline of communist authority might extend into the USSR itself. "What we have seen in Hungary and Poland in these recent days," he explained,

> could conceivably be the beginning of a disintegration which will carry deep into Russia itself. It could be the prelude to a great convulsion in the whole communist system. Or perhaps it may be the prelude of bad trouble in special areas, like the former Baltic states and the Ukraine. We must wait and see. . . . I don't think it's likely now, but I think it's going to

149

happen eventually. . . . Very often the things I and others who have lived in Russia have thought would happen *have* indeed happened in the end. But they have come to pass more slowly than we had anticipated.[59]

Recognizing the volatility of the Hungarian situation, Kennan told Alsop that this was "a tricky business, and it can take any sort of turn between this moment, when we sit talking here, and that moment in the future when our words will be printed." By the time the interview appeared—on November 24, 1956—the "tricky business" in Hungary had indeed taken a dramatic turn. Following Nagy's announcement that Hungary would withdraw from the Warsaw Pact, Russia launched a decisive air and ground offensive into Budapest, killing 40,000 Hungarian patriots and crushing the revolt. Nagy was hanged in 1958. Although the United States had given the impression through its propaganda that it would assist the revolutionaries, it was powerless to intervene without provoking a major war.[60]

Despite his insistence since 1948 that the division of Europe would endure in the absence of a negotiated political settlement in East-Central Europe, the events in Hungary had found Kennan once again predicting a demise of communist authority, possibly extending to the Soviet Union. The Kremlin's invasion of Hungary demonstrated that liberation was a farce and that negotiations offered the only hope of softening, much less terminating, Moscow's hegemony in Eastern Europe.

The Hungarian episode offers a dramatic example of the elusiveness of Kennan's diplomacy and his inability to resolve the conflict between his emotional and realistic perspectives. His emotional quest for the disintegration of communist authority led Kennan to predict that event even as his realism dictated that Moscow would never allow it. The right-wing *National Review* was the only publication that paid attention to Kennan's flip-flop, declaring that "it seems clear that the Kennan of six months past had not the vaguest idea of what he was talking about." Noting Kennan's reputation for expertise on Russia in the mainstream press, M. Stanton Evans charged that "in general, Kennan protects himself with what might be called 'prediction in depth'—i.e., predictions of any number of contradictory things, hung together in a meticulously loose style that leaves plenty of room for maneuver."[61] Although there is no evidence that Kennan consciously practiced this type of disingenuousness, his contradictory statements easily created such an impression.

After Moscow repressed the Hungarian revolt, Kennan reasserted that the satellite states could effect only gradual changes which stopped short of an open challenge to the Warsaw Pact. Polish reforms of such a limited nature survived under Gomulka in 1956 and although the Poles might prefer to adopt additional "Western ways and concepts," Kennan noted after a trip to Poland in 1958, "talk of 'liberation' and, in general, tactics designed to embarrass the precarious relationship now prevailing between the Gomulka government, and the Soviet government, can to the extent they are successful, have only one effect: which is to cause a tightening of the reins of the communist dictatorship."[62]

Although Europe, as always, remained at the center of Kennan's attention, he continued to think in global terms and to advance positions that reflected both his fears of communist expansion and his contempt for the aspirations of those on what he considered the periphery of civilization. He recommended an imperialistic policy in the Mideast, advising in 1952 that "we make up our minds at this time precisely what —in physical terms—it is that we and the British wish to hold onto in the Middle Eastern area" and then secure it by force from "local potentates" who understood only "the cold gleam of adequate and determined force." The Western powers should "not be ashamed or uncertain if we have to say that we require certain things and mean to retain them" and it was the responsibility of the lesser powers to "show some respect for our interests, even when they neither understand nor sympathize with them." Specifically, Kennan argued that the United States and Britain could seize control of the Suez Canal, which linked the Red and Mediterranean Seas, in the event that Egyptian nationalists threatened to close the waterway. The Anglo-Saxon powers could "consolidate their position with the utmost determination," he declared. "Who would be there to challenge it?"[63]

Such concerns became acute, of course, in 1956 when Egyptian president Gamal Abdel Nasser seized control of the canal, through which flowed the bulk of Mideast oil to the industrial West. Even before Nasser's action Kennan told Chester Bowles that he "resent[ed] the demands made upon us by people like Nasser, and have very little confidence in their type of nationalism or their sense of responsibility for the values I think indispensible to any stable world society."[64] As the United States contemplated events in Hungary and the presidential campaign, Israel, Britain, and France launched a surprise attack on Egypt a few days before the American election. Angered by the failure of the allies to consult with Washington, Eisenhower and Dulles condemned the invasion in the UN and cut back oil shipments to the aggressors. Opposed by the Americans, threatened by the Soviets, and denounced in the UN, the invaders pulled out in late December and Egypt retained control of the canal.[65]

Although Kennan called the invasion "ill-conceived and pathetic," the administration's response provoked a characteristic emotional outburst from him. To him the Suez crisis established the frightening precedent of a victory by dark-skinned third world nationalists over the forces of a superior Western civilization. Although he did not advocate American intervention, he did score Eisenhower for lacking the "grace and humility" to remain detached while the nation's allies attempted to extricate themselves from the conflict. "Instead of this," he wrote in the *Washington Post*,

> we have chosen to join, in part with the Communist nations, with Nasser, and with others who have only contempt and hatred for the Western world, in an effort which, if successful, can only pillory our oldest friends before world opinion, and destroy what remains of their positions in the Middle East and Africa, and to deny to the state of Israel—at the establishment of which we so eagerly assisted—the privilege of defending its existence in the face of a mortally dangerous encirclement.[66]

Kennan exaggerated the impact of Suez and feared that Washington's opposition to the Anglo-French invasion would weaken the bonds among the Western powers while increasing the possibility of war with Moscow. "The best we can expect," he declared on November 8, "is a grievous demoralization of the Western alliance and Soviet domination of the Middle East."[67] The Suez crisis also underscored the West's dependence on potentially hostile regimes for vital resources. Kennan deplored America's "comfortable, wasteful and uncoordinated habits" and called for action to make the country more self-sufficient. "The time for prattling has passed; and the Suez crisis should be the proof of this to any thoughtful person."[68]

Although he had opposed the 1955 Baghdad collective security pact and called the Eisenhower Doctrine "the purest nonsense," Kennan endorsed the President's decision to send 14,000 Marines to Lebanon to establish American credibility against putative communist expansion in 1958. Showing that his disdain for Arab nationalism had undergone no revision, the retired diplomat declared privately that same year that "if it were not for the possibility of war with Russia, I would be at this moment the most rabid of imperialists."[69]

In the Far East, Kennan's preoccupation with preserving American credibility led him to endorse containment to ensure that the contested offshore islands of Quemoy and Matsu remained independent of mainland China. "We cannot permit [Taiwan], as part of the island world of the Pacific and one whose fortunes have a powerful effect on the situation both in Japan and the Philippines, to be taken under control by the mainland communists," he declared in 1955. Still fearful of a bandwagon effect, he argued that a communist takeover would prove "disruptive of our position in the Pacific, for the maintenance of which a great many Americans died only a decade ago." Although he declared that Mao Zedong's regime displayed "the most profound arrogance, inhumanity and obstinate error in the understanding of the Western world," Kennan continued to rankle the foreign policy establishment by recommending U.S. neutrality on the issue of China's admittance to the UN.[70]

Despite his perception that the offshore islands were vital to containment, Kennan reversed himself when the Eisenhower administration raised the possibility of going to war over the issue. When the mainland resumed shelling the islands in 1958, Kennan condemned Jiang Jieshi— "a man who has lived for many years primarily out of our pocket and who owes to us all that he has today"—for risking war by clinging to the relatively insignificant atolls. When Eisenhower invoked the image of a "Western Pacific Munich," Kennan responded that "we have manufactured our own Czechoslovakia" and now declared that the whole affair was "very much an internal Chinese problem." He still wondered if Moscow "would have an interest in trading some sort of political and military neutralization of Korea for an American military evacuation of Japan and a similar neutralization of the Japanese islands," but neither Eisenhower and Dulles nor the Russians advanced negotiating positions with respect to Japan and Korea.[71]

The Eisenhower years had marked a transition period in which Kennan retired from the Foreign Service and reasserted himself in his accustomed role as outsider and critic of the foreign policy consensus. His dislike of Dulles and disagreements over the future of Germany distanced Kennan from the administration and his former colleagues in the State Department. But as important as his disagreement on substantive issues was the need Kennan felt to fulfill the role of an enlightened elite who found himself compelled to struggle against the whims of a misguided egalitarian republic.

Despite his efforts to distance himself from the foreign policy establishment, by the mid-1950s Kennan and other American statesman could agree that the cold war had entered a new phase. Although Kennan remained reluctant to acknowledge the division of Europe, Khrushchev had signaled Russia's acceptance of the status quo by supporting the neutralization of Austria and placing his hopes for the advancement of communism by supporting "wars of national liberation" in the developing world." Kennan still sought to contain communism across the globe but he doubted whether America possessed the maturity that was required to spearhead the struggle, particularly as he reflected upon the nation's hysterical response to the issue of domestic communism.

VIII

A Realist Confronts Hysteria

OF ALL the frustrations Kennan had experienced since he had begun to question the direction of American diplomacy in 1948, none was more wrenching than the anti-communist hysteria that plagued the United States in the wake of the "loss" of China, the successful Soviet atomic test, and the Korean War. Groundless charges of disloyalty against Foreign Service officers who had served in China before the communist takeover prompted a spirited defense of their actions from Kennan. Among those targeted by anti-communist zealots were John Paton Davies and Robert Oppenheimer, close friends of Kennan's whose purges from government service deepened his conviction that American democracy lacked the maturity required to conduct an effective foreign policy. The phenomenon known as "McCarthyism" thus eroded Kennan's support for American internationalism while reinforcing not only his fears about the decline of elite authority over foreign affairs but also his own marginality.

Domestic communism became a major issue in the United States as a result of World War I and the 1917 Bolshevik Revolution. The U.S. government, backed by private "patriotic" organizations, had stifled dissent, deported aliens, and conducted illegal raids against radicals in the first Red Scare, which left a legacy of restricted immigration, preoc-

cupation with domestic security, and a public perception equating radicalism with communist attempts to overthrow the government.[1] In the
late 1930s Texas Democrat Martin Dies chaired a new House Committee on Un-American activities that accused individuals of harboring
communist sympathies, employed the technique of guilt by association,
and laid the groundwork for McCarthyism. Harry Truman's executive
loyalty program fueled fears of internal subversion and by the fall of
1949, after Russia had exploded its first atomic bomb and Mao Zedong's forces assumed control of mainland China, allegations that communists had infiltrated the U.S. government had come back to haunt the
Truman administration. Revelations of "atom spies" and the sensational
case of Alger Hiss—a close associate of Dean Acheson who was con-
victed of perjury in 1950 for lying about a past communist affiliation—
gave credence to charges that the "reds" had infiltrated the U.S. government.[2]

Kennan had his own history of targeting domestic communists. While
serving in Moscow in the 1930s, he had combed the Soviet press to
report the names of Americans who offered praise of Russia and he
"personally brought some of these names to the attention of the government." The diplomat recommended revoking the passports of those
Americans "because it seemed to me evident that they had expatriated
themselves in every sense of the word."[3] During his cross-country speaking tour promoting containment in 1946, Kennan alerted superiors to
the existence of "Soviet agents" and "real Communist activity among
intellectual circles on the West Coast" and forwarded a list of names of
alleged radicals who attended one of his lectures in San Francisco,
although he did not say how he knew these people were communists.[4] A
major purpose of Kennan's 1946 speaking tour was to denounce the
"[Henry] Wallace movement," which he charged was part of "a neat
little arrangement" with the Kremlin to undermine administration policy, a charge that lacked substantiation. Embarrassed by his excesses in
later years, Kennan admitted in his memoir that some of his actions in
1946 "might suggest I was headed for a job as staff consultant to the
late Senator Joe McCarthy."[5]

As he assumed control of the Policy Planning Staff in May 1947,
Kennan aborted plans to hire Emile Despres as a consultant on German
economic problems because of the Williams College professor's activities
in behalf of an accused communist. After Depres's brief character testi-

mony at the trial of alleged communist Carl Marzini in 1947, Kennan, fearing that some zealous congressman might raise an outcry over Despres's appointment to the PPS, withdrew the offer in "the interests of the country." "I disagree thoroughly with the reasons which prompted your action," Despres told Kennan, adding, however, that he "appreciate[ed] the candor with which you stated them to me."[6]

Kennan showed little sympathy for the victims of anti-communist excesses until those victims included professional diplomats and other elites with whom he identified. His first direct involvement in the loyalty and security controversy came in the case of John Stewart Service, an Asian expert in the Foreign Service who was fluent in Chinese and had served under General Joseph Stilwell in the China-Burma-India theater during World War II. Service's loyalty came into question when he leaked copies of his classified reports on China to editors of the left-wing journal *Amerasia* in 1945 in an effort to publicize Jiang Jieshi's corruption. The FBI seized the documents and arrested Service along with several *Amerasia* editors, but none of Service's reports (most of which he had classified himself) contained national secrets and he returned to active duty after a grand jury voted unanimously against an indictment. Still, the highly publicized incident fueled cries that Washington's China policy was being sabotaged from within and Service underwent loyalty investigations in 1946, 1947, and 1949 as a result of his indiscretion. Review boards affirmed his loyalty in each case.[7]

Five years after the incident, Senator Joseph McCarthy resurrected the *Amerasia* case as part of his sensational charges of an "immense" communist conspiracy. On February 9, 1950, in his infamous speech at Wheeling, West Virginia, McCarthy declared that Service was among the 205 "known" Communist Party members who "are still working and shaping the policy of the State Department." The Wisconsin Senator asserted that the nation's "position of impotency" in the wake of the fall of China stemmed from the "traitorous actions of those . . . who have had all the benefits that the wealthiest nation on earth has to offer—the finest homes, the finest college educations, and the finest jobs in Government we can give."[8]

Service was the focal point of McCarthy's indictment of the Foreign Service "China hands," a group that also included O. Edmund Clubb, John Paton Davies, and John Carter Vincent. McCarthy also targeted Johns Hopkins University professor Owen Lattimore, an Asian expert and leftist who had been critical of Jiang. With promises of close postwar association with a "democratic" China having become ashes in their mouths, the congressional China lobby and Asia-first Republicans sought scapegoats for the shattering of American illusions in the Far East. Although McCarthy lacked evidence to substantiate his charges, he won popular support in his call for an investigation and on February 22 the Senate resolved "to investigate whether there are employees in the State Department disloyal to the United States."[9]

Although Service and Kennan had never met, the Asian expert knew of Kennan's reputation as a strong supporter of the integrity of the Foreign Serivce and reasoned that an endorsement from the architect of containment would undermine charges that he was a fellow traveler. The government's three-member Loyalty Security Board granted his request that Kennan be allowed to peruse documents written by Service from 1942 to 45 and comment on whether they were tainted with communist sympathies. After receiving the 126 documents on May 25, Kennan, then the State Department counselor, appeared before the board as an expert witness on May 29.[10]

He not only affirmed Service's loyalty but also complimented his "absolutely outstanding job of reporting" during the period in question. Kennan explained that Service had pointed out the weaknesses of Jiang's regime "because it was deliberate policy of the Chinese Government, as he saw it, to conceal this state of affairs from the United States public opinion, and he felt that unless he and other American observers did their part in bringing this situation to the attention of people at home, it would go unnoticed." Kennan added that in his own assessment Service's criticisms of Jiang were justified. Comparing Service's reports to communist literature, Kennan told the review board that they were free of the "extremes and distortions" and the "nasty little spins on the ball" for which Communist propagandists were infamous. Service's support for aid to the communists at Yenan needed to be understood in the context of wartime diplomacy, at which time, Kennan declared, recalling his own disgust with the Grand Alliance, aid to communists was "not only legitimate but was sacrosanct." Kennan testified that Service believed that it would be desirable for the United States "to take a greater interest in the [Chinese] communists, to help them in their operations against Japan, and to try to build up such a relationship with them as could constitute one of the foundations of our postwar policy toward China."

Kennan buttressed Service's case by discrediting one of the Asian expert's principal accusers, General Patrick J. Hurley, former American ambassador to Jiang's regime. Upon resigning that post in 1945, Hurley had charged that "the professional Foreign Service men sided with the Chinese Communist armed party and the imperialist bloc of nations whose policy it was to keep China divided against herself." Kennan depicted Hurley as naïve, recalling that during a trip to Moscow in 1944 he "didn't know that he was being given the usual run-around and the usual patter by Stalin and Molotov." He added that while in Moscow Hurley had sent a dispatch to Washington declaring that he was doing all that he could to promote a settlement between Mao's forces and the Chinese government. "What bewilders me," Kennan concluded, was that Service's reports "advocated, it seems to me, the same thing that General Hurley was advocating, which was political accommodation."

Kennan testimony was masterful. "The characterization of the reports has been so complete that there is very little to ask," loyalty board member Theodore Achilles declared after Kennan's presentation. Kennan had commended Service's reports and entered into evidence his own extensive notes on the documents, thus affirming Service's criticism of American support of Jiang, placing the dispatches in the context of the war, discrediting Hurley's charges, and defending a diplomat's prerogative to forward interpretations of events in foreign countries even if the reports reflected unfavorably on U.S. policy.[11]

On October 9 the Loyalty Security Board ruled unqualifiedly in Service's favor, but the controversy discouraged Truman from assigning Service to a new post. While he languished in Washington, the government's Loyalty Review Board, a higher court in such matters, summoned Service to a new round of hearings, rehashed the *Amerasia* case and decided that although there was no evidence of disloyalty, the leak to the left-wing journal "forces us with regret to conclude that there is reasonable doubt as to his loyalty." Secretary of State Dean Acheson fired Service in a matter of hours, thus denying him retirement benefits. "Good, good, good," McCarthy cooed upon hearing the news. Bitter, Kennan wrote to Service that his firing showed that "the Government itself does not really want anyone in its service who is imaginative and courageous and subject to the processes of intellectual growth." [12]

Kennan also testified before the Loyalty Security Board in the summer of 1951 in behalf of Asian experts O. Edmund Clubb and John Paton Davies, both of whom had been critical of Jiang's regime. In the hearings of both men Kennan pleaded for the integrity of the Foreign Service, declaring that

> if there ever creeps into our system an atmosphere in which men do not feel at liberty to state the facts as they see them, knowing that the greatest crime they could commit would be to state them as they did not see them; then, in my opinion, the successful operation of the democratic foreign policy will be out of the question. I feel very deeply about that, and I think that the first requirement we have of officers who are asked to report to the government is that they report honestly what they believe.

Judged a security risk in December 1951, Clubb was cleared upon appeal, but could remain in the Foreign Service only if willing to accept demotion to consul general. Instead he joined John Carter Vincent, the highest ranking Far Eastern expert to come under attack, in accepting early retirement with benefits in 1952. The loyalty board cleared Davies on this occasion, but he remained under fire. [13]

The campaign against his fellow professional diplomats left Kennan indignant and prompted him to take a public stand on the issue of domestic communism. The damage being done in the name of anti-communism outweighed the security threat posed by domestic radicalism, he charged in a *New York Times Magazine* article. Kennan began the piece by affirming his own anti-communist credentials, declaring that "we would have a complete moral justification for outlawing [the American Communist Party] and stamping membership in it as an offense to the country, but I doubt for several reasons that it would be wise or expedient to do so." He added that persons who were committed to Soviet ideology should be forbidden to teach in American schools and communist "fellow travelers" barred from government. He allowed that some communist sympathizers were merely guilty of "muddy thinking," yet "palpable damage has been done to our national interest in the past by agents of, or sympathizers with, the communist power."

The heart of Kennan's argument, however, was that the emotional preoccupations inherent in American democracy undermined the nation's ability to approach the problem of domestic communism with "restraint and realism." He deplored the "tendency among us to go whole hog, to assume that all our troubles stem from this single source, and to conclude that we have only to eliminate it from our society and everything will be all right." If the domestic communist issue was not "carefully moderated—if we permit it, that is, to become an emotional preoccupation and to blind us to the more important positive tasks before us—we can do more damage to our national purpose . . . than anything that threatens us today from the Communist side." If unable to curb the overreaction to the "tiny minority" represented by the American Communist Party, he concluded, the country would be "better off to go to the other extreme and put the communist problem out of our minds entirely." [14]

Columnist William Henry Chamberlain criticized Kennan's use of the term "witch-hunt" to describe the anti-communist campaign, declaring that investigations were in the national interest. "Do you really believe," Kennan responded, "that the formulation of policy in this government proceeds on so shallow and erratic a basis that great decisions are taken because some communist whispers something in some credulous person's ear?" The diplomat declared in June 1950 that "the attitudes and methods of which we have been the witnesses in past weeks and months are ones which have in them all the seeds of an American totalitarianism." [15] He found the anti-communist hysteria "more terrifying" than "the hostility of mind and the military preparations against us" on the part of the Soviet Union. [16]

While Kennan mounted a public defense of American Foreign Service officers, Acheson, plagued since Mao's victory by what he called "the attack of the primitives," appeased the critics by declining to defend the diplomats, thus allowing them to be subjected to repeated loyalty hearings. Kennan deplored the State Department's refusal to defend the Asian experts, declaring that he failed

> to see how the Department can permit thousands of faithful men to rest under the consciousness that if malicious and irresponsible charges are raised against them . . . the government will lift no finger to aid them in that situation but will put them in the position of having to stir around and drum up, in their own defense, information which is already the government's property. [17]

The change in presidential administrations in 1953 made matters worse, as Eisenhower and Dulles were even more committed to appeasing the right wing. "If this meant feeding an occasional body to the sharks," historian David Oshinsky observed, "Dulles was more than willing to supply it." After calling for "positive loyalty" from all federal employees, Dulles hired R. Scott McLeod to supervise State Department loyalty and security operations. An ex-FBI agent, McLeod was a "belligerent superpatriot" who believed the Foreign Service was little more than a haven for homosexuals and communists. He meant to get rid of them. "Fine appointment," McCarthy declared, "excellent man."[18]

Already indignant over the treatment of the Asian experts, Kennan grew even angrier as McLeod's investigators began following diplomats, opening their mail, tapping their telephones, and subjecting them to lie detector tests and outrageous interrogations.[19] Kennan lashed out against the wave of "triumphant and excited self-righteous anti-communism" in an off-the-record speech in New York. He blamed the Congress and its public supporters for creating

> an atmosphere in which simple alternatives of foreign policy (I am thinking here of such things as the admission of Communist China to the United Nations) cannot even be discussed without leading to charges of subversion and treason—an atmosphere in which name-calling and insinuation take the place of calm and free debate—an atmosphere in which the dog of government policy gets wagged by the tail of timid, childish and fantastic internal security arrangements which no one dares to question. Such conditions are not the mark of a mature political society, capable of exercising real world leadership.[20]

It was a melancholy time for Kennan, who had seen his colleagues drummed out of their jobs even as Dulles made it clear that the new administration had no place for him, either. Charles Thayer, whom Kennan had personally recruited into the Foreign Service in the mid-1930s, resigned rather than face a McCarthy hearing in which a love affair he had had with a Russian woman years before was to be the main topic of discussion.[21] "It will not be easy for either of us," Kennan wrote to Thayer, "for the government has been our home in a much more serious degree than we sometimes realized. But we will have to accustom ourselves to this situation and learn to live with it."[22]

Following his retirement from the Foreign Service, Kennan abandoned any reluctance to speak out publicly against the excesses of the anti-communist movement. He asserted in a May 1953 article in *Atlantic,* which featured his picture on the cover, that "communist penetration" was a "negligible" factor in American diplomacy. While communists had failed to influence "a single major decision of foreign policy," serious damage had been done "to public confidence and to governmental morale by the mishandling of our own measures to counter precisely this problem of communist penetration."[23]

Kennan decided to use an invitation to speak at Notre Dame University to denounce the accusers of treason. Although he did not mention McCarthy by name, the decision to speak out at Note Dame was a bold one as public opinion polls showed that a higher percentage of Catholics than other denominations supported McCarthy (himself a Catholic). In the speech, reprinted in several newspapers and magazines, Kennan declared that through the acceptance of "alarmed and exercised anti-communism . . . we begin to draw about ourselves a cultural curtain similar in some respects to the iron curtain of our adversaries." The intolerance and anti-intellectualism evident in the movement reflected "a deep-seated weakness in the American character. . . . There is a real and urgent danger here for anyone who values the right to differ from others in his interests or his associations or his faith."[24]

While Kennan spoke out publicly against McCarthyism he also worked behind the scenes in defense of John Paton Davies. Kennan credited Davies, who had served under him in Moscow in 1944 and again on the Policy Planning Staff, with teaching him "everything I know" about Asia.[25] Throughout Davies' loyalty ordeal, Kennan maintained regular contact with him, kept files on the case, and emerged as the targeted diplomat's chief supporter. An overriding reason for Kennan's concern was his involvement with the incident whose exploitation eventually hounded Davies out of the Foreign Service.

Davies was a target of the China lobby for the usual reasons: he had served under Stilwell, had criticized Jiang, and had recommended negotiations with the Chinese communists during the war. In addition, however, the allegations were fueled by charges that he had attempted to place known communists into a CIA covert operation against Communist China. In the fall of 1949, Lyle H. Munson of the CIA's Office of Policy Coordination approached Kennan, then the PPS director, with a proposal that the CIA and the Defense and State departments collaborate on a program of intelligence gathering about China in the wake of Mao's triumph. Kennan turned the chore over to Davies, who in a November 16, 1949, meeting suggested that journalists and intellectuals in the academic community who were familiar with the new Chinese leaders might be used to gain information. He mentioned Edgar Snow, Benjamin Schwartz, Agnes Smedley, and John King Fairbank. The proposed covert operation was code named "Tawny Pipit" after a small singing bird.[26]

News of the operation leaked to the China lobby, which then charged that Davies had intended to infiltrate the CIA with communist sympathizers (presumably Snow, Schwartz, Smedley, and Fairbank) in order to sway American policy toward accommodation with Beijing. Senator Patrick McCarran's Internal Security Subcommittee opened an investigation of Davies and on August 8 and 10, 1951, Davies refused to discuss the covert operation on national security grounds. However, on February 15, 1952, Munson outlined Davies' suggestions concerning Tawny Pipit to the subcommittee, adding that the CIA had rejected the idea. Following Munson's testimony, McCarran and the China lobby pressured the Justice Department to indict Davies for perjury because of seven discrepancies between his and Munson's statements. Munson's discussion of the classified material outraged Kennan, who contacted CIA officials to demand that he be fired.[27]

Seething over the entire incident, Kennan tried to use his influence in behalf of Davies. "I cannot stand by and consider myself unaffected by things that happened to a junior officer by virtue of his official activity under my authority," he told Paul Nitze. Kennan threatened to resign as ambassador to Moscow if a grand jury indicted Davies and told Nitze that Eisenhower and Adlai Stevenson, the two candidates for President in 1952, would "both find that the problem of replacing me here is not the simplest of problems and they might wish to have some warning of the fact that they may be faced with it."[28] Kennan doubted that his threat would carry any weight, but he was determined to intercede on Davies' behalf. "My faint hope," he wrote Davies from Moscow in July, "is that if people at home, including the President and the candidates for election as his successor, knew that a continuation on the path on which McCarran is embarked would jeopardize my usefulness as well as yours it might just possibly make a slight difference to them." The Justice Department declined to summon a grand jury because of lack of evidence, not because of Kennan's threat to resign.[29]

Kennan spent the late fall of 1952 alternately explaining why he had been removed from the Soviet Union and defending John Davies. He told official audiences that the anti-communist hysteria was "playing very dangerously into the hands" of the Kremlin and complained that one need only start a rumor to get an investigation that would ruin the career of a loyal official. "Are we so rich in talented public servants that we can afford to leave the ones we have vulnerable to this sort of danger?"[30] The hysteria carried the "real danger that the concepts necessary for the conduct of foreign affairs will be driven out and replaced by the clichés and epithets of the great oversimplifiers," he declared. "The very word 'diplomacy' has been semantically discredited in our American vocabulary; but I know of no other term that will replace it."[31]

On November 3 *Time,* long a forum for the China lobby, charged that Davies was among the diplomats who had misled General Douglas MacArthur on the eve of Chinese intervention in Korea, a baseless charge that Kennan publicly refuted. He explained in a letter to the editor that Davies had been serving under him on the PPS at the time in question, had been in no position to mislead MacArthur, and "your statement is therefore in error and constitutes a serious injustice to a professional civil servant." Kennan advised the editors to "allot responsibility where responsibility really resides" in their assessment of government policies and to "refrain from portraying the responsible heads of government as bewildered innocents manipulated at will by scheming subordinates."[32]

By this time Kennan himself had received a subpoena to appear before the McCarran subcommittee. Testifying on January 13, 1953, he defended Davies' loyalty and assured the senators that the diplomat had acted under his authority in the Tawny Pipit affair. The subcommittee then subjected him to hostile questioning which left no doubt that it entertained doubts as to *Kennan's* loyalty. The examiners "tried to trick me into a statement at odds with something else I'd said" in order to seek an indictment for perjury, Kennan recalled in 1984. "I've never forgotten that experience before the Senate [sub]committee. The methods these people used were extremely unpleasant." Asked if his reputation as an anti-communist, as manifested in the Long Telegram and the X-Article, shielded him from further harassment during the McCarthy period, Kennan replied: "No question, the X-Article saved my skin from McCarthyism. Yes, indeed, but I was very nearly gotten anyway."[33]

Outraged over his treatment by the McCarran subcommittee, Kennan demanded an "exhaustive" FBI examination of his loyalty. The diplomat sought to clear his name "in view of the serious damage that could be done to public confidence if it became known that a person who has held such high and sensitive positions as I have held, and still hold, did not enjoy full confidence in the Senate." Kennan, who had left Moscow four months previously but technically remained the U.S. ambassador, warned that he would be reluctant to accept a new post with the State Department in the absence of a review of his loyalty and fitness. As it turned out, of course, Dulles had no intention of offering him a new post.[34]

While Kennan denounced the anti-communist zealots, the McCarran subcommittee continued to push for a grand jury probe of Davies. In May 1953 the State Department responded to the pressure by removing Davies from his post as Assistant to the High Commissioner in Germany, exiling him to Peru as counselor of the American embassy in Lima. On September 9 Kennan expressed to the Justice Department his "shock" over the continuing harassment of Davies and demanded an interview with Attorney General Herbert Brownell, a request that was denied.[35]

The dam broke in the Davies case on November 24 when McCarthy interjected himself in spectacular public fashion. "Why is this man [Davies] still a high official in our State Department after eleven months of Republican administration?" he demanded. McCarthy declared that the administration had "struck out" on Davies, who was "part and parcel of the Acheson-Lattimore-Vincent-White-Hiss group which did so much toward delivering our Chinese friends into Communist hands." The alcoholic junior senator from Wisconsin asserted that Davies "lied under oath about his activities in trying to put—listen to this—in trying to put communists and espionage agents in key spots in the Central Intelligence Agency."[36]

"In view of the McCarthy stunt," Kennan wired Davies in Lima, "[I] have decided to throw myself publicly into your case." Although he was "not sanguine" about Davies' chances, Kennan pleaded the cause in a long letter to the *New York Times'* editors and to political reporter James Reston. On December 9 Reston published an analysis of the Tawny Pipit case and *U.S. News and World Report* followed with a long-winded account of "The Strange Case of John P. Davies."[37]

Meanwhile Kennan had sent his letter to the editor to Undersecretary

Robert Murphy in hopes that the State Department would come to Davies' defense. Murphy advised Kennan against "rushing into print," a charge that Kennan rejected. "For more than two years I have been repeatedly on the verge of coming out publicly in this case, but have been restrained each time by the hope that the government itself would take the necessary steps to protect Davies' reputation. My own fear now is that my action has been delayed for too long."[38] On December 17 the *Times* printed Kennan's letter, which explained the background of Davies' assignment to the Tawny Pipit case. He declared that Davies had suffered from "a seemingly endless series of charges, investigations, hearings and publicity—an ordeal which has brought acute embarrassment to Davies and his family, as well as a great sense of helplessness and concern to his friends and colleagues." Kennan called Davies "a talented and devoted public servant . . . whose departure from the governmental service would be a serious loss to the public interest."[39]

Scott McLeod was unimpressed. On December 29 the administration's security director called for a reinvestigation of Davies, the ninth such review of his loyalty. His family was exhausted—on one occasion his young children had been run out of a drugstore by a proprietor who called them "little communists." On August 30, 1954, a new Security Hearing Board recommended that Davies be terminated from government service for "lack of judgment, discretion, and reliability." Davies rebutted the charges but on November 5 Dulles fired him. Davies elected to live in Peru rather than return to the United States.[40]

While Davies' departure marked the end of the purge of the wartime China experts, Kennan joined the defense in a final and even more spectacular loyalty and security case—that of J. Robert Oppenheimer. On April 13, 1954, the public learned the shocking news that the scientist who had directed the wartime atomic bomb program had lost his access to secret government data on the charge that he was a security risk. Hearings had begun the day before to determine the security status of Oppenheimer, who was suspended from his position as a consultant to the Atomic Energy Commission (AEC).[41]

Kennan had known Oppenheimer since 1946 when he had heard the scientist lecture at the National War College and had worked closely with him on the issue of sharing information on raw materials for atomic energy with Britain and Canada. The diplomat had solicited Oppenheimer's views on other foreign policy matters during his tenure as PPS director and by the time Kennan left the government in 1950, accepting Oppenheimer's offer to join the Institute for Advanced Study, both men opposed the decision to develop the hydrogen bomb, shared deeper misgivings about the militarization of American diplomacy, and had become close friends.[42]

The security concern about Oppenheimer stemmed from revelations about his past forwarded by General Kenneth D. Nichols, general manager of the AEC. Nichols revealed that Oppenheimer had attended Communist Party meetings, contributed funds, and joined several front organizations in California between 1936 and 1946. His wife and brother had formally joined the party. Nichols charged, in addition, that Oppenheimer's opposition to developing the hydrogen bomb had been intended to sabotage the program or at least retard its progress.[43]

Oppenheimer did not deny his past communist associations, though he pointed out that he had not been a party member, but based his defense on the plea that his past political leanings should be viewed in the context of his entire life and career. That is, whatever security risk might flow from his past communist associations should be balanced against the worthiness of the tasks he had performed for the government without breaching security. Although he had opposed development of the hydrogen bomb, Oppenheimer denied that he had attempted to subvert or delay the program. He outlined his defense in a 10,000 word public statement which he released when the revelations of his past became known.[44]

In his April 20 testimony before the three-member AEC Personnel Security Board, Kennan admitted that Oppenheimer had displayed naïveté through his past communist sympathies but declared that in the matters on which he had worked with Oppenheimer—coordination of raw materials for atomic weapons and discussion of the hydrogen bomb—he had found no reason to question his loyalty or to consider him a security risk. "On the basis of what is known to me of Dr. Oppenheimer's qualities, his personality and his activities during the period that I have known him," Kennan testified, "I would know of no reason why he should not be permitted to have access to restricted data in the government."[45]

Kennan argued that Oppenheimer deserved special consideration because of his genius (in addition to his brilliance in theoretical physics, he displayed expertise in literature, painting, music, and spoke eight languages). "Really able and gifted people" such as Oppenheimer were "perhaps less apt than the others to have had a fully conventional life," Kennan declared, adding that the "higher types of knowledge and wisdom do not come without very considerable anguish and often a very considerable road of error."[46] After hearing testimony from Kennan and other witnesses totaling 3,300 typescript pages, the three-member committee on May 27 voted two-to-one against restoring Oppenheimer's security clearance. Oppenheimer did not appeal and his contract with the government expired on June 30.[47]

Kennan declared that Oppenheimer was another casualty of the "peculiar form of American extremism which holds it possible that there should be such a thing as total security, and attaches overriding importance to the quest for it." The costs of the recent wave of anti-communist hysteria—censorship, a chilling effect on intellectual expression, shattered careers—reflected an "unwillingness to accept the normal long term hazards and inconveniences of great power," A foreign policy aimed at the achievement of total security, Kennan declared, "is the one thing I can think of that is entirely capable of bringing this country to a point where it will have no security at all."[48]

Like historian Richard Hofstadter, who argued that McCarthyism reflected a "paranoid style" in American mass politics, Kennan saw evidence of "some deep inner crisis, some gnawing fear of ourselves" that confirmed his worst fears about democratic politics and mob psychology. The anti-communist hysteria was

> not just a question of the spectacle of a few men setting out to achieve a cheap political success by appealing to primitive reactions, by appealing to the uncertain, suspicious little savage that lies at the bottom of almost every human breast; it is more importantly the spectacle of millions of our citizens listening eagerly to these suggestions and then trotting off faithfully and anxiously, like the victims of some totalitarian brainwashing, to snoop and check up on their fellow citizens, to purge the libraries and lecture platforms, to protect us all from the impact of ideas.[49]

To Kennan the anti-communist hysteria reflected the decline of elite authority over the nation's diplomacy and called into question the ability of the United States as a mass democracy to summon the maturity required to conduct great-power diplomacy. The nation, he declared, had not been able "to conquer the habit of misusing our external relations for the satisfaction of domestic purposes."[50] By overreacting to what was in reality a minor security concern, the United States had shown that it lacked the sophistication required to carry out a program of ideological-political containment across the globe. Unless American statesmanship could "recover some relaxation and dignity and maturity," he declared in May 1953, ". . . then I look darkly and with with foreboding on our chances of finding an adequate answer to the challenge of Soviet policy at this juncture in world affairs."[51]

Unlike many, if not most, American artists, politicians, intellectuals, journalists, and academicians, Kennan had responded to the anti-communist hysteria in the years after 1947 with his personal integrity intact.[52] It had taken the purge of his fellow diplomats to get his attention, to be sure, but unlike Acheson, Dulles, and many lesser officials he was too principled and placed too much emphasis on good form and civility to succumb to anti-communist zealotry. "It was a terrible blow to me to see the mindlessness of this reaction," Kennan recalled in a 1984 interview. He insisted that he "had asked people to react thoughtfully to the reality of Soviet power," but "instead, what did I get—McCarthy and the China lobby." What Kennan did not say was that the nation's preoccupation with domestic radicalism flowed from the depiction of communists as devils incarnate that he himself had promoted in the early Cold War. McCarthyism was America's way of digesting the Truman Doctrine, the X-Article, the fall of China, the war in Korea and other manifestations of the global crusade against communism.

The anti-communist hysteria confirmed Kennan's darkest suspicions about democratic society and shook the foundations of his support for the nation's postwar internationalism. In the wake of his failed Moscow ambassadorship and retirement from the Foreign Service, McCarthyism also reinforced Kennan's marginalization in the foreign affairs establishment. Now firmly ensconced as an outsider and critic, he was powerless to prevent the purges of Davies, Oppenheimer, and other victims of the domestic security controversy. While McCarthy's censure in December 1954 following the televised Army-McCarthy hearings provided a symbolic burial of the domestic communist issue, Kennan's perceptions about American diplomacy would never be the same.[53]

IX

Challenging the Consensus

KENNAN CHALLENGED the fundamental assumptions underlying the postwar international system in a series of radio lectures in London over the BBC in late 1957. Delivered on the eve of a NATO decision to place nuclear weapons in Western Europe, the Reith Lectures sparked commentary throughout the West and called into question the containment consensus that Kennan himself had done so much to forge a decade earlier. As they had done since 1948, allied leaders rejected Kennan's call for German reunification, great-power disengagement, and the creation of a nuclear free zone in Europe. The rejection of his proposals reflected the West's fixation on the prospect of a Soviet invasion as well as the perception that the cold war provided a stable international system. Kennan's repudiation of the realist position reinforced his standing as an outsider and critic of the foreign policy establishment.

As the cold war became a permanent feature of international life in the 1950s, academics, journalists, and political figures requested Kennan's views on contemporary events in relation to the 1947 X-Article. Confessing his "guilt" at having written the containment policy, Kennan admitted that X had "overrated the ugliness of the problem" but added that since Stalin's death in 1953 the Soviet Union had undergone the "process of mellowing" that he had anticipated. Although "the doctrine is responding to my best hopes," he observed on another occasion, containment still focused too exclusively on the unlikely prospect of a Soviet attack. "The Reds deserve the closest watch," he explained, "but I'm sure there are ways of handling them . . . as one handles a psychotic person."[1]

In the summer of 1957 Kennan decided to use his invitation to deliver the annual Reith Lectures over the BBC "to tell how I feel today about the subjects I discussed in the original X article. The whole series would then be cast in terms of this tone and approach," he explained to the British radio network. Kennan later attempted to dismiss the lectures as a "weekend diversion," the response to which had shocked him. In actuality, he had anticipated the event "with unmitigated foreboding" and expected the lectures to be widely noted.[2]

Having failed since 1948 to convince Western statesmen of the wisdom of securing a negotiated settlement in Europe with the Russians, Kennan decided to go over their heads with an appeal to public opinion. The decision was hypocritical in view of his professed elitism and contempt for democracy, but now that he no longer commanded influence among them Kennan was less sanguine about leaving matters in the hands of diplomatic elites. "Obviously people are going to have to find better ways of solving international problems than simply developing weapons that would destroy us all," he declared in 1957. "I used to think we could safely leave such things to the government. Today, I no longer do." Kennan doubted that the government would "find its way out of these complexities unless it receives some useful support, both stimulus and encouragement, from public opinion."[3]

Kennan made an impression from the outset in Britain, as he spent the 1957–58 academic year as visiting Eastman Professor of History at Oxford University. Packed audiences heard him deliver classroom lectures on Soviet-Western relations from 1918 to 1939 and the *London Observer* noted that Kennan "has already startled the university: his lectures on Russia have been filled to the rafters with both dons and undergraduates."[4]

The attention Kennan received at Oxford foreshadowed the acclaim generated by his participation in the annual BBC lectures, which aired on six successive Sunday nights in November and December. Such previous lecturers as Bertrand Russell, Arnold Toynbee, and Robert Oppenheimer had established for the popular radio series a reputation of offering the views of controversial personalities on critical issues. Kennan lived up to their promise.

Recent international developments ensured that the retired diplomat would receive a large listening audience for his assessment of the East-West conflict. Nikita S. Khrushchev's decision to intervene in Hungary and his denunciation of Stalin had highlighted the prospects for change in the Soviet Union as well as instability in Eastern Europe. While the Soviets had reasserted authority over the Hungarian satellite in 1956, it was the launching of another, very different one in 1957 that created a panic bordering on hysteria in the West. This, of course, was *Sputnik*, the earth satellite whose launching on October 4 allowed the supposedly backward Slavs to embarrass the West with an advance in space technology. *Sputnik* created the illusion that Soviet scientists held a strategic advantage in the development of intercontinental ballistic missiles (ICBMs) and when Moscow followed up the launch by sending a dog hurtling into space, *Newsweek* asserted that "for the first time in history the Western world finds itself mortally in danger from the East."[5]

A Soviet diplomatic offensive coincided with the satellite shots. Appearing on American television on June 2, 1957, General Secretary Khrushchev offered to remove all Soviet troops from Eastern Europe if the United States and Great Britain reciprocated in the western half of the continent. Polish leader Wyladislaw Gomulka simultaneously blamed the presence of American troops in Europe for the presence of Soviet troops in his and neighboring countries. Two days before *Sputnik*, Polish Foreign Minister Adam Rapacki called for the declaration of a "denuclearized zone" comprising Poland, Czechoslovakia, and both Germanys. Under this proposal, "nuclear weapons would be neither manufactured nor stockpiled [and] the equipment and installations designed for their servicing would not be located there."[6]

Unlike Kennan, Western officials declined to consider these offers, which came on the eve of NATO's decision to add tactical nuclear weapons to its arsenal in Western Europe. Kennan endorsed the Soviet and East bloc proposals and declared that it was a mistake to regard the Kremlin leaders as men who were simply "looking for a moment to launch a military onslaught on the rest of the world." The Soviets had "recognized realities where they had to recognize them in the past," he told the Senate Foreign Relations Committee, and could be trusted to adhere to specific agreements. The Kremlin might welcome an opportunity to reduce an "awkward and embarrassing and dangerous" commitment in Eastern Europe, "provided it did not come as a great loss of face to them."[7]

Kennan set the tone for the BBC lectures by declaring at the outset, on November 10, that the X-Article was out of date. Noting that X had based his prescriptions on a belief in Soviet weakness, he "confess[ed] that Soviet economic progress in these intervening years . . . has surpassed anything I then thought possible." *Sputnik* was an example of Russia's "impressive" industrial and technological growth, so that the West could no longer hope to destroy the Soviet regime nor compel it to bow to Western demands. But one could negotiate the resolution of "specific problems."

In his third lecture Kennan came to the essence of disengagement by asserting that German reunification and mutual military withdrawal by the great powers offered the only means to resolve the conflict over Berlin and end Moscow's domination of Eastern Europe. "Only when the troops are gone," he declared, "will there be possibilities for the evolution of these nations toward institutions and social systems most suited to their needs." The refusal to consider German neutralization "renders permanent what was meant to be temporary" and "assigns half of Europe, by implication, to the Russians."

As in his 1948 disengagement proposals, Kennan's arguments centered on reducing the scope of the Western alliance and he agreed with the Russians that a reunified Germany could not become a member of NATO. Kennan declared that it was too much to ask Moscow to abandon "the military and political bastion in Central Europe which it won by its military effort from 1941 to 1945, and to do this without any compensatory withdrawal of American armed power from the heart of the Continent." The permanent partition of Germany, on the other hand, required "too much and for too long a time of the United States" and "does less than justice to the strength and the abilities of the Europeans themselves." A negotiated settlement would remove Soviet frontiers east of Poland, ending the need for a Western military presence in Central Europe. It was "far more desirable on principle to get the Soviet forces out of Central and Eastern Europe," Kennan argued, "than to cultivate a new German army for the purpose of opposing them while they remain there."

Kennan was not sanguine about achieving disengagement with Moscow and did not claim to be sure that the Soviet leadership really desired such a settlement. "But how much of this lack of enthusiasm is resignation in the face of the Western position," he added, "we do not know." Despite the emergence of separate polities in both Germanys, Kennan argued that a settlement could still be imposed on the two governments. He envisioned a united Germany but one in which East and West would maintain some aspects of the divergent social systems that had emerged since the war. "Whether or not, for example, the industries of [East Germany] should remain socialized would seem to me, compared with what else is at stake, one of the least important of the problems in question."

Turning to the military implications of the division of Europe in his fourth lecture, Kennan argued that the West held a sufficient nuclear deterrent and should abort plans to expand the arms race by placing tactical nuclear weapons on European soil. Their emplacement would simply provoke corresponding Soviet deployments in Eastern Europe, adding further impediments to reaching an agreement to end the division of the continent. He decried as illusory the argument offered in an influential 1957 book by Harvard professor Henry A. Kissinger that limited nuclear war was a plausible strategy. "The beginning of understanding rests, in this appalling problem, with the recognition that the weapon of mass destruction is a sterile and hopeless weapon which . . . cannot in any way serve the purposes of a constructive and hopeful foreign policy."

To Kennan, already troubled by the inability of enlightened elites such as himself to exercise authority, nuclear weapons were a potent symbol of the decline of order and civility in international relations. The first-use policy and the expansion onto European soil suggested that the arms race was already spinning out of control. "Are we to flee," Kennan asked,

> like haunted creatures from one defensive device to another, each more costly and humiliating than the one before, cowering underground one day, breaking up our cities the next, attempting to surround ourselves with elaborate electronic shields on the third, concerned only to prolong the length of our lives while sacrificing all the values for which it might be worthwhile to live at all?

Kennan advocated minimal nuclear deterrence, not unilateral disarmament, and called on the nations of Central and Western Europe to base their defenses on paramilitary "territorial-militia type" forces. Such forces, based on the Swiss model of defense, would provide initial response to invasion while the nation mobilized for all-out resistance. In a statement later subjected to ridicule, Kennan offered his "personal assurance" that with such forces no European nation would have "need of foreign garrisons to assure its immunity from Soviet attack."[8]

Kennan's lectures on disengagement and nuclear weapons prompted a spectacular response throughout Europe, but especially in Great Britain and West Germany. Britons who missed the radio lectures had ample opportunity to learn of the proposals from a slew of newspaper articles and editorials that appeared in the major London dailies. The print and broadcast attention devoted to the lectures made Kennan a prominent political figure in Britain—an opinion poll found that an extraordinarily high 73 percent of the British public recognized his name by the end of the series. The retired diplomat's words "had made quite a dent in public opinion," British Defense Minister Selwyn Lloyd declared. Feigning modesty, Kennan himself wrote Oppenheimer that he was "cringing with horror and remorse over the notoriety the Reith Lectures seem to have achieved. There was little in them that was new and nothing that was profound."[9] His alleged aversion to notoriety nothwithstanding, Kennan promptly published the lectures in book form under the title *Russia, the Atom, and the West.*

The London newspapers lauded the eloquence of Kennan's "magisterial" lectures, but rejected most of his arguments. The *Daily Telegraph* deemed disengagement "pitifully optimistic," asserting that it would force Europe to enter into "a loose and dangerous game of blind man's bluff." The editors did not share Kennan's "mystical faith in German unification as a step which would slowly but surely bring about a reformation in the fundamental aims of the Soviet Union's attitude to the West." *The Times* of London ridiculed Kennan's "utopian ideas of 'ending the Cold War,' " but agreed with him that the major powers "could agree not to put nuclear missiles near each side of the dividing line in Europe." The London *Observer* retained doubts about disengagement, but declared that Kennan's plan "remains the only suggestion which has ever offered a concrete prospect for restoring the freedom of the enslaved peoples" in Eastern Europe.[10]

In West Germany, Kennan's lectures inspired several weeks of public debate. The editor of the daily *Die Welt* responded favorably to his proposals in a lead article accompanied by a cartoon lampooning Dulles for his support of the status quo in Europe. "One may well say," North German Radio declared, that "scarcely ever before has any political lecture series anywhere in the world aroused such interest." Kennan's call for a neutral, nuclear-free Central Europe had made a "tremendous impact on the German mind." *The New Republic* declared that Kennan's lectures had a "greater impact on thinking Germans" than had the recent launchings of the Soviet satellites.[11]

The ruling Christian Democratic Party in West Germany had secured Bonn's membership in NATO and thus viewed Kennan's proposals with "distaste, misgivings and real alarm." The government of Konrad Adenauer insisted that West Germany retain membership in the Atlantic alliance and harbored the unrealistic expectation that NATO membership would not only deter Soviet aggression but eventually persuade the Kremlin to abandon East Germany. Officials in Bonn mounted public criticism against Kennan in order to allay the popular misperception in Europe that he remained an influential figure in the shaping of the Democratic Party's foreign policy. Foreign Minister Heinrich von Brentano assailed Kennan's "senseless proposals," declaring that criticisms of the retired diplomat in the United States showed that he was "an outsider" with whose views the West German government need not be concerned.[12]

Although Bonn, London, and Washington opposed disengagement and the preservation of a nuclear-free zone in Europe, "the evidence is that the three governments are running scared," the *New York Times* reported. "They are well aware of the tremendous acclaim with which the Kennan ideas have been received in West Germany and Britain." In London, Conservative Prime Minister Harold Macmillan supported the alliance and assailed Kennan's "neutralism" while Britain's NATO representative, Frank Roberts, declared that "every time a former diplomat leaves his job, he loses his practical sense." However, in both Britain and West Germany opposition parties embraced disengagement and demanded dialogue with Moscow. Aneurin Bevan, the probable foreign minister in the event of a British Labour government, publicly endorsed Kennan's proposals and the German Social Democrats adopted the call for a nuclear-free Central Europe as a major campaign issue in elections scheduled for July 1958.[13]

In American politics, most Democrats declined to attack Eisenhower on NATO, and while Kennan received some sympathy from American liberals, he found little actual support for disengagement. Adlai Stevenson typified the tepid response, telling Kennan that he opposed the Reith proposals but that anything the Soviet expert said "was significant and distinguished, and commanded our congratulations and warm respect." However, Minnesota Senator Hubert Humphrey praised Kennan's willingness to "probe relentlessly to see if there isn't some way that we can achieve the objective of reduced tensions without sacrificing security and at the same time get emancipation or liberation of people who have been literally enslaved."[14]

The American media reported the controversy over Kennan's proposals in Europe while tracking responses to disengagement in the United States. Richard Rovere found significance in Kennan's "repudiation" of containment in the *New Yorker* while the *Nation* commended the retired diplomat for conceding that some of the assumptions underlying the X-Article were "erroneous" and for being "responsive to new happenings and developments." The *Progressive* applauded Kennan for "seeking to let some fresh air into a room gone stale and musty with the negative concepts of Dulles-Acheson rigidity." Despite his friendship with Kennan, Joseph Alsop attributed the "plain silliness" of Kennan's proposals to his "almost neurotic horror of military power in all its modern forms." The diplomat suffered from "an attack of moral shingles at the mere sight of the Pentagon," Alsop declared. The *New Republic* criticized disengagement and pointed out that Kennan did not "represent the Democratic Party or any influential circle of American political leadership." The *National Review* called Kennan the "premier American apostle of appeasement" and the *Ukrainian Bulletin,* a publication of Soviet emigrés, featured an article entitled "Kennanism: The Road to Surrender."[15]

In Paris, the Congress of Cultural Freedom, a group of European anticommunist intellectuals with CIA affiliations, expressed divergent views on Kennan's proposals. French political theorist Raymond Aron, a leading realist, argued that the partition of Europe, while unfortunate in many respects, nevertheless offered stability against the outbreak of war because both sides recognized the dividing line. Aron doubted that the Russians could be trusted not to intervene in Eastern Europe even if they agreed to a negotiated disengagement. Richard Lowenthal, an authority on communism, defended Kennan's position, arguing that the status quo represented "the most pernicious form of coexistence" and "the point which George Kennan had at heart was to set us thinking about the possibility of an *active* Western policy."[16]

It was no surprise that Kennan's proposals found support in the Soviet Union, which had already advocated the declaration of a nuclear-free zone and great-power disengagement from Central Europe. Khrushchev endorsed disengagement on December 10 and declared on another occasion that it was "high time to reach agreement on the reduction of foreign troops stationed in Germany and other European states. . . . Eventually all foreign troops must be withdrawn from the territories of other countries." The Western leaders refused to take these statements seriously and depicted them as propaganda ploys designed to sow dissension within NATO as part of a Soviet master plan to dominate Europe.[17]

Unlike the opponents of disengagement, Kennan refused to dismiss the Soviet offers to negotiate as mere propaganda ploys. He pointed to a Soviet offer to withdraw Red Army contingents from East Germany and from the other Warsaw Pact countries in return for the withdrawal of American and British forces from Western Europe. "Now this may or may not be a proposition acceptable to us today," he advised, "but it indicates that they are prepared to go quite far." The diplomat perceived Khrushchev as a moderate, "a man whose sincerity, at least when it comes to the desire to see the competition between the two systems carried forward by means other than those of a major war, we need have no doubt."[18]

The Eisenhower administration ignored the Reith Lectures on the premise that an official denunciation would only legitimize debate over Western policy. Questioned by a BBC reporter, Dulles declined to comment on Kennan's proposals but did note that "the Soviets cannot be relied upon to live up to their promises." When a wisecracking American reporter asked Dulles at a news conference if he intended to return Kennan to a policy making role in view of the Reith proposals, the Secretary quipped in response: "Well, we have an opportunity to get his thinking anyway, don't we?"[19]

Disgusted with the administration, Kennan declared that the nation had lacked a coherent foreign policy since George Marshall had resigned as Secretary of State. Marshall's resignation, of course, had also marked the point at which *Kennan* had begun to lose influence. "The [Eisenhower] administration is anti-intellectual . . . concerned with the package rather than its content," Kennan declared. "It has no foreign policy." He complained that the Policy Planning Staff had "been scrapped"—an exaggeration at best since the planning unit continued to function—and the Foreign Service made "mute." "There's plenty of talent in the lower echelons of government; the vacuum is at the top," he declared, adding that Vice President Richard M. Nixon was the most able leader in the Republican administration.[20]

Although they refrained from comment on disengagement, the impact of Kennan's ideas concerned Eisenhower and Dulles as representatives of the fifteen NATO countries prepared to meet in Paris on December 16. *Time* spoke for the administration in depicting Kennan's lectures as little short of disloyal, claiming that his call for German reunification "came perilously close to undercutting the U.S. position by implying NATO was an obstacle to reaching an agreement with the Russians." Kennan indeed held that very view and hoped that his lectures would call into question the imminent NATO decision to locate tactical nuclear weapons on West European soil. "I delivered the BBC lectures on the eve of the final decision to place nuclear weapons on the continent," he recalled in 1984. "There was a note of desperation in those talks because I felt that once you did that, it prejudiced greatly the possibilities for any peaceful unraveling of the knot."[21]

Despite a last-minute plea from Soviet Premier Nikolai Bulganin for a nuclear-free Central Europe, on December 18 the NATO ministers authorized the basing of tactical nuclear bombs in Western Europe. The decision came three days after Kennan's final lecture but before the full impact of the debate he had unleashed had been felt.[22] Citing the Soviet Union's putative desire to dominate Europe, NATO rejected Moscow's —and Kennan's—proposal of a nuclear-free Central Europe. Eisenhower, who had attended the NATO meeting with Dulles, formally rejected the Soviet proposal on December 23, explaining that the Kremlin's "pretensions and their actions have all failed to inspire confidence in free men." Only spokesmen for Norway and Denmark among those who attended the NATO meeting encouraged a negotiated settlement with Russia. "It seems to me," declared Kennan, "that what has happened in these last days in Paris has served simply to make negotiation more difficult, without adding anything real to the defense of Europe."[23]

While Eisenhower and Dulles made no comment on the subject of disengagement, former Secretary of State Dean Acheson delighted the Republicans by taking the lead in rebutting Kennan's heresies. James B. Conant, the former Harvard President who now headed the private American Council on Germany, sought out Acheson, Harry Truman, and other prestigious men of foreign affairs for the express purpose of mounting a public campaign against Kennan's proposals. Truman complied with a public condemnation of disengagement but it was Acheson, who had always rejected Kennan's views on Germany, who delivered the sharpest polemic.

"Mr. Kennan has never, in my judgment, grasped the realities of power relationships but takes a rather mystical attitude toward them," Acheson declared on January 11, 1958, in a statement released by Conant's group. Clearly defensive of the alliance he had been instrumental in establishing, Acheson denounced any program which entailed "leaving Russian military power unopposed on the Continent." The allied presence alone permitted Western Europe to withstand Soviet pressure and Moscow's domination "could be accomplished by intimidation" if the West withdrew. Acheson ridiculed Kennan's pledge of his "personal assurance" against a Soviet invasion and declared that "as long as we are giving personal assurances, I think I can give mine that Mr. Kennan's opinion is not shared by any responsible leader in the Democratic Party." Acheson's public attack on the Reith lectures elicited a private note of praise from Foster Dulles.[24]

The public attacks stung Kennan, who told Adlai Stevenson he "was amazed and distressed to find how many indignant pigeons I had flushed out of the underbrush." He was "hard hit" by Acheson's and Truman's attacks, however, and insisted that he was "at a loss to explain this sudden vehement outburst of malevolence on the part of people whom I have never publicly criticized and who heretofore treated me only with cordiality." The rising tide of condemnation provoked a characteristic bout of illness, which left Kennan recuperating in Zurich for several days.[25]

Acheson's critique fueled more discussion over disengagement and delighted the press. "Mr. Kennan has started a debate and we haven't had a good debate on the assumptions of our present foreign policy for years," James Reston wrote. "Next to the Lincoln Memorial in moonlight," he added, "the sight of Mr. Dean G. Acheson blowing his top is without doubt the most impressive view in the capital." The *Washington*

Post, while opposed to disengagement, found Acheson's "savage" attack on Kennan "inexplicable" because it was "the same sort of unfair attack of which Mr. Acheson himself was so often the target."[26]

The Kennan-Acheson dispute reflected a broader rift over foreign policy within the Democratic Party. Acheson and Paul Nitze served as the chair and vice chair, respectively, of the party's Advisory Committee on Foreign Affairs and were determined that their perceptions of the Soviet Union should prevail in Democratic policy councils. Nitze declared that Moscow would use negotiations as "a wedge" designed to "knock the foundations out from under our current defense policy" and he and Acheson continued to advocate military power and multilateral alliances to bolster containment whereas Kennan, Hubert Humphrey and Mike Mansfield (D-Montana) argued that the new Kremlin leadership was more interested in domestic reform than overrunning Western Europe and thus they took seriously Moscow's expressions of interest in European negotiations and arms control.[27]

Acheson continued on the offensive against Kennan's views, declaring in the lead article in *Foreign Affairs* in April 1958 that disengagement was "a futile—and lethal—attempt to crawl back into the cocoon of history." There was only one disengagement possible, he declared—"the disengagement from life, which is death." Acheson asserted that Kennan's "vague" ideas and "seductive" style masked what was in reality a call for "a timid and defeatist policy of retreat. . . . a withdrawal from positive and active leadership in the creation of a workable system of states." Acheson insisted that disengagement would compel the Germans to seek a "a sort of new Ribbentrop-Molotov agreement" with Moscow which would confront "the free world . . . with what has twice been so intolerable as to provoke world war—the unification of the European land mass (this time the Eurasian land mass) under a power hostile to national independence and individual freedom."

The appeal of Kennan's "new isolationism," as Acheson labled disengagement, was "gravely disturbing" not only because it was "utterly fallacious, but because the harder course which it calls on us to forego has been so successful." American leadership had restored the West European economies and was exerting an "irresistible pull upon East Germany and Eastern Europe." In time this pressure would force the Russians to come to terms on "a united Germany, under honorable and healing conditions, and toward the return of real national identity to the countries of Eastern Europe."[28]

What bothered him most "about the views of my critics in this country, and particularly Mr. Acheson," Kennan declared in a rejoinder to Acheson in the January 1959 issue of *Foreign Affairs*, "is that in all he has said there is not the faintest trace of a suggestion that at any point we would have to come to any sort of political accommodation with Russia. We're supposed to remain strong and some day Russia is going to give us all we want." Kennan himself had expressed this view up to 1948 but since then he had argued that it was unrealistic to expect to "get everything without having to make any compromises, without having to pay any price."[29]

Acheson's response to disengagement illuminates once again the irony of Kennan and containment. More than a decade after the publication of the X-Article, Acheson employed the same arguments in the same journal to rebut the positions now advocated by Kennan. If the West continued to display its credibility through a program of military strength and economic assistance, Acheson argued, the Soviet Union would in time be forced to abandon its sphere of influence and settle on terms favorable to the West. Whereas Kennan had lost faith in the argument that containment could compel Moscow to change its foreign policy, Acheson remained wedded to that view.

Interestingly, Walter Lippmann, who had delivered the most trenchant critique of the X-Article in 1947, sided with Kennan in the disengagement debate. "Mr. Kennan's words have resounded and reverberated throughout the world," he declared, because the Western leaders "had come to a dead end on the road which they had been following in the postwar years." Consistent with the position he had taken in 1947, Lippmann argued that the Reith Lectures pointed to an alternative approach "which the Allies might have chosen at the defeat of Germany, had they not been in the grip of a war psychosis and, we may add, had they been lucid and realistic about Stalin." Critics of disengagement, Lippmann continued, based their opposition on the premise—"once held by Mr. Kennan—

> that Western power is paramount and that the Soviet power is certain to decline. On this premise, but only on this premise, can one arrive at the

official policy which expects Russia to withdraw while the Western powers advance. We are living in a time when the underlying premise of our postwar policy has been shown to be false.[30]

Thus Kennan and Lippmann advocated adjustments in the European status quo as the best means of calming international tensions and preserving a balance of power. Their position offered a more hopeful prospect for encouraging the eventual independence of the Soviet satellites than the continuing program of militarization, although prominent among the critics of disengagement were those, like Dulles, who insisted that they were morally committed to liberation in Eastern Europe. Disengagement also offered a means to resolve the dispute over Berlin, which Kennan feared, with good reason, might lead to war, and might have provided a foundation upon which to base nuclear arms control agreements.

Kennan blamed the rejection of disengagement on the Western "obsession" with a chimerical threat of a Soviet invasion and he despaired at the prospect of overcoming that perception. "I am afraid that the die is really cast," he explained to Hamilton Fish Armstrong.

> Our country, including most of my good friends at home, is committed to a view of the psychology of Soviet leaders which denies them all the common aspects of humanity, which fails to connect their intentions with any rational political motives, which views them as indistinguishable from Hitler and sees them as concerned only to destroy for the sake of destroying, to over-run for the sake of over-running, quite independently of what this might mean to them in terms of new responsibility, or even consistency with their own doctrines. On the basis of this view it is of course assumed that the second the Soviet leaders thought that they could destroy our country with relative impunity, they would at once plaster us all with hydrogen bombs; just as it is to be assumed, the evidence of Finland, Sweden, Austria and Switzerland (not to mention Yugoslavia) notwithstanding, that they would at once occupy any country not defended by an American garrison—or, alternatively, that the inhabitants of such a country would at once become demoralized at the consciousness of this certain doom, and would invite them in. I can argue myself blue in the face, but I cannot even dent this conviction. We have made our decision. The Russians are monsters, from which only the worst is to be expected.[31]

Critics of disengagement insisted that it would be irresponsible to fail to plan on the possibility that the Soviets might launch an invasion of the West. "Whoever says: they *might* instead of they *would*," Kennan responded, "implies another possibility, as well: namely, that they might not. But where is the recognition of *this?*" The retired diplomat explained that "if we act as though the possibility that they 'would' were the governing one—the only one that need preoccupy us—then we will compel similar behavior on their part, and we will make that contingency much more real—much more probable—than it needed to be." Kennan thus continued to oppose the militarization of thinking in the West and the insistence on basing national security policy on judgments about Soviet capabilities rather than intentions.[32]

Why, asked critics of Kennan's proposals, if the Russians had no desire for a military conflict in Europe, did they maintain a huge conventional military establishment? Apart from the historic Russian propensity to maintain a great standing army, he responded, "they also have a certain internal role: that this is, after all, a dictatorial government. It has, in its relation to the Russian people . . . a bear by the tail, and it can't let go, and it cultivates great armed forces partly as a form of reassurance for itself." Kennan urged military analysts to focus on the geographical deployment of Soviet troops—which would be 500 miles further east after a full disengagement—rather than on their numbers. "We have tended here consistently to underestimate the importance of getting the Soviet forces back behind their own borders," he declared.[33]

Acheson, among others, had criticized Kennan for the vagueness of his proposals and it was true that in the Reith Lectures, each of which lasted less than half an hour, he had only outlined the concept of disengagement. The radio lectures were not the proper forum to unfold a detailed plan, such as Kennan had devised in Program A on the Policy Planning Staff (see chapter 4) and he had meant only to offer a "positive" program, leaving the details to the respective governments to negotiate. When pressed for specific proposals, Kennan declared that he could "conceive of many variations of a disengagement" including a withdrawal of forces to garrison areas, as he had recommended ten years before, "or you could remove them from Germany and Eastern European countries and a certain number of Western countries." He declared that "no disengagement would be worth while which did not involve the evacuation of Poland and Hungary."[34]

The essential argument stressed by critics of disengagement—most notably Acheson, Eisenhower, and Dulles—was simply that the Soviet Union could not be trusted and that a mutual withdrawal of forces would not preclude the Kremlin from intervening in East-Central Europe. With the Western powers having disengaged from the continent, they argued, Russia would be free to reassert dominant military power on any recalcitrant neighbor. Kennan responded that the "very essence" of disengagement would be a specific prohibition of any unilateral reentry of troops into the neutral zone and that there would be "automatic sanctions against precisely this sort of violation." The United States would issue a unilateral guarantee of German sovereignty (Kennan's Monroe Doctrine for Central Europe) so that an all-out Soviet offensive would mean war with the West. In the event of "a gradual and piecemeal reintroduction of Soviet armed units, . . . there would be plenty of time for the Western powers" to reintroduce their own military power into Western Europe.[35]

While prepared to respond to these contingencies, Kennan doubted that intervention was a permanent feature of Soviet diplomacy. Those who cited Hungary as evidence of Russia's lust for military adventure "seem unaware that Soviet forces were already in Hungary, on a treaty basis, when the Hungarian uprising began" and that Soviet repression would be far more problematical once troops had been "disengaged" from that nation. "Nor does it seem to have occurred to many of them," he continued, "that the continued presence of United States forces in Western Germany, or the lack of any assurance that a Hungary released from the Warsaw Pact would not promptly join the Atlantic one, could have had any influence on Soviet policy in the Hungarian crisis."[36]

Kennan rejected the image of the Red Army poised and eager to launch an invasion and asserted that the West overestimated its own role in deterring Soviet aggression. "The Finns have existed for years in a state of complete vulnerability to Soviet power and without the faintest reason to expect that anyone in the West would come to their assistance," yet had avoided conflict with Russia since 1940. Yugoslavia had broken with Moscow without benefit of Western support; Poland had chosen its own "path to socialism"; Turkey had withstood Soviet pressure before entering the Atlantic Pact; and Austria now stood independent of Moscow's power. Kennan also disputed the contention that the USSR would intervene with indifference to world opinion, arguing that "the degree to which it has made the cause of 'peace' and 'noninterference' the basis of its propaganda, internally and externally, already represents a form of commitment to opinion within the Communist orbit and throughout the European world more serious than is generally recognized in the West."

Kennan's advocacy of disengagement implied no abandonment of the quest for a moderation of Soviet influence, if not a genuine liberation, in Eastern Europe. It was possible, he thought, to achieve a negotiated settlement whereby Moscow, in return for a demilitarized Germany and a Western military withdrawal across the Rhine, would withdraw the Red Army from Eastern Europe. Following disengagement the nations of East-Central Europe could realize some degree of independence, and while they might not be allowed to emerge as capitalist democracies on the Western model their social systems would be distinguishable from Moscow's. Kennan, of course, held both social systems in disrepute and argued that the distinctions between East and West were becoming obscure. "It would not really be so drastic a transition today from the institutions of contemporary Poland to those of the more extreme examples of the Western welfare state," he explained.

Opponents of disengagement offered a compelling argument—which elicited the visceral support of the millions of Americans and Europeans who remembered the last war—when they insisted that a reunified Germany would follow the familiar course of the interwar period and once again emerge as a belligerent European power. Kennan countered that "National Socialism is deader today in Germany than was Bonapartism in France twelve years after the fall of Napoleon," but he proposed that as part of disengagement, the great powers would allow only a small, internally directed police force in reunified Germany in order to prevent any form of pernicious military power from arising. Moreover, NATO would remain in force in Western (not Central) Europe to safeguard those nations from any aggressor, including Germany, and to provide a sense of security and psychological reinforcement to bolster Western European economic and political development.[37]

The "strongest argument" against disengagement, according to Kennan himself, was the possibility "that the Russians did not want an agreement about central and eastern Europe at this time, and that therefore there was no use considering making any concessions to them in order to obtain it." He did not claim to *know* the extent to which Moscow desired a settlement along the lines of his disengagement proposal but he believed the Soviet leaders were anxious to secure West Germany's withdrawal from NATO and "would be willing to pay a price to stop the atomic armament of Germany." On the other hand, Kennan told a Senate subcommittee on disarmament in 1959, that "our experience would indicate that on what might seem to be even the easiest of issues one must be prepared to negotiate long and not very pleasantly with the Soviet Government before one ever achieves anything."[38]

In the final analysis, what Kennan called for in the Reith Lectures was for the West to consider *the possibility* of a negotiated settlement with Moscow. "We could have made the effort to negotiate with the Soviet Union," he insisted in 1984. "How are you going to know [the terms of a settlement] before you ask them? You have to go beyond their asking price, their public statements," he explained. "The real problem was that the French and the British have never wanted to negotiate about a gradual disengagement. They could never imagine the withdrawal of our forces."[39]

The quest for "total unanimity" within NATO undermined the prospects of negotiations with Moscow, Kennan complained in 1959. He called for more pressure from Washington on the Western allies in order to "recover something of the independence of our policy . . . within the alliance." Despite Washington's position as the preeminent power within NATO, he charged, the allies actually dictated policy and left the United States in a position in which "we are gently blackmailed by every one of our friends and have no room for maneuver whatsoever."[40]

In addition to widespread distrust of the Soviet Union and fears of a reunified Germany, many statesmen who saw themselves as realists argued that the postwar international system offered stability and the prospect of a lasting peace. They did not share Kennan's quest to reunify Germany and saw only instability and trouble from tinkering with the balance of forces in Europe. The ritual professions of outrage over the absence of freedom in the East European satellites, as expressed by Truman, Acheson, Eisenhower, Dulles, Adenauer, and others, took a back seat to the requirement of a stable world order. These statesmen called for muddling through in Berlin and dealt with their own insecurities about nuclear weaponry by deploying still more bombs.

Kennan admitted in the midst of the disengagement debate that it was reasonable to argue that while the present division of Europe entailed risks and disadvantages, they were at least established and well understood, whereas if the situation were to be thrown wide open, new doubts and uncertainties would arise which might increase the prospects of armed conflict. It was also true that Russian intentions were shrouded in secrecy; that securing a mutual disengagement would have required long and tedious negotiations; that calming fears over German reunification would have been difficult; and that allowing for the coexistence of divergent social systems within Germany posed a daunting task. Despite these concerns, a year after he delivered the lectures Kennan was "still not convinced" that the Reith proposals had failed to offer a more promising future than the status quo and its attendant uncertainties.[41]

He remained convinced that only through a negotiated settlement with Moscow could the West hope to loosen the Soviet hold on the satellites, resolve the precarious situation in Berlin and, above all, come to grips with the accelerating nuclear arms race. The continued irresolution of these issues carried the possibility of another war in which there could be no victor. "This ... is the essence of my whole outlook on these problems," he told the Senate Foreign Relations subcommittee: "that we are running into an increasingly ugly and dangerous situation, and that it is worth a great deal of effort and some boldness on our part to try to avoid it."[42]

The situation in Berlin appeared particularly explosive on November 10, 1958, when Khrushchev announced Moscow's intention to conclude a separate peace treaty with East Germany. The proposed accord would terminate the Western powers' occupation rights in the former German capital, a proposal that the West found intolerable. While many in the allied capitals accused the Russians of seeking to secure Berlin as part of a master plan of global expansionism, Kennan declared that the Soviet proposal reflected "serious political motives and interests, partly of a defensive nature," which were "not adequately explained merely by saying that it wants to conquer the world." In the absence of a negotiated settlement, Khrushchev sought to close off Berlin to the Western powers, who were exploiting their enclave in the city to encourage defections and instability in the German Democratic Republic.

Kennan had promoted disengagement to reunite Berlin and all of Germany and to loosen Soviet hegemony over the satellites, but he also sought to create a climate of stability that would make agreements on nuclear arms control possible. In his thinking, a Berlin settlement followed by disengagement of the great powers from Central Europe were essential prerequisites to arms control, which could not take place while such issues remained unresolved. The development of ICBMs and tactical nuclear weapons, now being placed in Europe as a result of the NATO decision, represented, in Kennan's judgment, "a mortally dangerous predicament" which had resulted from a "failure to think through the dilemmas of this suicidal weapon." He blamed the West for the arms race, which was now "virtually out of control," and argued that the Soviet nuclear research and development program had been "in significant degree the response to our own attitudes and policies in this postwar period."[43]

Kennan called for a stronger conventional military establishment and territorial militias as alternatives to the growing reliance on nuclear weapons under Eisenhower's New Look. The dependence on nuclear weapons had gathered such momentum, Kennan lamented in the wake of the allied decision to place warheads in Europe, that "any renunciation of these things would appear quite preposterous. . . . There will be no possibility of action except with the unanimous concurrence of a wide circle of governments having the most varied interests and motives."[44]

While publicly calling for no "first use" and arms limitation agreements, Kennan was less restrained and more gloomy in private. "I profoundly regret our use of the atomic weapon against the Japanese," he wrote Eugene Rabinowitz, editor of the *Bulletin of Atomic Scientists*. "This seems to me to have been a mistake of tragic import, for which I think it wholly possible that we or our children may some day suffer a ghastly retribution."

To Kennan nuclear weapons were more than merely the agents of Armageddon, though that, of course, was bad enough. Like the automobile, television, and twentieth-century urban-industrial society as a whole, the weapons of mass destruction symbolized the tyranny of modern technology and could only destroy, not enhance, the quality of human life. Nostalgic and pessimistic, Kennan had little faith in the ability of human beings, especially those in a democratic society, to control the forces of modernization and declared that he

> would be personally greatly relieved, for my children more than for myself, if every form of development of nuclear energy or explosives (including, that is, all the 'peaceful uses') were to be terminated everywhere and in permanence. . . . But I am not publicly calling for any such renunciation. I realize the momentum that is behind all this, and the imponderables

involved. I understand how many people are committed, and how deeply, to playing with these toys.[45]

The Reith Lectures represented Kennan's most concerted effort since 1948 to challenge the perceptions that fueled the cold war. In 1948 he had failed to convince his colleagues in government of the logic of disengagement, and a decade later had taken his case before the public —with the same results. Kennan had shown once again that his eloquent appeals could arouse a powerful response, but also that he no longer influenced Western national security policy. Although he would soon rejoin the U.S. diplomatic corps, the rejection of disengagement confirmed Kennan's status as an outsider and critic of American diplomacy.

Kennan's proposals prompted some official support but mostly thundering denunciations from American and Allied leaders. Conversely, the man who had once targeted the Soviet regime for destruction now found himself in substantial agreement with the Kremlin's official positions on disengagement and denuclearization. While Moscow applauded his aims, Kennan's former colleagues in the national security establishment condemned him for apostasy.

The call for European disengagement had prompted an ephemeral debate on the West's approach to the cold war, but distrust of the Soviet Union on the part of the men in power in Paris, Bonn, London, and Washington had been too great to allow for serious consideration of Kennan's ideas. The militarization of thinking in the West and the fears fostered by *Sputnik* and the Soviet ICBM program overwhelmed his call for a rethinking of the cold war in the wake of the death of Stalin and the emergence of a reformist, albeit bumptious, regime under Khrushchev. Obsessed with the prospect of a Soviet invasion of Europe, the NATO powers were not to be deterred from their decision to lodge tactical nuclear weapons in Western Europe. Many of the allies, and especially France, also remained fearful that German militarism would be renascent in the event of reunification, and thus opposed disengagement.

It is impossible to say whether Kennan's proposals could have established a new and more stable balance of power while ameliorating the plight of the East bloc of satellites, the arms race, and the dispute over Berlin. Negotiations would have been long and difficult and the divergent national interests of East and West may well have prevented a settlement. Clearly it would have been more practicable to have disengaged in the early postwar period, as Kennan pointed out at the time, rather than a decade later after so much had been done, in actions as well as in the hardening of attitudes, to cement the cold war consensus and the division of Europe. Both Kennan and Lippmann soon acknowledged that the postwar European status quo had gained such permanence that it could not be undone by the type of negotiations Kennan had proposed. Lippmann backed off of disengagement after a tour of Europe in 1958 and Kennan, too, admitted that it was too late by then.[46]

Kennan's proposals for German reunification may well have been unrealistic, but Soviet and allied officials could have agreed to widen the neutral zone in Europe and they should have perceived the futility of extending the nuclear arms race onto European soil. While Soviet intentions cannot be known because of the unavailability of diplomatic records, in its public statements Moscow had a better record than the West. Khrushchev showed a willingness to explore neutralization and a nuclear-free zone but officials in Washington and the Allied capitals refused even to consider such proposals. Their rejection of negotiations perpetuated a depressing personal irony for Kennan, as the Western leaders clung to the perceptions of the Soviet adversary that had governed the Long Telegram and the X-Article. They showed little interest in any arrangement that stopped short of a virtual Soviet capitulation to Western demands, a posture that Kennan was now fully justified in castigating as unrealistic.

The rejection of disengagement ensured that Germany would remain divided and Eastern Europe Soviet-controlled for the foreseeable future. Stability in Berlin was bought at the price of freedom when Khrushchev ordered construction of the Berlin Wall in August 1961. The arms race not only continued but actually gained momentum as the Democratic Party made an arms buildup to close a fictional "missile gap" one of its chief issues in the late 1950s and in the 1960 presidential campaign.[47]

With the failure of disengagement, Kennan finally admitted defeat on the unification of Germany issue and in the future devoted his energies to advocating détente and nuclear arms control. He was far from sanguine about the prospects of achieving accord, however, and his thinking on international affairs for the next thirty years revolved around fears that nuclear war could happen. "The atom is capable, in the end, of destroying every rational consideration, even every political consideration, in favor of the impulses of an unreasoning fear," he warned. "Was not last autumn," he asked in the wake of the rejection of disengagement and the NATO decision to expand the arms race in Europe, "perhaps really the last point at which there was even a faint possibility that our predicament might have been taken in hand and altered by any single human will or any circle of human wills?" Haunted by the threat of nuclear war, Kennan saw "the walls of possibility narrow around the tiny human figures."[48]

X

New Frontier, Old Problems

Kᴇɴɴᴀɴ ʟᴏɴɢᴇᴅ to return to government service under the Kennedy administration in 1961 despite his last unhappy experience as ambassador to Moscow and the divergence between his views and those of the foreign affairs establishment. Supporters helped Kennan overcome opposition and Kennedy appointed him ambassador to Yugoslavia. Kennan took charge of the American mission in Belgrade and strove to forge closer ties with the Tito regime in hopes that it might serve as a model of independent national communism in Eastern Europe. Unable to abide the democratic political process in the United States, Kennan resigned over ill-conceived congressional economic sanctions against Yugoslavia. He blamed the influence of minority groups and advocates of liberation for Washington's pursuit of unrealistic objectives in the cold war. The Yugoslav ambassadorship brought an end to Kennan's Foreign Service career and compounded his doubts about the ability of the United States to conduct a mature foreign policy.

Following the rejection of disengagement Kennan completed his visiting professorship at Oxford and returned to the United States to pursue a successful career as a historian. Insisting that he had "said all I want to say" on contemporary diplomatic issues, Kennan resolved to study the past and remain mute about the present, a promise that he could not keep.[1] Already the retired diplomat's two-volume study of Russian-American relations from 1917 to 1920, published in 1956 and 1958, had earned him acclaim and a Pulitzer Prize. Kennan continued to employ realism as the guide to sound diplomacy and condemned the type of idealism that had led President Woodrow Wilson to embrace the illusion that democracy might triumph in authoritarian Russia. In the first volume of his study, *Russia Leaves the War,* he concluded that America's response to the Bolshevik revolution "illustrate[d] the infinite possibilities for misunderstanding, confusion, intrigue, and malevolent exploitation that are always present when inexperienced people . . . are permitted to dabble in the transactions between governments."[2]

Most reviewers welcomed the book. "The experienced foreign service officer is evident throughout," *Foreign Affairs* observed, "not only in the intimate feeling for the ways of international affairs but also in the acute, and often wry, recognition of familiar patterns of diplomatic behavior." Historian Dexter Perkins predicted that the book would have "a substantial and lasting value," but noted Kennan had become "unduly involved in the minutiae of the period." Cold war revisionist historian William A. Williams pointed to Kennan's preoccupation "with the undemocratic aspects of the Soviet government" and declared that he had assumed but not established the inveterate hostility of the Bolsheviks toward the West. "Kennan would be far more accurate," Williams declared, "if he referred to the leadership in Washington when he spoke of a government that had no intention of exploring the alternatives to unmitigated antagonism between the West and the Bolsheviks."[3]

In his second volume, *The Decision to Intervene,* Kennan assembled a mountain of evidence to bolster his conclusion that the allied intervention in Russia "could not . . . have been more confused, more futile, or more misleading." As with the first volume, the editors of *Foreign Affairs* declared, "an extraordinarily complex story is developed with great skill, scholarship and reflective analysis." The book was "great drama" and showed "remarkable deftness as an exposition of the processes of foreign affairs," the *New York Times* declared.[4]

While Kennan's monographs showed little reluctance to criticize Western governments for their limited understanding of Russia, his enmity for Soviet communism, as Williams pointed out, had undergone little revision. In *Russia and the West Under Lenin and Stalin,* a compilation of lectures published in 1961, Kennan embraced the traditional interpretation that Moscow's ideological pretensions, secrecy, and cynicism had provoked the cold war. Stalin's Great Purge, the Nazi-Soviet Pact, and the manipulation of Western Communist parties had destroyed any hope for normal relations. Kennan's essays were "brilliant, bold, and in some respects, baffling," wrote Herbert Feis, who shared Kennan's interpretation of the origins of the cold war but observed that in several instances "the author's meaning is difficult to discern because of skilled indirection of expression." Similarly, Edmund Wilson judged *Russia and the West* "one of the most important books" to have appeared since World War II, but added that careless writing had left "Mr. Kennan's expression sometimes limping behind his intellect."[5]

Most critics found Kennan's failures insignificant in comparison to his contributions and these books enhanced his reputation as one of America's top academic experts on Russia. In little more than a decade he had achieved critical success as a historian and received myriad offers from the nation's finest universities. While still affiliated with the Institute for Advanced Study at Princeton, Kennan lectured at Harvard and Yale. "I liked the academic life," he declared after returning to government in 1961, "but I became tired and stale writing in solitude. I missed diplomacy."[6]

Although critical of America's democratic society and the manner in which the nation conducted diplomatic relations, Kennan longed to rejoin the foreign affairs establishment despite his iconoclastic views. "America is the only thing we belong to," he explained to a group of intellectuals in May 1958. "We—the eggheads, the esthetes, the expatriates, the people who don't even know or care who's ahead in the American League—we have to recognize that in serving [the people], we are performing the best service we can to the things we care about." He declared that he was ready to "trot right back into the ring, like an old circus horse, do the old tricks, and pretend to like it and even to be hopeful about it," but in reality Kennan found it impossible to sustain such a deferential attitude.[7]

As the Democratic Party campaigned to reclaim the White House after Eisenhower's two terms, Kennan tried to rehabilitate his own image, which had been tarnished in the eyes of many Democrats after his twin heresies of pronouncing the finality of Soviet domination of Eastern Europe and calling for great-power disengagement. Although he was respected for his knowledge and expertise, many agreed with Acheson that Kennan, too far removed in the ivory tower of academe, had a "mystical" attitude and failed to understand "power relationships."[8] Moreover, in the wake of Stevenson's two humiliating defeats, the Democrats were not inclined to turn again to the former Illinois Governor who had been Kennan's chief benefactor.

The surprising choice of the Democratic Party in 1960 was Senator John F. Kennedy of Massachusetts, a Catholic whose father had been a confidant of Franklin D. Roosevelt. Although Kennedy was a war hero who claimed intellectual credentials—partly on the basis of his Pulitzer Prize-winning, but ghostwritten, *Profiles in Courage*—many resented the young patrician's rise to prominence. Expressing a "sense of bewilderment" early in the Democratic campaign, Kennan told Stevenson that "I used to have my ideas about the sort of person we ought to seek for the Presidency, but if it is royalty we are to elect, I am uncertain." After scoring a critical primary victory in West Virginia, Kennedy was on his way to a first-ballot nomination.[9]

Kennan first met JFK in 1938 when Ambassador Joseph P. Kennedy had arranged for his twenty-one-year-old son to tour the European capitals and Kennan received instructions to arrange the schedule of the young man whom he characterized at the time as an "ignoramus." When Kennan next heard from Kennedy the latter was a U.S. Senator who wrote that he had "read in full your Reith Lectures [and] I should like to convey to you my respect for their brilliance and stimulation and to commend you for the service you have performed." Although opposed to disengagement, Kennedy applauded the "comprehensive and brilliantly written set of alternative proposals and perspectives," adding that he deplored the "personal criticisms" leveled at Kennan.[10]

JFK sent another approving letter following Kennan's attempt to rehabilitate himself in the eyes of the cold war establishment by publishing an essay in the January 1960 issue of *Foreign Affairs* that was critical of Nikita S. Khrushchev's call for "peaceful coexistence." The Soviet leader had blamed the West for blocking improved relations—a position with which Kennan had agreed in the Reith Lectures—but the Soviet expert now blamed Russia for the perpetuation of the cold war. Moscow's domination of Eastern Europe, its promotion of "the science of insurrection" around the world, and its "irresponsible attitude toward objective fact" were the main impediments to peaceful coexistence. Although he often expressed his contempt for democracy in private, Ken-

nan asserted in the published essay that America's "liberal institutions
. . . embody something that lies close to the essence of human dignity"
and were among "the most precious attainments of civilized man."[11]

Following Kennedy's nomination, Kennan sent the candidate a long,
unsolicited letter of advice on world affairs that reflected Kennan's
efforts to position himself to receive a presidential appointment in the
event of a Democratic victory in November. He advised Kennedy that
the failure of the May 1960 U.S.-Soviet summit in Paris, which Khrushchev had aborted after disclosing that his country had shot down an
American U-2 spy plane, signaled a new hard line on Moscow's part.
The incident occurred in the midst of a dispute between Russia and
China over whether to pursue a strident campaign against "Western
imperialism" or Khrushchev's peaceful coexistence. "The U-2 incident
simply undermined Khrushchev's personal position, increased Chinese
influence within the bloc, and tipped the scales of Soviet policy-making,
for the moment, in the direction of acquiescence in standing Chinese
demands," Kennan told JFK. "The Russians have shown themselves,
since the U-2 and the summit breakdown, prepared to play much closer
than before to the edge of military conflict."

Reversing the argument he had offered in *Foreign Affairs,* Kennan
now once again put the onus on the Eisenhower administration, rather
than Khrushchev, for the failure to achieve détente and he advised
Kennedy to stress this issue in his campaign. The Republicans, he argued, had failed "to give Khrushchev sufficient support to enable him to
hold his own against contrary opinion within the [communist] bloc and
within his own entourage in Russia." Preoccupied with "such things as
solidarity with brother Adenauer, or such military information as the U-
2 flights could produce," Eisenhower had ignored "the favorable possibilities which Khrushchev's attitude did, after all, provide." Kennan
believed that Khrushchev's position as leader of the communist world
had been "seriously shaken, but not finally destroyed."

With the Soviet Union now attempting to maintain bloc solidarity by
sounding a bellicose line, Kennan advised "a quiet but unmistakeable
strengthening of our armed forces, particularly the conventional ones."
He urged "a prompt strengthening of the Marine Corps" and other
special forces, thus encouraging military reforms that soon distinguished
Kennedy's "New Frontier." Insisting that the United States remained
"greatly overextended," Kennan advised removing the new medium-

range missiles from Europe and dropping the defense of Quemoy and Matsu, "portraying our action as a generous contribution to the peace of the area." Such unilateral actions, as opposed to summit meetings or complex treaties, would be understood by the Russians and might allow Khrushchev to reassert the primacy of détente. Just before the November election JFK wrote that he had "profited greatly" from Kennan's advice, although the Democratic nominee had chosen to criticize Eisenhower and Nixon in strident tones for being too soft on communism rather than for failing to pursue détente, as Kennan had recommended.[12]

Through his correspondence with Kennedy and over the course of the presidential campaign, Kennan gained respect for the young Democrat's intellect as well as his emphasis on national service and the call to "get the country moving again." Putting aside his disdain for democratic politics, Kennan campaigned for JFK in the latter stages of the race and wrote letters in support of Kennedy and critical of Vice President Richard Nixon, the Republican nominee. The *New York Times* declined to print a letter from Kennan (it was too long and he refused to trim it) in which he charged Nixon with advocating a "double standard" by justifying the U-2 flight over Russia. "He would claim the right to do to others what we would not be prepared to permit others to do to us," Kennan explained.[13]

Despite his correspondence with Kennedy and his not inconsiderable efforts to position himself for an appointment in the new administration, Kennan had sunk into gloom by the end of the year after having heard nothing from the President-elect and his newly appointed Cabinet and advisers. "I can regard it only as a sign of deliberate repudiation" as a result of the disengagement debate, he wrote Lippmann, adding that he no longer intended to take part in public discussion of foreign affairs and held out no hope that Kennedy might make use of his services. Despite these statements, the letter could certainly have been read as an appeal to Lippmann to intercede on Kennan's behalf with the new administration.[14]

The disengagement debate had indeed undermined support for Kennan within the Democratic establishment, but friends interceded and secured a place for him. Kennedy himself had expressed interest in offering Kennan a position even before the narrow victory in November but, as he told Cyrus Sulzberger of the *New York Times*, "since George is involved with things like disengagement" he would be reluctant "to mention his name at this time." Whether Lippmann interceded is not known, but after the election California newspaper editor C. K. McClatchy did approach Adlai Stevenson, the new UN ambassador, in Kennan's behalf. "Writing without George's knowledge," McClatchy, who knew Kennan from Stevenson's previous campaign, asked "whether you have heard any plans afoot to use George Kennan in the new administration?" Although no one had approached Kennan, there was "no question" that he would like to return to government "if he is wanted," McClatchy wrote. "There is always the possibility," he added, "that a decision has been made not to use him, especially if Mr. Acheson really does have Mr. Kennedy's ear."[15]

McClatchy followed his letter to Stevenson with a phone call in which he recommended Kennan's appointment as the next ambassador to Yugoslavia. The newspaperman declared that Kennan "would be interested in doing anything that the new administration cares to have him do" but explained that Kennan "has a lot of friends and contacts" in Yugoslavia, "so what about Ambassador to Yugoslavia if nothing else turns up?"[16] The Belgrade ambassadorship was ideal for Kennan, who had long viewed Yugoslavia's independent national communism as a paradigm for Eastern Europe, and who had already established cordial relations with President Josip Broz Tito, who had welcomed him in Belgrade during a lecture tour the previous summer.

A few days after McClatchy's intervention on Kennan's behalf, Kennedy invited the diplomat to accompany him on a flight from New York to Washington and the two discussed foreign affairs and presidential appointments. On January 23 JFK called Kennan at Yale and offered him the post of ambassador to either Poland or Yugoslavia and Kennan accepted the latter. He declared that he looked forward to working with the President's new team but in fact he resented the weeks of silence and absence of support from Dean Rusk, the new Secretary of State, and Assistant Secretary George Ball. "They would not have selected me and they were not interested in what happened to me," he later declared.[17]

Despite the disengagement debate and the controversy over his last ambassadorial appointment, Kennan encountered little opposition to his nomination in Congress. Appearing before the Senate Foreign Relations Committee, he called for policies aimed at maintaining Yugoslavia's "maximum independence from the Soviet Union" and insisted that American aid should not have "a political price tag." If the Yugoslavs were "able to maintain true independence and conduct their foreign affairs so as to make it possible for us to cooperate with them," he declared, the divergence between the ideologies of the two nations was not sufficient reason for strained relations. Both the SFRC and the full Senate unanimously approved Kennan's nomination in early March and the diplomat told the press as he prepared to depart for Belgrade that disengagement was no longer an issue and that he was "very happy at this time to merge my views" with the new administration. Thrilled by the turn of events, the town council in East Berlin, Pennsylvania, near Kennan's farm, christened a new firetruck the "Ambassador George Kennan."[18]

While Rusk and others lacked enthusiasm for Kennan's appointment, the Yugoslavs interpreted the selection of a man of his prestige "as a sign that Washington finally was realizing the importance of Belgrade in the world picture," the *New York Times* reported. "The Yugoslavs were extremely cordial, and I think they were pleased with my assignment there," Kennan recalled. After arriving on March 8, he met with Marshal Tito, sixty-nine years old at the time and Yugoslavia's ruler since 1944. Tito appreciated Kennan's knowledge of European and Soviet affairs as well as his sensitivity to Yugoslavia's unique position in the communist world. Both Tito and Kennan were, at various times, public advocates of disengagement in Europe and both shared the desire to capitalize on Khrushchev's moderate tendencies.[19] Since assuming power after leading the wartime resistance to the Nazis, Tito had marshaled authority in a state which had existed only since World War I and whose tensions between competing nationalities and surrounding great powers were notorious. Twenty million people in six constituent republics inhabited Yugoslavia, one of the most beautiful countries in Europe. The U.S. mission over which Kennan was to preside included the embassy, two consulates, and a staff of 114.

Once a loyal Stalinist, Tito had rejected the Soviet model in 1948, an action that prompted Yugoslavia's ouster from the communist international and led Kennan to recommend at the time that the Truman Administration support Belgrade's independence. By the early 1950s, the United States had provided Yugoslavia with millions of dollars in economic and military aid to bolster its security and independence from the Kremlin.[20] After Stalin's death, Khrushchev forged a rapprochement with Tito in Belgrade in 1955 at which time he endorsed Yugoslavia's moderate reforms. The Eisenhower administration provided military and economic assistance even after Tito drew closer to Russia during a state visit to Moscow in 1956 and not even the Yugoslav leader's approval of the repression in Hungary swayed the Republican administration from trade relations with Belgrade. Several members of Congress complained, however, that Yugoslavia's "nonalignment" actually disguised a tilt toward Moscow and they secured passage of legislation restricting American military aid in 1956 and 1957. Eisenhower restored the aid provisions, but Tito himself abrogated the military agreement in the wake of the controversy in December 1957.[21]

Kennan and his Kennedy Administration colleagues sought to maintain normal relations with Yugoslavia in order to encourage polycentrism in the communist world, but they faced opposition in Congress and among Yugoslav exile groups which called for the overthrow of Tito's government. An anti-Tito policy was not only unrealistic, in Kennan's view, but would actually encourage unity rather than exploit differentiation in Eastern Europe. Whereas opponents of a moderate policy toward Yugoslavia branded the regime a typical communist dictatorship, Kennan deemphasized ideology and respected Tito's authoritarianism.[22]

Overt efforts to promote liberation and "legalistic-moralistic" declarations such as the annual "Captive Nations Week" resolution would succeed only in driving Yugoslavia and other nations of Eastern Europe closer to the Soviet Union, Kennan argued. Criticizing "the tyranny which the exile groups and the right-wing elements in both parties have heretofore exercised over the formulation of policy toward Eastern Europe," the diplomat urged the new administration to terminate the practice of declaring Captive Nations Week in June of every year. Congress had passed the first such resolution in 1953 and the Eisenhower Administration had professed its support for liberation every year since, but Kennan considered the declarations foolish and gratuitously offensive to Moscow. Included among the official list of "captive nations" were Ude-Ural and Cossackia, entities whose claims to independence stemmed from Nazi propaganda during the German invasion of Russia. Following Kennan's advice that Captive Nations Week represented "an unsound commitment" which could "hardly lead to anything other than misinterpretation," the administration at first decided to dispense with the annual ritual but Kennedy reversed his decision to avoid controversy and proclaimed the declaration in June 1961.[23]

While Kennan viewed the Captive Nations Resolution as another example of domestic political considerations undermining foreign policy, the issue was minor compared with a series of crises that carried the threat of war with Russia. The first year of the Kennedy Administration witnessed the sharpest U.S.-Soviet tensions since the Korean War as East-West conflicts surfaced in Berlin, Cuba, and the jungles of Laos and Vietnam. Before departing for Belgrade, Kennan joined JFK, Vice President Lyndon Johnson, Rusk, National Security Adviser McGeorge Bundy, Soviet Ambassador Llewellyn Thompson, and advisers Charles Bohlen and Averell Harriman for White House strategy sessions on means of defusing the crises while combating the Soviet and Chinese calls for "wars of national liberation."[24]

Opposed to summit conferences on principle, Kennan winced when he read transcripts in Belgrade of Kennedy's meeting with Khrushchev in Vienna in June 1961. Apparently the President had not been inspired by his reading of Kennan's *Russia and the West Under Lenin and Stalin* on the plane to Vienna, for the diplomat concluded that JFK "had not acquitted himself well" in response to Khrushchev's verbal assaults and had permitted the Soviet leader "to say many things which should have been challenged right there on the spot." While he was disappointed in Kennedy, Kennan encouraged the administration to pursue further negotiations and opposed the President's decision in the wake of the failed summit to terminate back-channel communications that Kennan had opened with the Soviet Ambassador to Yugoslavia, Aleksy Yepishev. A partisan of such informal communications, which he had employed in 1951 in an unsuccessful effort to stop the fighting in Korea, Kennan had hoped that the talks with Yepishev could contribute to resolving the Berlin and Laotian conflicts. "I felt the administration missed a chance," he recalled.[25]

The conflict over Berlin, which had long been anticipated by Kennan and upon which he based, in part, his advocacy of disengagement, came in the first months of the Kennedy administration. Terrified by the prospect of war with Russia, Kennan returned to Washington before Khrushchev resolved the crisis by ordering construction of the Berlin Wall. At the time Kennan told Kennedy adviser Arthur Schlesinger that he was "expendable" and that "the only thing I have left in life is to do everything I can to stop the war." After returning to Belgrade, Kennan rejected U.S. and allied statements blaming Russia for the impasse and now argued privately, as he had done publicly in the Reith Llectures, that the West's refusal to negotiate had left Moscow little choice but to take draconian action. The NATO demand for self-determination throughout Germany without a compensatory allied military withdrawal from West Germany may have been justified in moral terms, he allowed, but it was "not a realistic demand" because it required a unilateral Soviet withdrawal from Central Europe. Kennan declared that it should have been clear that "unless the West shows *some* disposition to negotiate," Moscow would pursue a "hard line . . . not only to the very brink but to the full point of a world catastrophe."[26]

In contrast to his revisionist perspective on the Berlin crisis, Kennan adopted a nationalist response to both the Bay of Pigs and Cuban Missile crises and showed no inclination to view those events from either the Cuban or Soviet perspective. Vacationing in Milan during the missile crisis, Kennan returned to Belgrade to defend Kennedy's Cuban diplomacy in a "briefing for Americans." His depiction of Fidel Castro's regime as "one of the bloodiest dictatorships [the] world has seen in entire postwar period" was a gross oversimplification of the Cuban revolution and Kennan falsely described the Bay of Pigs invasion as a grassroots exile movement. "What was [the] alternative?" he asked. "To forbid these people to move?" Blame for the Cuban missile crisis rested squarely with Moscow, he asserted, arguing that American missiles in Turkey offered no parallel because that nation had never been part of the Russian sphere of influence whereas Cuba had always been part of Washington's. "I have no apologies to make, and none of you need have, for what we have done," he declared after American ships instituted a blockade in the Caribbean. Still committed to upholding the nation's credibility against communism, Kennan asserted that Kennedy's brinkmanship was the only alternative to appeasement and compared the Cuban crisis to the "Nazi entrance into [the] Rhineland" in 1936. "How could people have confidence in our seriousness about [the] defense of Europe if we failed to take action in our own backyard?"[27]

The crises in Cuba, Berlin and Southeast Asia and the growing rift inside the communist world itself undermined Kennan's diplomacy in Belgrade. As China criticized Tito's moderate socialism and supported his hostile neighbor in Albania, the Yugoslav leader closed ranks with Moscow. Tito displayed his solidarity in 1961 by joining Khrushchev in denunciations of the Bay of Pigs invasion, supporting the Soviet position on Berlin, and initiating trade with Castro's regime. The administration responded to mounting congressional unrest by suspending export licenses and slowing trade with Yugoslavia.[28]

Tensions escalated when the Kremlin terminated a three-year-old moratorium on atmospheric testing of nuclear weapons and Yugoslavia hosted a conference of 25 "nonaligned" nations in Belgrade. As the Soviets contaminated a portion of Central Asia with a nuclear test blast on September 1, Tito opened the Belgrade Conference by denouncing the "fallacy" that the nonaligned nations supported either Washington's or Moscow's foreign policy. He called for a world disarmament conference and a superpower summit but criticized the "aggressive [U.S.] intervention in Cuba," advocated the seating of China in the UN, and called for great-power withdrawal from Berlin followed by German unification and demilitarization.[29]

Tito's proposals on Germany mirrored Kennan's own in the Reith Lectures, as well as the position still formally advocated by Moscow, but because the United States had rejected disengagement while the Soviets had not, American officials concluded that Tito was toeing the Soviet line. The Yugoslav leader's refusal to support an allied proposal for an atmospheric test ban agreement or to denounce the Soviet resumption of tests even as he criticized the West angered Kennan and other administration officials. Taken as whole, Tito's performance at the Belgrade conference, at a time of high tensions over construction of the Berlin Wall and the resumption of atmospheric tests, appeared decidedly unneutral to Western observers. Washington issued a formal protest, withdrew an offer for Tito to visit the United States, and ordered a review of economic relations with Belgrade.[30]

Tito's actions stung Kennan, who took the criticisms of the West as a personal affront. Tito had made himself unusually accessible to Kennan during the diplomat's first months in Belgrade and the two men—both proponents of authoritarianism and steeped in the traditions of old world dignity and charm—had enjoyed each other's company and expressed similar views on many issues. Although Kennan admired Tito's "distinguished qualities," he declared that the communist leader's "strong ideological tendencies" placed barriers in the path of the American-

Yugoslav relationship and complained that while the Yugoslavs requested economic assistance, in their next breath they advocated "the earliest possible dismantling of America's world position." He hoped that his ambassadorship would contribute to understanding so that "the great chasm of outlook may some day be bridged."[31]

Kennan resented the anti-Western tone of Tito's speeches at the Belgrade Conference because they were heard by the world press and the nonaligned representatives, for whose support both East and West competed. He complained to Yugoslav Vice President Mijalko Todorovic and, as he took an honored position next to Tito at dinner following the annual hunt for chiefs of diplomatic missions, expressed his displeasure directly to the Yugoslav president. Kennan, who took daily lessons in Serbo-Croatian and assiduously read the morning newspapers in Belgrade, also wrote letters to the editor charging the papers with misrepresenting American positions. The communist editors refused to print the letters but the party sheet *Borba* invited Kennan to a dinner and exchange of views. "The Yugoslavs have learned," one embassy diplomat told *Time*, "that Kennan won't allow the U.S. to be pushed around. Some of his predecessors just shrugged and said, 'Well, it's a communist country, and they don't like us.' Kennan's not like that, and now that they know it they have begun to show him extreme friendliness, deference and interest."[32]

Kennan appreciated the Yugoslavs' willingness to pay attention to his remonstrances, in marked contrast to the behavior of the Soviets in his last ambassadorship, and he was willing to make some allowances for Tito's anti-Western remarks in view of the Sino-Soviet split and China's support for Albania. Kennan concluded that he had defended his government against Tito's charges during the Belgrade Conference and the matter should be dropped in deference to ensuring Yugoslav security and independence from Moscow through closer ties with the West. Since his protests after the Belgrade Conference, Kennan advised Hamilton Fish Armstrong, "the U.S. has been treated with much more restraint in the Yugoslav press than had been the case for months, and I think years, prior thereto." In November Kennan assisted Belgrade in the purchase of additional U.S. wheat needed as a result of a drought in the country and the Yugoslavs appreciated his intervention and responded "with a series of friendly gestures."[33]

The relative openness in Yugoslavia was a refreshing contrast to the paranoid Stalinist atmosphere under which Kennan had languished in Moscow. Yugoslav socialism allowed for economic reforms, only limited collectivization of agriculture, religious toleration, relatively few political prisoners, and open borders, except with Albania. Belgrade allowed large U.S. information and aid missions to function, tolerated the sale of Western newspapers and magazines, declined to ban foreign broadcasts, and saw no need to impede the American ambassador's frequent strolls and travels in the countryside. "The first months of service have been a stimulating and enjoyable experience," Kennan told a friend. "The political differences are deep-seated . . . but aside from politics, people and country are wonderful, and life—full of interest."[34]

Far removed from the spectacular Balkan countryside, Congress was less willing than Kennan to distinguish between communist nations, refused to forgive Tito's unneutral behavior at the Belgrade Conference, and was determined to implement economic sanctions that soon undermined Kennan's ambassadorship. As Tito planned another visit to Moscow in 1962 and ordered the arrest of Milovan Djilas, whose call for democratic-style reforms threatened the supremacy of the Yugoslav Communist Party, the Congress blocked the proposed U.S. sale to Belgrade of 130 outdated jet fighters otherwise destined for the scrap heap. Senators William Proxmire (D-Wisc.) and Frank J. Lausche (D-Ohio) secured passage of an amendment to the Foreign Assistance Act of 1962 denying the President discretionary power to allocate surplus commodities as foreign aid and the House Ways and Means Committee contemplated a proposal to deny the President the authority to grant Most Favored Nation trade status to communist countries. The actions threatened to undermine the administration's efforts to aid Yugoslavia to facilitate its independence from Moscow and to promote schisms in the communist world.[35]

Congressional leaders who supported the economic sanctions argued that it was senseless to assist Tito, whom they viewed as a loyal proponent of Soviet diplomacy, as he attempted to undermine Western positions throughout the world. Noting that Tito had endorsed the repression in Hungary as well as Moscow's line on Cuba and Berlin, Senator Thomas Dodd (D-Conn.) charged that "the posture of ostensible independence from Soviet control has enabled Tito to serve the international purposes of the Kremlin far more effectively than he could have served it as an open lackey" and declared that Washington should not "help the tyrants forge more strongly on their subjects the bonds of dictator-ship." Denouncing Tito's "cheek to jowl collaboration with Khrush-chev," Proxmire asserted that the Yugoslav president's leadership of the nonaligned movement was "greatly serving international communism by proselytizing newly emerging countries in Asia and Africa."[36]

Kennan was unable to restrain his contempt over the congressional "meddling" in foreign policy. Opposed to the economic sanctions, he declared that he "would never play politics with Yugoslav stomachs" and insisted that the real issue was not one of aid or no aid to Yugoslavia but whether the executive branch would be allowed "sufficient latitude to handle intelligently and effectively a delicate problem of international affairs, and one which has the widest implications for our approach to the problem of world communism generally."[37]

He found it galling that he had received no forewarning of the congressional amendment to the Foreign Assistance Act. By the time Kennan learned of the action it was already a *fait accompli* and Yugoslav officials "acted incredulous" when he told them he had been unaware that the amendment was under consideration. After notifying Belgrade of the sanctions, Kennan sent a long memorandum to Washington in which he argued the merits of "continuing patience, restraint and sub-tlety of approach" in contrast to the "appalling ignorance" displayed by the Congress.[38]

In typical fashion, Kennan's words soon had him at the center of controversy over U.S. diplomacy. Kennedy took the unusual step of allowing Kennan and John Moors Cabot, the ambassador to Poland, to make public their opposition to the amendment to the Foreign Assis-tance Act. "Both of them regard this action as a major setback and a great asset to Moscow," the President explained. "I don't think we should do those favors for them if we can help it." The State Department allowed the diplomats to release their memoranda on the issue and granted Kennan's request to return to Washington to lobby for revoca-tion of the amendment. By the time his plane touched down, however, members of Congress were seething over his published reference to their "appalling ignorance."[39]

In the first two weeks of July, Kennan was at the center of a White House campaign to assert executive authority over Congress in matters of U.S. foreign policy. The diplomat wrote letters to the *New York Times* and the *Washington Post* declaring that the "dramatic and vindictive" congressional amendments threatened to drive Yugoslavia into Moscow's camp. JFK arranged for Kennan to meet with key legislators in both chambers and the diplomat also traveled to Gettysburg to receive Eisenhower's public endorsement of administration policy. Ike's former Secretary of State, Christian Herter, who had replaced Dulles upon his death in 1959, also publicly endorsed maintaining strong economic ties with Yugoslavia.[40]

Kennan attempted to persuade legislators that the United States should not let its Yugoslav policy be dictated by that nation's communist ideology. He sympathized with the need for authoritarianism in the multiethnic Yugoslav state and saw no reason to suppose that an alternative regime would be more favorably disposed toward the West than Tito. Instead of focusing on ideology or internal practices, congressmen should recognize the "shattering effect" of Yugoslav independence on the Soviet rationale for its domination of Eastern Europe. "The fact that a socialist country has been able to apply a reasonably mature and liberal regime to contacts between its people and the Western countries, without finding itself subverted and ruined in consequence," he explained, "has made it much more difficult for Moscow to persuade the other Eastern European peoples that the iron curtain is really necessary."[41]

Admitting that Yugoslavia failed to meet Western standards of political freedom, Kennan argued that government repression would only increase if the West forced Belgrade to tilt toward the East. Appearing on NBC's *Today* show, he asserted that since the break with Moscow in 1948 Yugoslavia had sought greater "liberalization" and although the arrest of Djilas was a setback, "Djilas is one man, and if we are to regard the arrest of one man for political reasons as something that should affect our relations with other countries, I'm afraid we'd have to take a closer look at a lot of other countries besides Yugoslavia, and perhaps at some of our allies as well."[42]

Kennan urged J. William Fulbright, chairman of the Senate Foreign Relations Committee, to persuade his colleagues that while ideological differences set limits on the Belgrade-Washington relationship they were not sufficient cause to alienate Tito by denying his regime normal economic and trade relations with the West. Secretary of State Rusk and National Security Adviser Bundy joined Kennan in emphasizing that Yugoslavia conducted most of its trade with the West and was not a member of the Soviet satellite economic system, COMECOM. Yugoslavia conducted $39 million in trade with the United States in 1961. The U.S. should not "produce a state of affairs," Kennan declared, "in which the Yugoslavs would be compelled to look exclusively elsewhere for support in their natural and understandable desire for economic advancement."[43]

Kennan offered examples of Yugoslavia's history of nonalignment and pointed to the strategic implications that would result from Belgrade's defection to the East. The diplomat credited Yugoslavia with having cooperated since World War II in resolving the Greek civil war, the dispute with Italy over Trieste, and the Austrian peace treaty. He insisted that Yugoslavia employed its huge land army, third largest in Europe, for defensive rather than offensive purposes. However, if Western actions drove the Yugoslavs into the Warsaw Pact, a hostile coalition would then extend to the Adriatic, where it would be more threatening to NATO members Italy and Greece.[44]

The Kennedy administration concluded early in the struggle with Congress that the limitation on American military and economic aid was less crucial than the proposal to deny Yugoslavia Most Favored Nation trade status. The MFN designation, pledged to virtually all nations outside of China and the Soviet bloc, stipulated that tariffs would not exceed those applied to any other (or the "most favored") trading partner. Yugoslavia had enjoyed the designation, Kennan pointed out, during the period when it had served as "a faithful Stalinist satellite," yet the Congress now threatened to take it away.[45]

The withdrawal of MFN would force Belgrade out of the General Agreement on Trade and Tariffs (GATT) which Washington had persuaded Yugoslavia to join as a provisional member in 1960 in an effort to pull the country toward the West. With some tariffs increasing 100 percent as a result of the withdrawal of MFN, officials estimated that 94 percent of Yugoslavia's exports to the United States would be priced out of the market. The action would leave Washington "in the most absurd of positions," Kennan advised Walter Lippmann: "namely, that of one who has loaned just enough to another government to help get it seriously indebted, and now moves to prevent it from earning by honest means the wherewithal to repay." Earning few dollars, Belgrade would be unable to meet its debts to the West and, Kennan argued, the economic hardships and enmity flowing from the withdrawal of MFN might compel Yugoslavia to orient its economy and diplomacy toward Russia.[46]

Already, as a result of congressional limitations on the shipment of new military equipment, Yugoslavia had expanded its trade in military hardware with Moscow. "They have now begun, as was to be expected, to acquire new equipment, including tanks and possibly planes, from the Soviet bloc," Kennan told Frederick G. Dutton, the assistant secretary of state in charge of congressional relations. "There are, I must assume, people in Washington who perceive some way in which our national interest is benefited by this state of affairs. I must confess myself unable to do so."[47]

Kennan complained to Harrison Salisbury of "the continued failure of the [New York] Times to give its readers adequate coverage of the Yugoslav situation" and wrote Lippmann in "near-despair" over the "indifference" of the American press to Tito's significance as a model for the Soviet satellites. Kennan charged that the media had failed to make an issue of the absence of a "coherent American policy" toward Eastern Europe out of its deference to the anti-communist right-wing. "Considerations of domestic-political advantage," he charged, had caused every administration since the war to advocate liberation in Eastern Europe despite their awareness that such a policy was unrealistic. "The result, of course, has been to irritate and repel the governments of Eastern Europe without bringing any effective relief to their respective peoples." Washington's policies toward Belgrade had provided "no encouragement to elements in other *bloc* countries who might wish to follow, in one respect or another, the recent Yugoslav example," Kennan declared. "This is why, seeing darkly for our relations with Yugoslavia, I also see darkly for our relations with Eastern Europe as a whole."[48]

Proponents of liberation in Congress and elsewhere had thus sacrificed, in Kennan's judgment, a realistic pattern of relations with Yugoslavia in favor of the "primitive concept" of seeking the overthrow of the Tito regime. At the same time, however, Kennan himself found it difficult to maintain his own realism in the face of ritual denunciations of the West in the Belgrade newspapers. Thus, as with Russia, Kennan could still be whipsawed by a communist "country of contradictions." "One day you get sore as hell at them and say, 'By God, the Congress is just about right'; and the next day you think, 'This is a great shame that we have to treat them this way because there are possibilities.'[49]

The arguments offered by Kennan and his colleagues influenced several legislators to withdraw their support of the economic sanctions, but many congressmen resented the administration's heavy-handedness and especially Kennan's intemperate remarks. Such feelings gave a hollow ring to the diplomat's belated call for "more of the spirit of partnership and less of suspicion and cross examination in our mutual exchanges on these subjects." Dodd complained that Kennan had painted the Senate as a bunch of ignoramuses" and he and Proxmire decried taxpayer financing for what one newspaper called the "unprecedented use of an Ambassador" in a domestic political fight. Rep. Thomas Curtis (D-Missouri) declared that "ambassadors should be envoys to foreign countries" rather than "lobbyists at home for State Department partisan programs." Another representative, scoring Kennan's support of Tito's "notorious communist regime," cited containment and the Reith Lectures as evidence that "the record of Mr. Kennan on foreign policy reflects a continuity of failures with respect to the Russian problem." The administration defended Kennan's role, however, as a spokesman told the press that "if we had more ambassadors willing to take up the cudgels in behalf of what they feel to be the nation's best interests, we'd be better off."[50]

Representative Wilbur Mills (D-Ark.), chairman of the House Ways and Means Committee, presided as House and Senate conferees met to forge a compromise between administration and congressional positions over the Yugoslav economic sanctions. In the final agreement, Mills dropped the amendment to the Foreign Assistance Act but insisted on the withdrawal of MFN from any country "dominated or controlled by communism." Thus, Yugoslavia and Poland failed to qualify for MFN under terms of the Trade Expansion Act, which became law on October 4.[51]

Informed in Belgrade in late September of Mills' intention to withdraw MFN, Kennan called the White House for a personal conference with the President. Kennedy explained that an entire package of legislation would fail if he insisted on deletion of the MFN clause, or vetoed the bill, and that his presidency could not afford an open breach in executive-legislative relations. Unmoved by the realities of democratic politics, Kennan declared "that this places in jeopardy my success and my whole mission out here," whereupon Kennedy transferred the call to Mills, who bluntly informed Kennan that the action was final and the issue no longer merited discussion.[52]

The day after the telephone conversations, Kennan sent a wire advising Washington of his intention to resign. He agreed to wait until the summer of 1963 so as not to embarrass the administration by quitting in the midst of a controversy. The rupture in U.S.-Yugoslav trade "really shattered" all of his efforts at improving relations, Kennan told Robert Oppenheimer. "I cannot recall any instance of an action more drastically and needlessly destructive, or more utterly without positive rationale."[53]

Despite his decision to resign, Kennan and the administration had not given up the effort to sway congressional opinion and in December Kennedy asked Congress to restore MFN to Yugoslavia and Poland and to allow the sale of military spare parts. Appearing before a House subcommittee on national security operations, Kennan declared that he would not have gone to Belgrade in the first place had "I known how little value Congress would assign to my own judgment, in the light of an experience of nearly thirty years in the Eastern European area." He called for the creation of "something in the nature of a Prime Minister" for foreign policy to provide the executive with greater authority over the nation's diplomacy.[54]

Although some legislators defended Kennan's views, most attacked him for his elitism and impatience with Constitutional limitations. Senator Wayne Morse (D-Ore.) welcomed Kennan's resignation and declared that diplomats who shared his views "ought to line up" with resignations in hand. Rep. Bob Casey (D-Tex.) suggested that Kennan "refresh his memory on how this country got started. . . . I am a bit weary of diplomats, and others who are not responsible to the people of this country, assuming the role of papa knows best and saying that they alone know what is good for the people of the United States." Kennan took such commentary as evidence that Congress had "been a bit sobered" by his criticisms.[55]

Despite the angry words, by the spring of 1963 the Kennedy Administration had overcome congressional opposition and won narrow approval of an amendment to the Trade Expansion Act restoring the MFN designation to Poland and Yugoslavia. After two long talks with Kennan, Tito in April 1963 wrote a letter assuring Kennedy of his nonalignment and calling for improved relations. Despite his opposition to hasty summits—"the State Department of that day viewed visits, so far as I could observe, as a substitute for statesmanship," he later commented—Kennan helped arrange Rusk's brief tour of Yugoslavia in the spring and Tito's visit to the United States in October.[56]

Thus, Kennan's departure from Yugoslavia in the summer of 1963 came on a note of rapprochement between Washington and Belgrade. On May 16 the White House announced that Kennan would soon resign his post after 27 months on "long standing plans" to return to academic life and Kennedy accepted the resignation with "deep regret" while McGeorge Bundy encouraged Kennan to remain as an unpaid consultant to the government. The resignation of Kennan, 59 at the time, "will deprive the nation's diplomatic corps of one of its ablest men," the *New York Times* editorialized. Washington was "paying a high price . . . for the limitations of past Congressional understanding of Yugoslavia's complex role in world politics."[57]

Kennan kept up his Serbo-Croation studies and a busy schedule until the last day of his ambassadorship. A few days before his departure he sent a "fiery" letter which secured approval of a long-standing request for funding for a swimming pool in the U.S. embassy. Nostalgic for the prewar era in which no oppressive foreign affairs bureaucracies prevailed, Kennan resented the delay in obtaining funds for the pool and for rebuilding a fence around the embassy. He later complained before Congress of the government's failure to trust an ambassador with the "pocket money" he needed to make "minor dispositions affecting government property at his post, without waiting for approval."[58]

Popular with the staff and the junior officers at the embassy, Kennan and his family departed to a sea of "tear-stained faces." The mood had been made even more somber by reports of a major earthquake the day before at Skopje, to which Kennan had responded by leading a delegation to give blood at a local center. Before leaving the country on July 28, the Kennans said farewells to Tito on the president's island retreat at Brioni. Regretting the diplomat's departure, *Borba* declared that "Yugoslavia has a friend in George Kennan."[59]

Kennan's formal tenure as ambassador would not end until the last day of 1963 and in the event he had not said his last words on the subject of Yugoslavia. Responding to a direct request from JFK, Kennan agreed to greet and escort Tito upon his arrival in the United States for a state visit in mid-October.[60] Kennan and his wife met the Yugoslav delegation in Williamsburg, Virginia, where Tito stayed in close proximity to the remnants of America's colonial past but, more to the point, far away from Washington where exile groups protested his visit. After the Yugoslav president proceeded to the capital by helicopter, Croatian nationalists—to whom Tito was a symbol of Serbian domination of the country—hurled insults from beyond the White House grounds in an incident which left Kennan shaken and horrified. "The manner in which they had to be whisked in and out of the White House lawn by helicopter, with the Croatians screaming at them from the nearby park, was humiliating," he declared.

Despite the demonstration, Kennedy and Tito enjoyed a pleasant luncheon in the White House, where the President delivered a short speech drafted by Kennan. Although Tito and Kennedy had an "excellent" meeting, the Yugoslav president had been "shocked by the violence and the incessantly hostile demonstrations." Tito and Kennan, both authoritarians who were offended by the affronts to civility on the part of the demonstrators, agreed that it should be the obligation of the host government to repress such protests.

From Washington Tito proceeded to a UN meeting in New York, where mobs of exiles stalked his delegation. "New York was an absolute nightmare," Kennan reported to the U.S. embassy in Belgrade.

> The members of the staff of the delegation found themselves with not even a place to eat: they couldn't leave the hotel because of the constant presence of the hostile demonstrators, who in one case beat up three of them; and if they went down to the coffee shop, there were hostile Yugoslavs occupying other tables who immediately rose up, hissed at them, called the women prostitutes, and drove them back to their rooms.[61]

To Kennan, the controversy over economic relations and the actions of the exile groups offered still more evidence of the weakness of democratic foreign policy. At a time when the Sino-Soviet conflict had opened new fissures in the communist world, the United States had bowed to domestic pressure groups instead of capitalizing upon the opportunity to exploit polycentrism. Kennan charged that too many members of Congress, "terribly sensitive to the charge that they are not sufficiently anti-Communist," had used Yugoslavia "as a target for hostile sentiments with a view, then, to going back and confronting their electorate and beating their breast and saying: 'Boys, you see how anti-Communist I was; I told them where to head in.' "[62]

An emotional anti-communism—as manifested by Captive Nations Resolutions and economic sanctions—only foreclosed opportunities to undermine Soviet hegemony in the satellites, Kennan declared. "The effect of this closed door has been to convey to the peoples and governments of Eastern Europe that even if they wanted to liberate themselves from an exclusive association with the communist world, there was nothing in the West [with which] they could hope to associate themselves . . . which would not require in effect a revolution at home and an abrupt, provocative change of alliances."

Western policy, particularly with respect to Yugoslavia, had served to strengthen the hand of hardliners in the Soviet Union and the bloc countries, the same forces that were in the process of undermining Khrushchev.

> They were in a position to turn to their liberal opponents, particularly to those who talked about cultivating a better relationship with the West, and to say: Where do you think you're going? The Yugoslavs have gone five times as far in cultivating a good relationship with the West as you will ever be able to go. They have remained aloof from the Warsaw Pact. They follow an independent military line. They no longer associate themselves with communist subversive efforts anywhere in the western world. What happens to them? Are the imperialists grateful? Nonsense. The Americans spit in their face.[63]

Thus the nation's foreign policy was "paralyzed" by the very word "communism," which had become "sort of a fetish symbol," Kennan wrote in a *Look* magazine article.[64] In Cuba, Vietnam, and the Dominican Republic as well as in Yugoslavia, too many Americans assumed that "if a new communist state came into existence anywhere in the world, it would assuredly conform to . . . a pattern largely identical with the Eastern European communist state of the Stalin period." By adopting such a reactionary perspective, the United States had failed to exploit weaknesses in the Soviet world position that communist polycentrism had presented.[65]

Kennan refined these points in three essays published as *On Dealing With the Communist World* in 1964. Originally a series of lectures sponsored by the Council on Foreign Relations, the essays were "intended as a polemic against those attitudes towards the communist countries which have had such extensive currency in right-wing circles of both parties." One reviewer observed that the essays did not "break new ground" and "suffered somewhat from [Kennan's] frustrations as ambassador and his preoccupation with right-wing views," but few serious observers could challenge Kennan's fundamental point.[66]

Kennan had been a forceful advocate of a moderate approach to Yugoslavia and Eastern Europe during the course of his ambassadorship, but despite his criticism of the exile groups and right-wing proponents of liberation his differences with them were more a matter of style than substance, a dispute over means rather than ends. Like them, Kennan had not abandoned the quest for liberation in Eastern Europe as part of a larger effort to undermine Kremlin influence if not promote a domestic change inside Russia itself. "The element which Eastern Europe adds to Russian power still seems to me in many ways to constitute the hair on the head of Sampson," he explained in an argument that echoed the Long Telegram, X-Article, and his wartime essays. Western policy could still give the Russians a "haircut," but it was idle to strive for liberation by military means and by failing to exploit communist polycentrism.

As he prepared to resume his life as a scholar in the wake of his final departure from the State Department, Kennan joined the rest of the nation in mourning the assassination of Kennedy in Dallas on November 22, 1963. Proud to have returned to government as one of the knights of Camelot, and unaware of the events that would later tarnish that image, Kennan praised JFK's patriotism, his sense of duty to the nation and his handling of the Cuban missile crisis. Admitting that he had longed for more support from the President during the Yugoslav controversy, Kennan declared that JFK had not done enough to educate the American public about foreign policy but he still considered Kennedy of "Lincolnesque" stature—a man of "old-fashioned gallantry" and the "highest degree of personal integrity of character." Kennan lauded JFK's scholarly qualities and found him to be "the best listener I've ever seen in high position anywhere." Not since George Marshall's stewardship of the State Department had Kennan felt as comfortable with the leadership of American diplomacy. Only a month before the assassination, Kennan had told JFK that he did not think "we have seen a better standard of statesmanship in the White House in the present century."[67]

Kennan realized in the wake of his experience as Kennedy's ambassador to Yugoslavia that after twenty-nine years of service he could no longer play a useful role as a professional diplomat. "My own public philosophy is so wildly at odds with the one that dominates public discussions in this country, and inspires governmental actions, and is regarded as respectable," he confessed, "that I am at a loss to go about trying to reconcile these two things at all." Kennan assessed his ambassadorship, altogether too harshly, as "a failure" and the experience only compounded his doubts about America's "ability to deal successfully with many of the problems that we seem to be taking upon ourselves."[68]

The escalation of U.S. involvement in Vietnam tested the limits of Kennan's critique of American globalism and showed that his doubts about the nation's approach to world affairs were fully justified.

XI

Vietnam: Containment on the Perimeter, II

THE VIETNAM WAR forced Kennan to grapple with the conflict in his thinking between his quest to preserve American credibility and his declining faith in U.S. internationalism. As in Korea, Kennan's preoccupation with credibility and bandwagoning won out and found him supporting U.S. intervention even though he expressed strong doubts about the prospects for success. The retired diplomat advocated ideological-political containment and condemned the militarization of American policy in Southeast Asia, but in the end even ideological-political containment was a failed proposition. Although Kennan condemned the war in highly publicized Senate hearings in 1966, he stopped short of advocating U.S. military withdrawal until the Nixon Administration re-escalated the conflict. Ultimately, America's defeat in Vietnam led Kennan to abandon containment and embrace the perception that the United States was a declining power that lacked the ability to pursue a successful international diplomacy.

Kennan's resignation as ambassador to Yugoslavia in 1963 marked the end of his service as a professional diplomat and left him free to comment on public affairs and pursue his award-winning career as a historian and man of letters. He garnered both the National Book Award and a Pulitzer Prize for *Memoirs, 1925–1950*, a compelling autobiography published in 1967. Kennan contributed glimpses behind the scenes of American diplomacy at a time when many documents remained unavailable to researchers and offered rich character portraits of the men who had shaped American diplomacy. *Memoirs* was vintage Kennan—didactic, nostalgic, and reflective of the tension between realism and ethical and moral preoccupations. More than a book on American diplomacy, *Memoirs* was, as the National Book Award committee put it, a "work of rare art which, in illuminating the time and the man, reveals the complex fate it is to be an American today."[1] Kennan carried the story from his initial retirement in 1950 through the Yugoslav ambassadorship in a second volume of *Memoirs, 1950–1963,* published in 1972. It received less attention than the first but, as historian Richard W. Leopold observed, together Kennan's two volumes formed "one of the most outstanding memoirs of our time."[2]

Like all memoirs, Kennan's were highly subjective and in the first volume he did attempt to distance himself from the conflict that raged over the American attempt to contain communism in Southeast Asia. The retired diplomat confessed that the containment strategy he had propounded in the 1947 X-Article had "suffered, unquestionably, from serious deficiencies" and among these was the failure to explain that the "main task of containment" had been to safeguard Great Britain, the Rhine valley, Japan and, of course, the United States.[3]

While Kennan did identify Western Europe and Japan as the centerpieces of America's postwar internationalism, he advocated a global containment policy, including U.S. intervention in Southeast Asia. Indeed, as in the Korean War, Kennan's preoccupation with American prestige and credibility and fear of a bandwagon effect overshadowed his doubts about the nation's ability to function effectively as a world power and led him to support containment on the perimeter. Kennan did distinguish between "strongpoint" and peripheral regions in theory, but in practice his support for global containment rendered such distinctions meaningless.[4]

Kennan was among the leading State Department advocates of containment across the "great crescent" of Asia in the early cold war and he viewed the preservation of noncommunist regimes in Indochina as vital to ensuring the economic recovery and Western orientation of Japan. Success depended on the development of economic interdependence between Southeast Asia as a supplier of raw materials and Japan, Western

Europe, and India as suppliers of finished goods. As Kennan explained in a 1949 Policy Planning Staff report, although Southeast Asia was only of "secondary strategic importance" by itself, it had become "a vital segment on the line of containment" in overall U.S. policy toward Asia. If containment succeeded in Southeast Asia, he explained, "the links will exist for the development of an interdependent and integrated counter-force to Stalinism in this quarter of the world." He stressed the need for an American policy "to contain and steadily reduce Kremlin influence," thereby allowing the region "to develop in harmony with the Atlantic community." While it is now clear that Ho Chi Minh and his followers were first and foremost Vietnamese nationalists committed to over-throwing a legacy of Chinese hegemony and European colonialism, Kennan and his colleagues in the national security establishment per-ceived them as Kremlin puppets and agents of international commu-nism.[5]

The communist triumph in mainland China in 1949 reinforced the perception of monolithic communism and created a political uproar in the United States that virtually assured Kennan's and the Truman Ad-ministration's commitment to containment throughout Asia. In the wake of what he termed a "grievous political defeat" in China, the loss of Southeast Asia would constitute "a major political rout the repercus-sions of which will be felt throughout the rest of the world, especially in the Middle East and in a then critically exposed Australia."[6]

By 1949 Kennan recognized the futility of France's effort to recapture its colonial *grandeur* in Indochina as Ho and the Vietminh built popular support by appealing for a revolt against French colonialism. Although he described the Western position as being "in an advanced stage of deterioration," Kennan argued that the Vietminh communists might yet be defeated through the creation of a third force—a non-Communist nationalist regime to replace the French. Should France yield nominal sovereignty to a native regime, he reasoned, the noncommunists would no longer side with Ho against European colonialism and the popularity of the Vietminh would decline. In the likely event of a prolonged civil war between Ho and a noncommunist nationalist force, Kennan wrote, in a blueprint for American involvement in Vietnam, that the United States would ally with noncommunist Asians "to ensure, *however long it takes,* the triumph of Indochinese nationalism over Red imperialism." [emphasis added][7]

The government of emperor Bao Dai, which the United States recognized in February 1950, was hardly the sort of "third force" he had in mind but Kennan joined a broad consensus in Congress and the Truman Administration in support of the French war in Vietnam. Despite a lack of popular support for Bao Dai in Vietnam itself, the diplomat advised that it was sometimes necessary to "hang on to what appears to be a hopeless situation" because very often "it turns out in the end to be a very good thing that you did hang on and didn't get out. A situation is always subject to change."[8] The outbreak of fighting in Korea and Soviet and Chinese recognition of Ho's regime in 1950 reinforced Kennan's commitment to holding the line in Indochina.

The Eisenhower Administration's response to the French defeat at Dienbienphu in 1954 fueled doubts in Kennan's mind about the prospects for successful ideological-political containment in Indochina. The Southeast Asian Treaty Organization (SEATO), called into being by Eisenhower and Dulles to provide a basis for U.S. intervention in the wake of France's withdrawal from Indochina, underscored the militarization of U.S. foreign policy since 1948. "Many of us seem to be unable to get it through our heads," Kennan complained, "that this is not a pure military threat" and that what really mattered were "political attitudes" and the "subjective states of mind" of whole nations. "So far as the situation in Indochina is concerned," he declared in 1955, "I would share the blackest apprehensions of our most distinguished prophets of doom."[9]

The Republican administration was not guilty of ignoring the ideological-political dimensions of containment in Vietnam, as Kennan had charged. Eisenhower and Dulles employed propaganda, covert operations, and economic assistance as well as the SEATO alliance in a successful campaign to sabotage the Geneva Accords (unsigned by the United States), which called for Vietnam's unification through national elections in 1956. While the CIA promoted instability throughout the country, Eisenhower and Dulles inaugurated a program of "nation-building" in the southern half of Vietnam and installed as president an American-educated Catholic mandarin, Ngo Dinh Diem who, like Bao Dai, lacked popular support.

Fearful of a bandwagon effect and the blows to U.S. credibility that a communist triumph in Southeast Asia might unleash, Kennan remained committed to containment in the region and throughout the developing world. However, the retired diplomat had developed strong doubts about the ability of the United States to lead the global struggle or to offer an attractive alternative to communist ideology, whose theoretical advocacy of ending exploitation appealed to the leaders of many developing nations. The "main problem" of U.S. national security policy, he explained, remained finding ways "to keep other areas, now mostly non-European, from falling into the Soviet orbit," but Washington could not achieve this aim through intervention alone. "Urgently necessary" was nothing less than a new "strategic doctrine" which would enable the United States to offer an alternative model to counter the spread of communism.

Kennan's doubts about the prospects for successful containment in Vietnam and the developing world stemmed from his linkage of foreign policy and domestic society, a linkage that was pivotal in his thinking. Long critical of Western society, Kennan was now well on his way to the conclusion that the United States could not hope to implement containment because of its own internal weaknesses. His domestic critique and doubts about the efficacy of containment were on a collision course with his fears of a bandwagon effect and preoccupation with U.S. credibility. The turmoil Kennan experienced in attempting to resolve these conflicts manifested itself in the contradictory advice that he offered during the course of the escalating American intervention in Vietnam.

Preoccupied by his ambassadorship to Yugoslavia, Kennan had played no role as the Kennedy Administration expanded the numbers and responsibilities of American troops and advisors in an effort to combat the infiltration of "Vietcong" guerillas into "South Vietnam." These efforts failed to produce a stable government in Saigon, as the 1963 Buddhist crisis followed by the American-sanctioned ouster of Diem—as well as his unsanctioned assassination—graphically illustrated. After resigning the Belgrade ambassadorship in the summer of 1963, Kennan found the Vietnam situation "full of contradictions" and advised leaving policy in the hands of professional diplomats. "We have intelligent people there, and intelligent people backing them up in Washington," he explained.[10]

Hostile relations between Washington and Beijing reinforced the misperception—embraced by Kennan—that Vietnamese communism was an extension of mainland China's power. He warned that a Vietcong victory would signal the drawing of an Asian "iron curtain no less cruel

and unnatural from that which the Eastern European peoples are beginning to emerge." Although Beijing did support the Vietminh, China and
Vietnam were historic enemies, dating to an attempted Chinese assimila-
tion of Vietnam in 200 B.C., and by the end of the war ancient enmities
once again prevailed in the Sino-Vietnamese relationship.[11]

The perception of a Chinese guiding hand behind the struggle in
Vietnam points to the limitations of the impact of communist polycentrism on Kennan's thought. Despite his pronouncements on the decline
of monolithic communism during his Yugoslav ambassadorship, he now
exaggerated the power and influence of Mao's regime. Calling the Chinese
leaders "a group of embittered fanatics wedded to a dated and specious
ideology," Kennan asserted that the Chinese Communist Party represented "the most formidable problem American diplomacy has ever
faced" and empathized with those who wished to take the war directly
to Beijing.[12]

Kennan endorsed the expanded American role in Vietnam after President Lyndon Johnson exploited two incidents in the Tonkin Gulf—one
real and one imagined—to obtain congressional authorization for a
wider war.[13] Kennan criticized opponents of the war who would opt for
"a panicky and ignominious withdrawal that could only present our
adversaries with a gratuitous bonanza," yet he also warned that ultimately Washington could succeed only by establishing viable clients in
the developing world. "In general, there has been nothing wrong, *in any
of these areas* in recent years, with America's willingness to extend
support," he explained. "The problems have arisen in connection with
the ability of other people to make effective use of that support." [em-
phasis added][14]

The Johnson Administration shared Kennan's concerns about the
ability of the South Vietnamese to create a viable government, but the
military means by which it chose to lend Saigon support horrified Kennan. On February 6, 1965, in response to a Vietcong attack on U.S.
Army installations at Pleiku, Johnson ordered retaliatory air strikes
against the North, which soon intensified into the massive bombing
campaign codenamed Rolling Thunder, and called for more troops to
protect U.S. air bases and support facilities in Vietnam.[15] In Kennan's
thinking, the bombing campaign reflected American overreliance on
military means and mass destruction, thus obscuring the ideological-
political dimensions of the struggle against communism. Even while

condemning excessive militarism, however, he allowed that the bombing might be justified "as a means of gaining elbow room and bargaining power" in order to negotiate a "satisfactory disengagement" from Vietnam. "If this is the purpose of our present bombing operations," he declared, "so be it—although my heart sinks every time I read of one of these raids, because this is not the sort of thing I like to see Americans doing."[16]

The escalation of U.S. military involvement in the early months of 1965 eroded Kennan's faith in containment in Indochina. "I am dreadfully worried about what our people are doing in Southeast Asia," he confided in March. As with European policy in 1948–49, Kennan diverged from the foreign policy consensus in part because of his opposition to the militarization of American diplomacy, although a decade-long effort since French withdrawal to produce the ideological-political conditions favorable to containment in Vietnam had also failed.[17]

Appearing before Congress as an expert witness on the Sino-Soviet conflict in March 1965, Kennan declared that the United States should not have "gotten involved in this way" in Vietnam. Mindful of the Korean experience, he warned that the American military escalation might well prompt Russian or Chinese intervention. Kennan expressed his eagerness to exploit fissures within the communist bloc and declared that a prolonged military intervention in Vietnam obscured this aim. Although he had been one of the original architects of containment across the great crescent, Kennan now declared that he could "think of nothing we need more, at this stage, than a readiness to relax, not to worry so much about these remote countries scattered across the southern crescent, to let them go their own way, not to regard their fate as our exclusive responsibility."[18]

In a view shared by other Eurocentric realists, Kennan warned that the war in Vietnam would prevent the United States from pursuing other foreign policy goals, erode relations with the Western allies, and reduce the chances of détente with China and the Soviet Union. Still, although he and other realists decried the "unbalanced concentration of resources and attention" in Vietnam, they opposed American withdrawal. As Kennan put it, "no one can question the thesis that a precipitate withdrawal representing the total capitulation of our entire proposition in that region, would be one of the worst alternatives before us." He called instead for a "simmering down" of the conflict "through a series of reciprocal unilateral actions on the part of the main protagonists." If the United States were to "place some limited restraints" on its military efforts, and do so "quietly and without publicized time limits and ultimata," North Vietnam might reciprocate.[19]

Kennan recommended maintaining a fortified American presence in Saigon and in other strategic areas, mostly along the southern coast, while continuing to support and equip the government in the South. This "enclave strategy" would limit the American resources available to Saigon, reduce the chances of Chinese or Soviet intervention, and maximize opportunities for a favorable political settlement. Ultimately, however, Kennan underestimated North Vietnamese resolve and his assumption that a program of limited containment would bring the communists to the bargaining table to make a settlement that would be acceptable to the United States proved ill-founded.

Although many of his arguments, including those delivered in celebrated Senate hearings in 1966 and 1967, suggested that America should withdraw from Vietnam, Kennan rejected this alternative. As reluctant as the majority of his fellow countrymen to admit defeat, he reflected the "arrogance of power" that led Americans to assume that they could compel an acceptable settlement, and he still feared a bandwagon effect. Thus the enclave strategy was "a dictate of the policy of containment" even as Kennan admitted that he was no longer "capable of imagining" an outright American victory in Vietnam.[20]

Among those who still called for a clearcut "victory over aggression" was President Johnson himself, who in February 1966 pledged unqualified support to the Saigon government now headed by Nguyen Cao Ky. Ever mindful of the domestic impact of his foreign policies, LBJ arranged a meeting with Ky in Honolulu, hoping that this might divert media attention from the administration's congressional critics, most notably Senator J. William Fulbright (D-Arkansas). Alarmed by the expansion of executive power inherent in the 1965 intervention by U.S. Marines in the Dominican Republic as well as in Vietnam, Fulbright sought to use his position as chairman of the Senate Foreign Relations Committee to enhance Congress's role in shaping U.S. foreign policy. In January 1966, when the administration submitted a request for $415 million, most of which was earmarked for Vietnam, Fulbright called public hearings on the war.[21]

Kennan had expressed contempt for congressional meddling in foreign policy during his service in both the Truman and Kennedy Administrations, but now that he was an outsider himself the retired diplomat agreed to testify before the Fulbright committee. "It is far more important that this debate take place, even though it has undesirable side effects," he explained, "than that we move into such realms of danger without it." An imposing, articulate man, the sixty-two-year-old Kennan made a striking impression on national television viewers and created something of a public sensation.[22] In a devastating attack on the administration's policy, Kennan called for "a resolute and courageous liquidation of unsound positions" in Vietnam, criticized Johnson for linking American prestige to Ky in Honolulu, and flatly declared that the United States could not win in Vietnam. To use the scale of force needed for victory would require an unacceptably high level of destruction, "almost certainly" provoke Chinese intervention, and involve the United States in an expanded military conflict in "one of the most unfavorable theaters of hostility" possible.[23]

By the time of his testimony Kennan had virtually abandoned all hopes of implementing ideological-political containment in Southeast Asia. The American campaign in Vietnam had "failed to win either enthusiasm or confidence even among peoples normally friendly" to the United States. Although he viewed the Vietnamese Communists as "ruthless fanatics" with no legitimate claim to rule the nation, Kennan cautioned that the United States "should not be asked, and should not ask of itself, to shoulder the main burden of determining the political realities in any other country, and particularly not in one remote from our shores, from our culture, and from the experience of our people. This is not only not our business," he added, "but I don't think we can do it successfully." Dispensing with the image of an iron curtain in the Far East, Kennan now maintained that "a communist regime in South Vietnam would follow a fairly independent course" and would not be a "passive puppet and instrument of Chinese power." He called on the United States to make broad concessions in its negotiations with North Vietnam, concessions that would demonstrate its willingness to accept a "less than ideal" settlement of the conflict.[24]

Alluding to his own historical study of the Allied intervention in Russia from 1918 to 1920, Kennan warned about the perils of sending American forces into conflict unless it could be seen "how and at what point" they could be withdrawn, and unless the point of withdrawal appeared "fairly plausible and immediate." America's failure to secure these guarantees had doomed the Russian intervention just as it had doomed the intervention in Vietnam, and both actions illustrated that a foreign invader only strengthened the resolve and increased the popular support of the forces opposing it. Neither bombing nor counterinsurgency operations could change this reality, Kennan declared. "The Vietcong will go on controlling at night the villages which we control during the daytime."[25]

At the conclusion of his congressional testimony, Kennan joined Army General James Gavin, who had testified earlier, in recommending adoption of the enclave strategy. Asked why this approach could be expected to lead to an acceptable settlement, Kennan admitted that he could not envision a peaceful solution at the present time. "But I have seen too many international situations in which possibilities of this sort were not visible at one time, but in which they were visible at another time if one showed a little patience and had a reasonably strong position." He had first offered this advice in 1948, but Hanoi had shown no inclination to settle for a divided Vietnam either then or in the ensuing eighteen years.[26]

As in the X-Article and Reith Lectures, Kennan displayed through his testimony his penchant for sparking debate and evoking a sensational public response to his words. The ABC and NBC television networks carried his testimony live, while CBS News President Fred Friendly resigned over his network's failure to do so. For one of the few times in his life, Senator Wayne Morse, who had welcomed Kennan's resignation over the Yugoslav controversy, found that "words simply fail me" in an effort to convey his appreciation of Kennan's testimony. The Oregon Democrat, one of two men who voted against the Tonkin Gulf Resolution, predicted that Kennan's "scholarly, intellectual statesmanship . . . is going to be referred to for generations to come." Kennan's appearance prompted international press attention and a spate of editorials filled with both praise and condemnation. The New York Times, which featured a large photograph of Kennan alongside the page one story on the hearings, also editorialized in favor of the "strikingly parallel analysis" of Gavin and Kennan. Moderate magazines such as the New Republic welcomed Kennan's dissent and offered reprints of his congressional testimony. Consistent with its postwar advocacy of American intervention in Asia, Time attacked Kennan for "an attitude that evokes distant echoes of Neville Chamberlain's dismissal of Hitler's plans to rape Czechoslovakia." One box of Kennan's personal papers in Princeton, bulging with mostly favorable letters, attests to the public interest generated by his testimony.[27]

While most accounts played the Gavin-Kennan testimony as a sharp break from the administration's Vietnam policy, the President himself emphasized the essential similarities and underscored the limitations of Kennan's dissent. "No one wants to escalate the war and no one wants to lose any more men than is necessary," Johnson explained. "No one wants to surrender and get out. . . . So I don't see that there is any great difference of opinion." While Kennan and Johnson were divided on the means employed and the extent of the U.S. commitment, the President was justified in pointing out that even critics of the war agreed with him that the United States should not withdraw and accept defeat. "I don't want to debate with Mr. Kennan," LBJ declared the day after Kennan's appearance in the Senate but when reporters continued to make reference to the retired diplomat's testimony Johnson suggested that the views of "Kee-nin" were not to be credited since the diplomat had never actually been to Vietnam to survey the situation first-hand.[28]

In addition to aggravating the President, Kennan's Senate testimony brought him into direct conflict with his longtime Foreign Service colleague, Secretary of State Dean Rusk. The Secretary had defended the administration position before the Fulbright committee, arguing that the SEATO pact obliged America to intervene and that the nation would risk losing credibility with its allies if it did not. "Dean is a nice man, sincere and intelligent," Kennan observed in a *New York Times Magazine* interview, "but his historical parallels are completely misconceived." Despite his own preoccupation with a possible bandwagon effect, Kennan asserted that Rusk's "notion that we stand up and fight in Vietnam or risk losing the allegiance of our allies around the world is flagrantly unsound." Noting that Kennan had crafted the containment policy in 1947, Marvin Kalb, who conducted the interview, observed that "throughout the conversation, Kennan seemed like a father trying desperately to disown a child." Indeed, on another occasion Kennan downplayed his link with containment, calling it "one of those semantic vulgarizations to which our mass media are prone when they lack the patience and inclination to look at things carefully." Privately, however, Kennan still defended containment, as when he encouraged Princeton

University Press to publish Robert J. Maddox's intemperate book attacking revisionist accounts of the origins of the cold war.[29]

The Fulbright hearings marked a significant step in the erosion of the domestic consensus for containment in Vietnam and led some to urge Kennan to run for the U.S. Senate. As a national debate erupted between Vietnam "hawks and doves," a group of anti-war Democrats in New Jersey, no doubt unaware of Kennan's anti-democratic values, encouraged him to challenge incumbent Republican Senator Clifford Case. After meeting with a steering committee of the New Jersey Democratic Council, Kennan, perhaps recalling his abortive campaign for Congress in 1954, declined to make the race.[30]

Despite mounting domestic criticism, the Johnson Administration continued to escalate the war in Southeast Asia, much to Kennan's discomfort. By 1967 gargantuan B-52 bombers had rained more bombs on Vietnam than had been dropped in all theaters of World War II and nearly a half a million American combat troops were conducting "search and destroy" operations in the Vietnamese jungles. Many of the "grunts" patrolled in areas sprayed with cancer-causing defoliants—under operation Ranchhand 100 million pounds of herbicides were dumped on the Vietnamese landscape in an effort to deprive the enemy of natural cover.[31]

International opinion echoed Kennan's protest of the massive American bombing campaign, now condemned by allies and enemies alike. Although Kennan had long warned against relying on the United Nations and other international forums in the pursuit of America's national interests, he now argued that a bombing halt would bolster UN Secretary General U Thant's efforts to mediate a settlement of the war. Kennan himself advocated an end to the bombing regardless of whether this led to any "reciprocal action either by Ho or by the Russians."[32]

Filled with a sense of "miserable unhappiness and helplessness," the retired diplomat foresaw only "catastrophic possibilities, and no favorable ones," as a result of the escalating conflict. Johnson and Rusk lashed out at domestic dissenters even as advisers George Ball and Bill Moyers and Defense Secretary Robert S. McNamara turned against the war. In the face of the growing opposition, Kennan found it "particularly shocking to see the President and the Secretary of State doing all in their power to stimulate and enlist behind this hopeless effort the most violent sort of American patriotic emotionalism."[33]

Although he had long shared the Johnson administration's ultimate goal in Southeast Asia—the preservation of an independent, noncommunist government in Saigon—the failing American intervention found Kennan backing away from that position. As early as November 1966 he declared that he "personally could not care less" if a united Vietnam called itself communist and advocated for purposes of negotiation that Washington ignore internal Vietnamese politics and focus instead on assuring Vietnam's "international status" and relations with foreign powers. He did insist that the United States had a right to participate to ensure at least that much, although he offered a revisionist caveat of his own by declaring that "if comparable difficulties were to arise in Mexico or in the Caribbean area, I wonder how many people in our country would be prepared to concede the Chinese communists an equivalent right to have a voice in their settlement."[34]

Kennan now opposed the administration's commitment to securing an independent South Vietnam because he recognized that the Saigon government could survive, if at all, only as an extension of American power. An American "victory" would thus result in an unwanted "colonial responsibility" for the territory of Vietnam. Moreover, Kennan was contemptuous of the leadership in Saigon, frequently scoring its corruption and abject dependence on the United States. "It is a great mistake to think that the devils are all on one side or the angels on the other," he told the Foreign Relations Committee. Despite billions of dollars in assistance and half a million American troops, the southern government was still "too weak, too timid, too selfish, too uninspiring, to form a stable or promising object of our support. . . . We should have recognized at the start that this patient was beyond saving."[35]

Kennan, Fulbright, and other "doves" argued that the root of the problem was the administration's inability to distinguish between an international conflict and a civil war. Whereas Johnson and Rusk depicted the war as a campaign against Soviet- and Chinese-sponsored "aggression," a perception that Kennan himself had now outgrown, the retired diplomat pointed to its internal dynamics and to the restraint shown by China and the Soviet Union. In his view, the conflict was "a civil war with a very complex set of origins—not, so far as I can see, one deliberately sparked as a move on the international chessboard by any of the great communist powers." As he explained to Arthur Schlesinger, Jr., however, the hypothetical man from Mars ... would never suppose from the Administration's statements that North and South Vietnam were not two separate and long established neighboring countries, one of which had suddenly launched a military attack across the frontier against the other in defiance of all the established concepts of international propriety.[36]

Despite his sweeping condemnation of the war in Southeast Asia, the importance Kennan attached to preserving U.S. credibility and his fear of a bandwagon effect precluded his advocacy of a unilateral American withdrawal in 1967. Kennan struggled to overcome his preoccupation with credibility, however, and offered conflicting advice on the subject. Questioned by senators after delivering his statement before the Fulbright committee in February 1966, he declared that although he believed that a defeat in Vietnam "would be exploited mercilessly by the Chinese and the North Vietnamese" to humiliate America, the negative repercussions "would be a six month sensation" and even in defeat the United States would remain a great power. Even if Washington were to withdraw unilaterally from Vietnam—a step that Kennan reminded the senators he still opposed—he was confident that "three or four years hence the world would not look quite so different as we think."[37]

In contrast with these statements, however, Keenan invoked credibility and his fears of a bandwagon effect in an appearance on "Meet the Press" in November 1967. If the United States "were to turn tail and simply withdraw from Vietnam," he explained, other Southeast Asian nations might fall to communism because of the psychological repercussions of Saigon's defeat. For all his realism about the "grievously unsound" commitment in Vietnam, Kennan's fears of a bandwagon effect led to his "support [for] the administration in its unwillingness to get out of Vietnam in any ignominious way, in any way that would be a rout or a capitulation of our position."[38]

Thus by the end of 1967 Kennan, like the overwhelming majority of his contemporaries in the foreign affairs establishment, offered little in the way of a hopeful solution of the conflict. He continued to adhere to the enclave strategy, yet contradicted himself by declaring that it was a "complete miscalculation" to assume that Ho and his associates would accept South Vietnamese independence if they could "only be persuaded of our 'determination' to 'stay the course.' " Kennan believed that ideology compelled the North Vietnamese leaders "to think in long-term rather than short-term concepts" and he thought it possible that they might "prefer to go down fighting." Moreover, he was not optimistic about negotiations and reproached people for acting as if there were, in the word "negotiation," "some magic that promised the solution of this problem."[39]

The Tet offensive launched by Hanoi on January 30, 1968, marked a turning point in the war. The United States beat back the communist assault on South Vietnamese strongholds, but Americans were shaken by the widespread destruction that had taken place and by the spectacle of a gun battle in the U.S. embassy compound in Saigon. Tet deepened skepticism about promises of certain victory and turned moderates against the war. When news of a request for 206,000 additional troops leaked to the press, the antiwar movement gained momentum and in March an embattled LBJ announced a reduction in the bombing, a new push for a negotiated settlement, and his unexpected decision to decline to seek another term as President.[40]

In April, Kennan endorsed the liberal Democrat, Senator Eugene McCarthy (D-Minnesota), who had announced in November his presidential candidacy on an antiwar platform. Both men were mavericks and public critics of American militarism in Vietnam. Kennan, who spearheaded McCarthy's New Jersey campaign, declared that the Minnesota senator was the "sort of man who will stand forth in public life and offer himself as a spokesman for the millions of Americans who would like to see this war terminated as rapidly and as peacefully as possible."[41] Both McCarthy and Robert F. Kennedy, who entered the race on March 16, called for a ceasefire, a negotiated settlement, and international mediation, without advocating outright withdrawal and thus defeat in Vietnam.

Kennan offered no public statements on the war for more than a year following the 1968 election of Republican Richard M. Nixon, who temporarily placated the antiwar movement with his "Vietnamization" plan for the phased withdrawal of American troops. Although touted as the means for extricating the United States from Vietnam, Nixon's initiative still committed the nation to South Vietnamese independence, a commitment that required the continued presence of some American troops and an increase in bombing to reinforce Washington's credibility even as thousands of U.S. soldiers returned home.[42]

When it became evident that Nixon was no less committed to containment than his predecessors—and far more deeply committed to raining devastation from the air—Kennan had finally had enough. Breaking a long silence on the war, he overcame his preoccupation with credibility and fears of a bandwagon effect, repudiated the enclave strategy, and called for a unilateral American pullout. The United States should effect a "military withdrawal from Vietnam" he advised in November 1969, and should supply Saigon with no more than military training and equipment. "What remains is their task," he declared, "not ours."[43] Nixon's insistence on South Vietnamese independence was neither "necessary, [n]or wise" and, in the event, the government of Nguyen Van Thieu "might do better" without American help, particularly since the Vietnamese used U.S. assistance "as an excuse for relaxing their own efforts." Kennan declared that it was unrealistic to demand that the Vietcong cease its "aggression" as a condition for a settlement even as the United States intensified its own bombing. "We have, in the past, made withdrawals in wartime, when it suited our interests, without waiting for an agreement with the enemy," he asserted. "This is not defeat."[44]

Thus, as the Nixon Administration pursued a futile effort to preserve American credibility in Southeast Asia, Kennan put aside his fears that a unilateral withdrawal would trigger a rash of communist triumphs throughout Asia and the developing world. He no longer recommended holding southern redoubts in the vague hope that a negotiated settlement with Hanoi would somehow materialize. He even came close to endorsing Senator George Aiken's (R-Vermont) advice to "declare victory and get out."

Kennan offered little public comment on the war as Nixon, exceeding the escalatory boundaries set by his predecessors, announced the 1970 Cambodian "incursion" and the mining of Haiphong Harbor in the North and the punishing Christmas bombing of Hanoi in 1972. By the time National Security Adviser Henry Kissinger and Le Duc Tho initialed the Paris Accords, providing a temporary stay of execution to the Saigon government,[45] Kennan could barely speak of the conflict. "As for Vietnam," he wrote in the fall 1972 issue of *Foreign Affairs,* "the less said at this point, the better." The war, he bemoaned, was "the most disastrous of all America's undertakings over the whole 200 years of history." The only course of action for the nation now was "total withdrawal, followed by silence and detachment, leaving initiatives to others."[46]

The Vietnam War shattered the containment consensus that Kennan had helped forge in 1946–47 and called into question the nation's approach to the cold war. Intent on maintaining American prestige and credibility in order to head off a bandwagon effect, Kennan had for two decades advocated containment on the Southeast Asian perimeter. Recognizing that no policy could succeed in Vietnam without building an economic and political structure able to win over a plurality of "hearts and minds," he condemned the SEATO pact, military assistance programs, and use of combat troops and aerial bombardment for obscuring efforts to implement ideological-political containment in Southeast Asia. His persuasive criticism of the war during the Fulbright hearings contributed to an urgently needed reassessment of U.S. policy, and Kennan deserved credit for perceiving the dangers of American escalation earlier and with greater clarity than most of his colleagues.

It is clear, however, that ideological-political containment itself failed in Vietnam. Although the United States succeeded in rebuilding the economies and political structures of Western Europe and Japan after the Second World War, Washington did try but failed to establish a viable government in South Vietnam. Despite the expenditure of millions of dollars, the United States initiated programs and policies and supported a succession of governments that failed to promote containment in southern Vietnam. Given the preoccupation with credibility on the part of Kennan and the U.S. government, it is no surprise that a faltering program of ideological-political containment gave way go a military campaign, a point that Kennan failed to acknowledge as he condemned U.S. militarism in Vietnam. The retired diplomat and his colleagues paid too little attention to Vietnamese history and culture, the study of which may well have been sufficient to convince them that "South Vietnam" was a fiction and that American intervention was doomed.

Kennan himself recognized by the mid-1960s that America would fail in Vietnam and he acknowledged that the Saigon regime could survive only as an extension of Washington's power. He also reminded himself that world communism was polycentric rather than monolithic and that Ho's revolution was neither Chinese- nor Soviet-inspired and thus constituted little if any threat to U.S. national security. Yet despite the changes in his perceptions, Kennan's preoccupation with credibility and fear of a bandwagon effect caused him to hesitate to follow through on his own call in February 1966 for "a resolute and courageous liquidation of unsound positions" in Vietnam.

Like nothing else in his experience, Vietnam had unearthed all the contradictions of containment and found Kennan unable to recommend a consistent approach to the war. He called on the United States to hold the line in Vietnam to avoid a prestige defeat even as he admitted the hopelessness of the U.S. position there. He defended Lyndon Johnson's quest to head off blows to U.S. credibility by remaining in Vietnam even as he publicly condemned the administration's policy and argued that such a prestige blow would be a mere "six-month sensation." He advocated the enclave strategy even as he poured cold water on the prospects for achieving a negotiated settlement. Torn by conflicting emotions, Kennan found his way out only when he threw in the towel on the whole enterprise and called for a unilateral American withdrawal.

When the Vietnam communists culminated their long struggle by pouring into Saigon in April 1975, their triumph revealed that the postwar containment policy had outlived its usefulness. In the wake of Vietnam, Kennan himself abandoned containment and overcame his preoccupation with preserving the nation's credibility through global intervention. The ordeal in Southeast Asia thus confirmed many of his doubts about the efficacy of U.S. internationalism. Kennan turned his attention to American domestic society, which he was sure was at the root of the nation's declining international position.

XII

The Decline of the West

KENNAN'S ATTITUDES about American culture and society structured his views on the nation's approach to world affairs. Nostalgia for the age of European aristocracy fueled disenchantment with post-industrial democratic society in the United States and contributed to the erosion of his support for containment. While his elitism and nostalgia made him more of a reactionary than most social critics, many American intellectuals of the 1950s shared Kennan's perception of a culture dominated by materialism, conformity, and declining spiritual and artistic values.

While Kennan found American culture in the 1950s disturbing, the "counter-culture" that emerged during the next decade horrified him. The outbreak of dissent over cultural conformity, civil rights, and the Vietnam War disrupted life on college campuses and authority in the cities and enraged Kennan, who feared for the stability of the American government and could not abide the style and means by which youthful dissidents expressed themselves. Already disturbed by the militarization of U.S. diplomacy and soured on containment in the wake of Vietnam, he had concluded by the 1970s that America could no longer hope to be effective in foreign affairs. Kennan's alienation from American culture —indeed his conclusion that all of Western civilization was in decline—

underlay his rejection of U.S. internationalism for a foreign policy of neo-isolation.

A sharp critic of American democracy since the 1930s, Kennan had expressed himself mostly in private on this subject in deference to his Foreign Service career. During his formulation of containment from 1944 to 1947, he had called for greater collectivism and argued that the success or failure of U.S. diplomacy hinged on the quality of the nation's domestic life.[1] The linkage was paradoxical in view of Kennan's anti-democratic values and alienation from post-industrial society, but he hoped that the global confrontation with Moscow would prompt the United States to resolve its domestic social and political problems along the lines of the type of benevolent authoritarianism that he had advocated since the 1930s. In this context Kennan was fond of quoting Shakespeare's King Henry V, including the lines:

> There is some soul of goodness in things evil.
> . . . For our bad neighbor makes us early stirrers,
> Which is both healthful and good husbandry.[2]

Gratified by his own rise to prominence in the early cold war period, Kennan had expressed some confidence in America's ability to meet the challenges of international diplomacy, but that confidence began to wane as he lost influence during the Truman Administration. By mid-1949 he was advocating retrenchment, observing that the "first task of foreign policy is really the ordering of our own internal house in such a way as to render us capable in a far greater degree of exercising leadership by precept and example in the community at large." Turning to the visiting nineteenth-century European critics James Bryce and Alexis de Tocqueville for inspiration, he rejected the notion of an "American Century" and declared that "people in this country are calling on us to be wiser than American tradition calls upon us to be." The nation's institutions had "not yet met their final test" nor had the question raised by Lincoln as to whether "any nation so conceived and so dedicated can long endure" been answered. "Not being the masters of our own soul," he observed, "are we justified in regarding ourselves as fit for the leadership of others?"[3]

At the root of Kennan's declining faith in American internationalism were his anti-democratic values and the alienation he shared with other intellectuals over the materialism and conformity that characterized the nation during the postwar years. With his retirement from the Foreign Service in 1953, Kennan was free to indulge his penchant for scholarship and social criticism during a decade in which such pursuits were very much in vogue in intellectual circles. He joined film and literary critic Dwight Macdonald, philosopher Sidney Hook, historians Daniel Boorstin, Louis Hartz, and Richard Hofstadter, economist John Kenneth Galbraith, sociologist David Riesman, journalist William Whyte, theologian Reinhold Niebuhr, and other writers who probed beneath the surface of America's postwar prosperity, illuminated social ills, and lamented the decline of standards in a mass material culture.[4]

More nostalgic and romantic than these critics, Kennan found it difficult to accommodate himself to change in American society. He lamented the passing of "a rural America, an unmechanical America, an America without motor cars and television sets, an America of the barefoot boy and the whitewashed board fence." Although he urged his audience on this occasion to adjust to the realities of modern American society, Kennan himself clung to the image of that "wonderful old America" and "sometimes wonder[ed] whether those of us who knew it will ever really adjust to any other."[5]

The postwar economic boom buried the vestiges of "old America," fueling unprecedented growth and social change as interstate highways, jet planes, suburbs, television, and consumerism changed the face of the United States and redefined what it meant to be an American. As the Gross National Product more than doubled from 1945 to 1960, Americans who had lived through the trials of depression and global war were happy to accommodate themselves to the opportunities and pleasures afforded by higher education, white collar jobs, a home in the suburbs (complete with outdoor barbeque and two-car garage), the cozy patriarchy embodied in *I Love Lucy* and *Father Knows Best,* and all manner of recreational opportunities from new golf courses at the country club, to boating, to Disneyland.

Kennan and other intellectual critics took little pleasure in the dynamic transformation of American society, however, and raised disturbing questions about underlying psychological and cultural ramifications. Kennan shared the concerns of David Riesman, whose 1950 book *The Lonely Crowd* identified a predominance of "other-directed" Americans who compromised their "inner-directed" individuality for conformity to "groupism" in a mass material culture. Kennan deplored the growing sameness of American society stemming from the rise of what author William Whyte called "the organization man." In the offices of corporate America and in the suburbs, Whyte identified an alarming but "unmistakable similarity in the way of life."[6]

While economic expansion raised living standards and increased social mobility for millions of Americans, Kennan focused on the negative implications of rapid population growth, materialism and uncoordinated development, environmental pollution, and declining communal and spiritual values. He deplored the growing sameness and vulgarity of American mass culture and wondered "how deep or solid is a prosperity that expresses itself so largely in sales of new automobiles and television sets, in expensive recreations." As the economic boom chewed up ground for the development of new superhighways, motels, and amusement parks, Kennan condemned the "absolutely absurd wastefulness of American society. . . . the relative thoughtlessness with which this society exhausts its natural resources, in deference to the dictatorship of commercial considerations." Criticizing "the cult of production for production's sake," he advised a "thoroughgoing skepticism about all technological innovation beyond what is necessary to satisfy basic material needs, and a readiness to take all this under the strictest sort of public control."[7]

Kennan's critique of American economic expansion echoed arguments made by the liberal economist John Kenneth Galbraith, whose 1958 book *The Affluent Society* called attention to the greed, wastefulness, and absence of social balance underlying the postwar boom. Like Galbraith, Kennan rejected the conventional wisdom that the quest for private-sector profits contributed to the public good and condemned much production as frivolous. A concern for the plight of the impoverished and economically disadvantaged did not, however, characterize Kennan's critique, as it did Galbraith's and later Michael Harrington's.[8]

Kennan was more concerned about environmental destruction than poverty and still considered the automobile the greatest scourge on the landscape. As car registration soared throughout the 1950s, a system of interstate highways displaced the passenger railroad and changed the face of the city as parking lots, drive-ins, suburbs, and shopping malls sprang up across the nation. Kennan had complained for years that the profusion of automobiles represented an appalling waste of resources and a source of community and environmental devastation. "It is not absolutely essential that one or two tons of machinery . . . should be employed to haul the individual American body around the streets and highways of our country," he declared in 1956. "There are more economical—some would even say more pleasant—means of conveyance."[9] As an octagenarian in the 1980s, Kennan could still be seen pedaling his bicycle amid a haze of automobile exhaust on Princeton's busy Nassau Street—he was a picture of alienation.

The "naked and undiluted materialism" of modern American society came at the expense of "deeper and worthier" values, not least of which was the natural environment. Kennan dreamed of a

> civilization in which there would be no dreary urban deserts, no wastes of stone and steel and dust and filth, no people living and working day in and day out in cubicles of concrete and metal; no over-population, no desolation and plundering of natural resources, no individual human life that did not stand in close association with the plants and animals to whose world we still in part belong.[10]

Years later he declared that "what really set me off" as an environmentalist was the 1944 purchase of his 235-acre Pennsylvania farm, which alerted him to "how much of a unit the ecosystem was." Also a lifelong sailor and lover of the sea, Kennan recalled lapsing into "depression" after witnessing garbage being dumped from a trawler into the Norwegian Sea while sailing in 1964. By that time the retired diplomat was well on the way to the conclusion that preservation of the natural environment was a greater priority than containing communism.[11]

Environmental pollution, the automobile, population growth, and urban sprawl had caused "the disintegration of real community almost everywhere" and left Americans confused and disordered. Urban blight, chaotic traffic conditions, community demoralization, and disregard for aesthetic values where costs of the nation's uncoordinated development. Kennan advocated regional and municipal planning and broadening the powers of government agencies to rein in private transportation and development. "Today," he explained, "we see all around us the chaotic and depressing effects of this failure on our part to insist on public responsibility for the control of processes that are certainly matters of public concern in their effects."[12]

Close behind the automobile in Kennan's catalogue of the ills of post-industrial culture were television and commercial advertising. Advertisers capitalized on revolutionary developments in communication to reach mass audiences, but their motivation had "little, if anything, to do in the deeper sense with human welfare," he observed. In calling for "freeing literature and art and journalism from the tyranny of advertisers," Kennan anticipated recommendations offered by sociologist Vance Packard, whose 1956 book, *The Hidden Persuaders,* condemned the machinations of advertisers who were "systematically feeling out our hidden weaknesses and frailties in the hope that they can more efficiently influence our behavior."[13]

In his cultural critique as well as in his views on diplomacy, perceptions concerning mass psychology often dominated Kennan's thinking. He declared that Americans were victims of a "cloying mass culture" and warned of damaging psychological repercussions as a result of mass indulgence in the "vast spectacle of pretended life in which we are constantly being asked vicariously to share." The images and symbols of television, movies, and advertising had the effect of "a tremendous, easy, and insidious narcosis, quietly eating away at our capacity for direct experience and at the same time lulling us into a lazy imperviousness to what it is that is really happening to us." The influence of Hollywood and Madison Avenue meant that "much of our emotional experience is too indirect and too passive. . . . As we share the loves and excitements of the television screen," he explained,

> we become less and less capable or having real love and excitements of our own; and this vacuum leaves us unsatisfied and gives to all of life that sense of anti-climax you get when you come out from a good afternoon movie and are suddenly confronted, again, with the dust and disillusionment of the sunlit street.[14]

Many intellectuals in the 1950s shared Kennan's concerns over the commercial media's usurpation of the prerogative once held by the traditional elite of dominating the arts and leisure and establishing popular tastes. The mass production and marketing of books, magazines, radios, televisions, and the movies made it impossible for cultural elites to influence popular tastes as they had done in the pre-industrial era. Kennan, author Clement Greenberg, Dwight Macdonald, and other intellectuals argued that America's mass-produced popular culture undermined standards and obscured distinctions between quality and shoddy works of art and literature. They were "distressed by the corruption of high culture in its losing battle with the tastes of the 'mob.' "[15]

America's rampant materialism and the commercialization of the arts and leisure confirmed many of Kennan's worst suspicions about democratic society. He did not consider Americans "a bad people or a weak one or even a consciously unhappy one," but a people who were "becoming sluggish intellectually, underdeveloped emotionally, creative only where commercial interest raises its capricious demands, . . . dull and uninteresting to others and, what is worse, not terribly interesting to ourselves." As long as this situation prevailed Americans would be preoccupied by their own "inner restlessness and dissatisfaction" and thus "incapable of integrating our full strength and bringing it to bear where it is most needed," and least of all in foreign affairs.[16]

As he advanced his views on American culture in the 1950s, Kennan proposed myriad "reforms," some of which might be described as liberal or progressive, others conservative and reactionary, and all of which were aimed, as he saw it, at the redemption of American society. He advocated authoritarian government by a cultured elite; a streamlined federal and state bureaucracy; increased regional and municipal planning and limitations on urban-industrial growth; state control of transportation facilities; universal military training; restrictions on labor unions; restraints on gambling and luxury recreation; public controls on television and all forms of advertising; "drastic reform of . . . the moral cess pools we call prisons"; state promotion of birth control; and strict laws against pollution.[17]

He continued to advocate a benevolent authoritarianism in his private correspondence and had little expectation of achieving meaningful reforms through the nation's two-party political system. Despite his association with Adlai Stevenson, Kennan insisted in 1958 that he was neither a Democrat nor a Republican and noted only "relative distinctions" between the *Soviet* and *American* political systems. He argued that the two U.S. political parties were "ideologically indistinguishable"; that their positions comprised "one integral body of banality and platitude; [and] whoever does not care to work within their framework is also condemned, like the non-person in Russia, to political passivity— to an internal emigration." As he had done in 1938, Kennan called for the country to be governed by a "cultural elite . . . of mind and character" instead of being led by "mediocrities, selected out of mediocrity." It was an "illusion" to suppose

> that in this day of technological complexity, the average man is capable of surveying and understanding the influence by which his experience is formed or of shaping his environment usefully on the strength of his own concept of his needs and interests. The trees of the jungle have grown too high around him.[18]

Kennan had long advocated empowering elites within the central government through constitutional reform, but had been reluctant to express this controversial view publicly. As he observed in 1963, what was required were "reforms and changes in our actual system of government, which would be very, very far reaching, which, if I were to try to describe them publicly as I think they might look, would sound very shocking and probably land me before Congressional investigating committees." In 1968 Kennan called for "a high degree of *dirigisme,* a strengthening of the hand of government, which is quite foreign to our habits and concepts."[19]

Kennan's desire to remake the nation's political system was not shared by most intellectual critics of the 1950s, most of whom preferred liberal reform and amelioration to radical change. Like them, Kennan had been more effective in illuminating the social problems of post-industrial capitalist society than in formulating viable solutions. While Kennan and other intellectual critics had brought to light myriad social and psychological problems that lurked beneath the surface of the postwar prosperity, they were shocked by the changes that their social criticism helped to unleash in the next decade.

The New Left of the 1960s—like Kennan and the 1950s intellectuals—condemned America's mass produced consumer culture, questioned the power and lack of social responsibility on the part of corporate America, decried the "organization man," and sought "inner-direction" and the revitalization of art and literature. The youthful dissidents of the 1960s expressed themselves differently, to be sure, and the intellectual elites of the 1950s could muster little understanding of hippies, drugs, and rock 'n' roll; yet a linkage existed between the cultural criticism of the two decades and the New Left sprang from the groundwork laid by the 1950s critics. Still, the older social critics—and Kennan most outstandingly—could not abide the style and tactics of the new "counterculture" that emerged in the 1960s.[20]

The civil rights movement and the Vietnam War fused with the critique of 1950s culture and the sense of activism inspired by John F. Kennedy's New Frontier to give rise to the New Left. Demonstrations against segregation and the disfranchisement of blacks as well as the failed campaign to contain the Vietcong sparked domestic protest that paralyzed the universities, disrupted the 1968 Democratic national convention in Chicago, and polarized American society. The convergence of the antiwar and civil rights movements and the emergence of the hippie counter-culture opened a "great schism" which found America "coming apart" as a society by the late 1960s.[21]

As long-haired students demonstrated against the war and African-Americans took to the streets to protest racial inequality, Kennan came down firmly on the side of the "establishment" in the domestic political struggle. The long hair, beards, beads, sandals, open sexuality, and unconventional language of the youth movement aroused a visceral response from Kennan. Years later he recalled arriving at a Danish port with his family and encountering a youth festival "swarming with hippies, motorbikes, girl-friends, drugs, pornography, drunkenness, noise— it was all there. I looked at this mob and thought how one company of robust Russian infantry would drive it out of town."[22]

As an exponent of Old World civility, the retired diplomat attached "overriding importance [to] good form as an essential of civilized living," a style for which the New Left had little sympathy. He resented the "disregard, if not contempt, for serious discussion and respectful appeal to normal channels of authority" that characterized the activities of student radicals and civil rights activists, whose tactics included sit-ins, boisterous and sometimes violent demonstrations, American flag and draft-card burnings, and other forms of civil disobedience. Kennan denounced activism on college and university campuses, which he insisted should be reserved, like monasteries, solely for study and contemplation in an atmosphere of "detachment and seclusion" from contemporary events.[23]

Enraged by the actions of radical students, Kennan lashed out against them on the lecture circuit and in print. He railed against the "banners and epithets and obscenities," "meaningless slogans," "total permissiveness," and "angry militancy" of the day's "perverted and willful and stony-hearted youth." After Kennan made these statememts in a lecture at Swarthmore College, "a group of angry young men, mostly bearded," confronted him and "hissed their disagreement and resentment at me like a flock of truculent village geese." When, in January 1968, he published his talk in the *New York Times Magazine,* it appeared under the headline "Rebels Without a Program," and provoked a barrage of angry rejoinders. Never one to shirk a good controversy, Kennan published his original speech along with 39, mostly negative, responses (out of more than 200 received) and concluded with a 104-page reassessment of his differences with radical students.[24]

In *Democracy and the Student Left,* Kennan denied the legitimacy of the student protests and invoked his penchant for mass psychology to offer a Freudian explanation of their behavior. He asserted that the unrest on college campuses stemmed from "obviously far deeper, and largely subconscious, sources of discomfort" than the political issues of the day. Invoking his own cultural critique, Kennan declared that overpopulation, rampant urbanization, advanced technology, and the proliferation of automobiles, televisions and "gadgetry" had left American youth confused and dissatisfied. The radical student "senses in his parents, and feels in himself, the malaise of material society without the balancing influence of any inner security." As victims of the "appalling shallowness of the religious, philosophic and political concepts" of contemporary society, radical students had adopted an "embittered pseudo-revolutionary nihilism" as an expression of their internal frustrations.[25]

Kennan not only deplored the style and most of the substance of the New Left, but also feared that the unrest and violent demonstrations would destroy the fabric of American society. The union of white student radicals and black-power activists aroused in his mind the specter of violent revolution and totalitarian government and led Kennan to draw historical parallels which were tenuous at best. "It was out of just such radical students, frustrated in their efforts to help the Russian peasant," he charged in *Democracy and the Student Left,* "that Lenin forged his highly disciplined faction. It was in part from people of just this desperate and confused state of mind that Hitler recruited his supporters." The burning of draft cards—"an extravagant and indefensible act"—was the kind of flouting of authority that Kennan found intolerable, although he did agree with the argument, resolved by the twenty-sixth amendment, that persons of draft age should have the right to vote. Overall, however, Kennan mustered little sympathy for the demands of the New Left and called for "a stricter code for student behavior" on campuses, including a willingness to "resort fairly extensively to expulsion." He called for an end to the "excess of tolerance" toward protesters and found charges of police brutality "simply ludicrous" in light of the provocations.[26]

Although the student radicals did display considerable confusion, recklessness and naïveté, as Kennan had charged, their advocacy of civil rights, an end to the war and the draft, greater responsibility on the part of corporate America, and broadening of political power in the nation offered something resembling a coherent program for change. Kennan, in contrast, had failed to offer a realistic scenario for ending the war, favored racial segregation (as will be seen below), and trusted elites to govern an authoritarian society. One might reasonably conclude that Kennan was the real "rebel without a program" as well as the one most disturbed by "the malaise of material society." In this respect *Democracy and the Student Left* might be best understood as a work of psychological projection on the part of Kennan himself.

Reviewers of the book observed that the retired diplomat had shown himself to be a "temperamental conservative" whose ideas "do not even remotely apply to the most clamorous of contemporary realities." One critic found it "disturbing to see Kennan making an issue of beards" and expressed amazement at his call for students to display more of a sense of humor and *joie de vivre,* "as if these qualities were appropriate to the occasion, or as if his own treatise abounded in hilarity."[27]

Unchastened, Kennan appeared with student leader Sam Brown for another "direct clash of the generations" at a December 1968 meeting of the International Association of Cultural Freedom. As unkempt student demonstrators chanted outside, he appeared at the meeting wearing a grey suit with a silk tie and a gold watch chain dangling across his vest. Through his dignified bearing, *Newsweek* observed, Kennan "personified a lifestyle for which the young could muster little sympathy or understanding. He reciprocated completely." After becoming "visibly angered" as Brown excoriated the American "establishment" during his speech, Kennan reiterated his claim that American students were "dreadfully like" their Russian counterparts in 1917 and had no sense of the consequences they might suffer when "the right wing comes back at you." He explained that the disorder flowing from the student and black protest movements might easily create a climate conducive to reaction. According to *Newsweek*, Kennan, who had supported Democrat Eugene

McCarthy early in the 1968 campaign, "thought a cool dose of Nixon-ism might be just the thing for an America grown weary of 'political hysteria.' "[28]

Just as he thought students should stick to their textbooks and muzzle themselves on the issues of the day, Kennan, as president of the American Academy of Arts and Letters in 1968, urged the literary community to avoid allowing the arts to become "polluted by the passions and myopia of the moment."[29] Poet Robert Bly rejected the advice and savaged American policy in Vietnam at National Book Award ceremonies in March. Kennan offered a stark contrast as he accepted his own award for the first volume of *Memoirs* and lamented in a nostalgic reverie the decline of the "grace of expression" in diplomatic dispatches as well as in the affairs of "our own raucous egalitarian republic." In accepting his award Kennan declared that he longed for the days when diplomats displayed their respect by concluding dispatches, "I have the honor to be, Sir, your humble and obedient servant."[30]

The poverty of Kennan's romantic-nostalgic worldview was nowhere more evident than in his advocacy of an outmoded paternalism and separate-but-equal formula in response to the drive for African-American equality. Opposed to integration, he urged a system of "voluntary separate development and local self-government" for African-Americans, but offered no suggestion as to how such a program could emerge on a voluntary basis. Speaking in honor of American independence at Williamsburg, Virginia, in the summer of 1968, he declared that it was unrealistic

> to suppose that the American Negro is going to find his dignity and comfort of body and mind by the effort to participate and to compete as an individual in a political and social system he neither understands nor respects and for which he is ill-prepared.

Kennan added that the current generation had inherited rather than created the race problem and declared that he was "a little tired of being told how endlessly guilty I am with relation to this situation."[31] The retired diplomat displayed little sensitivity, much less guilt, in relation to the African-American experience and his prescriptions would have sanctioned what the presidential Kerner Commission warned against, but what occurred anyway: the emergence of "two societies, one black, one white—separate and unequal."[32]

Kennan was sympathetic to the concept of racial segregation in southern Africa as well as in the United States. "With my whole proclivity for thinking the wrong things," he told a West German editor in 1965, "I am bound to say I have a soft spot in my mind for apartheid—not as practiced in South Africa but as a concept."[33] After a tour of South Africa on a leadership exchange program two years later, he declared that apartheid was "foolish" and "doomed to eventual failure," but argued that "any sudden introduction of majority rule in South Africa would be a disaster for all concerned." Kennan not only believed the African majority "quite unprepared" for self-government, but also opposed a "general mingling of the races in all aspects of residence and education, where this does not rest on a general natural acceptance and preference by both parties."[34] Similarly, Kennan opposed calls for majority rule in what was then Rhodesia, declaring that it would be a "miracle" if black Africans under the influence of "Marxist extremists" effected peaceful change and respected the rights of the white minority without a bloodbath. The "miracle" of transition to majority government without a bloodbath occurred with American support in 1980 with the emergence of Zimbabwe.[35]

NAACP President Roy Wilkins declared that Kennan's "emotional clinging to the past" on southern Africa represented "precisely the under-the-rug tactics which Americans have learned, in great spiritual and physical pain, produce nothing except dissatisfaction among both whites and blacks." Ernest R. Gross, a former assistant secretary of state, also criticized Kennan for his "catalogue of clichés" and rejected the argument that "the black man would be the first to suffer" from American economic sanctions against repressive white minority governments in southern Africa.[36]

Kennan's attitudes on race relations mirrored the perceptions he had adopted throughout his career toward peoples of the developing world. He was not a visceral racist but he did seem to feel that African-Americans—like so many Arabs, Asians, Africans, and Latin Americans—should be content with their positions on the periphery of civilization and neither demand nor expect to achieve equality with a superior white civilization. When these peoples insisted on making themselves heard, Kennan usually responded with indignation, less often with historical understanding.

The wrenching impact of the student disorders and the struggles over

African-American equality in the 1960s reinforced Kennan's image of a chaotic democratic society that had little hope of being effective in foreign policy. "We know from personal life," he explained, "that only he is capable of exercising leadership over others who is capable of some real degree of mastery over himself."[37] Given his linkage between domestic and foreign affairs, Kennan's sweeping critique of American culture and society led inexorably to the conclusion that Washington should scale back its involvement in world affairs.

Kennan first contemplated an isolationist foreign policy after withdrawing to Princeton in the fall of 1950. His "External Relations Project" at the Institute for Advanced Study began with the premise that "foreign relations are by and large troublesome and undesirable and represent something that one should accept only reluctantly and when the alternatives are worse." Kennan began to probe the feasibility of a "continentalist" foreign policy centered on the Western Hemisphere, a variant of isolationism popularized by the progressive historian Charles A. Beard.

A neutral "porcupine" defense which had allowed Switzerland to remain a nonbelligerent in the two world wars also impressed Kennan. "Our own geographic situation is one of the most favorable that could be conceived" for a foreign policy of armed neutrality, he wrote.

> We must remember that in such a state of complete isolation many— though by no means all—of the sources of hostility and resentment and danger to us might no longer exist. Why should it not be a better policy than one which plunges into the complexities of world leadership, for which we are ill-prepared, and into the risks of atomic rivalry with the USSR?[38]

Unlike prewar isolationists, many of whom, disillusioned by World War I and Wilsonianism, wanted to preserve American democracy from the corrupting influence of Europe, Kennan's neo-isolationism blamed American democracy for undermining the nation's ability to conduct a realistic diplomacy. To conduct foreign policy, he wrote in 1955, was "merely to shape the behavior of a nation, in relation to its external environment," but there was "no society that is less susceptible of being shaped to any coherent foreign-political purpose than our own." Again citing the "devastating insights" of Tocqueville, who had argued in 1835 that America's simple political institutions would not accommodate great-power status, Kennan declared that "it is to these institutions that we owe the inflexibility, frequent contradictions, the lack of privacy, and the slowness of decision that characterize our performance in foreign affairs."[39]

In unpublished drafts of his second volume of memoirs, Kennan attacked the American political system for its failure to empower people who were "intellectually equipped" for statesmanship and for denying elites "sufficient control over our national behavior to make possible the conception and the consistent pursuit of enlightened and consistent policies." The implications for foreign policy were clear: an unenlightened mass democracy such as the United States could not expect to pursue a consistent foreign policy and therefore ought to accept limitations on what it hoped to achieve in world affairs.[40]

As he approached his seventies, Kennan declared that the older he got the more sympathy he had for the "isolationist principles of my forefathers." The retired diplomat explained that he was not "an isolationist in their sense, but I understand much better than I did twenty or thirty years ago why a country like ours should exercise a great degree of prudence before it involves itself in complicated affairs far from its own borders." On another occasion Kennan called himself a "semi-isolationist" and observed that "people greatly exaggerate the degree to which a country can really control other countries far from its shores."[41]

The erosion of Kennan's support for containment and his rising interest in neo-isolationism stemmed from the conclusion that America could not effectively conduct an internationalist diplomacy. He had not gone "soft" on communism—which he still considered evil and theoretically indefensible—but had concluded that the United States lacked the maturity required to shape world affairs and had no paradigm to offer developing nations within whose borders the struggle with communism was being waged. A policy of global containment was, as he put it in 1955, "more than utopian" because it reflected the "deep and rather fateful philosophic error" of viewing communism "as exclusively an external danger, having nothing to do with ourselves." In reality the West could not hope to combat communism unless it offered a superior model for developing nations to emulate. "I would submit that the fuel of communism has always consisted of the deficiencies of the western example and western influence, and of the weaknesses and illnesses and follies of the West itself," he explained. "The mote is still in our eye."[42]

Marxists sought to expand their influence by fomenting disorder in politically unstable and vulnerable areas of the world, Kennan explained, and thus the communist challenge required a Western response to the needs of peoples in the noncommunist world. He had envisioned the United States serving as a model in which "the quality of our leadership and the tone of our national life generally . . . would radiate themselves to the world at large" and thereby frustrate the drive for communist expansion. His idealistic vision was as venerable as white civilization in America and echoed the Puritan leader John Winthrop's call for the Massachusetts Bay Colony to serve as "a city upon a hill" in which "the eyes of all people are upon us."[43]

Kennan invoked John Quincy Adams in defense of his call for America to pursue a noninterventionist foreign policy and to rely on the power of example in efforts to influence other nations. During his 1966 testimony at the Fulbright Committee hearings on the Vietnam War, Kennan recalled Adams' 1821 warning against America going "in search of monsters to destroy." Adams, often cited as the greatest statesman in U.S. history, had advised that America was

> the well-wisher to the freedom and independence of all [but] the champion and vindicator only of her own. She will recommend the general cause by the countenance of her voice, and by the benignant sympathy of her example. She well knows that by once enlisting under other banners than her own, were they even the banners of foreign independence, she would involve herself beyond the power of extrication, in all the wars of interest and intrigue, of individual avarice, envy, and ambition, which assume the colors and usurp the standards of freedom. The fundamental maxims of her policy would insensibly change from liberty to force. . . . She might become the dictatress of the world. She would no longer be the ruler of her own spirit.[44]

By the mid-1950s, however, Kennan had concluded that the West had little hope of serving as a shining example to others. America's "wasteful, self-indulgent and highly permissive social system" offered "little relevance and little charm for the peoples of Asia and Africa." The nation's material generosity had "already come to be widely taken for granted, and scoffed at as evidence of her weakness and naïveté." Although Kennan himself embraced racial segregation in the United States, he did recognize that it placed a "tremendous barrier" in the path of influencing developing nations.[45]

Instead of implementing a realistic foreign policy and developing an alternative paradigm to Marxism for developing nations to emulate, Kennan charged the United States with conducting its foreign affairs recklessly and more often than not for the satisfaction of domestic needs. The nation had failed to leave foreign affairs in the hands of competent experts such as himself and instead of marshaling its resources for the struggle against communism had embarked on a wasteful and psychologically damaging era characterized by materialism and cultural conformity. If the nation could devise "a broader purpose than the mere provision of facilities for [the] physical enrichment of the individual," and if it could "begin to take into account the more subtle aspects of the effect of environment on his emotional health and inner happiness," he declared, only then could the "external behavior of the nation . . . begin to be shaped to a positive end, to accord with its internal purpose."[46]

A country as disordered as the one perceived by Kennan had little hope of being effective in international affairs: it had no example to offer to others and had little to protect for itself. Unless and until the nation reordered its domestic life to establish a sound basis for the conduct of foreign relations, it should adopt a posture of neo-isolation, Kennan argued. "There comes a time in the lives of nations, as in the lives of individuals," he explained, "when the best they can say is nothing and when the best they can do is to make themselves as inconspicuous as possible. I would suggest that this is the situation of the United States today." Americans should desist from "incessant claims to virtue [that] we ourselves understand very poorly" and allow peoples throughout the world to pursue their interests free of Washington's interference.[47]

The theorist of containment now admitted he could "forsee a time when the major portion of our recent pretensions to influence in Europe and Asia will indeed have been dismantled and yet the world situation will still not be too catastrophic." The "natural state" of U.S. foreign policy was not one of complete isolation from world affairs but the nation should settle for being "a power among powers," should abandon its leadership at the center of the Western alliance, and become "a somewhat detached attendant at the quarrels and rivalries of peoples on other continents." The country needed to "learn to mind its own business" and "recognize the uniqueness of its own national experience and the irrelevance of many of its practices for the problems of others" while addressing itself to "the ordering and sanification of its own life." Kennan was "tempted to think" that had Washington adopted a foreign policy of complete armed isolation in 1900, "the world would not be worse off today and many confusions would have been avoided."[48]

Kennan outlined his neo-isolationist posture in *The Cloud of Danger,* a book that offered "something resembling a grand design of American foreign policy," published in 1977. The retired diplomat blended sober warnings about America's limited ability to shape world events with his own iconoclastic views on democracy and the third world in what historian Ronald Steel aptly described as an "alternately irritating and sensible book." Kennan called for retaining American commitments to the security of Western Europe and Japan, but for eliminating them in Greece and Turkey, South Korea, the Philippines, Taiwan, and southern Africa. Israel was a "serious" but not a "vital" interest of the United States, which should do what it could "short of direct military involvement" to preserve Israeli security. Kennan declared that Moscow had a right to play a role in negotiations toward an Arab-Israeli settlement and called for both major powers to curb arms sales to the Middle East. The septuagenarian diplomat deplored America's "self-flagellation" over the plight of poor countries and insisted that the democratic form of government was irrelevant to the solution of their socioeconomic problems. Declaring that foreign policy "begins at home," he outlined a "whole series of domestic phenomena" that needed attention before the country could expect to achieve success in foreign affairs and he insisted that America could not be "a source of hope and inspiration to others against a background of resigned failure and deterioration of life here at home."[49]

Kennan made it clear in an interview published in 1979 that he had abandoned containment as a result of his loss of faith in American culture and society. "Show me first an America which has successfully coped with the problems of crime, drugs, pornography, and decadence of one sort or another—show me an America that is what it ought to be," he declared, "then I will tell you how we are going to defend ourselves from the Russians." Americans had to face the reality that "we have nothing to teach the world" and "have not got the answers to the problems of human society in the modern age."

Once the architect of a policy of global containment, Kennan was now committed to the view that America—"honeycombed with bewilderment" and "internal decay"—had little hope to be effective in foreign affairs.[50] He urged a foreign policy of neo-isolation that would allow the nation to focus its energies on reining in the nuclear arms race, combating environmental pollution, and reforming a destructive commercial culture. These were the critical problems confronting the United States and the Western world—containment and the cold war were no longer of primary importance.

XIII

An Ephemeral Thaw

K ENNAN WAS a strong and early proponent of détente with the
Soviet Union, but efforts to mold a new relationship between East and
West faltered in the mid-1970s. The retired diplomat opposed the policy
of "linkage," which made negotiations conditional on Soviet "behavior,"
arguing that such an approach would undermine détente. The positions
Kennan adopted during the era of détente cemented his position as an
outsider and critic of American internationalism. Despite his support for
improved East-West relations, however, Kennan continued to struggle
to reconcile the internal competition between his emotional and realistic
responses to world affairs.

Since 1948 Kennan had been a forceful, but inconsistent, advocate of
negotiations with Russia. He found it inexcusable in 1967 that so many
officials, "still stewing in the trauma we received from Stalin's seizure of
Eastern Europe," were unable to take "bold and generous and imaginative courses." One of the reasons he found Vietnam so disturbing was
that Washington's preoccupation with the war had prevented America
from capitalizing on the "real possibilities for a genuine and greatly
exciting and constructive form of understanding" with Russia which
could be "one of the great developments in world affairs. If I did not

believe this was a possibility," he declared, "I wouldn't have led the life I have led for the last forty years."[1]

Following the brinksmanship over the Cuban missiles, John F. Kennedy and Nikita S. Khrushchev opened the era of détente when they agreed to install a direct communications "hotline" and signed the Limited Test Ban Treaty in July 1963, which terminated atmospheric and underwater nuclear tests. Kennan blamed Western timidity and Soviet intransigence regarding on-site inspection for the failure to achieve a comprehensive test ban, but the limited accord at least showed the Soviet interests were "not always and in all circumstances in conflict" with those of the West. "We must get over the naïve concept that whenever you have a rival or adversary in international life, the conflict of interests is always total, so that nothing can be good for him which is not bad for you, and vice versa."[2]

Kennedy's assassination, Khrushchev's ouster by the Communist Party Central Committee in October 1964, and the escalating conflict in Vietnam combined to undermine prospects for détente in the mid-1960s. Kennan considered the leadership changes little short of tragic: he had viewed Kennedy as the best President in his lifetime and Khrushchev as "a diamond in the rough." Although the Soviet leader still embraced Marxist dogmas, he had "thought it worthwhile to talk with us and to try to get agreement between our respective outlooks," Kennan explained. "This was a great change and a very important one" but Washington had failed to exploit it out of deference to "our military preoccupations." Kennan attributed Khrushchev's fall to his failures in Soviet domestic issues, however.[3]

Foreign affairs had been "a new field of responsibility" to President Lyndon Johnson and he and Secretary of State Dean Rusk were "more interested in organizing consensus" and following "the well-worn paths of recent years" than in achieving accord with Moscow, Kennan declared. Preccupied with Vietnam, the administration could not be expected to achieve a breakthrough in East-West relations. Moreover, Kennan told a West German editor, the United States was "a provincial society, remote from European affairs, preoccupied with our own problems, dizzy and confused over the impact of over-rapid technological change" and thus "the sort of leadership needed to solve Europe's problems is not apt to come out of our midst."[4]

Kennan was right: the impetus for détente came not from Washington but from French President Charles De Gaulle and West Germany's Willy Brandt. Distrustful of the Americans, De Gaulle called on Europe to take the initiative and did so himself in 1966 by visiting Moscow and withdrawing France from NATO's integrated military command. Noting that he had been "a Gaullist before De Gaulle," Kennan welcomed the possibility that France might "assume more of the burden of leadership in Western Europe."[5] Despite De Gaulle's initiatives, France was no longer a great power and could not compel a change in the European status quo.

Defenders of American domination of NATO attempted to counter De Gaulle's criticisms with the Multilateral Nuclear Force (MLF), under whose authority a polyglot crew representing all member nations of the alliance would serve on nuclear-armed ships. To Kennan "this nonsense" put "the requirements of the ideal military posture ahead of the desirability of a political accommodation" and undermined Washington's ability to conduct arms control negotiations with Moscow. "Any agreement on such matters would be hard enough to arrive at, God knows, if it were only primarily ourselves and the Russians who were involved," he explained in a letter to National Security Advisor McGeorge Bundy. The Johnson administration soon abandoned the MLF.[6]

As a scholar dividing his time between Princeton and Harvard in 1966, Kennan exerted only marginal influence on policy as Western officials continued to integrate West Germany into the NATO military command while refusing to recognize the East German communist regime. This approach was expected somehow to result in German reunification on terms favorable to the West, but such a position "has never struck me as realistic," Kennan complained to Henry Kissinger, who advocated German reunification under Western terms in his 1965 book, *The Troubled Partnership*.[7] If disengagement was not to occur, Kennan told another realist scholar, Hans J. Morgenthau, then Washington should recognize East Germany. Refusal to recognize the GDR or negotiate over Germany with Moscow even as the United States continued to ship arms to Bonn was "just about the most dangerous position I can think of," he declared.[8]

As Kennan and his fifteen-year-old son toured Russia on a "sentimental" journey in the summer of 1965, the retired diplomat appeared to be accommodating himself to the perpetuation of Soviet influence in Eastern Europe. Kennan blamed the Kremlin's domination of the region

on the refusal of the Western powers to assume a reasonable negotiating posture and he seemed sure that the Khrushchev reforms and
the emergence of communist polycentrism marked the end of "decisive Russian influence" in Eastern Europe and left Russia "very little
expansionist today."[9] The picture "differs quite fundamentally from
that which I assumed" in the Reith Lectures, he explained in 1965.
In the absence of a supranational European federation, it was "perhaps better that Germany, in particular, should not be reunited at
this stage in her history, and that Russia should continue to bear a certain responsibility for the preservation of the order of Eastern Europe
and the Balkans."[10] Reporters noted that the appearance of Foreign
Minister Andrei Gromyko at a luncheon for Kennan at American Ambassador Foy Kohler's Moscow residence was a "special tribute at a
time when Soviet officials are avoiding unnecessary contacts with
Americans here to show their displeasure over Washington's Vietnam
policy."[11]

The Soviet invasion of Czechoslovakia in August 1968 shattered
Kennan's perception of only moderate Russian influence in Eastern Europe. As the Red Army poured across the Carpathian Mountains, the
Kremlin showed that its attitudes toward the region had, in certain
fundamental respects, undergone little revision since Stalin's time. A
Soviet-led force of 600,000 intervened on the night of August 20, terminating the reforms of Alexander Dubcek's "Prague Spring." Unlike the
Hungarian reformers of 1956, the Czechs had carefully avoided threats
to withdraw from the Warsaw Pact. Instead, it was Dubcek's domestic
reforms, his call for "socialism with a human face," that prompted the
Soviets to intervene and replace him with Gustav Husak.[12]

The Czechoslovak intervention prompted another spectacular reversal
in Kennan's perceptions, one that reflected his penchant for emotional
outbursts rather than realistic assessments in response to Soviet imperialism. In a nationally circulated Associated Press interview, he called for
the United States to "send 100,000 troops to West Germany and say 'we
will not take them out until you leave Czechoslovakia.'" Calling on
Johnson to cancel a proposed summit with the Soviet leaders, Kennan
now asserted that he had "never understood this talk about détente. I
have not seen any evidence of détente and I wouldn't trust any so-called
détente if it is not supported by free contacts between governments and

peoples." Russia's "conspiratorial methods of diplomatic action" ruled out any possibility of relaxing East-West tensions, he declared.[13]

The Czechoslovak invasion prompted Kennan to view as real the possibility of a Soviet invasion of Western Europe, something he had long considered a remote contingency. Asked if Western Europe faced the prospect of invasion, he responded: "A year ago I would have said: definitely not. Now I don't know. Recent Russian behavior has not been rational." Kennan suspected that "some curious internal struggle" fomented by the secret police had prompted Moscow's actions and he speculated that "rational" leaders in the Kremlin must have opposed the invasion, which constituted "the greatest blow since the Hitler-Stalin pact" to Russia's international prestige.[14]

The Kremlin, citing defensive considerations to justify the invasion, pronounced the "Brezhnev Doctrine," which arrogated to Moscow the right to intervene to protect socialist states from counterrevolution. The Soviet explanation was "specious" and "shameless," Kennan declared. "There was no effort on the part of any other power to place military installations in Czechoslovakia, nor were other powers in any way involved in the political developments in that country to which Russian action was a response."[15] He charged that it was "against the rules of the game for them to intervene when a Communist regime evolves as the Czech Communist regime has evolved. There was no challenge to the Warsaw Pact." He lamented that Washington's preoccupation with Vietnam had prevented a show of force in Europe and "we are apparently not even reinforcing our troops there, though there are now about half a million more Russians in the area." Washington had failed to "recognize that whereas it was obliged to tolerate such aggression in 1956, it cannot and should not pass it over in the same way in 1968." As the *National Review* gleefully observed, it was "as if Mr. X had returned."[16]

Kennan's outrage was understandable in view of the brutal Soviet repression and the absence of threatening gestures on the part of the Prague regime. Still, America more than matched Soviet aggression through its own militarism in Southeast Asia and in the smaller scale but perhaps more analogous Dominican intervention. Kennan's call for sending American troops to Central Europe would have increased the prospect of war for the sake of a region that America had written off since 1938.

In the wake of the Czechoslovakian intervention, a still fuming Kennan held out little hope that the Soviet leadership would pursue détente. He described Communist Party General Secretary Leonid Brezhnev as "a man never, to my knowledge, reported to have said a single interesting thing, utterly devoid of a sense of humor: obviously a sly, adroit political chameleon." Although Brezhnev was "excellently adjusted to life in the jungle of Soviet politics," he knew nothing about the West. As for Premier Alexi Kosygin, he was a "dreadfully pedestrian . . . reflection of a weary, faithful, plodding unimaginativeness." Both men were "characteristic representatives of the party system which governs that country and has governed it for fifty years" and their successors were "apt to be the same sort of people." The post-Brezhnev Soviet leadership has itself echoed Kennan's assessment, although he did underestimate Brezhnev's potential to emerge as a keen supporter of détente.[17]

The Czechoslovakian intervention caused a temporary setback to efforts to achieve East-West accord but prominent statesmen and Kennan himself soon overcame their anger and once again advocated détente. The elections of Richard Nixon and Willy Brandt in 1969 brought to power two men intent on improving East-West relations. Brandt's election as chancellor in October 1969 marked the triumph of *Ostpolitik* (Eastern Policy) in the Federal Republic, as the former Mayor of West Berlin renounced the rigidities of Konrad Adenauer's legacy, including the "Hallstein Doctrine" which mandated nonrecognition of any government that recognized East Germany. Before Brandt's election, Kennan had applauded *Ostpolitik* for putting East Germany's Walter Ulbricht, whom many called "the last Stalinist," on the defensive. "The mere fact that Ulbricht got so frightened when one began to talk seriously of East-West contacts shows that Brandt's policy was correct," he explained. *Ostpolitik* spurred an agreement on Berlin, long the pivot of East-West tensions, as Ulbricht's resignation and replacement by Erich Honecker facilitated the 1971 Quadripartite Agreement in which Moscow guaranteed access to West Berlin in return for a pledge that West Germany would not attempt to make its sector of the city a vital part of the Federal Republic.[18]

Brandt's diplomacy worried Nixon and National Security Adviser Kissinger, both of whom feared that a West German-led détente would undermine U.S. leadership in Europe. Already Senator Mike Mansfield (D-Montana) had introduced resolutions calling for significant reductions in U.S. troop deployments on the continent. Still ill at ease about Soviet intentions in the wake of the Czech invasion, Kennan joined the new administration in opposing Mansfield's proposals, declaring that unilateral American troop reductions "would plainly constitute a further disturbance to our disadvantage of the strategic balance in Europe." In an effort to undercut Mansfield's appeal, the administration proposed and received Soviet endorsement for opening talks on Mutual Balanced Force Reductions as well as a conference on security and cooperation in Europe.[19]

While easing tensions in Europe was one of the major features of détente, Kennan was leery as Nixon and Kissinger moved with secrecy followed by fanfare toward normal relations with China. Having narrowly averted war with Moscow in 1969, Beijing reversed twenty years of enmity and crossed ideological lines in an effort to improve relations with Washington. Nixon went to China for discussions with Zhou Enlai and Mao Zedong and signed the "Shanghai Communiqué," which pledged that both nations would move toward normal relations and seek to curb "hegemony," a euphemism for the Soviet Union.[20]

The Nixon Administration applauded itself loudly for the accomplishments of the new "triangular diplomacy," but Kennan declared that China was "not a suitable ally or associate of this country in world affairs" and feared that the Nixon summit would produce "unreal dreams of intimacy" similar to the perceptions held by many Americans in the first half of the twentieth century. "For reasons only a social psychologist could explore," he observed, "euphoric dreams of this nature have long been a congenital weakness of American opinion." Anxious to achieve a meaningful détente with Russia and doubtful about forging close ties with "Orientals," Kennan warned against expecting China "to constitute a major factor in the solution of the problems of our relationship with the Soviet Union."[21]

Kennan welcomed the Nixon Administration's arms control initiatives but recognized their limited value. As historian Raymond L. Garthoff has observed, although "neither Nixon nor Kissinger put much stock in arms control," they opened the Strategic Arms Limitation Talks as a "political enterprise" designed to deflect attention from continuing U.S. involvement in Vietnam. SALT was part of a strategy of "linkage" under which the United States dangled trade agreements and arms control measures to induce the Soviets to alter their policies in the Middle

East, withdraw support for revolutionaries in the developing world, and help the United States achieve an "honorable" exit from Vietnam. The concept was flawed, however, as Moscow expected to negotiate on equal footing in recognition of its achievement of strategic parity with the United States.[22]

Kennan declared that SALT "may prove to be the greatest opportunity . . . to bring this dreadful and expensive and dangerous weapons race to an end, or at least to prevent its further development." However, when Nixon made it clear that Washington intended to deploy a defensive antiballistic missile (ABM) system as well as offensive missiles with multiple, independently targeted warheads (MIRVs), Kennan declared that he could not "believe that the inauguration of new weapons systems of this sort on our side, just while these talks are getting underway, is going to be useful and conducive to their success."[23] The SALT I accord signed in the Kremlin on May 26 during Nixon's second dramatic summit of 1972 did restrict ABM deployment, thus containing an explosive avenue of strategic competition, and both powers agreed to measures reducing the risk of accidental war and upgrading the hotline. However, SALT I failed to achieve meaningful limitations on offensive weapons, including MIRVs, or to limit qualitative improvements to existing systems.[24] Because SALT allowed so many avenues of strategic competition to remain open, Kennan correctly observed that the negotiations "had more of a symbolic than real value."[25]

Brezhnev pursued trade and economic relations with the West, but found that Nixon and Kissinger intended to use trade as a "political instrument" to reward or punish Moscow, depending on how it "behaved" in world politics.[26] Kennan now favored the expansion of Soviet-American trade as a means to promote détente, supported granting Most Favored Nation status to Moscow, and opposed administration efforts to link economic relations with Soviet political behavior. Once Moscow had paid for American goods, he explained, "we cannot then logically come along afterwards, as a government, and say in effect, 'You must pay for this all over again in the form of this or that political price, before you can have the goods.' Either we believe in free enterprise and the validity of the market or we do not."[27]

While the administration sought to influence Russia's diplomacy, critics of détente linked East-West trade to Soviet domestic policy, especially Jewish emigration, in a move that Kennan condemned.[28] He suffered few illusions about the treatment of Soviet Jews and political dissidents, but recognized that political and religious persecution was not so much a communist as a Russian phenomenon. Moreover, as a result of his direct experience with Stalinism, Kennan argued that Soviet human rights policies, while "far from satisfactory," were still "far better" than under Stalin. "There is just no comparison."[29]

The potential benefits of détente "dwarf in importance the comfort and well-being of individual minorities" in either country, Kennan argued. Moreover, the chances were "less than poor" that Moscow could be compelled to change its domestic political practices for "no government could afford, if only for reasons of prestige, to make its internal policies a subject of bargaining with outside powers. We ourselves would not do it." Thus, an insistence on linking détente with such issues as Soviet dissidence and Jewish emigration carried the risk of "forfeiting the remaining possibilities for shaping Soviet-American relations in a manner favorable to the solution of world problems, without bringing any appreciable relief to the people in Russia who are the object of this solicitude."[30]

The logic of Kennan's position failed to impress Senator Henry M. Jackson (D-Washington) and Representative Charles Vanik, who secured overwhelming congressional approval for an amendment linking the granting of MFN with higher levels of Jewish emigration. As a result of successful negotiations by Kissinger, Jewish emigration rose from a minimal level in 1970 to 35,000 in 1973 but Jackson, a presidential aspirant, insisted on making Soviet-American negotiations public, trumpeted his role in altering Moscow's domestic policy, and pressed for additional concessions. As Kennan had predicted, the Kremlin rejected the entire package of trade expansion that had been an integral component of détente rather than allowing foreign interference in its domestic affairs. Linkage had failed and Jewish emigration plummeted to 13,000 in 1975.[31] In congressional testimony, Kennan declared that Washington had singled out Moscow for discriminatory treatment. "Why only the Soviet Union?" he asked. "Are we sure there are no other countries where citizens would have difficulty in obtaining permission to leave the country at will?"[32]

Despite their anger over linkage on human rights, the Soviets still hoped to maintain a higher level of trade with the West and to perpetuate détente. Thus at the conclusion of the Helsinki Conference on European Security and Cooperation in 1975, Moscow promised to "respect human rights and fundamental freedoms, including freedom of thought, conscience [and] religion." These pledges conflicted with the regime's actual policies on civil liberties, but the Soviet leaders signed the document in return for formal Western recognition of the territorial and political boundaries of postwar Europe, as well as economic cooperation among states. "Helsinki was a sterile two-year exercise in semantics which was bound to lead to very little," Kennan declared. "The idea of saying that we are both going to behave like good democrats, that we are both going to recognize human rights and so forth, is a mistake from the beginning." Such accords violated realist precepts against seeking ideal agreements based on "general principles."[33]

The Watergate scandal, which forced Nixon's resignation on August 9, 1974, undermined détente by removing from office a man whom the public trusted in dealings with the USSR. Unable to fathom American politics, Moscow interpreted Watergate as a plot engineered by the U.S. "ruling circles" to undermine a moderate Soviet policy.[34] By this time détente had already been "oversold," as Kennan put it, alluding to an exaggerated public perception of accomplishment flowing from the SALT treaty and the two dramatic summits with the communist powers. Conservatives opposed to détente had been quieted by Nixon's "formidable credentials as a hardliner, which bewildered many critics, and by Henry Kissinger's diplomatic fireworks, which dazzled them," Kennan explained. He now recognized that a renascent right-wing would exploit public misperceptions of détente to discredit the policy.[35]

One reason détente became a dirty word under Nixon's successor, Gerald R. Ford, was Soviet and Cuban support of a successful communist revolt in Angola. Despite an absence of evidence that Moscow ordered the Cuban intervention in Angola, Ford and Kissinger charged that the unprecedented use of Soviet "proxy" troops warranted $28 million in emergency military aid to American-backed forces there, but Congress turned down the request.[36] Declaring that it was America's "responsibility to contain Soviet power," Kissinger advocated U.S. intervention even though Angola was strategically insignificant. "If the United States is seen to waiver in the face of massive Soviet and Cuban intervention," he explained, "what will be the perception of leaders around the world as they make decisions concerning their future security?" Kennan, of course, had long been an advocate of containment on the perimeter and had offered this very argument in support of U.S. intervention in Korea and Vietnam, but defeat in Southeast Asia had taught him that such preoccupations with credibility and bandwagoning could be self-defeating.[37]

Despite his respect for Kissinger's "intellect" and "demonstrated competence" in foreign affairs, Kennan publicly challenged the Secretary of State's call for direct U.S. intervention in Angola. The United States "has still to evolve methods for asserting its influence in overseas territories which would save it from the sort of failures it has experienced in the past," he declared. Kennan doubted that the Cubans had "acted as Soviet puppets" and, in the event, he was "not greatly worried about this situation." To the extent Moscow was involved, he advised Congress in 1980, "I think that they are only going to have trouble in there. These countries do not really like any of us big powers, and they are not noted for their gratitude for the arms and military support you give them."[38]

Opponents of détente charged that events in Angola and the Horn of Africa, where Moscow and Havana supported the Ethiopian communist government in a brief war with Somalia in 1977–78, reflected a Soviet plan to expand its influence under the cover of reducing East-West tensions. The Kremlin and supporters of East-West accord, including Kennan, argued, however, that such ideological-political competition in the developing world was inevitable and could coexist with détente. Nor did they see such competition as one-sided. "I find, in principle, nothing in recent Soviet actions in Angola or the Horn of Africa," Kennan explained, "which we ourselves have not done in other areas, on a number of instances, in recent years."[39]

By 1976, however, the perception that détente enhanced Soviet ascendancy in world affairs put supporters of improved East-West relations on the defensive. Former California Governor Ronald Reagan challenged Ford for the Republican nomination, charging that recent American diplomacy threatened to transform the nation into a second-rate power. A new Committee on the Present Danger, a lobby of veteran cold warriors, found the Russians' dedication to "a Communist world order" comparable to Nazi Germany's aggression in the 1930s and declared that "if past trends continue, the USSR will within several years achieve strategic superiority over the United States."[40]

To Kennan this was pure nonsense. He rejected the notion that Moscow sought military superiority or to conquer or "Finlandize" Europe, much less the entire globe. The men in the Kremlin pursued détente not to gain unilateral advantage but because "they are coming to realize that they cannot advance themselves to the point of a really great economic power . . . without a much more fluid and extensive access to Western technology than they have today." The Soviets had their own problems, Kennan advised a congressional subcommittee in 1977, including "a certain skepticism, a certain demoralization, a good deal of corruption, a great deal of drunkenness, a great deal of absenteeism in labor." In view of the serious domestic challenges, he emphasized that "they have a great many things to think about other than doing us under, and some of these things are much more intimately associated with their interests at the moment than these ideas about the future of world revolution." Rather than seeing the Soviet Union as "a static, unchanging phenomenon," he advised, policy makers needed to realize that "it, too, evolves, and the direction in which it evolves is influenced to some degree by our vision of it and our treatment of it."[41]

Kennan played no role in the 1976 presidential campaign but hoped that the new Democratic administration of Jimmy Carter would offer a sensible Soviet policy. Following the election, he drafted a statement for the American Committee on U.S.-Soviet Relations, a group formed in 1974, whose arguments countered those of the Present Danger lobby. Kennan's statement urged a "resolute abandonment of the stale slogans and reflexes of the cold war" and new attention to a Soviet policy that had been "neglected, adrift and devoid of initiative." The Committee called on Carter to pursue détente, and especially arms control, in an effort to halt the "suicidal proliferation of nuclear and other weapons."[42]

Kennan approved of the appointment of veteran diplomat Cyrus Vance as Secretary of State,[43] but soon realized that the Carter Administration would do little to salvage détente. Carter made human rights the centerpiece of his diplomacy and publicly embraced the cause of Soviet dissidents, thus creating, as Raymond Garthoff observed, "the impression in the minds of the Soviet leaders that the United States would be satisfied only with a fundamental change in their system." Carter and his National Security Adviser, Zbigniew Brezinski, a Polish emigré whom the Russians distrusted, emphasized Soviet violations of the Helsinki Final Act from the moment they took office. Kennan admitted that the Kremlin had "asked for trouble" by signing the human rights pledge and that the new administration was "formally on good ground" in making an issue of Moscow's violations of the Helsinki provisions, but he opposed sacrificing détente over the issue of Soviet domestic policy.[44]

Although increased tensions characterized Soviet-American diplomacy under Carter,[45] the administration did negotiate a second SALT accord, which set ceilings on MIRVs, Cruise missiles, and strategic bombers, and also arranged for record numbers of Jews to emigrate. However, a bipartisan coalition of conservatives led by Paul Nitze, Henry Jackson, and Reagan opposed SALT II, endangering its chances of Senate ratification. "I am not aware of any of the dangers that people see in the treaty which would not be greater if there were no treaty at all," Kennan declared.[46] The "discovery" of a Soviet troop brigade in Cuba in the late summer of 1979, accurately described as a "false alarm" by Kennan, further poisoned the international atmosphere.[47]

The events of November and December 1979 shattered whatever hopes remained for perpetuating détente. On November 4 Islamic fundamentalists seized the American embassy in Teheran and held hostage its fifty-three occupants.[48] On December 27 the Soviet Union invaded neighboring Afghanistan, provoking nearly universal condemnation and a return to East-West confrontation. These conflicts reinforced a perception of American impotence in world affairs first set in train by defeat in Vietnam and subsequent events across an "arc of crisis" stretching from Africa and the Near East to Southeast Asia.[49] The events in Iran and Afghanistan, as might be expected, prompted a characteristic blend of emotional and realistic responses from Kennan.

Kennan's response to the Iran hostage crisis reflected both his anger over the Iranians' affronts to accepted international behavior and his contempt for third world peoples on the periphery of civilization. Outraged by the actions of the "howling mobs," who made American flag burnings and shouts of "death to Carter" a daily ritual outside the U.S. embassy, Kennan castigated Iran for its "grievous affront to international law, to diplomatic practice, and to the entire international community." Recalling his own five and one-half month internment by the Nazis in 1941–42, Kennan warned that Washington should not "temporize with this problem indefinitely" in view of "the psychic stress that these people are under." He proposed to free the hostages "in such a way as to deprive [Iran] of any illusion that it could ever again resort to this totally indefensible, unacceptable and barbaric practice."[50]

In Kennan's view, a proper response to the hostage seizure would have been for the President to ask Congress for a declaration of war. Such action would have acknowledged the existence of "a state of hostilities brought on by the Khomeini regime and, I may say, by the never ending flood of insults to this country from the mouths of the chiefs of state there, something I have never seen the likes of at any time." After declaring war Washington should have interned all Iranian official personnel in this country and turned over its interests in Iran to a third power as normally during a state of war. "We would then be in a position to play it by ear from that time out," Kennan explained, "including the use of certain military pressure."

After interning Iranian officials in the United States, Washington might have been able to trade them for the American hostages, Kennan argued. In the event, he preferred such a course to continued demonstrations of American impotence while the Iranians "diddled" the UN during its deliberations over the issue. Asked if he had made his views known to the Carter administration, Kennan elicited laughter during the Senate committee hearing by responding, "no, sir, I have not detected any inordinate curiosity on their part."[51] With the exception of the aborted rescue mission across the Iranian desert, Carter chose to negotiate for the hostages' freedom, which he secured after more than 400 days of their confinement.

Kennan's call for a declaration of war was not without logical foundation, but neither was there any assurance that such an approach would have achieved any more than an escalation, and perhaps a prolongation, of the crisis. A declaration of war on the part of the "Great Satan" may well have made the the Khomeini regime even more obdurate and the Ayatollah showed in the subsequent war with Iraq that he was willing for his countrymen to endure extended suffering in the service of Allah. Kennan's call for a declaration of war delighted the editors of the *National Review*, however, as William F. Buckley called the proposal a "wonderful demystifier, sucking up the smoke from the room, so that you are left there with your objective in very plain view."[52]

Kennan's response to the Soviet invasion of Afghanistan contrasted sharply with his outrage over the events in Iran or, for that matter, those in Czechoslovakia in 1968. He did not approve of the Afghan intervention but was far more critical of the American reaction, which wiped out the remnants of détente. Kennan called for a sober recognition of Moscow's legitimate security interests in Afghanistan and recommended restraint in contrast to the feverish response of the administration. Calling the Soviet action "the greatest threat to peace since World War II," Carter shelved the SALT II treaty, authorized a military buildup and economic sanctions against Russia, ordered a U.S. boycott of the 1980 Moscow Olympics, and propounded the "Carter Doctrine" asserting that America would employ "military force" to secure its "vital interests" in the Persian Gulf. "Never since World War II has there been so far-reaching a militarization of thought and discourse in the capital," Kennan declared. "A war atmosphere has been created."[53]

Kennan rebuked the administration for a "serious lack of balance" in its interpretation of events and insisted that Carter had ignored "geographic proximity, ethnic affinity [and] political instability in what is, after all, a border country of the Soviet Union." The Kremlin had acted in part to secure its border against the spread of Islamic fundamentalism into the Soviet Muslim population, and Kennan was sympathetic to the Russians, a more "civilized" people than the dark-skinned, robed, and bearded Afghan rebels whom they opposed. As early as 1947 he had declared that the Russians had a sense of "mission" which prompted them to "come to the peoples along their Asiatic borders as a civilizing force" and he could "not blame the Russians greatly for their attitude."[54]

Kennan also charged that Washington's cultivation of the Shah as an American client in the Persian Gulf encouraged the Kremlin's decision to invade Afghanistan. "I suspect that we frightened them considerably by what we did in the period of the rule of the Shah," he explained, citing U.S. military cooperation and arms sales to Teheran. "I think if the converse of that had been done in Mexico there would have been a lot more excitement in this country" and thus Americans were "not entirely without responsibility for the creation of the atmosphere, the anxieties, and the troubles that have led to our situation today."[55]

It required "a lively imagination" to suppose that Moscow intended to occupy and seal off the Persian Gulf, Kennan told a Senate subcommittee. While many viewed the Afghan invasion as the initial thrust of a Soviet plan to seize the gulf and halt the flow of oil to the West, Kennan argued that even if successful in dominating Afghanistan, the Soviets would be closer to the Gulf, but "still separated from it by 500 to 600 miles of some of the most inhospitable territory in all of southern Asia." Moreover, Moscow knew that any attempt to dominate the Persian Gulf would mean war with the West and there were "many other considerations both internal and external to which they have to give attention, which would argue against anything so dramatic and so tremendously destabilizing in its effects as going down there, conquering the Persian Gulf, and cutting off the oil to all the rest of the industrialized world." Long a critic of American dependence on Mideast oil, Kennan added that "if the Persian Gulf is really vital to our security, it is surely we who, by our unrestrained greed for oil, have made it so."[56]

Convinced that Moscow had "made a mistake" with the Afghan invasion, Kennan advised an aloof American posture. "I think this is a situation that they backed into and may come to regret very bitterly." Carter Administration efforts to make Pakistan the focal point of Afghani resistance reflected "questionable wisdom, not only from the standpoint of our relations with the Soviet Union, but also from the standpoint of our relations with India," a bitter opponent of Pakistan. "I wish I could understand better why some of this is necessary," Kennan bemoaned. He recommended "no help" for the *mujahdeen* guerrillas who mounted resistance against the Soviet-backed government. "This is far from our shores. It is not really our quarrel" and Washington had little "in common with these Afghan resistance groups." American officials rejected this advice and supplied the *mujahdeen* with modern weaponry that contributed to their eventual victory culminating in a Soviet withdrawal from Afghanistan.[57]

In typical fashion, Kennan qualified his moderate response to the Afghan war by agreeing with conservatives who advocated intervention against Cuba in response to the Soviet invasion. The Caribbean island had long been a source of consternation to Kennan, who had defended the Kennedy Administration's handling of the Cuban missile crisis, yet admitted that it constituted a "double standard" to place nuclear weapons near Soviet borders while proscribing their deployment in Cuba.[58] By 1970 Kennan termed the Soviet relationship with Cuba "not very menacing" and advised "keep[ing] out of their affairs." While not wanting "to be facetious," he wondered "whether we know when we are well off." After all, he explained, equating third world peoples with troublesome children, "somebody else is today paying the bills for Cuba and has to argue with the Cubans."[59]

Appearing on television's *60 Minutes* in 1980, however, Kennan sounded a different line. Asked about Republican presidential candidate Ronald Reagan's call for action against Cuba in response to the Afghan invasion, he declared that "it's not on every question of foreign affairs that I would agree with Governor Reagan, but I—in this case, I rather would." If the Soviets remained in Afghanistan and attempted to use the country "for strategic purposes further afield," then military action against Cuba might be justified. "As a matter of fact, this might have been a more logical reaction to what they did in Afghanistan than what we have actually done," Kennan declared.[60] On other occasions he reiterated that the Soviet-Cuban relationship was "in conflict with our traditional concept of the security of this hemisphere and particularly the Caribbean" and was therefore "not indefinitely compatible with our national interests." Kennan had thus been unable to resolve his contempt for communists and third world nationalists even as he occasionally admitted the hypocrisy of Washington's attitudes toward them.[61]

As in the case of Afghanistan, but not in Czechoslovakia, instability in Poland found Kennan willing to give Moscow the benefit of the doubt in its relations with neighboring countries. In Poland the independent trade union Solidarity challenged the authority of the Polish Communist Party, prompting many Western observers to predict a Soviet invasion of the country. Moscow did not intervene but its presence was felt in December 1981 when General Wojciech Jaruzelski seized power and imposed martial law. The Reagan Administration placed the blame for this event squarely on the Soviet Union and imposed economic sanctions against both Warsaw and Moscow.[62]

Kennan showed little sympathy for the striking trade unionists and asserted that their renunciation of socialism and repudiation of Poland's membership in the Warsaw Pact was inevitably self-defeating. As he had done for years, Kennan argued that Poland and the other states of Eastern Europe would inevitably remain within the Soviet sphere of influence in the absence of an agreement to establish a neutral zone in East-Central Europe. If the United States "really wanted" to guard against Soviet intervention, it would have to address itself to "the Kremlin's basic strategic stake" in the region, he argued. Washington could have encouraged Soviet moderation had it assured Moscow that any liberalization in Poland "would not be taken advantage of by the NATO powers, to the detriment of the Soviet strategic position in Eastern and Central Europe as a whole."

Kennan preferred the stability of marital law under Jaruzelski to the combination of "a semiparalyzed Communist government and a Solidarity well set up to obstruct this Government, but in no way prepared to replace it." He declared that Jaruzelski's seizure of power was "bad—of course," yet preferable to direct intervention by Moscow. "Jaruzelski is, after all, a Pole, surrounded by Poles," he explained. Economics sanctions accomplished nothing and the United States should have "reserve[d] judgment in the face of a rapidly moving and unpredictable situation that we have little capability of influencing in any case."[63]

Critics condemned Kennan for his response to the Polish and Afghan crises, which were symptoms of his abandonment of American internationalism since Vietnam. Writing in the *New Republic,* Leon Wieseltier criticized Kennan for speaking "only about the interests of the Soviet Union" and declared, in an absurd charge, that Kennan's response to the Polish crisis was consistent with the containment policy which had delivered "a death sentence for the people of Eastern Europe." Conservative academics Hugh Seton-Watson, Richard Pipes, Michael Novak and others contributed to a book entitled *Decline of the West? George Kennan and His Critics* (1978) that scored Kennan for abandoning containment as well as for his critique of Western culture and society. Novak declared that whereas "in 1947 Mr. X was bold and assertive" in the modern era "Mr. Y is weary, timid, and ready to yield" to Soviet demands. Seton-Watson doubted that pollution, crime, drug abuse and other Western social problems were, as Kennan now argued, "more urgent or more menacing than the danger of Soviet imperialism." Eugene V. Rostow saw Kennan as "exhausted, disillusioned and nearly without hope" in his reflection of "a fashionable post-Vietnam mood about foreign affairs" that came "perilously close to preaching that we don't really need a foreign and defense policy at all." The most vicious attack came from the British journalist Henry Fairlie, who declared that Kennan practiced the "politics of senility" and should be "put out to pasture."[64]

The criticism of his positions showed how much distance separated

Kennan from the renascent cold war consensus that swept Reagan into the White House in 1980, thus terminating détente. The effort to mold a new relationship had depended too much on "empty demonstrations of friendship" and too little on "offering real initiatives to the Soviet Union," Kennan concluded.[65] Thus, as he had done more often than not since 1948, the retired diplomat blamed militarization and rejection of negotiations by the Western powers for the failure to ameliorate Soviet-American tensions. Kennan was right: Soviet insecurities and aggressiveness contributed to the failure of détente; but Washington had fueled those insecurities by forging close ties with China (including the exchange of military intelligence), taking a timid approach to arms control, and attempting to restrict Soviet ideological-political competition while supporting its own clients in the developing world. The policy of linking détente with Soviet domestic practices presupposed an American superiority in world affairs which the Russians, having achieved strategic parity, were not bound to accept.[66]

Still respected as an expert on Soviet behavior, Kennan had expressed his views before congressional committees, in opinion articles, and on television; but he served in no official capacity, exerted only marginal influence on American diplomacy, and often undermined his own limited appeal by embracing quirky positions on world affairs. The retired diplomat relished his role as an outsider and took particular pleasure in debunking conventional wisdom. Thus, he advocated détente before it was popular in the mid-1960s but then chastised American statesmen for considering negotiations with Russia and failing to bolster U.S. military forces in Europe after the Soviet invasion of Czechoslovakia. Kennan voiced his suspicions about the normalization of relations with China while denouncing linkage and the Carter Administration's focus on human rights, all of which were popular at the time that he expressed his dissent. His call for a declaration of war on Iran and his refusal to criticize the Soviet Union for the Afghan invasion were not without elements of realism but these positions also reflected Kennan's efforts to distinguish himself outside the foreign affairs establishment. He felt a strong need to distance himself from the mainstream of American diplomacy, which was, as he saw it, the product of a chaotic democracy that had paid insufficient attention to cultivated elites such as himself.

Although Kennan still struggled to resolve the conflict between his realistic and emotional responses on most issues of world affairs, his views on nuclear weapons did not lack consistency. He devoted his energies in the 1980s to efforts to curb the arms race and steer American diplomacy toward a posture of neo-isolationism and cooperative internationalism.

XIV

The Diplomacy of Survival

THE LANDSLIDE ELECTION of Ronald Reagan in 1980 ensured a return to Soviet-American confrontation and thus further marginalized Kennan. The new President, whose perception of a global communist threat had undergone little revision since the early days of the cold war, ordered a massive military buildup, shelved arms control negotiations, and vowed to make America once again "stand tall" in the world.[1] Firmly entrenched as a critic of the foreign affairs establishment, Kennan condemned Reagan's diplomacy and devoted his energies in the 1980s to efforts to counteract what he perceived as a drift toward nuclear war. Although forced to swim against a tide of militant nationalism, Kennan influenced the national debate over arms control and Soviet policy.

The Reagan Administration enjoyed popular support for a return to confrontation in the wake of the Soviet invasion of Afghanistan, unrest in Poland, and the desire of many Americans to cast off the "Vietnam syndrome"—a perception of impotence in world affairs that had become acute during the Iran hostage crisis. Reagan asserted that the Soviet regime was "the focus of evil in the modern world" and that Kremlin machinations were at the root of "all the unrest that is going on." He claimed that Moscow had achieved strategic superiority, but the putative "window of vulnerability" was as illusory as the "missile gap" trumpeted by Democrats in the 1960 campaign.[2]

To Kennan it was obvious that fundamental misperceptions about Soviet capabilities as well as intentions underlay the "dramatic and very serious deterioration" of U.S.-Soviet relations. "It was never easy to deal with [the Soviet] government," he declared, "but it is no harder today than it used to be."[3] Reagan's Soviet policy rested on an "endless series of distortions and oversimplifications"; "systematic dehumanization" of the Kremlin leadership; "routine exaggeration of Moscow's military capabilities"; and a "reckless application of the double standard to the judgment of Soviet conduct and our own."[4] Speaking at Dartmouth in November 1981, he added that the popular perception of Moscow's foreign policy was "so extreme, so subjective, so far removed from what any sober scrutiny of external reality would reveal," that it was "dangerous as a guide to political action."[5]

While the Reagan Administration and much of the public were content to view the Soviet Union as an "evil empire" bent on world domination, Kennan emphasized the defensive motives underlying Kremlin actions. The Soviet leaders were a "group of troubled men" and "prisoners" of Russia's past. General Secretary Leonid Brezhnev and his comrades presided over a stagnant and demoralized society, whose internal weaknesses heightened traditional insecurities about international isolation and "capitalist encirclement." The ruling elite confronted hostile border regimes in Iran, Pakistan, and China and feared the disintegration of Soviet hegemony in Eastern Europe.[6]

As he juxtaposed attacks on American policies with his explanations of Soviet behavior, Kennan infuriated conservatives. "Wherever he looks he finds exculpatory reasons for Soviet expansionism," fumed Paul Hollander in *Policy Review*. Writing in the *New Republic*, Paul Seabury criticized Kennan for opposing American efforts "to countervail a relentless Soviet nuclear arms buildup," a position that amounted to unilateral disarmament. Noting that Kennan had once championed containment, both men now condemned him for apostasy—Seabury's article even carried the subtitle, "the great container springs a leak."[7]

To these critics, and to the Reagan Administration itself, the Soviet war in Afghanistan, competition in the developing world, and Moscow's history of intervention in Eastern Europe evidenced an ideological commitment to global expansion. They believed that the United States, as the leader of the Western world, had an obligation to contain the Soviet Union. Kennan rejected this interpretation of Soviet behavior and had lost faith in containment and U.S. intervention since Vietnam. He declared that the persistent "demonizing" of Soviet leadership reflected "an intellectual primitivism and naïveté unpardonable in a great government" and typified the immaturity that prevented America from exercising effective world leadership.[8]

While critical of American diplomacy, Kennan also scored the Kremlin for habits of secrecy, paranoia, and espionage. He charged Moscow with impeding efforts to improve East-West relations through an "inability to take account of [its] own past" as well as a tendency to view all forms of authority not under Soviet control as "wicked, hostile, and menacing." Even as the Soviets walled themselves off "like some ancient Oriental despotism," the regime authorized damaging intrigues such as sending nuclear submarines into Swedish territorial waters. He also criticized the Kremlin for an obsession with espionage and systematic abuse of traditional diplomatic institutions and channels.[9]

Kennan had long accused Moscow of bearing major responsibility for the cold war, but since 1948 he had also blamed the West for basing its planning on worst-case military scenarios. If Americans insisted on viewing the Russians as "incorrigible enemies, consumed only with their fear or hatred of us and dedicated to nothing other than our destruction," he declared, "that, in the end, is the way we shall assuredly have them." By adhering to the most negative perceptions of the adversary, the West would fail to encourage moderates while strengthening the hand of anti-détente forces in the Soviet hierarchy.[10]

Shortly after Reagan took office, the seventy-seven-year-old Kennan declared that the older he got the more he realized that such events as the Afghan invasion and the imposition of marital law in Poland were ephemeral, even trivial, in comparison with the dangers posed by the nuclear arms race. "The one thing that could be really final and could destroy all our values," he explained, "is the use of the weapons of mass destruction." In view of the threat posed by nuclear weapons, it was senseless "to work ourselves up in a lather of military apprehension" over characteristic examples of Soviet behavior along its borders, such as Afghan war. Neither could the West afford to make an issue of Soviet domestic practices. "Whoever subordinates the interests of world peace to the chimera of an early democratization of the Soviet Union," he declared, "will assuredly sacrifice the first of those values without promoting the second."[11]

To a man long disturbed by democratic politics, industrial growth, and modern technology, nuclear weapons were a powerful symbol of the failure of human beings to provide for the health and sanity of their own environment. The arms race, population growth, and environmental pollution all fused together in Kennan's mind to create the image of Western civilization in decline. As the elderly Kennan confronted his own mortality, he became more outspoken in his calls for actions to ensure the preservation of human civilization.

More than ever before, the perception that events in the 1980s reflected the "unfailing characteristics of a march toward war" dominated the elder statesman's thinking.[12] As both nations augmented their stockpiles of nuclear weapons and the arms control process broke down with the American refusal to ratify the SALT II treaty, Kennan warned in a speech in Garmisch, West Germany, in October 1980 that modern governments had become "the servants rather than the masters" of nuclear weapons. Modern history offered no example of such a buildup of armed forces by rival powers that did not result in the eventual outbreak of war and there was "no reason to believe we are greater, or wiser, than our ancestors." In a peroration that newspapers and magazines throughout the West reprinted, Kennan implored both Soviet and American leaders to "cease this madness. . . .

> You are mortal men. You are capable of error. You have no right to hold in your hands—there is no one wise enough and strong enough to hold in his hands—destructive powers sufficient to put an end to civilized life on a portion of our planet. No one should wish to hold such powers. Thrust them from you. The risks you might thereby assume are not greater—could not be greater—than those which you are now incurring for us all.[13]

While the Reagan Administration rejected SALT II as a "fatally flawed" treaty that would benefit the Soviet Union,[14] Kennan proposed to scrap the SALT process on grounds that it failed to encourage meaningful arms reductions by either side. He had "no illusion that [SALT] negotiations could ever be adequate to get us out of this hole. They are not a way of escape from the nuclear weapons race; they are an integral part of it."[15]

After his outspokenness against the nuclear arms race earned him the $50,000 Albert Einstein peace prize in 1981, Kennan asserted in a widely quoted acceptance speech delivered in Washington that the United States and the Soviet Union had embarked on a "collision course" toward nuclear war. "We have gone on piling weapon upon weapon, missile upon missile ... like the victims of some sort of hypnosis, like men in a dream, like lemmings headed for the sea." Calling for a bold and sweeping departure from the arms buildup, he advocated scrapping SALT in favor of an immediate across-the-board reduction by 50 percent of the nuclear arsenals of both powers. The "complete elimination" of nuclear weapons should be the ultimate goal of American diplomacy, he declared on another occasion.[16]

Kennan had remained steadfast in his opposition to the cultivation of nuclear weapons since 1949. At that time he had opposed development of new weapons systems and had called for a policy of "no first use" of nuclear weapons. He had long advocated a comprehensive nuclear test ban and argued that deterrence should rest on a strengthened conventional capability as well as a system of militias and reserves within individual nations.[17] Kennan had sharply opposed the placement of nuclear weapons in Europe and continued to advocate a nuclear-free zone on that continent and in other parts of the world. He still believed, as he had argued in opposition to the hydrogen bomb in 1949, that nuclear weapons could not "be reconciled with a political purpose directed to shaping, rather than destroying, the lives of the adversary."[18]

Although he continued to publish in *Foreign Affairs* and made his views known before small gatherings of international relations experts, Kennan's pleas for arms control and a "stable" Soviet policy increasingly appeared in newspapers and popular magazines such as the *New Yorker*, *Harper*'s, and the *Atlantic*. He granted more interviews than in the past and showed a willingness to work with individuals and groups in pressing his views, something he had not done in the State Department. The retired diplomat also founded the Kennan Institute for Advanced Russian Studies (named for his distant cousin and namesake rather than himself) in Washington D.C. in an effort to promote greater understanding of the Soviet Union.

Despite his advanced age, Kennan was more prolific than ever and undertook an ambitious three-volume study of European diplomacy on the eve of World War I.[19] The retired diplomat once declared that "every work of history ... is at least as revealing of the person who wrote it, and of the period in which it was written, as it is of the people it portrays, and of the epoch in which they lived," a statement that certainly applied to his study on the background of the Great War. Kennan meant to alert his readers to the parallels between the "self-destructive madness" that overtook Western civilization in 1914 and the same trends of modern-day diplomacy. "How fine it would be," he declared, "if it could be said of us that we had pondered these ominous lessons and had set about, in all humility and seriousness, to avoid the bewilderments that drove our fathers and grandfathers to these follies."[20]

As he noted in the introduction to his first volume, *The Decline of Bismarck's European Order,* published in 1979, the study stemmed from the author's "long-standing preoccupation with the First World War . . . as a factor in the life of our own time." The Great War, he declared, was *"the* great seminal catastrophe of this century—the event which, more than any other, excepting only perhaps the discovery of nuclear weaponry and the development of the population-environmental crisis, lay at the heart of the failure and decline of this Western civilization."[21]

Kennan's diplomatic experience and language skills—he exploited French, German, Russian, and English sources—enabled him to assess the emergence between 1875 and 1890 of the Franco-Russian entente. He condemned the "misguided and self-destructive Russian statesmanship" which had needlessly involved the nation in the European conflicts and ultimately in war and revolution. Despite the growing destructiveness evident in nineteenth-century warfare, virtually all the powers approached the coming of another war with a "lightheartedness" reflective of the "romantic-chivalric concept of military conflict." Like the great powers of his own day, Kennan declared, the leaders of the time had failed to appreciate that a modern war would be so incomparably destructive as to outweigh any gains that might be realized.[22]

Kennan's second volume, *The Fateful Alliance,* published in 1984, was even more present-minded than the first. His research suggested that France and Russia had cemented their "fateful alliance" behind the premise that Germany planned aggression against them when in fact Berlin was a satiated power. The alliance, which Kennan saw as central to the initiation of hostilities in Europe in 1914, thus showed "the pitfalls that lie in wait for statesmen who try to look too far into the future and to meet distant and imagined contingencies by the devices of military alliance." This conclusion complemented Kennan's own opposition to NATO and other collective security pacts. He also found that the statesmen of the World War I generation, like the Reagan Administration, had succumbed to a "nationalistic euphoria" that served only to increase the chances of war. Indulgence in these "mass emotional compulsions" had obscured from the European leaders of the World War I generation a realistic view of the national interest and thus led to catastrophe. One difference between the epochs was that weapons of the earlier time had been "only partially, not totally, self-destructive" whereas if modern-day governments continued to indulge in militant nationalism and nuclear arms competition, they "will be preparing, this time, a catastrophe from which there can be no recovery and no return."[23]

Critics welcomed Kennan's volumes as fine additions to the history of European diplomacy. One reviewer lauded his "impressive research" and skill of presentation and another declared that the "masterly contribution to diplomatic history" had illuminated the goals and illusions of statesmen during the diplomatic realignment of 1880s and 1890s. Critics praised Kennan's writing skills, especially his vivid character portraits, geographical imagery, and his ability to display the "insights of a tragic ironist."[24]

Less scholarly but more accessible to a popular audience was Kennan's 1982 book, *The Nuclear Delusion*. In this collection of essays on arms control and Soviet policy—most of which had been written in previous years—he argued that the arms race had placed the planet on the brink of "the abyss of total nuclear catastrophe." Although as a realist historian Kennan had long ridiculed the 1928 Kellogg-Briand pact outlawing war, he now called on all governments to recognize that war was "simply no longer a rational means of affecting the behavior of other governments." He condemned the "profoundly cynical" and "debauching" business of arms exports to developing countries as an "enormous evil" for which there was "no justification whatsoever."[25]

As the arms race, arms sales, and environmental deterioration undermined Kennan's outlook on the fate of human civilization, he showed a greater inclination to invoke Christian morality. In *Nuclear Delusion*, he branded the arms race "unacceptable from the Christian standpoint" and asserted that the stockpiling of weapons of mass destruction constituted "nothing less than a presumption, a blasphemy, and indignity— an indignity of monstrous dimensions—offered to God!" A longtime Presbyterian, Kennan embraced original sin and had grown even more doubtful about the ability of human beings to combat evil than when he had endorsed Reinhold Niebuhr's Christian realism in the early 1950s.[26]

Like Jonathan Schell's *The Fate of the Earth*—a popular and, in

Kennan's estimation, "powerful book"—*Nuclear Delusion* was both a polemic against the arms race and a call to transcend the cold war.[27] Historian Martin Sherwin found Kennan's book "replete with wisdom and learning" and *Time*'s Strobe Talbott noted that while Kennan was "too sanguine" in his perceptions of Soviet behavior, he was "quite right" in the assertion "that strident, bellicose countermeasures have played into the hands of the Soviet propaganda and diplomatic campaign to split NATO."[28]

Many Americans and Europeans shared Kennan's fears of Armageddon, as evidenced by the increasing numbers of anti-nuclear protesters in the early 1980s. The Reagan Administration's renunciation of détente and plans to deploy Pershing II missiles in Western Europe had heightened the fear of nuclear war within allied nations, prompting tens of thousands to participate in street demonstrations and to demand the closure of American military bases in Europe.[29] The popularity of books such as *Nuclear Delusion* and *Fate of the Earth* and of the ABC television production, *The Day After,* which depicted the grisly aftermath of a nuclear exchange, attested to the mounting public fear of nuclear war.

As a professional diplomat Kennan had long expressed his aversion to public involvement in diplomatic affairs, but private citizen Kennan had a different view. While the foreign affairs establishment was, as always, unnerved by such demonstrations, Kennan declared with approval that the "gathering strength of the anti-nuclear movement here and in Europe is to my mind the most striking phenomenon of this beginning of the 1980s." Once revolted by the sight of long haired protesters, he still found the dissenters "ragged, confused and disorganized" but he endorsed the "very fundamental and reasonable and powerful motivations" behind their actions and rebutted statements by Reagan, Secretary of State (until mid-1982) Alexander Haig and Defense Secretary Caspar Weinberger, which dismissed the West European and American anti-nuclear protesters as witless victims of Soviet propaganda. Kennan insisted that they instead reflected a "deep, instinctive, insistence . . . on sheer survival—on survival as individuals, as parents, as members of a civilization."[30]

Kennan endorsed the major aim of the protest movement: a freeze on the deployment of additional nuclear weapons. "At the very least," as he put it in the *New York Review of Books,* "one could accept a temporary freeze on the further build-up of these fantastic arsenals." The Reagan Administration attempted to arrest the momentum of the Freeze movement by initiating negotiations on intermediate range nuclear forces in Europe and by opening strategic arms reduction talks, or START. However, the President's lack of enthusiasm for these negotiations and political infighting among his charges prevented any progress from being made during his first term.[31]

Sign-toting and public rallies were still not Kennan's style, of course, but he did attempt to mount a campaign against the NATO policy that embraced the "first use" of nuclear weapons. At the heart of Western deterrent strategy was the plan to respond to a Soviet conventional attack against Western Europe by employing nuclear weapons, a position that Kennan found "pernicious and indefensible." In June 1982 Brezhnev renounced "first use" in Soviet strategic doctrine on grounds that "should a nuclear war start it could mean the destruction of world civilization, and, perhaps, the end of life itself on earth." Proponents of retaining the first use option in Western strategy still argued, however, that it was necessary to offset Soviet advantages in conventional armaments.[32]

Having opposed "first use" since 1949, Kennan spearheaded a campaign against the policy in the 1980s and soon found himself in his accustomed position at the center of controversy over Western strategy in the cold war. The retired diplomat provided the impetus behind a 1982 *Foreign Affairs* article against "first use" which ignited controversy throughout the West. Three prominent figures in the history of the nation's foreign affairs establishment joined Kennan as co-authors: Gerard Smith, the chief U.S. SALT negotiator from 1969 to 72; Robert S. McNamara, defense secretary under Kennedy and later president of the World Bank; and McGeorge Bundy, who had been JFK's national security adviser and president of the Ford Foundation.

It was Kennan, normally prone to working in isolation, who had put the coalition together. "I realized the voices of all four of us would be more powerful than the voice of any one of us," he explained. McNamara—who had abandoned the war-fighting component of his 1967 "flexible response" strategy—and Smith both shared Kennan's opposition to first use, but he had to persuade Bundy to join them in 1981.

Once united, the four chose to make their argument in *Foreign Affairs,* the premier journal of the Western diplomatic establishment with which Kennan had been closely associated since the X-Article.[33]

Kennan, Smith, McNamara, and Bundy argued that "first use" no longer constituted a credible deterrent because any actual use of nuclear weapons carried "unacceptable risks to the national life that military forces exist to defend."[34] If NATO employed nuclear weapons to halt a Soviet conventional attack in West Germany, for example, the Federal Republic itself would likely be destroyed by the very act of its defense, or in an ensuing nuclear counterresponse by the Soviet Union. Furthermore, "first use" was not credible because the Soviets would have reason to doubt that American policy makers would risk a nuclear attack *against the United States* by initiating the use of nuclear weapons in Europe.

The "gang of four," as critics promptly dubbed Kennan and his colleagues, declared that "a policy of no-first-use would not and should not imply an abandonment" of America's guarantee of the security of Western Europe, and particularly of West Germany. The four elder statesmen did not oppose *second* use, or a retaliatory nuclear strike, but hoped to prevent such a macabre scenario from being played out by bolstering conventional deterrence in Western Europe. "There has been a tendency, over many years," they argued, "to exaggerate the relative conventional strength of the USSR and to underestimate Soviet awareness of the enormous costs and risks of any form of aggression against NATO."[35]

The essential rationale for NFU was to create a climate conducive to arms control. If conventional deterrent capabilities were such that only a credible second nuclear strike was needed, they explained, requirements for the modernization of major nuclear systems would become more modest and "we can escape from the notion that we must somehow match everything the rocket commanders in the Soviet Union extract from their government." Although large, varied and survivable nuclear forces would still be necessary to ensure deterrence, once "first use" had been renounced "we shall find that our requirements are much less massive than is now widely supposed." An NFU policy would encourage the Soviet Union to adopt restraints of its own, they argued. Although Moscow had already renounced "first use," the four called for a joint declaration of the policy.[36]

Kennan and his three colleagues thus presented a compelling case for revising Western strategy and creating a climate conducive to arms control while maintaining security through a still formidable deterrent arsenal. The problem with their proposals, they recognized, was political and psychological rather than strategic, but these obstacles were sufficient to defeat NFU. Many West Europeans feared that renouncing "first use" was a step toward "decoupling" America from NATO, although Kennan and his colleagues insisted that conventional rearmament would ensure deterrence and unity within the Western alliance.[37]

Having learned of the imminent release of the *Foreign Affairs* article to the press, Secretary of State Alexander Haig launched a "preemptive strike" against NFU. The retired general summoned reporters to a news conference at Georgetown University and released a statement declaring that NFU was "tantamount to making Europe safe for conventional aggression." Making only an indirect reference to Kennan and his co-authors, whose own news conference publicizing their argument was scheduled for the next day, Haig asserted that "those in West who advocate the adoption of 'no first use' seldom go on to propose that the United States reintroduce the draft, triple the size of its armed forces, and put its economy on a war footing." The former NATO commander insisted that NFU would undermine deterrence, cripple the Western alliance, and leave the United States and its allies vulnerable to "nuclear blackmail" and "political intimidation."[38]

Haig's criticism backfired, however, as his news conference only publicized the argument offered by Kennan, McNamara, Bundy, and Smith. The four expressed regret for Haig's actions in their own meeting with the press the next day, declaring that they did not seek "polarization" with the Reagan Administration. Still, the combination of a cogent argument offered by four senior statesmen and a counterattack by the administration had set in train a public debate over Western nuclear strategy. "From the start we knew it would attract a very considerable amount of attention," declared *Foreign Affairs* editor William Bundy, the older brother of co-author McGeorge Bundy.[39]

The essay in *Foreign Affairs* prompted a spate of angry rejoinders and the publication of several articles on NFU in other national security journals. In an attempt to ensure numerical parity in authorship as well as in strategic arsenals, four representatives of the West German security establishment rebutted Kennan and his three colleagues in *Foreign Af-*

fairs. Karl Kaiser, Georg Leber, Alois Mertes, and Franz-Josef Schulze argued that a destabilizing policy of NFU "would liberate the Soviet Union from the decisive nuclear risk"; undermine confidence of Europeans and especially of Germans in the European-American alliance; and endanger the strategic unity of the Alliance and the security of Western Europe. The German leaders charged that Kennan, McNamara, Smith, and Bundy had offered an argument that was "tantamount to suggesting that 'rather Red than dead' would be the only remaining option."[40]

In addition to the rebuttals from the State Department, the White House, and the European allies, NFU was publicly rejected by the Joint Chiefs of Staff and leading Democrats, including 1984 and 1988 presidential nominees Walter Mondale and Michael Dukakis. Despite the opposition, Kennan insisted that NFU offered increased assurance against the outbreak of nuclear war. "After all," he explained in an interview in *U.S. News,* "if there is no first use of these weapons, there will be no use of them at all." The retired diplomat scoffed at the notion that renouncing "first use" would make Western Europe vulnerable to Soviet control and insisted that the very concept of nuclear superiority was "empty of meaning so long as both sides have these stupendous quantities of long-range nuclear weapons." Western Europe was fully capable of deterring Soviet aggression through conventional means and retention of the "first use" option only made Russia "unduly suspicious" of American intentions. "If we both declare that we won't be the first to use nuclear weapons—and they have repeatedly offered to do this," he explained— "a far more relaxed atmosphere might emerge in which serious talks about nuclear arms reductions could take place."[41]

The Reagan Administration refused to reconsider "first use" and insisted, despite the Soviet Union's offers to make substantial reductions in its own missile forces, on deploying intermediate range missiles in Western Europe. When the deployment began in November 1983, the USSR terminated discussions over intermediate-range nuclear forces (INF) and suspended START. While his chief arms control advisers remained divided on negotiating strategy, Reagan held to the position that the deployments were necessary to counter putative Soviet strategic advantages.[42]

Rejecting the President's attempts to justify the arms buildup, Kennan declared that there were "no 'widows of vulnerability' that could be opened or closed. We are vulnerable—totally vulnerable." Kennan sided with Moscow in its insistence that French and British nuclear stockpiles be counted as part of the Western arsenal, explaining that "either those two powers are NATO allies or they are not. One cannot have it both ways. Alluding to the administration's quest for liberation against indigenous Marxists in Central America, Kennan charged that it was hypocritical to attempt to disassociate the United States from French and British nuclear weapons even as the administration "insists[s] on viewing every weapon discovered in Nicaragua as being under direct Soviet control."[43]

Having at least captured some attention with their campaign against "first use," Kennan and his three co-authors attempted to build a broader coalition behind NFU. Under the auspices of the Aspen Institute for Humanistic Studies, they joined with several West European leaders in issuing a statement calling for the renewal of arms talks to be conducted by a strategic panel comprising a small number of high-level U.S. and Soviet representatives. The Aspen group urged the removal of intermediate and short-range weapons from Europe; an emphasis on conventional deterrence; outlawing of chemical weapons; and a breakthrough on the stalemated conventional arms reduction talks in Vienna. In an effort to woo support from European allies, they agreed to promote an initial policy of "no early use" of nuclear weapons before pressing for the adoption of NFU.[44]

By 1986 Kennan had joined a new "Project on No First Use" which argued in a policy statement that although NATO's "first use" policy had been intended to reduce the risk of conventional war, in effect it had actually "increase[d] the risk of nuclear war" by heightening the Soviet incentive to launch a first strike in a time of crisis. The authors declared that a program of conventional rearmament would keep America "coupled" with the security of Western Europe and would reduce the risks of the major powers "tumbling into war," as they had done in 1914. Termination of the "first use" policy would hardly inspire aggression from Moscow, they argued, because despite any renunciation of using nuclear weapons, as long as they existed "the possibility of their use exists and cannot be discounted by the East or the West." After all, it was hardly likely that Moscow would rely on Washington's pledge of NFU though such a statement could create a climate conducive to arms reductions.[45]

While Kennan and his colleagues attempted to build consensus for new departures in arms control, the Reagan Administration was proceeding in the opposite direction. In March 1983 the President glibly opened a new avenue of strategic competition by calling for a comprehensive space-based defense system that he insisted could some day make nuclear weapons "impotent and obsolete." Reagan thus authorized the Strategic Defense Initiative, initially a $26 billion, five-year program—fittingly dubbed "Star Wars" in honor of the popular movie fantasy. The new research promised to carry the arms race into space and constituted a renunciation of the 1972 Anti-ballistic-missile portion of the SALT I accord. A wide majority of scientists denounced Star Wars as dangerous and unfeasible, but Reagan refused to compromise on the issue. The proposed space-based defense system alarmed the Soviets and posed an obstacle to arms control reductions.[46]

Reagan's Star Wars proposal prompted another challenge from Kennan and the "gang of four" in *Foreign Affairs*. Decrying the administration's "technological hubris," they declared that "no one has been able to offer any hope that it will ever be easier and cheaper to deploy and defend large systems in space than for someone else to destroy them. . . . The inescapable reality is that there is literally no hope that Star Wars can make nuclear weapons obsolete." Like the hydrogen bomb, MIRVs, Cruise missiles, and other arms race innovations, Star Wars was "a prescription not for ending or limiting the threat of nuclear weapons, but for a competition unlimited in expense, duration and danger." The four chastised Reagan for announcing the new system without first informing the Kremlin and for undermining the ABM accord, which had reflected "a common understanding of exactly the kinds of danger with which Star Wars now confronts the world." In deference to Reagan's tremendous personal popularity—the President captured 49 states in his 1984 reelection—the four statesmen called for a "long, hard damage-limiting effort by Congress."[47]

Kennan blamed the American "military-industrial complex" for the "first use" policy and innovations such as Star Wars that were designed to perpetuate the arms race. The term "military-industrial complex" was hackneyed, he admitted, "but the reality has never been more imposing or more ominous than it is today." The "defense" establishment, both public and private, had become accustomed to record-high levels of spending, as well as corrupt procurement practices under Reagan and Weinberger. "In my experience," Kennan observed, "there is no inertia, once established, as formidable as that of the armed services." The retired diplomat cited the military services, defense industries, individual lobbies, and labor unions as examples of groups that put economic and political self-interest ahead of arms control in the national interest.[48]

While he conducted a restrained debate in publications such as *Foreign Affairs,* Kennan continued to score Reagan's "inexcusably childish" policies in public forums. Speaking before the Committee on East-West Accord in May 1983, he asserted that the administration's "almost totally militarized" policies were based on a "grotestquely overdrawn caricature" of the adversary and had led to an atmosphere characterized by "antagonism, suspicion and cynicism." With Soviet ambassador Anatoly Dobrynin seated in the audience, Kennan added that in Moscow a "high general sense of insecurity, a positively neurotic passion for secrecy, a marked sensitivity to conditions in border regions and a tendency to overdo in the cultivation of armed forces" had contributed to the breakdown in superpower relations. He urged new initiatives in arms control, an increase in official exchanges, and an end to American economic sanctions put into effect in the aftermath of the imposition of martial law in Poland.[49]

The death of Soviet leader Yuri Andropov in February 1984 placed further obstacles in the path of restoring détente, however. The former head of the KGB had replaced Brezhnev in 1982 and had been committed to a program of domestic reform and decreased international tensions.[50] To Kennan, Andropov had appeared "a little more flexible, a little more pragmatic, less ideologically fanatical, more willing to ask what works rather than to look and see what Marx said 140 years ago."[51] However, Andropov's illness—whether a "cold" or something more sinister—and the debacle over the shooting down of a Korean Airlines passenger jet over Soviet airspace on September 1, 1983, prevented him from seizing the diplomatic initiative. The Soviets took 269 lives by ordering the destruction of KAL 007, while the Reagan Administration promptly deepened the crisis by asserting, without evidence, that Moscow knew the target was a civilian airliner and shot it down anyway.[52]

Like many observers, Kennan realized that Andropov's death confronted the Kremlin with a "serious problem" in choosing between old and new leadership. The Politburo selected the decrepit apparatachik Konstantin Chernenko, whose own death in 1985 ushered in the reform-minded leadership of Mikhail Gorbachev. Kennan declared that Gorbachev's elevation showed that Chernenko had been "a compromise choice for the position and largely a figurehead" and he accurately predicted that Gorbachev would "produce a much higher order of vigor, flexibility and thoughtfulness in the leading position." Now the dean of American "Kremlinologists" after the death of Averell Harriman in 1986, Kennan reminded reporters that the Politburo was a "collective body" and that Gorbachev would face restraints in implementing his reform program.[53]

The rise of Gorbachev signaled revolutionary changes in Moscow and created the opportunity for a breakthrough in U.S.-Soviet relations. The Soviet leader's policies of *glasnost* (openness) and *perestroika* (restructuring) required applying resources to domestic rather than foreign affairs and he was thus eager, as Kennan put it, to "shift away from international political and military involvements and into internal investment." In reviewing Gorbachev's book *Perestroika,* Kennan characterized the reform program as "revolutionary" and "far-reaching" in its implications for both Soviet domestic and foreign affairs. Gorbachev was "something of an idealist" and a "true believer" in socialism who could not hope to implement the full array of reforms that threatened the Soviet bureaucracy and the *nomenklatura,* or Communist Party elite. However, Kennan predicted that even in the event of Gorbachev's immediate ouster, "it is safe to say that Russia would never again be the same as it was before his passage" and the changes that flowed from *perestroika* "could hardly be other than for the better."[54]

Although Kennan adopted his realist persona in branding Gorbachev an idealist, he had himself first called for an end to the cold war at a time when the Soviet leader was still reciting his Marxist-Leninist catechisms at Moscow State University. Kennan rejected as "border[ing] on the bizarre" Western claims that Gorbachev was advancing *perestroika* as part of a disengenuous campaign to lull the West to sleep in advance of new Soviet initiatives to expand communist influence. Gorbachev's calls for sweeping reductions in nuclear arms, withdrawal of the Red Army from Afghanistan, noninterventionism, and revision of Marxist thinking on such issues as class conflict and support of third world revolutions—all were reforms that impressed Kennan. Here, he realized, was a statesman committed to domestic recovery and reduced international tensions and Kennan blamed the United States for failing to respond with meaningful proposals of its own. To "a substantial, politically influential, and aggressive body of American opinion," Kennan explained, "the specter of a great and fearful external enemy, to be exorcised only by vast military preparations and much belligerent posturing, has become a political and psychological necessity."[55]

After the Soviets renewed INF talks in Geneva in 1985 and Gorbachev urged deep cuts in each nation's nuclear arsenal, Kennan advised American negotiators at Geneva—including his longtime friend and foe Paul Nitze—to capitalize on the Soviet leader's initiatives rather than to engage the Russians in "futile wrangling over human rights issues and over the ins and outs of the respective political and military involvements —theirs and ours." Kennan deplored the Reagan Administration's tendency to dismiss Soviet calls for a comprehensive nuclear test ban and other arms control measures as "just propaganda," as if the Kremlin could have "no serious interest in mitigating the dangers of the nuclear weapons race." Quite the contrary, he added, it was Gorbachev who could reasonably be expected to have "profound skepticism about Ronald Reagan's professed commitment to the reduction and control of nuclear weaponry."[56]

Reagan decided, however, that he did want to achieve an arms control agreement in his second term and entered into a new round of discussions with the Soviets. The President's refusal to compromise on testing of Stars Wars torpedoed Gorbachev's proposal for sweeping reductions at the Reykjavik, Iceland, summit in October 1986, but that meeting established a framework that allowed the two leaders to sign an accord in Washington in December 1987 that led to the removal of intermediate and short-range missiles from Europe.

Although there were thus stirrings of progress by the end of the Reagan Administration, the perpetuation of the nuclear arms race and the inability to effect a realistic Soviet policy during the 1980s underscored Kennan's doubts about American internationalism. The enduring appeal of cold war orthodoxies and the military-industrial complex continued to deflect attention from serious domestic problems such as the deterioration of the natural environment, the "devastating budgetary deficit," and the "inability to control immigration" into the United States.[57]

Although Kennan had devoted much of his professional life to combating the spread of Soviet influence, that issue was no longer central to his thinking. "What most needs to be contained," he declared in 1985, ". . . is not so much the Soviet Union as the weapons race itself."[58] The "morbid nuclear preoccupations" of the great powers combined with "the devastating effect of modern industrialization and overpopulation on the world's natural environment" were, in Kennan's judgment, "the problems of the future. The others—the ones flowing from the ideological conflicts of the turn of the century which produced the Russian Revolution—are the problems of the past."[59]

Kennan advised that domestic issues receive top priority while the nation pursued a "more modest, less ambitious American foreign policy" centered on arms control and nonintervention. The United States should confine its involvement in world affairs to a cooperative internationalism in which it would work with other powers, and especially the Soviet Union, in behalf of population control, environmental protection and reducing international tensions. Beyond that, the onetime architect of global containment predicted that sooner or later the United States would discover the "virtue of minding our own business whenever there is not some overwhelming reason for minding the business of others."[60]

XV

Kennan and Postwar Internationalism

GEORGE F. KENNAN became one of the most influential diplomats in American history because he established the intellectual
framework that governed U.S. foreign policy in the cold war. But containment, like Kennan himself, was plagued by contradictions and specious assumptions. The quest for liberation, global implementation,
and the militarization of U.S. policy made containment a flawed approach to the problems posed by the Soviet Union in the postwar
era.

A major contradiction of containment—and one central to understanding Kennan—flowed from the conflict between his anti-democratic
and his anti-communist values. Students of U.S. foreign policy have long
been perplexed by Kennan's elusiveness: how could the perfervid anti-
communist Mr. X have become one of the earliest advocates of détente
and an outspoken critic of American internationalism? I suggest that the
central contradiction in Kennan's thinking was the unresolved conflict
between his quest for global containment and his belief that America's
democratic society lacked the subtlety and sophistication required to
conduct an activist foreign policy. In one of the most striking paradoxes
of cold war history, the architect of global containment ultimately resolved this conflict by abandoning containment, pronouncing the "de-

cline of the West," and calling for America's "extensive withdrawal" from world affairs.[1]

Kennan expressed nothing but contempt for communist ideology as a result of his early Foreign Service training, his nostalgia for pre-revolutionary Russia, and because Marxism-Leninism targeted for ruin the upper classes of society with which he identified. As a Russian expert who had lived for several years in the USSR before World War II, Kennan understood better than most the reality of what he called the "horrors of Stalinism."[2] Sensitive to Western misperceptions about Russia, particularly under the Grand Alliance, he intended his essays and lectures on Soviet-American relations as a corrective to the attitudes that prevailed at home. Less than a year after the end of World War II, the Truman Administration responded to Kennan's amalgam of scholarship, strategy, and the call for a moralistic crusade against evil and made containment the essence of American national security policy. The X-Article, consistent with Kennan's earlier writings, declared an ideological-political war against world communism and implied that history was on America's side and thus victory was certain.

Revisionist historians of the cold war have demolished the orthodox depiction of the United States as a bewildered innocent responding to the machinations of the international communist conspiracy.[3] They have demonstrated that Americans seized the opportunity afforded by victory in World War II to attempt to create an international system oriented around the supremacy of the U.S. dollar and determined to contain communism on every front. Washington made an issue of Soviet hegemony in Eastern Europe, to which it had acquiesced during the war and could do nothing about, while arrogating to itself the right to act unilaterally in its own spheres of influence. That America pursued its own selfish interests is hardly surprising nor does it imply that Stalin was any less an evil dictator whose obsession with class struggle would have complicated efforts to achieve East-West accord under any circumstances. Still, the United States should have accepted as inevitable ideological-political competition with the Soviet Union while trying harder than it did in the immediate postwar period to negotiate a settlement. Such a settlement might have been based on economic assistance to Russia and agreement on Soviet neutralization of the Near East in return for a U.S.-sponsored neutralization of the Far East, whereupon both nations might have withdrawn from Central Europe and attempted to come to terms on control of atomic weapons.

Kennan himself had long ruled out any such détente, which he equated with appeasement, and argued that the Western powers could undermine Soviet influence without meeting the Russians at the bargaining table. His faith in liberation, or a Soviet capitulation, rested on dubious assumptions and was a major flaw of the containment strategy. In several essays and addresses—including but not limited to the Long Telegram and the X-Article—he predicted that containment would unleash disintegrative forces that were rumbling beneath the surface not only in Eastern Europe but in the heart of Stalin's totalitarian regime as well. He was less sanguine on other occasions, predicting that if not destroyed the Soviet Union would at least "mellow," reduce the scope of its ambitions in foreign affairs, and capitulate to Western terms.

Kennan realized that the Soviet threat was ideological-political rather than military and helped formulate the Marshall Plan in an effort to counter Stalin's effort to exploit war-weariness in order to extend Soviet influence into Western Europe. Kennan urged Russia's exclusion from the European Recovery Program and until 1948 opposed negotiations on the assumption that once relegated to its own borders and surrounded by a superior Western model, the Kremlin would either collapse or capitulate. As he soon realized, however, liberation sacrificed the possibilities, however limited they might have been, of loosening the Soviet grip on the satellites through normalization of East-West relations. A policy focused on rolling back Soviet hegemony served only to deepen divisions while ensuring that no real liberation would occur. Thus, a dramatic overestimation of both Russian weakness and the strength of the Western position characterized Kennan's early thinking on containment.

A second major flaw in Kennan's strategy concerned the geographic scope of containment. Because of limited resources and cultural and political barriers, he argued that containment should be restricted to the five military-industrial regions of the world that could be mobilized for war. The advocacy of "strongpoint" containment was clear enough in theory, but in practice Washington pursued a global foreign policy that carried containment onto the perimeter. This was first manifested in the Near East under the Truman Doctrine and ultimately through military intervention in Korea and Southeast Asia. Kennan promoted containment in these peripheral regions because he feared a "bandwagon" effect and believed that intervention was required to establish American credibility to oppose the spread of communism. He viewed Marxist-Leninist ideology as a cancer which if allowed to take hold in any one place would continue to spread until it undermined Western interests throughout the world.

Kennan invested so heavily in such psychological constructs as bandwagoning and credibility that they overwhelmed his theoretical desire to confine containment to vital regions. Like most of his colleagues in the national security establishment, he was willing to commit tens of thousands of lives and millions of dollars to perimeter wars on the assumption that the fate of developing nations hinged on the psychological repercussions of a Western victory or defeat in the struggle against communist insurgents in some other part of the world. Kennan's Victorian racial attitudes and determination to contain communism caused him to underestimate the more immediate concerns that prevailed in the developing world, such as overcoming legacies of European and Japanese colonialism and raising living standards. Kennan and his colleagues failed to understand that third world nationalism and local cultural tradition carried more weight than alliances based on ideology.

The importance Kennan attached to cold war psychology undermines the argument that he advocated "realist" diplomacy in the early cold war period. It was no accident that the original X-Article was entitled *"Psychological* Background of Soviet Foreign Policy," as Kennan's arguments rested on psychological assumptions, specious lessons drawn from Russian history, and exaggerations of Kremlin weaknesses, none of which were consistent with classical realism. The quest for liberation and the globalization of American diplomacy violated realist precepts advocating the "end of ideology" as well as those opposing "ideal blueprints" and overextension of American power. Kennan sought not a realistic "balance of power," but Soviet defeat and isolation and Western dominance.[4]

The attempt by Kennan, Hans Morgenthau, Reinhold Niebuhr, and others to base diplomacy on the realist paradigm ignored the role of American culture and was itself an exercise in idealism that was doomed from the start. The realists sought to resurrect a timeless diplomacy that would be focused almost exclusively on power and national interest, but such an approach ignored American racial attitudes, the role of mission and exceptionalism, fear of revolution, the search for profits and open markets, and other forces that historians have identified as lying at the root of U.S. diplomacy. As Kennan himself discovered as the cold war unfolded, the United States could not abandon its cultural roots in order to conform to the realist paradigm.

Just as the nation could not be expected to transcend its cultural values, Kennan could not divorce himself from his own anti-democratic and anti-communist values. His alienation from American culture and his enmity for the Soviet Union and communist ideology made it impossible for him to follow through on the realist quest to eschew ethical and moral preoccupations in the formulation of policy. Although he attempted to disassociate himself from crusading American anti-communism, Kennan's own attitudes and perceptions established linkage between ideology and foreign policy. A strong commitment to anti-communism, rather than an objective view of the role of power in world affairs, structured Kennan's approach to the cold war.

Thus, although his writing helped found the theory of political realism, Kennan himself will not be best understood as a realist. He postured as a cool and detached geopolitician but his romantic attachment to the past, enmity for Marxism-Leninism, and desire for America to redeem itself reflected his own concern with ethical and moral considerations. Historian Lloyd C. Gardner was close to the mark when he observed many years ago that "in George Frost Kennan the Presbyterian elder wrestled with the Bismarckian geopolitician."[5] The tension between Kennan's realism and his emotional preoccupations manifested itself in contradictory advice, ulcer attacks, repeated threats to resign from the Foreign Service, and outrage over the march of Western civilization.

The positions Kennan adopted toward postwar Germany, nuclear weapons, and the cold war itself further distanced him from the realist tradition. Whereas most realists accepted the division of Germany and nuclear deterrence as foundations of a stable postwar international system, Kennan could abide neither. A Germanophile since his childhood, he had been slow to condemn Nazism in the 1930s and longed even a decade after the end of World War II to establish Germany at the center of a trans-national European federation. A successful containment strategy, in Kennan's view, depended on a reunited and nonaligned Germany replacing Russia as the preeminent power in East Central Europe. Thus, the permanent division of Germany and the cementing of Soviet hegemony in Eastern Europe marked the failure of Kennan's postwar strategy and formed the basis of his dissent from the cold war consensus after 1948.

Toward the end of that year Kennan realized—his claims to consistency over the course of the cold war notwithstanding—that the momentum of world events worked against liberation and German reunification and toward a prolonged power struggle with the Kremlin. Although he had summoned the nation into the cold war against Moscow, the truth was that such a state of perpetual hostility violated Kennan's desire for order and civility in international discourse. Nuclear weapons were the symbols of the abandonment of gentlemanly codes of conflict to the forces of militarization and modernization that threatened to overwhelm all political considerations and ultimately to destroy the human race. Kennan had paid little attention to atomic weapons during the early cold war period—he later noted that the containment strategy "did not address itself to [the] dialectics of [the] weapons race"—but by 1949 he considered cultivation of nuclear weapons not only "sterile and hopeless," but amoral as well.[6] Whereas most realists have viewed the cold war as a stable "long peace,"[7] Kennan has since 1948 advocated (with certain lapses, to be sure) a negotiated settlement of the U.S.-Soviet conflict, which carried, as he saw it, the constant threat of Armageddon.

To his credit Kennan acted on the changes in his perceptions, reversed course, and advocated as the State Department's Policy Planning Staff director immediate negotiations with the Kremlin. He called for talks aimed at restoring international stability, ending the impasse over Berlin and the division of Germany, and to provide a basis for arms control and the erosion of Soviet hegemony in Eastern Europe.

Kennan blamed the rejection of his initial disengagement plan of 1948 on American intransigence and on the "militarization" of containment in the West. The perpetuation of a divided Europe, creation of NATO, NSC-68, and the thermonuclear bomb all reflected the predominance of military considerations in American strategic planning. Kennan was thus one of the first American statesmen to call attention to the rise of the national security state and the military-industrial complex that have dominated American foreign policy since World War II. Ironically, underlying these developments were the perceptions of the Soviet adversary that Kennan himself had popularized in the early cold war period but had since called into question.

Concerned about his historical reputation, Kennan insisted that the militarization of containment had prevented his original strategy from succeeding, but American policy evolved logically from the perceptions that he had laid down. It is difficult to imagine any American approach that could have achieved his aims of liberation, or a Soviet capitulation, but Kennan blamed American society rather than accepting any responsibility for the misperceptions that governed U.S. policy. By the time Kennan realized that domestic political considerations and American cultural values placed barriers in the path of a cold war settlement, he exercised only marginal influence over American foreign policy.

Kennan's forty-year quest to distance himself from the containment consensus smacks of a self-serving apology—and it is partly that—but in a sense it is also true that he has been misunderstood. The fame achieved by the Long Telegram, the X-Article, and containment overshadowed the fact that Kennan was not a consensus figure. Indeed, it was ironic that Kennan—a congenital outsider and critic of American society, a man wedded to anti-democratic values—should have become the intellectual spokesman for United States' diplomacy. Thus, Kennan's divergence from the cold war consensus, while in part an effort to disassociate himself from containment, also reflected his alienation from American culture and his lifelong penchant for challenging the conventional wisdom on foreign affairs.

Departure from the State Department in 1950 and emergence as a scholar and public critic of the cold war marked Kennan's return to his accustomed role of outsider as well as the beginning of his transformation from advocate of global containment to neo-isolationist. He called American policy since World War I a "vast and historic failure," referred to the cold war as a "cosmic misunderstanding," and lamented that he had not advocated détente in the early postwar period. "I was so concerned about combating fatuous appeasement," he recalled in 1984. "I should have stressed negotiations more [in an effort to achieve] a hard-boiled agreement on their forces and ours."[8] It was tragic for Kennan personally that he influenced American foreign policy for only a relatively brief period of time—from 1946 to 1948—and that the rejection of his calls for disengagement ensured that he would be long remembered primarily for the stridency of the X-Article rather than for the statesmanship of his plea for détente.

The rhetoric of liberation, appeasement of Senator Joseph McCarthy and the domestic right-wing, and the rearmament of Germany all worked against Kennan's call for a negotiated settlement in East-Central Europe. Eager to devise an alternative to West Germany's inclusion in NATO, he proposed a Monroe Doctrine for Central Europe in which Washington would issue a unilateral American guarantee of the sovereignty of West Germany and the independence of Berlin, thus defining Western security demands while limiting the militarization of the continent. This proposal and many of the arguments advanced by Kennan in the Reith Lectures might have provided a basis for the type of détente that Washington and Moscow eventually pursued more than a decade later, but perceptions of the Soviets were so hostile in the West that Kennan proved unable to mobilize support for negotiations even after the death of Stalin. As Soviet and American leaders struggled to negotiate nuclear arms reductions in Europe in the late 1980s, one may well reflect how much easier it would have been to have avoided placing them there in the first place, as Kennan had urged in his radio lectures. Although ridiculed at the time, his call for bolstering conventional deterrence, including the development of defensive militias, offered a feasible alternative to the reckless buildup of nuclear arms.

That the United States and its Western allies declined to consider a negotiated disengagement reflected the exalted stature that NATO had achieved in its first decade. The alliance, once conceived as a means to an end, now became the end itself and it was already a well-established practice in Washington to conclude that Soviet offers of compromise were nothing more than disengenuous ploys designed to disrupt Western security arrangements. Given the perceptions underlying the militarization of containment, the NATO command would not be denied the opportunity to integrate nuclear weapons into its arsenal and to maintain the prerogative of their first use. As Kennan observed at the time, Western leaders could not remove their gaze from the specter of a Soviet blitzkrieg.

Kennan has advocated détente from his Yugoslav ambassadorship to the present (except after the 1968 Soviet invasion of Czechoslovakia) and has opposed linkage and the embrace of worst case scenarios that have undermined normalization of relations with Moscow. Cold war realists found the transformation in Kennan's thinking disturbing, especially since he commanded attention as one of the nation's preeminent Soviet experts. The retired diplomat thus found himself subjected to repeated attacks from the right while liberals often welcomed, but rarely acted upon, his dissent from the conventional wisdom on foreign affairs.

The changes in Kennan's perceptions as reflected in his advocacy of disengagement and détente did not amount to a complete revolution in his thinking, however. His enmity for Marxism-Leninism, attachment to order and what he considered proper international behavior, and contempt for third world nationalism continued to structure his outlook on foreign affairs. Although he advocated a negotiated settlement of the cold war, Kennan's support of military containment on the perimeter in Korea and Southeast Asia reflected the persistence of his concerns about credibility and bandwagoning. He condemned the Johnson Administration's militarism in Vietnam during his Senate testimony, but the Southeast Asian war also revealed the limitation on efforts to implement ideological-political containment in the developing world and confirmed the desperate need for the United States to reduce the scope of its involvement in world affairs. After Vietnam, Kennan abandoned containment on the perimeter and in the case of civil war in Angola, for example, he argued that neither Washington nor Moscow could control events in a state so remote from their borders and cultural experience.

By the early 1970s the threats posed by the arms race, world population growth, environmental deterioration, and the "decline of the West" dominated Kennan's thinking. In view of his sweeping critique of American culture and society and his linkage between foreign and domestic affairs, containment of communism was no longer central to his worldview. "It could, in fact, be said," he remarked on the fortieth anniversary of the X-Article, "that the first thing we Americans need to learn to contain is, in some ways, ourselves."[9]

This statement illuminates the central contradiction in Kennan's thought, one that flowed from his linkage of foreign and domestic policy. In his essays and lectures formulating containment from 1944 to 47, he had stressed that the United States required a healthy society in order to provide an effective alternative to developing nations in the global struggle against communism. But Kennan's own anti-democratic values and his alienation from post-industrial commercial society ensured that America would never measure up to that requirement in his own eyes.

Leaving aside for a moment Kennan's critique of Western society, he was certainly justified in calling attention to the cultural roots of the nation's foreign policy. As historian Michael Hunt has recently argued, faith in national greatness, racial stereotypes about foreign peoples, and fear of revolution have comprised an ideology of American foreign policy that often clashes with international realities.[10] Along the same lines, Kennan's charge that the West suffered defeats in the global struggle against communism because it failed to develop an alternative philosophy—aside from the abstract notion of freedom that had little relevance to the needs of peoples in the developing world—merits serious consideration. It is also true that domestic political considerations and the need to depict an evil adversary in order for Americans to feel better about themselves both exercise a pernicious influence on the conduct of U.S. diplomacy. Examples abound: the exaltation of Stalin's image during the war; the militarization of containment; the nuclear arms race; the anti-communist hysteria after the fall of China; the controversy over trade relations with Yugoslavia; intervention in Southeast Asia; the insistence on linkage in détente; the "first use" policy; and the early Reagan Soviet policy—all reflected shortcomings in the nation's effort to respond with balance and maturity to the demands of an activist diplomacy. Kennan's own preference would have been to do away with democratic foreign policy altogether in deference to empowering elites such as himself, reactionary advice that was inimical to the American political tradition.

Nostalgic and reactionary throughout his career, Kennan clung to the perception that Western civilization began to decline as the European and American aristocracies lost their dominance in the late eighteenth and early nineteenth centuries and to the tragic view of history that this outlook entailed. Rarely did he probe beneath the surface to ask why the *ancien regime* itself had disintegrated nor did he empathize with the plight of working people and disadvantaged classes. Kennan's elitism and *nostalgie du temps perdu* found him clinging to Victorian racial attitudes and advocating segregation at home and imperialism abroad.

Kennan leavened his reactionary positions on American culture and society with some progressive recommendations. One can sympathize with his abhorrence over the destruction of the natural environment and applaud his call for strong central government authority to coordinate growth, allocate resources, and inhibit pollution. By the end of his career Kennan realized that environmental degradation and other domestic economic and social problems outweighed the putative communist threat and called for a critical rethinking of America's approach to world affairs. As an elder statesman, the retired diplomat advocated a cooperative internationalism in which the United States would take the lead in promoting such issues as world population control and environmental protection.

Kennan's greatest skills lay in the forcefulness of his arguments and the power of his prose. He is the only Foreign Service officer in American history to influence policy and promote himself to high positions almost solely on the power and persuasiveness of his pen. The Long Telegram, the X-Article, the Reith Lectures, the Fulbright hearings and the "no first use" campaign were impressive displays of his ability to move mass audiences with his literary and oratorical skills. From the publication of *American Diplomacy* in 1951 to his volumes on the diplomatic setting before the Great War in the late 1980s, Kennan enjoyed an uninterrupted pattern of literary achievement. His two-volume memoir, polemics, and works of scholarship have secured for him a lasting reputation as a scholar, critic, and reflective man of letters.

Kennan displayed his skills as a diplomat on several occasions in Moscow during the 1930s; during his internment by the Nazis and in Portugal during the war; in the secret discussions over Korea with Jacob Malik; and in his service in Belgrade. He was capable of brilliant political reporting and his talent for languages enhanced his effectiveness as a diplomat. Kennan displayed the ability, essential for effective diplomacy, to understand and respect the perspective of the adversary, although his emotional preoccupations overwhelmed this attribute on many occasions.

Kennan has earned his reputation as one of the West's preeminent experts on the Soviet Union. Such a distinction does not, of course, mean that he was always right or "amazingly accurate" in his forecasts of all things Soviet, as his friends in the press sometimes argued. As we have seen, Kennan exaggerated the Kremlin's vulnerability in the early cold war, yet even here he identified some of the sources of instability in the Soviet political system. These problems were not sufficient to undermine the communist regime, as Kennan had once believed they would be, but they did necessitate the type of sweeping reform agenda that Mikhail Gorbachev has now taken before his nation.

After repeated threats to resign, Kennan's actual departure from the Foreign Service, first in 1950 and then for good in 1963, reflected his maturation as a scholar and intellectual. The halls of the State Department and America's foreign embassies had grown too narrow for the wide-ranging and iconoclastic mind that became a source of aggravation to Dean Acheson, Foster Dulles, and other prestigious men of foreign affairs. Kennan made a greater contribution as an outsider and intellectual than as a professional diplomat. Out of the profound disillusionment over the realization that he had helped to launch the cold war came years of reassessment that shed light on the history of postwar American internationalism. Kennan thus made his greatest contribution not through some detached geopolitical realism, much less through the consistency of his positions, but for the questions he asked, the ideas that he probed, and the ultimate transformation in his thinking over the course of the cold war.

For all of his confusion, contradiction, and romantic eccentricity, there was a certain logic to Kennan's transformation from containment to neo-isolation and cooperative internationalism. He was right to abandon containment, a strategy whose formulation rested in too great a degree on fear of communism and an exaggerated perception of the potential for the spread of Soviet power. As Kennan himself came to understand, containment also expected too much of the United States, a nation whose penchant for putting domestic political considerations first and whose provincialism and embrace of romantic myths about its own past undermined its ability to conduct an effective international diplomacy. The rehabilitation of the venerable isolationist strain in American foreign policy by the architect of global containment ought to set Americans thinking about their place in world affairs.

Kennan contemplated American diplomacy across an epoch which began as the United States moved beyond its preoccupation with the domestic economic and political problems of the 1930s and embraced a global foreign policy. By the end of his career, the nation had muddled through an era of geopolitical supremacy and found itself once again confronted with the overarching domestic issues such as economic inequality, reemergence as a debtor nation, the overweening influence of the military-industrial complex, a deteriorating natural environment, and myriad social problems.

By calling attention to the primacy of these issues in the post-Vietnam years, Kennan anticipated the "decline school" that emerged in the 1980s and argued that the United States, like other empires before it, was passing into the sunset. The burden of this scholarship was that the United States, entering into a phase of "relative decline," would have to learn to accommodate itself to diminishing influence in world affairs, a role not far removed from Kennan's neo-isolationism.[11] Perhaps it would be the ultimate measure of his influence if Kennan were found to have once again anticipated a major transition in the character of American diplomacy.

NOTES

Preface

(See complete references in Bibliography)

1. Kennan, "The Sources of Soviet Conduct," p. 99.

2. Steel, "Man Without A Country," p. 8; *New York Times*, Jan. 12, 1958 (Acheson); Rostow, "Searching for Kennan's Grand Design," in Herz, ed., *Decline of the West?*, p. 114; Gardner, *Architects of Illusion*, pp. 270–300; Gaddis, "Containment: A Reassessment," p. 886; Buckley, *National Review*, April 4, 1980, p. 432.

3. John Kenneth Galbraith, review of Kennan, *Memoirs, 1950–1963*, in *New York Times Book Review*, Pct. 8, 1972, p. 1; Kennan, *American Diplomacy, 1900–1950*, p. 82.

4. On realism, see Morgenthau, *Politics Among Nations;* Thompson, *Political Realism and the Crisis of World Politics;* Smith, *Realist Thought from Weber to Kissinger;* and Coffey, *Political Realism in American Thought;* on corporatism, see McCormick, "Drift or Mastery?"; Gaddis, "The Corporatist Synthesis"; Hogan, "Corporatism: A Positive Appraisal"; for an overview on revisionism and post-revisionism, see Gaddis, "The Emerging Post-Revisionist Synthesis" and the responses by Gardner, Kaplan, Kimball, and Kuniholm.

5. Gaddis, *Strategies of Containment*, pp. 25–88; Mayers, *Kennan and the Dilemmas of U.S. Foreign Policy;* see also the relevant portions of Isaacson and Thomas, *The Wise Men;* Gellman, *Contending With Kennan;* and Stephanson, *Kennan and the Art of Foreign Policy.*

1. Worldly Prejudices, 1904–1944

1. Interview with Jeanette Hotchkiss, Sept. 26, 1960, Highland Park, Ill., Box 8, C. Ben Wright Biography Project, George C. Marshall Library, Lexington, Va.

2. George F. Kennan, *Memoirs, 1925–1950*, p. 4; Hotchkiss interview.

3. On Kennan's childhood, see the revealing portrait in Isaacson and Thomas, *The Wise Men*, pp. 72–76.

4. *Old Boys Review: Alumni Bulletin of St. John's Military Academy* (Winter 1960–61), in Box 8, Wright Biography Project; Kennan, *Memoirs, 1925–1950*, pp. 9, 16.

5. Kennan, *Memoirs, 1925–1950*, pp. 9–11.

6. Isaacson and Thomas, *The Wise Men*, pp. 78–79; Kennan, *Memoirs, 1925–1950*, pp. 15, 12.

7. Kennan, *Memoirs, 1925–1950*, p. 17.

8. Schulzinger, *Making of the Diplomatic Mind*, pp. 74–78; Kennan, *Memoirs, 1925–1950*, p. 18.

9. Weil, *A Pretty Good Club;* Schulzinger, *Making of the Diplomatic Mind*, p. 125.

10. Kennan, *Memoirs, 1925–1950*, p. 20.

11. Kennan to Charles W. Thayer, May 22, 1935, Thayer Correspondence, Harry S. Truman Library Institute (HSTL), Independence, Mo.

12. Kennan 123 Personnel File, 1930–1939, Department of State Files (DSF), Record Group 59 (RG59), National Archives (NA), Washington DC; Isaccson and Thomas, *The Wise Men*, p. 163.

13. Kennan to Thayer, May 22, 1935; Isaacson and Thomas, *Wise Men*, p. 154; Kennan threatened to resign at least three times in the prewar years: in 1928, 1933 and again in 1938. See Kennan, *Memoirs, 1925–1950*, p. 23, and Charles Bohlen interview by C. Ben Wright, Sept. 29, 1970, Wright Biography Project.

14. Kennan, *Memoirs, 1925–1950*, pp. 8–9; George Kennan to Robert Lansing, May 26 and June 28, 1918, Box 4, Robert Lansing Papers, Seeley G. Mudd Manuscript Library, Princeton University; George Kennan, *Siberia and the Exile System* (introduction by George F. Kennan).

15. Kennan 123 Personnel File, 1930–1939; Propas, "Creating a Hard Line Toward Russia," p. 215; De Santis, *The Diplomacy of Silence*, pp. 27–44; Kennan *Memoirs, 1925–1950*, pp. 23–34; on Versailles, see Levin, *Woodrow Wilson and World Politics* and Gardner, *Safe for Democracy*.

16. DeSantis, *Diplomacy of Silence*, p. 29; Loy W. Henderson interview by C. Ben Wright, Oct. 3, 1970, Wright Biography Project; Propas, "Creating a Hard Line," p. 218; Kennan 123 Personnel File, 1930–1939.

17. Kennan, *Memoirs, 1925–1950*, p. 29; Kennan, "Flashbacks," *"The New Yorker,* February 25, 1985, p. 52; on Kennan's reports on Americans, see his testimony before the United States Atomic Energy Committee, "In the Matter of J. Robert Oppenheimer, Transcript of a Hearing Before the Personnel Security

Board," Washington D.C., April 12–May 6, 1954 (Washington: U.S. Government Printing Office, 1954), p. 354.

18. See Kennan's comments on Marxism in his *Memoirs, 1925–1950*, p. 7, as well as much that follows in this study.

19. Kennan, "The Prerequisites," proposed chapter of his manuscript, "Notes on the Problems of the United States in 1938," Box 25, Kennan Papers, Mudd Library.

20. Kennan, "Fair Day, Adieu," unpublished manuscript, Box 25, Kennan Papers.

21. Kennan, "The Prerequisites."

22. Members of these groups were sometimes arbitrarily flunked on oral examinations to keep them out of the Foreign Service. See Schulzinger, *Making of the Diplomatic Mind*, pp. 107–09, 129.

23. Kennan, "The Prerequisites."

24. Kennan, *Democracy and the Student Left*, p. 206.

25. Mayer, ed., Tocqueville, *Democracy in America*, p. 229.

26. For a survey of the literature on the decline and fall of Rome, see Grant, *The Fall of the Roman Empire* and Jordan, *Gibbon and His Roman Empire;* on Kennan's "decline of the West," see chapter 12.

27. Kennan to Volodia Kozhevnikoff, Oct. 20, 1930. I have relied on C. Ben Wright, who quoted this material extensively in his unpublished doctoral dissertation, "George F. Kennan: Scholar-Diplomat." Wright found a copy of this letter in Kennan's papers at Princeton, but Kennan himself apparently removed it, along with several other documents, after Wright's dissertation appeared.

28. Kennan, "Washington, 1937–38," unpublished manuscript, Box 25, Kennan Papers.

29. Kennan, *Memoirs, 1925–1950*, p. 8.

30. Kennan to Walt Ferris, Jan. 12, 1931. Once again I am relying on C. Ben Wright's quotation of this letter, which he found among the Kennan Papers but which Kennan himself apparently removed from the collection at Princeton. See Wright, "Scholar-Diplomat," p. 21.

31. *FRUS: The Soviet Union, 1933–1939*, pp. 1–60; Dallek, *FDR and American Foreign Policy*, pp. 39, 80–81.

32. Kennan to Walt Ferris, Jan. 12, 1931.

33. Kennan, *Memoirs, 1925–1950*, p. 57.

34. Dec. 16, 1933, Memorandum from William Bullitt in Kennan 123 Personnel File, 1930–1939; Bullitt to J. V. A. MacMurray, Dec. 12, 1933, Box 135, MacMurray Papers, Mudd Library.

35. Kennan, "Flashbacks," p. 57; Kennan, *Memoirs, 1925–1950*, p. 81.

36. Kennan, "Fair Day, Adieu."

37. On Stalin's rise to power, see Tucker, *Stalin As A Revolutionary; FRUS, Soviet Union*, p. 74; Stephen F. Cohen, "Bolshevism and Stalinism, "Tucker, ed., *Stalinism: Essays in Historical Interpretation*, pp. 3–29, as well as Cohen's observations in *Rethinking the Soviet Experience* (New York: W. W. Norton and Co., 1985); Conquest, *The Great Terror*, pp. 525–35; Medvedev, *Let*

History Judge, pp. 152–286; for a revisionist view, see Getty, *Origins of the Great Purges,* pp. 196–210.

38. *FRUS: Soviet Union 1933–1939,* p. 369; Joseph Davies to Cordell Hull, Feb. 17, 18, 1937, DSF 861.00/11675 and 861.00/11676, RG 59, NA; Kennan, *Memoirs, 1925–1950,* p. 83.

39. Kennan quoted in DeSantis, *Diplomacy of Silence,* pp. 34–35; Kennan, *Memoirs, 1925–1950,* pp. 82–85; Weil, *A Pretty Good Club,* p. 93.

40. Kennan, "Russia," May 20, 1938, Foreign Service School lecture, Washington, Kennan Papers.

41. *FRUS, Soviet Union,* p. 446; Wright, "Scholar-Diplomat," pp. 107–35; Charles Thayer to Cordell Hull. Aug. 10, 1937, DSF 124.61/114; Kennan memorandum, Mar. 24, 1938, DSF 124.61/130, both in RG59, NA; Stiller, *George S. Messersmith,* p. 75.

42. Kennan, *Memoirs, 1925–1950,* pp. 21–23, 34–39; Kennan to Walt Ferris, Jan. 12, 1931.

43. Kennan, "The War Problem of the Soviet Union," March 1935, Box 1, George F. Kennan Papers, Mudd Library; David Mayers, "Nazi Germany and the Future of Europe: George Kennan's Views, 1939–1945, *International History Review* 8 (November 1986): 550–72.

44. "Excerpts from a Despatch of Feb. 17, 1939, from George F. Kennan to Department of State on the Jewish Problem in the New Czechoslovakia," reproduced in Kennan, *From Prague After Munich,* pp. 43–57.

45. Kennan, "Personal Notes on the Munich Crisis Written in Early October 1938," in Ibid., pp. 3–6.

46. Quoted in *Memoirs, 1925–1950,* pp. 118, 133.

47. Kennan, "The Internment and Repatriation of the American Official Group in Germany, 1941–42," Box 1, Kennan Papers; Wright, "Scholar-Diplomat," pp. 160–61; Frederick C. Oeschner to Cordell Hull, June 24, 1942, DSF 124.623/1012, RG59, NA.

48. Kennan to G. Howland Shaw, Aug. 18, 1942, Box 3, Kennan Papers; Kennan, *Memoirs, 1925–1950,* pp. 139, 142–63; Kennan, "Russia and the Postwar Settlement," Summer 1942, Box 25, Kennan Papers. On Roosevelt's wartime diplomacy, see Dallek, *FDR and American Foreign Policy, 1932–1945* (New York: Oxford University Press, 1981), pp. 406–441.

49. *FRUS: The Conferences of Cairo and Tehran, 1943,* pp. 394–95, 790–93; *FRUS 1943,* 2: 527–76; Kennan to Cordell Hull, Oct. 18, 1943, 124.623/1012, RG59, NA; DeSantis, *Diplomacy of Silence,* pp. 92–94.

50. Kennan, *Memoirs, 1925–1950,* pp. 164–71; *FRUS 1944,* 1: 207–9; Kennan to John G. Winant, March 1944, Box 3, Kennan Papers; Wright, "Scholar-Diplomat, pp. 210–11; DeSantis, *Diplomacy of Silence,* pp. 109–110.

51. Kennan, "Russia and the Postwar Settlement," Summer 1942, Box 25, Kennan Papers; Kennan to John G. Winant, March 1944; Wright, "Scholar-Diplomat," pp. 229–31; on unconditional surrender, see Dallek, *FDR and American Foreign Policy,* pp. 373–76, and O'Connor, *Diplomacy for Victory.*

2. Forging the Consensus

1. Harriman to Cordell Hull, Dec. 19, 1943, Charles Bohlen 123 Personnel File, Department of State Files (DSF), Record Group (RG)59, National Archives (NA), Washington DC; George F. Kennan, *Memoirs, 1925–1950*, pp. 181, 187.

2. Examples of these disputes appear in *FRUS 1944*, 4: 801–1273; see also Harriman and Abel, *Special Envoy to Churchill and Stalin*, quote page 317, and Deane, *The Strange Alliance*, pp. 20, 53–55.

3. Kennan notes, Summer 1944, quoted in Kennan, *Memoirs*, p. 209.

4. Kennan, "Soviet Policy," Sept. 18, 1944, Box 25, Kennan Papers, Seeley G. Mudd Manuscript Library, Princeton.

5. Ibid.

6. Mastny, *Russia's Road to the Cold War*, pp. 183–86.

7. Kennan, "Russia—Seven Years Later," reprinted in *Memoirs, 1925–1950*, pp. 503–31; portions reprinted in *FRUS 1944*, 4: 902–914.

8. *FRUS 1944*, 4: 951, 988–98, 1012–15; *FRUS 1944*, 1: 826–28; on Harriman's attitudes toward Kennan, see K. Tolley, "Memorandum for Captain Smedberg," Feb. 26, 1946, Box 70, James F. Forrestal Papers, Mudd Library, and William A. Crawford interview by C. Ben Wright, Sept. 29, 1970, Box 8, Wright Biography Project; on changes in Harriman's attitudes toward Russia, see Larson, *Origins of Containment*, pp. 66–125.

9. Under terms of the Churchill-Stalin agreement, Russia would have 90 percent influence in postwar Romania and 75 percent influence in Bulgaria while Britain would retain 90 percent influence in Greece. The two leaders agreed that each would have 50 percent influence in Yugoslavia and Hungary. See Churchill, *Triumph and Tragedy*, p. 227; Resis, "The Churchill-Stalin Agreement on the Balkans"; and Dallek, *FDR and American Foreign Policy*, pp. 479–80.

10. See Levering, *American Opinion and the Russian Alliance*.

11. *FRUS 1944*, 4: 923–24.

12. Ibid., pp. 253–75.

13. *FRUS 1945*, 3: 110; *FRUS 1945*, 4: 453–54, 532–33; *FRUS 1945*, 7: 343.

14. The term "liberation" was popularized by the Republican Party in the 1950s (see chapter 7) to criticize the Democratic containment policy for sanctioning the "enslavement" of peoples in Russia and Eastern Europe. Despite the political connotations, I employ this term throughout the book because it provides a direct and generally accepted means of expressing the American quest to "roll back" communism.

15. Kennan to Bohlen, Jan. 26, 1945, Box 28, Kennan Papers; Bohlen to Kennan, Feb. 3, 1945, Box 3, Bohlen Papers. On the Open Door thesis, see the Williams' classic, *The Tragedy of American Diplomacy* (New York: Dell Publishing Co., 1972 [1959]).

16. *FRUS 1945*, 5: 231–34; Yergin, *Shattered Peace*, pp. 82–83.

17. Kennan, *Memoirs, 1925–1950*, pp. 239–43; *FRUS 1945*, 5: 849.

18. "Russia's International Position At the Close of the War with Germany," reprinted in Kennan, *Memoirs, 1925–1950*, pp. 532–46.

19. Ibid.

20. Kennan, *Memoirs, 1925–1950*, pp. 269–70; on economic aspects of Soviet-American relations in this period, see Herring, *Aid to Russia* and Paterson, *Soviet-American Confrontation*.

21. Kennan, "Comments on the Results of the Crimea Conference as Set Forth in the Published Communiqué," Box 23, Kennan Papers. Kennan was not briefed on the Yalta Conference by Harriman, much to his discomfort. See Sulzberger, *A Long Row of Candles*, pp. 250–51.

22. Quoted in *Memoirs, 1925–1950*, pp. 258, 263–65; *FRUS 1945*, 5: 277–78; Kuklick, *American Policy and the Division of Germany*, pp. 143–44.

23. Kennan, "The United States and Russia," Winter 1945–46, Box 23, Kennan Papers.

24. Kennan to Bohlen, Jan. 26, 1945; Kennan to Matthews, Aug. 21, 1945, Box 28, Kennan Papers.

25. *FRUS 1945*, 5: 888–91.

26. Quoted in Kennan, *Memoirs, 1925–1950*, p. 287; Messer, *The End of Alliance*, pp. 137–80; Donovan, *Conflict and Crisis*, pp. 155–62.

27. On Soviet actions in the Near East, see Kuniholm, *The Origins of the Cold War in the Near East*; Messer, *End of Alliance*, pp. 156–94.

28. Donovan, *Conflict and Crisis*, pp. 160–62.

29. Kennan to Department of State, Jan. 29, 1946, "Subject File, Foreign Affairs—Russia," George Elsey Papers, Harry S. Truman Library Institute (HSTL).

30. DSF 761.00/2–1146 and 861.00/2–1246, RG59, NA.

31. Kennan, *Memoirs, 1925–1950*, p. 293.

32. Kennan, "Telegraphic Message of February 22, 1946," reprinted in *Memoirs, 1925–1950*, pp. 547–65; also in *FRUS 1946*, 6: 696–723; *FRUS 1945*, 5: 867.

33. Kennan, "Long Telegram."

34. Matthews to Kennan, February 25, 1946, DSF 861.00/2–2246, RG59, NA; Halle, *The Cold War As History*, p. 105; on the impact of the Long Telegram, see also Yergin, *Shattered Peace*, pp. 168–71; Jones, *The Fifteen Weeks*, p. 133; Acheson, *Present at the Creation*, p. 151; Larson, *Origins of Containment*, p. 256.

35. Paterson, *Soviet-American Confrontation*, pp. 177–183; Harbutt, *The Iron Curtain*; Churchill's "iron curtain" speech can be found in, e.g., LaFeber, ed., *Origins of the Cold War: Interpretations and Documents*, pp. 135–39.

36. *FRUS 1946*, 6: 716; *New York Times*, March 12, 1946.

37. Kennan to Elbridge Durbrow, March 7, 15, 1946, Kennan 123 Personnel File, 1945–49, RG59, NA.

38. DSF 861.00/2–2246 and 861.00/4–346, Box 6462, RG59, NA; William T. Stone interview by John T. Mason, Aug 6, 1980, Columbia University Oral History Project, Bakmateff Archive.

39. Kennan to Elbridge Durbrow, April 2, 1946, Kennan Personnel File,

1945–49; K. Tolley, "Memorandum for Captain Smedberg" attached to the Long Telegram in Box 70, James V. Forrestal Papers, Mudd Library; Interview with Harry Hill, Dec. 16, 1968, by John T. Mason Jr., Columbia University.

40. Millis, ed., *The Forrestal Diaries*, p. 57; Truman received information on Forrestal's "nervous breakdown" in a March 31, 1949, memorandum: President's Secretary's Files, Papers of Harry S. Truman, HSTL; Kennan, *Memoirs, 1925–1950*, p. 306; Kennan to John Osborne, July 31, 1962, Box 31, Kennan Papers.

41. Kennan report to Francis Russell, Aug. 23, 1946, Box 27, Dean G. Acheson Papers, HSTL.

42. Reports and comment on Kennan's tour can be found in DSF 711.61/11–1246, Box 3428, RG59, NA.

43. See "American Relations with the Soviet Union: A Report to the President by the Special Counsel to the President" and Kennan's "Comments on the Document" in Subject File, Foreign Affairs, Elsey Papers, HSTL; Krock, *Memoirs*, also contains a copy of the Clifford Report, pp. 419–82; Oral history interview with George M. Elsey, April 9, 1970 by Jerry N. Hess, HSTL.

44. Kennan to Waldemar J. Gallman, March 14, 1947, Box 28, Kennan Papers.

45. Kennan, *Memoirs, 1925–1950*, pp. 306–7; Kennan to John Osborne, July 31, 1962.

46. Kennan to Acheson, Oct. 8, 1946, Box 27, Acheson Papers, HSTL; on Wallace's ouster, see Walker, *Henry Wallace and American Foreign Policy*, pp. 149–162; Acheson to Kennan, Oct. 11, 1946, Kennan 123 Personnel File, 1945–49.

47. Kennan, "Measures Short of War," Sept. 16, 1946 National War College (NWC) lecture, Box 16, Kennan Papers; Kennan, *Memoirs, 1925–1950*, p. 308; Fitzpatrick, "George F. Kennan and the National War College."

48. Kennan, "Russia," Oct. 1, 1946, NWC lecture, Newport, R.I., Box 16, Kennan Papers.

49. Kennan, "Measures Short of War."

50. On totalitarianism, see the essays, including one by Kennan, in Friedrich, *Totalitarianism: Proceedings of a Conference;* on the Stalin-Hitler comparison, see Adler and Paterson, "Red Fascism;" Kennan quoted in Brooks Atkinson, "America's Global Planner," *New York Times Magazine*, July 13, 1947, p. 33; Kennan, "Preparedness as Part of Foreign Relations," Jan. 8, 1948, NWC lecture, Box 17, Kennan Papers; Arendt, *Totalitarianism* is the classic work on this subject.

51. Kennan, "Preparedness as Part of Foreign Relations;" Kennan, "Estimate of the International Situation," Joint Orientation Conference in Secretary Forrestal's office, Washington, Nov. 8, 1948, Box 17, Kennan Papers; Kennan, "Contemporary Problems of Foreign Policy," Sept. 17, 1948, NWC lecture, Box 17, Kennan Papers.

52. Kennan, "Russia's National Objectives," lecture at Air War College, Maxwell Field, Ala., April 10, 1947, Box 17, Kennan Papers.

53. Kennan, "Presentation to Select Leaders of Industry," Jan. 8, 1948, NWC lecture, Box 17, Kennan Papers." Kennan, "Background of the Marshall Plan," Feb. 18, 1948, speech to Chicago Businesman's Luncheon, Box 17, Kennan Papers; Kennan, "The Sources of Soviet Conduct," in his *American Diplomacy*, p. 100.

54. Kennan, "Background of the Marshall Plan;" Kennan, *The Marquis de Custine and His Russia in 1839*, pp. 120, 124.

55. Kennan talk to National Defense Committee, U.S. Chamber of Commerce, Washington, D.C., Jan 23, 1947, Box 16, Kennan Papers; Kennan, "Preparedness as Part of Foreign Relations."

56. Sherry, *Preparing for the Next War,* quote on p. 55; see also Leffler, "The American Conception of National Security and the Beginnings of the Cold War.

57. Kennan, "Preparedness as Part of Foreign Relations"; Kennan, "Where Are We Today"; Kennan, "Factors Affecting the Nature of the U.S. Defense Arrangements in Light of Soviet Policies" (PPS 33), in Nelson, ed. *Policy Planning Staff Papers*, 2: 292.

58. Kennan, "Presentation to Select Leaders of Industry."

59. "Recommendations on Offer of U.S. Forces to UN and on Disarmament" (PPS 29), in Nelson, ed., *Planning Staff Papers*, 2: 244; *FRUS 1946*, 1: 861–64; *FRUS 1947*, 1: 608–13.

60. Kennan talk to National Defense Committee; Herken, *The Winning Weapon;* Gerber, "The Baruch Plan and the Origins of the Cold War"; Holloway, *The Soviet Union and the Arms Race*, pp. 15–29.

61. Kennan, "Measures Short of War"; Kennan, "Long Telegram, quoted in *Memoirs, 1925–1950,* p. 559.

62. Kennan talk to Foreign Service staff at the American Legation, Lisbon, June 1944, Box 16, Kennan Papers. Kennan predicted turmoil at home in the immediate postwar era and declared that "it would be a miracle if we could survive this crisis without violence and disorder." Kennan, "American Capitalist Democracy in a Collective Environment," May 2, 1947, Williams College speech, Box 17, Kennan Papers.

63. John T. Connor, "Impressions of the Secretary," Oct. 23, 1961, Box 31, Arthur M. Krock Papers, Mudd Library.

64. Kennan to Connor, Oct. 30, 1946, Box 70, Forrestal Papers; Allen W. Dulles Papers, Box 30, Mudd Library; Minutes of discussion group on Soviet Foreign Policy, Jan. 7, 1947, Records of Groups, vol. 22, 1946–47, Council on Foreign Relations, New York; Kennan, "The Soviet Way of Thought and Its Effect on Foreign Policy," Jan. 24, 1947, NWC lecture, Box 16, Kennan Papers.

65. Connor, "Impressions of the Secretary."

66. Kennan, "Psychological Background of Soviet Foreign Policy," Box 1, Kennan Papers; also in Box 18, Forrestal Papers; Connor, "Impressions of the Secretary."

67. Lloyd C. Gardner has made this point in *Architects of Illusion,* p. 283; see also Halle, *The Cold War as History,* p. 107. Halle, also a professional

diplomat, served with Kennan on the PPS in the late 1940s and Kennan read drafts of Halle's manuscript before its publication in 1967.

68. Correspondence, Box 33, Hamilton Fish Armstrong Papers, Mudd Library.

69. Kennan, "Sources of Soviet Conduct," in *American Diplomacy*, p. 96.

70. Ibid., pp. 92, 97–99.

71. Ibid., pp. 102–5.

72. *Life*, July 28, 1947, pp. 53–63; *Newsweek*, July 21, 1947, pp. 15–17; *Reader's Digest* 51 (Oct. 1947): 25–31. Kennan at first opposed publication of excerpts by *Reader's Digest*, but relented when the magazine paid him $1,200 (Box 33, Armstrong Papers).

72. Kennan, *Memoirs, 1925–1950*, pp. 357–59; for analyses of the X-Article, see C. Ben Wright, "Mr. 'X' and Containment," *Slavic Review* 35 (March 1976): 1–36; John L. Gaddis, "Containment: A Reassessment," *Foreign Affairs* 55 (July 1977): 873–887, and a reply by Eduard Mark in Ibid. 56. (January 1978): 430–441; also see Gaddis, *Strategies of Containment: A Critical Appraisal of Postwar American National Security Policy* (New York: Oxford University Press, 1982), pp. 25–53 and Charles Gati, "What Containment Meant," *Foreign Policy* (Summer 1972): 22–40; Paul Seabury, "Reinspecting Containment," in *Beyond Containment: Alternative Policies Toward the Soviet Union* (San Francisco: Institute for Contemporary Studies, 1983); and David Mayers, "Containment and the Primacy of Diplomacy: George Kennan's Views, 1947–1948," *International Security* (Summer 1986): 124–162.

74. On this point, see chapters 3, 5, 11, and the conclusion; Kennan, *Memoirs, 1925–1950*, p. 359; Kennan, "Problems of U.S. Foreign Policy After Moscow."

75. Kennan, *Memoirs, 1925–1950*, pp. 354–67; Gaddis, "Containment: A Reassessment," p. 873; Gaddis, *Strategies of Containment*, pp. 25–53.

3. The Global Planner

1. Kennan contrasted the "universalistic" and "particularlized" approach to foreign affairs in his "Review of Current Trends in U.S. Foreign Policy" (PPS 23), Feb. 24, 1947, in Nelson, ed., *Policy Planning Staff Papers*, 1: 103–34, one of the early expressions of his realism; see also Kennan, *American Diplomacy, 1900–1950*, and *Realities of American Foreign Policy*. The classic study of realism is Morgenthau, *Politics Among Nations*, but see also Thompson, *Political Realism and the Crisis of World Politics*; Smith, *Realist Thought from Weber to Kissinger*; and Coffey, *Political Realism in American Thought*. The quotation is from Thompson, *Political Realism*, p. 250.

2. Smith, *Realist Thought from Weber to Kissinger*, pp. 1–22, 54–67; Kennan, *American Diplomacy*, passim and pp. 82, 95; Kennan, *Realities of American Foreign Policy*, pp. 13–27.

3. Smith, *Realist Thought from Weber to Kissinger*, pp. 99–164, 218–38.

4. Kennan, "Where Are We Today?" Dec. 21, 1948, National War College (NWC) lecture, Box 17, Kennan Papers.

5. Kennan to Dean Acheson, Nov. 11, 1949, Box 23, Records of the Policy Planning Staff (PPS Records), Record Group 59 (RG59), National Archives (NA).

6. Kennan, "Where Are We Today?"

7. Kennan, *Memoirs, 1925–1950,* p. 359; Kennan, "Contemporary Problems of Foreign Policy," Sept. 17, 1948, NWC lecture, Box 17, Kennan Papers.

8. Kennan, "An Estimate of the International Situation," Jan. 14, 1948, National Defense Building, Box 17, Kennan Papers.

9. Nelson, ed., *Planning Staff Papers,* 1: 130–32; *FRUS 1947:* 1: 770–71.

10. Pogue, *George C. Marshall: Statesman,* pp. 168–96; Donovan, *Conflict and Crisis,* pp. 286–91.

11. R. B. Reams to Harry Hill, March 7, 1947, Kennan Personnel File, 1945–49, Record Group 59 (RG59), National Archives (NA), Washington DC; Pogue, *Marshall: Statesman,* pp. 87, 150, 202.

12. Kennan, *Memoirs, 1925–1950,* p. 345; George C. Marshall to Kennan, Jan. 6, 1948, Box 7, Wright Biography Project, Marshall Library, Lexington, Va.

13. *FRUS 1947,* 3: 220; *Department of State Bulletin,* May 11, 1947, p. 1007; "GFK on PPS Origins," 1959, Documents loaned by Kennan to Forrest Pogue, Verifax 358, Marshall Library; Charles Bohlen, Benjamin V. Cohen, William A. Crawford, and Paul Nitze interviews by C. Ben Wright, Wright Biography Project; *U.S. News and World Report,* Oct. 10, 1947, pp. 52–55 and July 25, 1947, p. 17; *New York Times Magazine,* July 13, 1947, p. 63; Kennan, *Memoirs, 1925–1950,* p. 313.

14. Kennan, "Report on the Activities of the Policy Planning Staff" (PPS 15), Nov. 13, 1947, in Nelson, ed., *Planning Staff Papers,* I, p. 143; Nelson, "Truman and the Evolution of the National Security Council," 360–78.

15. *Department of State Bulletin,* May 18, 1947, p. 1001; see also *FRUS, 1947:* 1: 733; Nelson, ed., *Policy Planning Staff Papers,* 1: vii.

16. Nelson, ed., *Planning Staff Papers,* 1: viii; for an example of Kennan forwarding dissenting views, see Dorothy Fosdick's UN memorandum, April 29, 1947, Records of the PPS, Box 33, RG59, NA.

17. Kennan, "Background to the Marshall Plan," Feb. 18, 1948, Box 17, Kennan Papers.

18. Kennan, "Problems of U.S. Foreign Policy After Moscow," May 6, 1947 NWC lecture, Box 17, Kennan Papers.

19. PPS 23, pp. 112, 118.

20. Kennan, "Policy with Respect to American Aid to Western Europe" (PPS 1), May 23, 1947, in Nelson, ed., *Policy Planning Staff Papers,* 1: 3, 5, 9; Kennan, "Problems of U.S. Foreign Policy After Moscow"; *FRUS 1947,* 3: 220–30, 235.

21. Kennan, *Memoirs, 1925–1950,* pp. 335–45; Bohlen, *Witness to History,* pp. 263–67; Jones, *Fifteen Weeks,* p. 253.

22. Kennan, "Soviet-American Relations Today," May 12, 1947, lecture at Army Information School, Carlisle, Pa., Box 17, Kennan Papers.

23. Kennan, "Problems of U.S. Foreign Policy After Moscow"; Hogan, *The Marshall Plan*, p. 44.

24. Kennan, *Memoirs, 1925–1950*, p. 342; Bohlen, *Witness to History*, pp. 263–67; Jones, *Fifteen Weeks*, p. 253; Freeland, *The Truman Doctrine*, pp. 169–70; Yergin, *Shattered Peace*, p. 314–15; Bohlen, The *Transformation of American Foreign Policy*, p. 91; *FRUS 1947*, 3: 266.

25. *FRUS 1947*, 3: 294–95, 318–20; Donovan, *Conflict and Crisis*, p. 290; Ulam, *The Rivals*, pp. 126–36; Yergin, *Shattered Peace*, pp. 314–26.

26. *FRUS 1947*, 3: 335; Kennan, "Certain Aspects of the European Recovery Problem from the United States' Standpoint" (PPS 4), July 23, 1947, in Nelson, ed., *Planning Staff Papers*, 1: 31–34.

27. *FRUS 1947*, 3: 397–405.

28. Kennan, "Notes on the Marshall Plan," Dec. 15, 1947, Box 23, Kennan Papers; Kennan, "The Time Factor in a European Recovery Program" (PPS 6), Aug. 14, 1947, in Nelson, ed. *Planning Staff Papers*, 1: 71.

29. Donovan, *Conflict and Crisis*, pp. 340–41; Paterson, *Soviet-American Confrontation*, p. 221.

30. Hogan, *The Marshall Plan*, p. 445; Leffler, *The Elusive Quest*.

31. *FRUS 1947*, 3: 294–95; Taubman, Stalin's American Policy, pp. 171–79; Yergin, *Shattered Peace*, pp. 317–24; Ulam, *The Rivals*, p. 130.

32. Kennan, "Problems of U.S. Foreign Policy After Moscow."

33. Kennan, "Current Problems of Soviet-American Relations," May 9, 1947, U.S. Naval Academy lecture, Box 17, Kennan Papers.

34. Kennan, "Where Are We Today?"; Kennan, "What Is Policy?" Dec. 18, 1947, NWC lecture, Box 17, Kennan Papers; on Kennan's early involvement with the CIA, I am relying in part on Wright, "Scholar-Diplomat," p. 436, which cites a memorandum from Vandenberg dated June 26, 1946. Wright found the document in the Kennan Papers, but the letter is no longer in the collection.

35. Kennan to Lovett, May 25, 1948, and Oct. 29, 1948, both in PPS Records, Box 33, RG59, NA.

36. Church Committee (U.S. Senate) Final Report, Book IV, Supplementary Detailed Staff Reports on foreign and Military Intelligence, p. 29; Etzold and Gaddis, *Containment: Documents on American Policy*, pp. 126–27.

37. Church Committee Report, Book IV, pp. 29–31.

38. Kennan, "Estimate of the International Situation."

39. Kennan, "United States Policy in the Event of the Establishment of Communist Power in Greece" (PPS 8), Sept. 18, 1947, in Nelson, ed. *Planning Staff Papers*, 1: 92–127; *FRUS 1947*, 3: 1091–95.

40. Jones, *The Fifteen Weeks*, p. 133.

41. Kennan, *Memoirs, 1925–1950*, pp. 313–14; Truman Doctrine quoted in LaFeber, ed., *Origins of the Cold War: Interpretations*, pp. 154–55; *FRUS 1947*, 5: 45; *FRUS 1947*, 3: 229; Kennan, *Memoirs, 1925–1950*, p. 317; Jones,

Fifteen Weeks, p. 155; Acheson, *Present at the Creation*, p. 221; the extension of aid to Turkey is examined in Leffler, "Strategy, Diplomacy, and the Cold War: The United States, Turkey, and NATO, 1945–1952."

42. Freeland, *The Truman Doctrine and the Origins of McCarthyism*, pp. 70–150.

43. Ibid.; Wittner, *American Intervention in Greece, 1943–1949*; Iatrides, *Revolt in Athens*.

44. PPS 23, pp. 115–16.

45. Kennan, quoted in PPS 8, p. 94; on bandwagoning see Walt, *The Origins of Alliances*, pp. 17–49.

46. Kennan, "Orientation and Comments on the National Security Problem," March 14–28, 1947, NWC exercise and lecture, Box 16, Kennan Papers.

47. Kennan, "What Is Policy?"

48. Kennan, "Comments on the General Trend of U.S. Foreign Policy," Aug. 20, 1948, Box 23, Kennan Papers.

49. PPS 23, pp. 121–22.

50. Schaller, *The American Occupation of Japan*.

51. *FRUS 1948*, 6: 486–87; Kennan to W. W. Butterworth, Feb. 10, 1948, Box 33, PPS Records; on the reverse course, see Dower, "Occupied Japan and the American Lake, 1945–1950," in Friedman and Selden, eds., *America's Asia*, pp. 186–206, and Schaller, *American Occupation of Japan*, pp. 122–40.

52. Kennan, "Recommendations With Respect to U.S. Policy Toward Japan" (PPS 28/2), May 26, 1948, in Nelson, ed., *Planning Staff Papers*, 2: 175–243.

53. Kennan to W. Walton Butterworth, Mar. 14, 1948, quoted in Schaller, *American Occupation of Japan*, pp. 124–25.

54. PPS 28/2; *FRUS 1948*, 6: 719.

55. *FRUS 1948*, 6: 776, 793.

56. Kennan, "The Present Situation In Japan," May 19, 1948, NWC lecture, Box 17, Kennan Papers.

57. Kennan, "Department of State Comments on Current Strategic Evaluation of U.S. Security Needs in Japan (NSC 49)," in Nelson, ed., *Planning Staff Papers*, 3: 183–86.

58. Kennan to Rusk, July 18, 1950, Department of State Files, 611.61/5-2252, Box 2825, RG59, NA.

59. *FRUS 1950*, 6: 1248–50, 1276–77; Kennan interview by Richard Challener.

60. Kennan, "United States Policy Toward China" (PPS 39), Sept. 15, 1948, in Nelson, ed., *Planning Staff Papers*, 2: 431, 450–51; Kennan, "United States Policy Toward China in Light of the Current Situation" (PPS 45), Nov. 26, 1948, pp. 509–18; *FRUS 1948*, 8: 211, 224–25. Kennan called Davies "the soundest man we've had on China in this century. I learned everything I know about [Asia] from him." (Kennan interview by Hixson).

61. Kennan, "United States Policy Toward Formosa and the Pescadores" (PPS 53), July 6, 1949, in Nelson, ed., *Planning Staff Papers*, 3: 63, 65.

62. On this point, see Tucker, *Patterns in the Dust*.

63. *FRUS 1949*, 7, (part II): 26–27; Kennan to Acheson, June 28, 1949, Box 33, PPS Records; Kennan, "Current Problems in the Conduct of Foreign Policy," May 15, 1950, *The Department of State Bulletin*, pp. 747–51.

64. PPS 23, p. 123.

65. Kennan, "United States Policy Toward Southeast Asia" (PPS 51), May 19, 1949, in Nelson, ed., *Planning Staff Papers*, 3: 32–58; see McMahon, *Colonialism and Cold War*.

66. PPS 51, pp. 38–39.

67. Kennan, "Position of the United States with Respect to Palestine" (PPS 19), Jan. 20, 1948, in Nelson, ed., *Planning Staff Papers*, 2: 34–57; *FRUS 1948*, 5(2): 545–554, 1020–21, 1113–14, 1213; Donovan, *Conflict and Crisis*, pp. 312–31, 369–87; Cohen, *Palestine and the Great Powers, 1945–1948*.

68. Kennan, "French North Africa" (PPS 25), Mar. 22, 1948, in Nelson, ed., *Planning Staff Papers*, 2: 146–47.

69. Kennan, "Anti-Communist Measures which Could be Planned and Carried Out Within the Inter-American System" (PPS 26), March 22, 1948, in Nelson, ed., *Planning Staff Papers*, 2: 157.

70. The President's speech and notes from Truman are in Box 36, PPS Records, RG 59; Kennan, "Comments on NSC 56, 'U.S. Policy Concerning Military Collaboration Under the Inter-American Treaty of Reciprocal Assistance" (PPS 63), Sept. 20, 1949, in Nelson, ed., *Planning Staff Papers*, 3: 182.

71. *Chicago Tribune*, March 9, 1950; *New York Times*, March 9, 1950.

72. *FRUS 1950*, 2: 598–624; Kirkpatrick, "Dictatorships and Double Standards."

73. Walt, *The Origins of Alliances*, pp. 17–49, 147–80, 262–85.

4. The Militarization of Containment

1. Lippmann interview by Nevins and Albertson; Lippmann, *The Cold War*, pp. 11, 13, 21, 34, 38, 40, 46, 50; Steel, *Walter Lippmann and the American Century* is an outstanding biography.

2. Kennan to Lippmann (unsent), April 6, 1948, Box 17, Kennan Papers.

3. See, for example, Taubman, *Stalin's American Policy*, pp. 171–79; Yergin, *Shattered Peace*, pp. 317–24; Ulam, *The Rivals*, p. 130.

4. Kennan, "Resume of the World Situation" (PPS 13), Nov. 6, 1947, in Nelson, ed., *Planning Staff Papers*, 1: 132–34.

5. Shulman, *Stalin's Foreign Policy Reappraised*, pp. 14–15; Ulam, *Expansion and Coexistence*, p. 455; Donovan, *Conflict and Crisis*, p. 358.

6. Donovan, *Conflict and Crisis*, pp. 357–61.

7. Kennan, "Presentation to Selected Leaders of Industry," Jan. 14, 1948, lecture, Box 17, Kennan Papers, Mudd Library; *FRUS 1948*, 3: 848–49.

8. *FRUS 1948*, 3: 40–42, 48; Donovan, *Conflict and Crisis*, p. 363.

9. *FRUS 1948*, 3: 7, 8, 109.

10. Kennan to Marshall and Lovett, May 24, 1948, Box 27, PPS Records; *FRUS 1948*, 3: 128–29.

11. Kennan, "Considerations Affecting the Conclusion of a North Atlantic Security Pact" (PPS 43), Nov. 24, 1948, in Nelson, ed. *Planning Staff Papers*, 2: 490–95.

12. *FRUS 1948*, 3: 157, 165, 182, 225–27; PPS 43, pp. 490–91.

13. PPS 43, pp. 490–95.

14. *FRUS 1948*, 3: 100, 116–18, 128–29, 140–42; Kennan, "Western Union and Related Problems" (PPS 27 and 27/1), Mar. 23 and April 6, 1948, in Nelson, ed., *Planning Staff Papers*, 2: 161–74.

15. *FRUS 1948*, 3: 283–84; Kennan, "Assessment of Foreign Policy," June 23, 1950, Box 24, Kennan Papers.

16. Kennan to Marshall, Aug. 25, 1948, Box 33, PPS Records; Kennan, "An Estimate of the International Situation," Jan. 14, 1948, Box 17, Kennan Papers.

17. Yergin, *Shattered Peace*, pp. 368–80; Murphy, *Diplomat Among Warriors*, pp. 312–15.

18. Kennan, "Draft Statement for Secretary," July 21, 1948; Kennan to Robert Lovett, Aug. 2, 1948, both in Box 15, PPS Records; FRUS 1948, 2: 1210–11.

19. *FRUS 1949*, 1: 271n.; Kennan, "Factors Affecting the Nature of the U.S. Defense Arrangements in Light of Soviet Policies" (PPS 33), June 23, 1948, in Nelson, ed., *Planning Staff Papers*, 2: 282; Kennan, "United States Objectives With Respect to Russia" (PPS 38), in Ibid., pp. 372, 387.

20. *FRUS 1949*, 1: 271–85; 381–84, 662–69.

21. Kennan, "Assessment of Foreign Policy."

22. Kennan to George C. Marshall, Sept. 8, 1948, Box 23, PPS Records, RG 59, NA; Bruce Kuklick, *American Policy and the Division of Germany: The Clash with Russia Over Reparations* (New York: Cornell University Press, 1972); Paterson, *Soviet-American Confrontation*, pp. 235–259.

23. Kennan, "Policy Questions Concerning a Possible German Settlement" (PPS 37), Aug. 12, 1948, in Nelson, ed., *Planning Staff Papers*, 2: 325–32.

24. *FRUS 1948*, 2: 1287–88; Kennan to Secretary, Sept. 8, 1948, Box 33, PPS Records.

25. Kennan, "Military Implications Deriving from the Establishment of a Free and Sovereign German Government"; Kennan to Marshall, Oct. 18, 1948, both in Box 15, PPS Records; *FRUS 1948*, 2: 1320–38; Kennan, "Position To Be Taken by the United States at a CFM Meeting (PPS 37/1), Nov. 15, 1948, in Nelson, ed., *Planning Staff Papers*, 2: 335–40.

26. PPS 37/1, pp. 335–71.

27. *FRUS 1949*, 3: 858–59; Kennan to Marshall, Oct. 18, 1948, Box 15, PPS Records.

28. PPS 37/1, pp. 335–71

29. Bohlen, *Witness to History*, pp. 285–86; *FRUS 1948*, 2: 1320n.

30. Kennan to Murphy, Dec. 24, 1948, Box 15, PPS Records.

31. Kennan quote Box 15, PPS Papers; *FRUS 1948*, 2: 1320n.

32. Kennan, "Contemporary Problems of Foreign Policy," Sept. 17, 1948, NWC lecture, Box 17, Kennan Papers.

33. Kennan, "Economic Relations Between the United States and Yugoslavia" (PPS 49), Feb. 10, 1949, in Nelson, ed., *Planning Staff Papers*, 3: 14, 17. In a 1984 interview Kennan noted that "I did not predict or anticipate the Tito break; we were weak on the analysis of political developments in the Balkans by 1947–48." Kennan's eventual awareness of Tito's defection changed his perception of the communist threat, although it took the Sino-Soviet split several years later to confirm for him the myth of monolithic communism (Kennan interview by Hixson).

34. Kennan, "Estimate of the International Situation"; PPS 49, p. 18.

35. Kennan, "Yugoslav-Moscow Controversy as Related to U.S. Foreign Policy Objectives" (PPS 60), Sept. 10, 1949, in Nelson ed., *Planning Staff Papers*, 3: 139–49.

36. Kennan, United States Policy Toward the Soviet Satellite States in Eastern Europe," Aug. 25, 1949, in Ibid., pp. 124–38.

37. Ibid., p. 134; PPS draft working paper "United States Policy Toward Communism" March 8, 1949, Box 8, PPS Records.

38. Kennan to Acheson, Jan. 3, 1949, Box 64, Acheson Papers, Harry S. Truman Library Institute (HSTL), Independence, Mo.

39. *FRUS 1949*, 3: 88–93, 96–104; on Acheson, see McLellan, *Dean Acheson: The State Department Years* and Acheson's own *Present at the Creation*.

40. *FRUS 1949*, 3: 137; "Report on George Kennan's Visit to Germany," Box 23, Kennan Papers.

41. Ibid.; Kennan to Bohlen, Oct. 12, 1949 and Bohlen to Kennan, Oct. 29, 1949, both in Bohlen Papers, RG 59, NA. (Kennan's letter to Bohlen also appears in Box 23, Kennan Papers.)

42. Kennan, Notes from Oct. 18, 1949, PPS meeting, Box 27, PPS Records.

43. *FRUS 1949*, 3: 872–73, 884–85; Donovan, *Tumultuous Years*, p. 42.

44. *FRUS 1949*, 3: 890.

45. Kennan, "Estimate of the International Situation"; Donovan, *Tumultuous Years*, pp. 40–43, 51.

46. Donovan, *Tumultuous Years*, pp. 41–43.

47. Miscamble, "George F. Kennan, the Policy Planning Staff, and American Foreign Policy, 1947–1949," pp. 181–82; Kennan to Sidney W. Souers, Dec. 3, 1948, Box 33, PPS Records.

48. Kennan, *Memoirs, 1925–1950*, p. 465; *Department of State Bulletin*, May 26, 1949, p. 734; Nitze interview by Wright.

49. Kennan to Dean Rusk, Dec. 15, 1949, Box 23, PPS Records; Kennan, "Assessment of Foreign Policy."

50. Kennan to Bohlen, Oct. 12, 1949, Bohlen Papers, RG 59, NA; Kennan, "Is War With Russia Inevitable."

51. *FRUS 1949*, 1: 422, 443–61, 469, 475–76, 543, 550–51.

52. Herken, *The Winning Weapon*, pp. 304–14; *FRUS 1949*, 1: 573–74.

53. Kennan, Oct. 11, 1949 PPS meeting, Box 1, Bohlen Papers, RG 59; *FRUS 1949*, 1: 402.

54. *FRUS 1949*, 1: 222–23; Herken, *Winning Weapon*, pp. 306–7; Kennan

statement, Nov. 18, 1949 and Kennan to Oppenheimer, June 5, 1950, both in Box 43, Oppenheimer Papers, Library of Congress.

55. *FRUS 1950,* 1: 22–44.

56. Kennan, "Presentation to Select Leaders of Industry," Jan. 14, 1948, Washington DC, Box 17, Kennan Papers.

57. *FRUS 1950,* 1: 22–44.

58. Ibid., pp. 40. 1, 2, 10–11.

59. Ibid., pp. 13–17; Herken, *Winning Weapon,* pp. 319–21; Holloway, *The Soviet Union and Arms Race,* pp. 24–25.

60. Rearden, *The Evolution of American Strategic Doctrine,* pp. 7–31; Kennan to Norman Graebner, May 16, 1959, Box 31, Kennan Papers.

61. Rearden, *The Evolution of American Strategic Doctrine,* pp. 7–31.

62. Ibid., pp. 27–29.

63. Kennan, "Where Do We Stand," Dec. 21, 1949, NWC lecture, Box 17, Kennan Papers.

64. Kennan to Norman Graebner, May 16, 1959; Acheson, *Present at the Creation,* p. 446.

65. Dennison interview by McKenzie; *Time,* Dec. 19, 1949. p. 12; *New York Times,* Dec 13, 1949, p. 20.

66. Bohlen interview by Wright; Laukhuff interview by McKenzie.

67. Nitze interview by Wright.

68. Kennan to Robert Oppenheimer, Feb 13, 1951, Box 43, Oppenheimer Papers.

5. Korea: Containment on the Perimeter I

1. "Summary by George F. Kennan on Points of Diference Between His Views and Those of the Department of State," Sept. 1951, Box 24, Kennan Papers, Mudd Library, Princeton.

2. Kennan, "Assessment of Foreign Policy," June 23, 1950, Box 24, Kennan Papers.

3. Kennan comments in June 6, 1949 PPS meeting, Box 27, Records of the Policy Planning Staff, Record Group (RG59), National Archives (NA); Kennan, "How New Are Our Problems," Jan. 29–30, 1951, Box 2, Kennan Papers.

4. Kennan, "Basic Factors in American Foreign Policy" Feb. 14, 1949, Box 17, Kennan Papers.

5. *FRUS 1946,* 8: 619–20.

6. Kennan, "Resume of the World Situation," in Nelson, ed., *Planning Staff Papers,* 1: 135; Kennan "U.S. Policy Toward a Peace Settlement with Japan" Sept. 22, 1947, Box 32, PPS Records, RG59, NA; *FRUS 1947,* 6: 814; Cumings, *Origins of the Korean War.*

7. Kennan testimony (June 16, 17 and 20, 1949), "Hearings Into Military Assistance in Korea, Selected Executive Sessions of the [House] Committee on International Relations, 1943–1950," Vol. 8, United States Policy in the Far East, Part II, pp. 32–33, 46–47, 50, 57, 80, 102; for background on the conflict

in Korea, see the following: Cumings, *Origins of the Korean War* and his edited volume, *Child of Conflict* Matray, *The Reluctant Crusade;* Stueck, *The Road to Confrontation;* Dobbs, *The Unwanted Symbol.*

8. On this point, see Matray, *The Reluctant Crusade,* pp. 217–18.

9. Kennan testimony, "Hearings Into Military Assistance in Korea," pp. 32–33, 46–47, 50, 57, 80, 102.

10. Matray, *The Reluctant Crusade,* p. 235; Cumings, ed., *Child of Conflict* p. 55; Kaufman, *The Korean War: Challenges in Crisis, Credibility, and Command;* Talbott, ed. *Khruschev Remembers,* p. 368; see also Dobbs, *The Unwanted Symbol,* pp. 160–92.

11. Kennan interview Hixson; Tucker, *Patterns in the Dust,* pp. 195–96, 200, 205–7.

12. *FRUS 1950,* 1: 325–30, 358–59, 615; Foot, *The Wrong War,* pp. 82–83.

13. *FRUS 1950,* 4: 1224–29 and *FRUS 1950,* 1: 361–67.

14. Kennan, "Possible Further Danger Points in Light of the Korean Situation," June 26, 1950, Box 24, Kennan Papers.

15. Kennan to Dean Acheson, Aug. 21, 1950, Box 65, Acheson Papers, HSTL; *FRUS 1950,* 7: 623–29.

16. *FRUS 1950, 7:* 574–76.

17. Kennan to Acheson, Aug. 21, 1950, Box 65, Acheson Papers, HSTL; for a shortened version of this memorandum, see *FRUS 1950,* 7: 623–29; Kennan, "Estimate of the International Situation."

18. *FRUS 1950,* 6: 1248–50, 1276–77.

19. Stueck, *The Road to Confrontation,* pp. 223–50.

20. *FRUS 1950, 7:* 1385; Kennan, *Memoirs, 1950–1963,* p. 34.

21. Donovan, *Tumultuous Years,* p. 314; Kennan memorandum, Dec. 3, 1950, Freedom of Information Act request.

22. Memorandum of Conversation, Dec. 5, 1950, Box 65, Acheson Papers, HSTL; Kennan, *Memoirs, 1950–1963,* p. 34.

23. Kennan to Paul Nitze, Jan 6, 1951, Freedom of Information Act request.

24. Foot, *The Wrong War,* pp. 88–130.

25. *FRUS 1951,* 7: 242–44.

26. *FRUS 1951,* 7: 406, 421–22, 460–62; Acheson, *Present at the Creation,* p. 532.

27. Acheson, *Present at the Creation,* p. 533; *FRUS 1951,* 7: 483–86, 241–43; Foot, *The Wrong War,* p. 133.

28. *FRUS 1951,* 7: 483–86; Acheson, *Present at the Creation,* p. 533.

29. *FRUS 1951,* 7: 536–38.

30. Acheson, *Present at the Creation,* pp. 534–38.

31. *FRUS 1952,* 15 (1): 431–35.

32. Foot, *The Wrong War,* pp. 174–88, 195.

33. Ibid., pp. 204–31; Kennan quoted on page 227.

34. Gaddis makes this argument in *Strategies of Containment,* pp. 30–31, 57–65.

35. Foot, *The Wrong War,* pp. 204–31.

6. An Appointment with Evil

1. Kennan to Charles Thayer, Sept. 4, 1950, Thayer Correspondence, Harry S Truman Library Institute (HSTL); Albert Einstein to Kennan, March 8, 1954, Box 89, Einstein Papers, Mudd Library.

2. Kennan, "United States External Relations Project," Box 26, Kennan Papers; Kennan, *American Diplomacy, 1900–1950.*

3. Kennan, *American Diplomacy;* Hanson Baldwin, *Great Mistakes of the War.*

4. Kennan to Acheson, Sept. 1, 1951, Box 29, Kennan Papers.

5. *Time,* Dec. 3, 1951, p. 20.

6. Kennan to Acheson, Nov. 24, 1950, Box 32, Acheson Papers, HSTL; Bohlen, *Witness to History,* p. 312; Richard Rovere, "Letter from Washington," May 17, 1952 *New Yorker,* p. 21.

7. "Nomination of George F. Kennan as ambassador to the Soviet Union," Executive Sessions of the Senate Foreign Relations Committee: 82nd Cong., 2nd Sess., 1952, 4: 189; *Time,* Dec. 3, 1951, p. 20.

8. *Washington Evening-Star,* Dec. 8, 1951; Official File, Box 3278, HSTL; *Fortune* 44 (December 1951): 117; *Department of State Bulletin,* March 24, 1952, p. 479.

9. *Department of State Bulletin,* April 21, 1952, p. 643; Richard Davies interview by Jessup, Nov. 9, 1979; Kennan off-the-record news conference, April 1, 1952, Freedom of Information Act request.

10. Kennan diary entry quoted in Kennan, *Memoirs, 1950–1963,* p. 111.

11. Barnet, *The Alliance,* pp. 127–43; Kaplan, NATO and the United States, pp. 63–66; Acheson, *Present at the Creation,* pp. 551–560.

12. Kennan to David K. Bruce, Sept. 26, 1952, Box 29, Kennan Papers, Mudd Library, Princeton.

13. Kennan, *Memoirs, 1950–1963,* pp. 161–62.

14. Rovere, "Letter from Washington," p. 111.

15. Davies interview; Rounds interview by Swerdloff; Franks Rounds, "Diary of a U.S. Embassy Man," *U.S. News and World Report,* Nov. 28, 1952, p. 106.

16. *U.S. News and World Report,* Nov. 28, 1952, p. 106; Rovere, "Letter from Washington"; Harrison Salisbury, "The View from Mokhovaya Street," *New York Times Magazine,* June 1, 1952, p. 33.

17. Rovere, "Letter from Washington," p. 117.

18. *Time,* June 30, 1952, p. 25; *Current Digest of the Soviet Press,* July 17, 1952, 4(23): 6.

19. Kennan's reports on the anti-American campaign appear in the State Department Files (SDF), 611.61/5–2252, 611.61/6–1952, and 611.61/5–3052, Record Group 59 (RG59), National Archives, (NA).

20. SDF 611.61/5–2252, RG59, NA; Kennan to Truman, Aug. 11, 1952. President's Secretary's Files, Box 188, HSTL; June 6, 1952, memorandum of conversation, Dean G. Acheson Papers. HSTL.

21. Kennan to H. Freeman Matthews, June 6, 1952, Box 24; Kennan to

Lewis Douglas, Aug. 12, 1952, Box 29, both in Kennan Papers; Davies interview.

22. Kennan, *Memoirs, 1950–1963*, pp. 114–18; Davies interview.

23. Kennan, *Memoirs, 1950–1963*, pp. 135, 154–56; Davies interview.

24. de Silva, *Sub Rosa*, pp. 71–74. de Silva's account coincides with the months Kennan spent in Moscow, but placed the events in 1953 instead of 1952.

25. *FRUS 1952–54*, 1: 864–65.

26. Kennan to "Doc" Matthews, July 15, 1952, Freedom of Information Act request; Kennan to Bernard Guffler, Aug 12, 1952, Box 9, Kennan Papers.

27. Kennan to Elin O'Shaughnessy, Oct. 29, 1952, Box 29, Kennan Papers.

28. *Time*, Oct. 13, 1952, pp. 21–22.

29. *Current Digest of the Soviet Press*, Nov. 18, 1952, 4(39): 17.

30. Kennan clip file, Box 33, Kennan Papers; *Department of State Bulletin*, Oct. 13, 1952, p. 557; Ibid., Oct. 20, 1952, p. 603; *Time*, Oct. 13, 1952, p. 10.

31. Davies interview.

32. Kennan to Bohlen, Sept. 27, 1952, Box 29, Kennan Papers.

33. Kennan to Robert Oppenheimer, Oct. 14, 1952, Box 43, Oppenheimer Papers.

34. *Baltimore Sun*, Oct. 6, 1952; *San Francisco Chronicle*, Oct. 7, 1952; *New York Times*, Oct. 6, 1952; *The Nation*, Oct. 11, 1952, p. 313.

35. Kennan to Bernard Guffler, Oct. 27, 1952, Box 29, Kennan Papers; Kennan, *Memoirs, 1950–1963*, p. 159.

36. Kennan to McGeorge Bundy, Feb. 11, 1953; see also Kennan to Walter Lippmann, Jan. 26, 1953, both in Lippman Papers, Box 81, Manuscripts and Archives, Yale University Library, New Haven.

7. The Politics of Liberation

1. Quoted in Kovrig, *The Myth of Liberation*, p. 112; attacks against containment and in favor of liberation also materialized in academic circles. See, for example, Burnham, *Containment or Liberation?*.

2. Kennan, "Draft Statement for London Conference," Sept. 23, 1952, Box 26 Kennan Papers.

3. Kennan, "Tasks Ahead in U.S. Foreign Policy," Dec. 18, 1952 NWC lecture, Box 18, Kennan Papers.

4. Kennan to Dean Acheson, Feb. 24, 1950, Box 65, Acheson Papers, HSTL; Kennan interview by Challener.

5. *New York Times*, Jan. 16, 1953.

6. Dulles Papers, Selected correspondence and related material, Box 61, Mudd Library; Kennan interview by Challener; Kennan to Louis J. Halle, April 20, 1966, Box 31, Kennan Papers.

7. Kennan, Pennsylvania Bar Association speech, Jan. 16, 1953, Box 2, Kennan Papers.

8. *Washington Post*, Jan. 17, 1953; *Washington Daily-News*, Jan. 17, 1953.

9. Kennan interview by Challener.

10. *New York Times,* Jan. 24, 1953; *Washington Post,* Jan. 23, 1953; *Chicago Tribune,* Jan. 23, 1953.

11. Kennan to John Foster Dulles, Jan. 23, 1953; Roderic O'Connor to Carl McCardle, March 27, 1953, both in Dwight D. Eisenhower Library, JFD Files, Subject Series, Alphabetical Subseries, Box 5, copies in Mudd Library.

12. *New York Times,* Jan. 13, 1953; Allen interview by Edwin.

13. *New York Times,* March 13, 1953; Kennan to Oppenheimer, March 15, 1953, Box 43, Oppenheimer Papers.

14. Kennan interview by Challener.

15. Kennan Clip File, Box 34, Kennan Papers.

16. Bohlen, *Witness to History,* pp. 309–36; see also Ruddy, *The Cautious Diplomat;* Allen interview.

17. Hughes memorandum to Sherman Adams, July 2, 1953, Emmett J. Hughes Papers, files relating to Dwight D. Eisenhower, correspondence, speech drafts and related materials, 1952–53, Box 1, Mudd Library.

18. Kennan to Charles Thayer, April 9, 1953, Thayer Correspondence, Harry S. Truman Library (HSTL); see Kennan's April 25, 1953, report to Allen Dulles, "USSR 1953", 64D563, Records of the Policy Planning Staff, Record Group (RG) 59, National Archives (NA).

19. In the draft, reminiscent of the report following his 1950 tour of Latin America, Kennan asserted that Soviet-dominated communists in the region sought to "foment and heighten every possible source of suspicion, resentment and dissension in the American world. . . . The fact that these intrigues and manipulations may be confusingly mingled with many legitimate and honest causes only makes them the more, rather than the less, dangerous, and increases our obligation to give them the most careful attention and to repulse them in the most firm and incisive manner." (See Kennan, "Draft for a speech by Mr. Foster Dulles," Feb. 28, 1954, Box 26, Kennan Papers.)

20. *FRUS 1952–1954,* 2: 349, 442.

21. Ibid., pp. 350–51, 388–89, 399–412.

22. Ibid., pp. 432–42; 488–534; Kennan, *Memoirs, 1950–1963,* p. 182.

23. Kennan report to Allen Dulles, April 25, 1953.

24. Kennan, Century Club address, May 7, 1953, Box 18, Kennan Papers; on the succession of Stalin, see Talbott, ed., *Khruschev Remembers,* pp. 306–41.

25. Kennan to Cecil B. Lyon, Jan. 28, 1955, Box 31, Kennan Papers

26. Kennan letter on German Problem, Oct. 16, 1955, Box 5, Kennan Papers.

27. Kaplan, *NATO and the United States,* pp. 63–66.

28. Kennan, "For the Defense of Europe: A New Approach," Sept. 12, 1954, *New York Times Magazine,* p. 7.

29. Ambrose, *Eisenhower the President,* pp. 215–17; Barnet, *The Alliance,* pp. 161–62.

30. Kennan, "Western European Integration," Dec. 3, 1954, Woodrow Wilson School, Box 18, Kennan Papers.

31. Kennan, "Notes for Address to Princeton Alumni Club, St. Louis, March 22, 1955, Box 19, Kennan Papers.

32. Kennan, speech to Sunday Breakfast Club (Philadelphia), Nov. 3, 1954, Box 18, Kennan Papers.

33. *Newsweek,* August 27, 1956, p. 92.

34. Kennan to Charles Thayer, Sept. 4, 1953, Thayer Correspondence, HSTL.

35. Matthews interview by McKenzie, July 7, 1973, HSTL; *New York Times,* March 14, 1954; "The Picture in Pennsylvania," *The Nation* March 27, 1954, inside cover; Kennan, *Memoirs, 1950–1963,* pp. 77–80.

36. Martin, *Adlai Stevenson and the World,* pp. 96–97, 138; Chester Bowles to Adlai Stevenson, [undated but reference made to Sept. 27, 1954 meeting between Stevenson and his advisers, including Kennan], Box 141, Chester Bowles Papers, Yale University Manuscript Library.

37. Kennan to Adlai Stevenson, Jan. 26, 1954, Box 401, Stevenson Papers, Mudd Library.

38. Cronin, *Great Power Politics and the Struggle over Austria.*

39. Ambrose, *Eisenhower the President,* pp. 248–49, 257–69; Talbott, ed., *Khrushchev Remembers,* pp. 392–400; on the U-2, see Ambrose and Immerman, *Ike's Spies,* pp. 265–78 and Michael R. Beschloss, *MAYDAY.*

40. Kennan, "After Geneva I," Oct. 31, 1955, Box 26, Kennan Papers.

41. *New York Times,* Jan. 16, 1953; Kennan, "Overdue Changes in Our Foreign Policy."

42. *New York Times,* Feb. 26, 1956.

43. *Newsweek,* Aug. 27, 1956, p. 92; Kennan interview by Hixson.

44. Martin, *Adlai Stevenson,* pp. 276–77; Adlai Stevenson to Kennan, March 31, 1956, Box 434, Stevenson Papers.

45. Kennan to Chester Bowles, May 28, 1956, Box 141, Bowles Papers, Yale University Manuscript Library.

46. Kennan to Stevenson, March 28, 1956, Box 31, Kennan Papers; Kennan to Tom Finletter, April 12, 1956, Box 434, Adlai Stevenson Papers, Mudd Library.

47. Kennan to Finletter, April 12, 1956; Kennan memorandum, "Dear Governor," Aug. 24, 1956, Box 434, Stevenson Papers.

48. Divine, *Blowing on the Wind,* pp. 3–35.

49. Kennan to Finletter, April 12, 1956.

50. Martin, *Adlai Stevenson,* pp. 308–12; Divine, *Blowing on the Wind,* pp. 84–112.

51. *Time,* June 4, 1956, p. 25.

52. Kennan to Tom Finletter, April 12, 1956.

53. *U.S. News and World Report,* June 29, 1956, p. 74.

54. *U.S. News and World Report,* June 29, 1956, p. 78; Kennan to M. Louis Brandt-Peltier, Jan. 28, 1957, Box 31, Kennan Papers

55. *Chicago Tribune,* May 11, 1956; *U.S. News and World Report,* June 29, 1956, p. 71.

56. Kovrig, *The Myth of Liberation,* pp. 139–52.

57. Talbott ed., *Khrushchev Remembers,* pp. 341–53; speech reprinted, pp. 559–618.

58. Kovrig, *The Myth of Liberation*, pp. 169–79.

59. "The Soviet Will Never Recover," Kennan interview by Joseph Alsop, *Saturday Evening Post*, November 24, 1956, pp. 32–33.

60. Ibid., p. 117; Kovrig, *Myth of Liberation*, pp. 180–222.

61. M. Stanton Evans, "The Liberal Against Himself," *National Review*, Dec. 22, 1956, p. 11.

62. Kennan, "Memorandum: Impressions of Poland, July, 1958" sent to State Department, Box 26, Kennan Papers; see also Kennan's comments of Jan. 3, 1957, on the prospects for reform in Hungary at Council on Foreign Relations meeting, Box 33, Hamilton Fish Armstrong Papers, Mudd Library.

63. Kennan, Memorandum on Mideast Policy, Jan. 22, 1952, Box 24, Kennan Papers.

64. Kennan to Chester Bowles, May 28, 1956, Box 141, Bowles Papers.

65. Ambrose, *Eisenhower the President*, pp. 347–75.

66. Kennan letter to editor, *Washington Post*, Nov. 3, 1956.

67. Kennan to Hamilton Fish Armstrong, Nov. 8, 1956, Box 33, Armstrong Papers.

68. Kennan, "Certain Long Term Implications of the Suez Crisis," Oct. 17, 1956, Johns Hopkins University lecture, Box 19, Kennan Papers.

69. Kennan to Charles Thayer, July 17, 1958, Thayer Correspondence, HSTL.

70. Kennan, "Background of the Present World Situation," April 19, 1955, Haverford College lecture, Box 19, Kennan Papers; *U.S. News and World Report*, June 29, 1956, p. 73.

71. *New York Herald-Tribune*, Sept. 21, 1958, Box 7, Kennan Papers; Kennan, "Alternate Strategic Concepts and Policies for the U.S.," Nov. 26, 1958, NWC lecture, Box 20, Kennan Papers.

8. A Realist Confronts Hysteria

1. Kennedy, *Over Here*; Murray, *Red Scare*.

2. Griffith, *The Politics of Fear*, p. 32; Theoharis, *Seeds of Repression*.

3. See Kennan's testimony in United States Atomic Energy Commission, "In the Matter of J. Robert Oppenheimer, Transcript of A Hearing Before Personnel Security Board," Washington, D.C., April 12–May 6, 1954 (Washington: U.S. Government Printing Office, 1954), p. 354.

4. The names of the accused communists did not appear with the copy of Kennan's report. See Kennan's report to Francis Russell, Aug. 23, 1946, Box 27, Acheson Papers, Harry S Truman Library (HSTL).

5. Kennan to Walter Bedell Smith, June, 18, 1948, Box 28, Kennan Papers; Kennan, *Memoirs, 1925–1950*, p. 301.

6. Kennan to James P. Baxter, June 11, 1947; Emile Despres to Kennan, June 15, 1947; and related papers in "Consultants, 1944–1951," "Box 8, Records of the Policy Planning Staff, RG 59, National Archives.

7. Kahn, *The China Hands*, pp. 165–72; Oshinsky, *A Conspiracy So Immense*, pp. 96, 128–29.

8. Oshinsky, *A Conspiracy So Immense*, pp. 108–9.

9. Kahn, *The China Hands*, p. 213; Oshinsky, *A Conspiracy So Immense*, pp. 137–57.

10. Loyalty Security Board meeting on John S. Service in "Hearings Before a Subcommittee of the Committee on Foreign Relations," United States Senate, 81st Cong., 2nd Sess., pursuant to SR 231, Part II, Appendix (U.S. Government Printing Office: Washington, D.C., 1950), pp. 2112–13.

11. Ibid., pp. 2115–26.

12. Kahn, *The China Hands*, pp. 222–24, 237–38; Oshinsky, *A Conspiracy So Immense*, p. 209; Kennan to Service, Dec. 14, 1951, Box 3, Kennan Papers, Mudd Library, Princeton.

13. Kahn, *The China Hands*, pp. 230, 241–43; see also May, *China Scapegoat*.

14. Kennan, "Where Do You Stand on Communism?" *New York Times Magazine*, May 27, 1951, p. 7.

15. Kennan to William Henry Chamberlain, June 21, 1950, Box 28, Kennan Papers.

16. Kennan, "The International Situation" April 25, 1951, Princeton graduate school lecture, Box 18, Kennan Papers.

17. Kennan to Charles B. Marshall, Feb. 25, 1952, Box 29, Kennan Papers.

18. Oshinsky, *A Conspiracy So Immense*, p. 262.

19. Ibid., p. 263.

20. Kennan, Century Club (New York) address, May 7, 1953, Box 18, Kennan Papers.

21. Bohlen, *Witness to History*, p. 323.

22. Kennan to Charles Thayer, April 9, 1953, Thayer Correspondence, HSTL.

23. Kennan, "Training for Statesmanship."

24. Oshinsky, *A Conspiracy So Immense*, p. 306; Kennan, "The Liberal Arts in Contemporary American Society," May 15, 1953, address at Notre Dame, Box 3, Kennan Papers; excerpts from Kennan's speech appeared in *The New Republic*, June 1, 1953, pp. 14–16 and *Saturday Review*, May 30, 1953, p. 20.

25. Kennan interview by Hixson.

26. *New York Times*, Dec. 9, 1952; Kahn, *The China Hands*, pp. 244–45.

27. *New York Times*, Dec. 9, 1952; Kahn, *The China Hands*, p. 246.

28. Kennan to Paul Nitze, July 26, 1952, Box 29, Kennan Papers.

29. Kennan to Davies, July 26, 1952, Box 29, Kennan Papers; *New York Times*, Dec. 9, 1953.

30. Kennan, "Tasks Ahead in U.S. Foreign Policy," Dec. 18, 1952, NWC lecture, Box 18, Kennan Papers.

31. Kennan speech, Feb. 7, 1952, Box 18, Kennan Papers.

32. *Time*, Dec. 29, 1953, p. 6.

33. Kennan interview by Hixson; the transcript of the McCarran subcommittee hearing remains classified and Freedom of Information Act requests were rejected.

34. Kennan to Acheson, Jan. 28, 1953, Box 29, Kennan Papers.

35. Kennan to Herbert Brownell, Sept. 6, 1953, Box 29, Kennan Papers.
36. *New York Times*, Dec. 9, 1953.
37. Kennan to John Paton Davies, Nov. 25, 1953, Box 29, Kennan Papers; Kennan to Charles Thayer, Dec. 5, 1953, Thayer Correspondence, HSTL; "The Strange Case of John P. Davies," *U.S. News and World Report*, Dec. 11, 1953, pp. 26–32.
38. Kennan to Robert Murphy, Dec. 14, 1953, Box 29, Kennan Papers.
39. *New York Times*, Dec. 17, 1953.
40. Kennan, "Loyalty and the Public service," Feb. 23, 1956, Princeton Adult School address, Box 19, Kennan Papers; Kahn, *The China Hands*, pp. 257–61.
41. Major, *The Oppenheimer Hearing*, p. 12.
42. Kennan testimony, "In the Matter of J. Robert Oppenheimer," pp. 355–56.
43. Major, *The Oppenheimer Hearing*, pp. 13, 91–146.
44. Ibid., p. 14.
45. Kennan testimony, "In the Matter of J. Robert Oppenheimer," p. 370.
46. Ibid., pp. 365, 386.
47. Major, *The Oppenheimer Hearing*, pp. 177–210.
48. Kennan, "The Illusion of Security," June 16, 1954, Radcliffe commencement address; also published in *The Atlantic* 194 (August 1954):31–34.
49. Hofstadter, *The Paranoid Style in American Politics*; Kennan, *Realities of American Foreign Policy*," p. 118.
50. Kennan, "After Geneva I," Oct. 31, 1955, Box 26, Kennan Papers.
51. Kennan, Century Club Address.
52. On this point, see Pells, *The Liberal Mind in a Conservative Age*, pp. 262–345; Navasky, *Naming Names*; and Schrecker, *No Ivory Tower*, among an abundant literature.
53. Kennan interview by Hixson; Oshinsky, *A Conspiracy So Immense*, pp. 472–94.

9. Challenging the Consensus

1. Quoted in *Progressive* 19 (October 1955): 17; Kennan interviews with the *Michigan Daily*, June 26, 1957, and International News Service, both in Box 35, Kennan Papers, Mudd Library, Princeton.
2. Kennan to Anna Kallin, June 29, 1957, Box 31, Kennan Papers; Kennan to Adlai Stevenson, Feb. 19, 1958, Box 750, Stevenson Papers, Mudd Library: Kennan to Robert Oppenheimer, Oct. 24, 1957, Box 43 Oppenheimer Papers, Library of Congress.
3. Kennan, Dedication of VFW post, East Berlin, Pa., June 22, 1957, Box 19, Kennan Papers.
4. *London Observer*, Nov. 3, 1957, Box 35, Kennan Papers.
5. *Newsweek*, Nov. 11, 1957, pp. 35–36.
6. Ulam, *Expansion and Coexistence*, pp. 611–12.
7. Kennan testimony in Hearings Before a Subcommittee of the Committee

on Foreign Relations, U.S. Senate, 85th Cong., 1st Sess., Part II, Jan. 9 and 10, 1957, 1000–21.

8. Kennan, *Russia, the Atom and the West*, pp. 25–65.

9. *FRUS 1955–1957*, 4:227; Thompson, "The Kennan-Acheson Debate," *Commonweal* 78 (April 4, 1958).

10. *London Daily Telegraph*, Dec. 16, 1957; *The Times* (London), Dec. 16, 1957; *London Observer*, Dec. 22, 1957, all in Box 35, Kennan Papers.

11. Kennan, *Memoirs, 1950–1963*, pp. 236–37; *New York Times Magazine*, Dec. 29, 1957; Prittie, "Have the 'Kennan Plans' Come Too Late?," p. 13.

12. Ibid.; *New York Herald-Tribune*, Jan. 21, 1958.

13. Ibid., Jan. 10, 1958; *New York Times Magazine*, Dec. 29, 1957, p. 5; Quester, *Nuclear Diplomacy*, p. 119.

14. Kennan to Adlai Stevenson, Feb. 11, 1958, Box 750, Stevenson Papers; "Hearings Before a Subcommittee of the Committee on Foreign Relations," U.S. Senate, 86th Cong., 1st sess., Part II, Feb. 4, 1959, p. 241.

15. Rovere, "Letter from Washington," March 22, 1958 *New Yorker*, p. 36; "Cold War Diehards," *Nation* 186 (Jan. 25, 1958): 62; "The Russians and Ourselves," *Progressive* 22 (March 1958): 5; *Chicago Sun-Times*, Jan. 21, 1958, Box 35, Kennan Papers; *The New Republic*, Jan. 20, 1958, p. 7; *National Review*, Nov. 19, 1960, p. 18; *Ukrainian Bulletin*, Feb. 1, 1958, p. 35.

16. Transcript of discussion by the Executive Committee, Congress of Cultural Freedom, Jan. 18, 1958, Box 35, Kennan Papers.

17. Levitt, "Musings of a Retired Diplomat; *The New Republic*, April 7, 1958, p. 15.

18. *New York Times Magazine*, Dec. 29, 1957, p. 5; Kennan, "Proposal for Western Survival," *The New Leader*, Nov. 16, 1959, p. 14.

19. *New York Times Magazine*, Dec. 8, 1957, p. 5; Dulles news conference, Dec. 10, 1957, Box 113, John Foster Dulles Papers, Mudd Library.

20. Levitt, "The Musings of a Retired Diplomat," p. 19.

21. *Time*, Jan. 20, 1958, p. 16; Kennan interview by Hixson.

22. *New York Times*, Dec 20, 1957.

23. *New York Times*, Dec. 17, 24, 29, 1957.

24. *New York Times*, Jan. 12, 1958; Acheson to John Foster Dulles, Box 131, John Foster Dulles Paper, undated [1958].

25. Kennan to Stevenson, Feb. 19, 1958; Kennan to Dorothy Hessman, Jan. 16, 1958, in Box 43, Oppenheimer Papers.

26. *New York Times Magazine*, March 2, 1958, p. 1; *Washington Post*, Jan. 14, 1958; Thompson, "Kennan-Acheson Debate."

27. *The New Republic*, Nov. 2, 1959, pp. 4–6; Schlesinger, *A Thousand Days*, p. 300.

28. Acheson, "The Illusion of Disengagement."

29. Kennan to Hamilton Fish Armstrong, Feb. 26, 1960, Box 33, Armstrong Papers; Kennan interview in the *Harrisburg (Pa.) Patriot-News Magazine*, Sept. 7, 1958, Box 7, Kennan Papers.

30. Lippmann, "Mr. Kennan and Reappraisal in Europe," pp. 33–35; on the

convergence of their views at this time, see also Lippmann to Kennan, Feb. 1, 1958, and Kennan to Lippmann, Feb. 10, 1958, both in Lippmann Papers, Box 81, Yale University Manuscript Library, New Haven.

31. Kennan to Hamilton Fish Armstrong, Jan. 3, 1958, Box 33, Armstrong Papers, Mudd Library.

32. Ibid.

33. *U.S. News and World Report,* Jan. 10, 1958, p. 69; "Hearings Before a Subcommittee of the Committee on Foreign Relations," U.S. Senate, 86th Cong., 1st sess., Part II, Feb. 4, 1959, p. 237.

34. *U.S. News and World Report,* Jan. 10, 1958, p. 70.

35. See Kennan's responses in "A Round-Table Discussion of the Views of George F. Kennan," Executive Committee, Congress for Cultural Freedom, Jan 18, 1958, Box 35, Kennan Papers; Kennan, "Disengagement Revisited."

36. Ibid.

37. Ibid., pp. 192–93.

38. Kennan, "The Argument About Disengagement," Oct. 5, 1958, lecture, Phillips Exeter Academy, N.H., Box 19, Kennan Papers; Kennan, *Russia, the Atom and the West,* pp. 235, 239.

39. Kennan interview by Hixson.

40. Kennan to Frank Altschul, Nov. 3, 1959, Box 31, Kennan Papers.

41. Kennan, "The Argument About Disengagement."

42. Kennan, "Hearings Before a Subcommittee of the Committee on Foreign Relations," p. 233.

43. Kennan to Robert Matteson, Dec. 4, 1958, Box 31, Kennan Papers; Kennan statement in *The Listener* (BBC weekly), Oct. 29, 1959, Box 8, Kennan Papers; Kennan testimony, "Hearings Before a Subcommittee of the Committee on Foreign Relations," Feb. 4, 1959, p. 204.

44. "A Round-Table Discussion of the Views of George F. Kennan."

45. Kennan to Eugene Rabinowitz, Sept. 11, 1956 and undated (1959), Box 31, Kennan Papers.

46. Steel, *Walter Lippmann and the American Century,* p. 509; Kennan, *Memoirs, 1950–1963,* p. 255.

47. There was a huge missile gap—in America's favor. See, for example, Costigliola, "Nuclear Arms, Dollars, and Berlin" in Paterson, *Kennedy's Quest for Victory,* p. 32.

48. "A Round-Table Discussion of the Views of George F. Kennan."

10. New Frontier, Old Problems

1. Kennan to Chester Bowles, April 26, 1958, Box 141, Bowles Papers, Yale University Manuscript Library.

2. Kennan, *Russia Leaves the War,* p. 410.

3. *Foreign Affairs* 35 (October 1956): 151; *American Historical Review* 62 (January 1957), 367–8; Williams, "The Convenience of History," pp. 223–24.

4. Kennan, *The Decision to Intervene,* II (Princeton: Princeton University Press, 1958), p. 470; *Foreign Affairs* 36 (July 1958): 686; *New York Times,* March 9, 1958.

5. *American Historical Review* 67 (October 1961): 68; *New Yorker,* Sept. 9, 1961, p. 140.

6. *Princeton Packet,* July 20, 1961.

7. Kennan, "Diplomacy, Scholarship and Politics" May 13, 1958, Oxford, Box 19, Kennan Papers.

8. Jan. 12, 1958 *New York Times.*

9. Parmet, *Jack: The Struggles of John F. Kennedy;* Kennan to Adlai Stevenson, Jan. 5, 1960, Box 789, Stevenson Papers, Mudd Library, Princeton University.

10. Kennan, *Memoirs, 1925–1950,* p. 91–92; John F. Kennedy to Kennan, Feb. 13, 1958, Kennedy Oral History Project, John F. Kennedy Library, Boston.

11. Khrushchev, "Peaceful Coexistence;" Kennan, "Peaceful Coexistence: A Western View."

12. Kennan to John F. Kennedy, Aug. 17, 1960 and Kennedy to Kennan, Oct. 30, 1960, both in appendix of transcript of Kennan interview by Louis Fischer.

13. Kennan to *New York Times,* unpublished, Oct. 20, 1960, Box 31, Kennan Papers; Kennan complained about the *Times'* refusal to publish his column-length letter—Kennan to Lippmann, Oct. 18, 1960, Box 81, Lippmann Papers, Yale Library.

14. Kennan to Lippmann, Dec. 28, 1960, Box 81, Lippmann Papers, Yale Library.

15. C. K. McClatchy to Adlai Stevenson, Jan. 2, 1961, Stevenson Papers, Box 832, Mudd Library.

16. William Blair to Adlai Stevenson, Jan. 5, 1961, Box 832, Stevenson Papers, Mudd Library.

17. Kennan comments, JFK Oral History Project, p. 40, 114.

18. *New York Times,* March 7, 1961; *Washington Post,* March 7, 1961.

19. *New York Times,* Jan. 5, 1961; Kennan, JFK Oral History Project, p. 55.

20. Wilson, *Tito's Yugoslavia;* Kennan, "Yugoslav-Moscow Controversy as Related to U.S. Foreign Policy Objectives" (PPS 60), in Nelson, ed., *Planning Staff Papers,* 2:139–49; also see Brands, "Redefining the Cold War."

21. Brands, "Redefining the Cold War," pp. 50–51; Kovrig, *The Myth of Liberation,* pp. 234–6.

22. Kennan, Shapex presentation, June 19, 1963, Box 31, Kennan Papers.

23. Kennan to Walter Lippmann, Feb. 8, 1963 and Kennan to George Mc-Ghee, April 20, 1961, both in Box 31, Kennan Papers; Kennan, *Memoirs, 1950–1963,* pp. 292–93.

24. *New York Times,* Feb. 11, 1961.

25. Kennan, Kennedy Oral History Project, p. 108, 124.

26. Schlesinger, *A Thousand Days,* p. 397; Kennan to Chester Bowles, Sept. 22, 1961, Box 299, Bowles Papers, Yale Library.

27. Allison, *The Essence of Decision;* Walton, *Cold War and Counterrevolution;* Kennan, "Briefing for Americans," Oct. 27, 1962, Belgrade, Box 24, Kennan Papers.

28. Kubricht, "Politics and Foreign Policy."

29. *New York Times,* Sept. 2, 4, 1961.

30. *New York Times,* Sept. 4, 1961.

31. Memorandum of conversation, Kennan and Veljko Micunovic, June 22, 1962 and Kennan to David Riesman, Oct. 3, 1961, both in Box 31, Kennan Papers.

32. *New York Times,* Oct. 16, 1961 NYT; Kennan, JFK Oral History Project, pp. 59–63; *Time,* Jan. 12, 1962, p. 20.

33. Kennan to Hamilton Fish Armstrong, Sept. 1, 1961, Box 31, Kennan Papers; *New York Times,* Jan. 5, 1962; Kennan, JFK Oral History Project, p. 69.

34. Kennan to Max Beloff, Oct. 2, 1961, Box 31, Kennan Papers.

35. Kovrig, *Myth of Liberation,* pp. 242–43; Kubricht, "Kennedy's Eastern European Diplomacy," pp. 61–62.

36. *Congressional Record* 108, July 9, 1962, V, Part 10, 87th Cong., 2d sess., p. 12926; Ibid., July 9, 1963, p. 12038; *New York Times,* June 22, 1962.

37. *Time,* Jan. 12, 1962, p. 19; Kennan letter to the editor, *New York Times,* July 2, 1962.

38. *New York Times,* June 15, 1962.

39. Ibid.

40. Memorandum of conversation, Kennan and Veljko Micunovic, June 22, 1962; *New York Times,* July 1, 2, 1962; *Washington Post,* July 8, 1962; Kennan, JFK Oral History Project, p. 83.

41. Kennan notes for National War College briefing, March 27, 1963, Box 20, Kennan Papers.

42. See "Today" show transcript in *Congressional Record* 108 (July 9, 1962), V, 2d sess., p. 12930.

43. Kennan to J. William Fulbright, July 6, 1962, Box 31, Kennan Papers; Kennan, JFK Oral History Project, p. 76.

44. *Washington Post,* July 8, 1962.

45. Kennan, JFK Oral History Project, p. 76.

46. *Washington Star,* May 19, 1963, Kennan Clip File, Box 36, Kennan Papers; Kennan to Lippmann, Dec. 2, 1962, Box 81, Lippmann Papers, Yale Library.

47. Kennan to Frederick G. Dutton, Sept. 11, 1962, Box 31, Kennan Papers.

48. Kennan to Harrison Salisbury, Dec. 12, 1963 and Kennan to Walter Lippmann, Feb. 8, 1963, both in Box 31, Kennan Papers.

49. Kennan notes for NWC briefing, March 27, 1963, Box 20; draft notes on Yugoslavia, Dec. 23, 1961, Box 31; Background press briefing, May 4, 1963, Box 21, all in Kennan Papers.

50. Ibid., *Stars and Stripes* and *Philadelphia Enquirer,* both July 11, 1962,

both in Kennan Clip File, Box 36, Kennan Papers; *Congressional Record,* Appendix Vol. 4, 87th 2d sess., A5253; *Congressional Record,* op. cit., p. 13122.

51. Kubricht, "Kennedy's Eastern European Diplomacy," p. 63; Kovrig, *Myth of Liberation,* p. 243.

52. Kennan, JFK Oral History Project, pp. 86–93; Kennan telephone conversation regarding Amendment to Trade Bill, Sept. 27, 1962, Box 31, Kennan Papers.

53. Kennan, JFK Oral History Project, 93, 86; Kennan to Robert Oppenheimer, Nov. 16, 1962, Box 31, Kennan Papers.

54. Kennan testimony, "Hearing Before the Subcommittee on National Security Staffing and Operations," 86th Cong., 1st sess., Part V, Dec. 11, 1963, p. 360.

55. *Congressional Record* 109 (Nov. 4, 1963), Part 16, 88th Cong., 1st sess., p. 20930; *New York Times,* Nov. 5, 1963; Kennan to Walter Roberts, Jan. 8, 1964.

56. *New York Times,* April 20, 1963; Kennan JFK Oral History Project, p. 313.

57. *New York Times,* May 17, 25, 1963; May 22, 1963 memorandum, White House Name File, John F. Kennedy Library, Boston.

58. *New York Times,* Nov. 3, 1963.

59. *New York Times,* July 29 and Nov. 7, 1963.

60. Kennan, JFK Oral History Project, p. 104.

61. Kennan to Walter Roberts, Jan. 8, 1964, Box 31, Kennan Papers.

62. Kennan interview, "Our Foreign Policy Is Paralyzed" Nov. 19, 1963 *Look,* p. 26; Kennan, JFK Oral History Project, p. 71.

63. Kennan, "The Communist State As A Problem in American Foreign Policy," Feb. 7, 1966, College of Wooster address, Box 22, Kennan Papers.

64. Kennan, "Our Foreign Policy Is Paralyzed," p. 27.

65. Kennan, "The Communist State As a Problem in American Foreign Policy" Feb. 7, 1966, College of Wooster, Box 22, Kennan Papers.

66. Kennan to Cass Caufied, July 2, 1964, Box 31, Kennan Papers; *New York Times Book Review,* May 10, 1964, p. 6.

67. Kennan, JFK Oral History Project, p. 99, 34; Kennan to John F. Kennedy, Oct. 22, 1963, Box 31, Kennan Papers.

68. Kennan to Walter Roberts, Jan. 8, 1964; Kennan comments, Mount Kisco conference, June 1963, Box 21, Kennan Papers.

11. Vietnam: Containment on the Perimeter, II

1. Kennan, *Memoirs, 1925–1950; New York Times,* Mar. 7, 1968.

2. Kennan, *Memoirs, 1950–1963;* see Leopold's reviews of both volumes in the *American Historical Review* 74 (December 1968):762; 78 (April 1973):510.

3. Kennan, *Memoirs, 1925–1950,* 357–59.

4. See chapters 3 and 5 above.

5. Kennan, "United States Policy Toward Southeast Asia" (PPS 51), in Nelson, ed., *Planning Staff Papers*, 3:38–40, 52; on American perceptions of Ho and early involvement in Southeast Asia, see Kahin, *Intervention*, pp. 3–33; Hess, *The United States' Emergence as a Southeast Asian Power;* Rotter, *The Path to Vietnam;* and Blum, *Drawing the Line.*

6. June 6, 1949 PPS meeting, Box 27, Records of the Policy Planning Staff, Record Group 59, National Archives; Kennan, "Basic Factors in American Foreign Policy," Feb. 14, 1949, Box 17, Kennan Papers; PPS 51, p. 39.

7. PPS 51, pp. 48–49.

8. Kennan, "An Estimate of the International Situation," Nov. 8, 1948, Box 17, Kennan Papers.

9. Herring, *America's Longest War,* pp. 43–58; Kennan, "Background of the Present World Situation," April 19, 1955, Box 19, Kennan Papers.

10. Kahin, *Intervention,* pp. 146–202; *The Daily Princetonian,* Oct. 22, 1963.

11. Kennan, "The Historical Development of American Foreign Policy," April 4, 1964, Tokyo University speech, Box 10; Kennan to A. J. Muste, January 4, 1965, Box 11, both in Kennan Papers; Stanley Karnow, *Vietnam: A History,* pp. 99–104, 151–53.

12. Kennan, "A Fresh Look at Our China Policy," *New York Times Magazine,* Nov. 22, 1964, pp. 27, 140.

13. Herring, *America's Longest War,* pp. 119–22; Gelb with Betts, *The Irony of Vietnam,* pp. 100–104.

14. Kennan, "A Fresh Look at Our China Policy."

15. Herring, *America's Longest War,* pp. 128–30; on LBJ's decision to escalate American involvement in Vietnam, see Berman, *Planning A Tragedy.*

16. Kennan, "Some Lessons in American Diplomatic History," Feb. 11, 1965, Box 21, Kennan Papers.

17. Kennan to Sir Llewellyn Woodward, Mar. 4, 1965, Box 31, Kennan Papers.

18. Kennan, "The Communist State as a Problem in American Foreign Policy," Feb. 7, 1966, Box 22, Kennan Papers; Kennan testimony, U.S. Congress, House Subcommittee on the Far East and the Pacific of the Committee of the Foreign Affairs Committee, *Report on the Sino-Soviet Conflict and Its Implications,* 89th Cong., 1st sess., March 11, 1965, p. 89; and Kennan, "The United States and the Communist Giants," Feb. 25, 1965, Box 11, Kennan Papers.

19. *Washington Post,* Dec. 12, 1965.

20. Kennan, "Containment: Russia and China," Feb. 9, 1966, Box 11, Kennan Papers; Fulbright, *The Arrogance of Power.*

21. *New York Times,* Feb. 18, 1967; Brown, *J. William Fulbright, Advice and Dissent,* p. 75.

22. *New York Times,* Jan. 12, 1966.

23. Kennan testimony, U.S. Congress, Senate Committee on Foreign Relations, To Amend Further the Foreign Assistance Act of 1961: Hearings on S. 2793, 2 pts. 89th Cong., 2d sess., Feb. 10, 1966, pp. 332–33.

24. Ibid., pp. 332–36.

25. Ibid., pp. 354, 422.

26. Ibid., pp. 334, 352.

27. Ibid., p. 339; *New York Times*, Feb. 11, 1966; *New Republic*, Feb. 26, 1966, p. 19; *Time*, Feb. 18, 1967, p. 20.

28. Kalb, "The Vital Interests of Mr. Kennan," p. 31; *New York Times*, Feb. 11, 1966.

29. Kalb, "The Vital Interests of Mr. Kennan," pp. 31, 77; Kennan, "Concept in Foreign Policy," *Harvard Today* (Autumn 1967): 14; Kennan, Notes, Seminar on the Origins of the Cold War, Feb. 15, 1968, Box 22, Kennan Papers; Maddox, *The New Left and the Origins of the Cold War*.

30. *New York Times*, Feb. 28, 1966.

31. Herring, *America's Longest War*, pp. 146–52.

32. Kennan testimony, U.S. Congress, Senate Committee on Foreign Relations, The Communist World in 1967, 90th Cong., 1st sess., Jan. 30, 1967, pp. 51, 60 (hereafter cited as Communist World in 1967); and Kennan to John Crocker, Nov. 9, 1967, Box 31, Kennan Papers.

33. Kennan to Emmet John Hughes, May 31, 1966, Box 31, Kennan Papers.

34. Kennan dinner address, Nov. 5, 1966, Woodrow Wilson School, Princeton, N.J., Box 22, Kennan Papers.

35. Communist World in 1967, pp. 40, 67; *New York Review of Books*, April 11, 1968, p. 14; and Kennan to Arthur Schlesinger, Jr., Oct. 17, 1967, Box 31, Kennan Papers.

36. Communist World in 1967, p. 66; Kennan to Schlesinger, Oct. 17, 1967.

37. Kennan testimony, Fulbright hearings, Feb. 10, 1966, pp. 343–45.

38. Transcript, "Meet the Press," Nov. 5, 1967, Box 13, Kennan Papers; Communist World in 1967, p. 29.

39. Kennan to Schlesinger, Oct. 17, 1967.

40. Herring, *America's Longest War*, pp. 183–205.

41. Kennan speech reprinted in *New York Review of Books*, April 11, 1968, p. 16.

42. Gelb and Betts, *Irony of Vietnam*, pp. 172, 217; Herring, *America's Longest War*, pp. 217–51.

43. *New York Times*, Nov. 10, 1966.

44. Ibid.

45. Herring, *America's Longest War*, pp. 229–72; Porter, *A Peace Denied*.

46. Kennan, "After the Cold War," p. 219.

12. The Decline of the West

1. See chapters 1 and 2.

2. The quotation is from Act IV, Sc. I of Shakespeare's play and is quoted in Kennan, "Russia," Oct. 1, 1946 NWC lecture, Box 16, Kennan Papers.

3. Kennan comments, June 6, 1949, Policy Planning Staff meeting; Kennan

to William Hooker, Oct. 17, 1949, Box 23, PPS Records, both in Record Group 59, National Archives.

4. See Pells, *The Liberal Mind in a Conservative Age.*

5. Kennan, *Realities of American Foreign Policy,* p. 109.

6. Riesman, *The Lonely Crowd;* Whyte, *The Organization Man.*

7. Kennan interview by Melvin J. Lasky, in Moynihan, ed., *Encounters With Kennan,* p. 198.

8. Galbraith, *The Affluent Society;* Harrington, *The Other America.*

9. Kennan, "Certain Long-Term Implications of the Suez Crisis," Oct. 17, 1956, Johns Hopkins lecture, Box 19, Kennan Papers.

10. Kennan, "Credo of a Civil Servant," *Princeton Alumni Weekly,* Feb. 12, 1954.

11. Kennan interview by Hixson.

12. Kennan, "Commencement, 1955," *Social Research,* p. 135.

13. Kennan, "Notes on Diplomacy, Scholarship and Politics," American Association, Oxford, May 13, 1958, Box 19, Kennan Papers; Vance Packard, *The Hidden Persuaders* (New York: David McKay Co., 1957).

14. Kennan, "Connecticut College for Women Commencement Address," June 10, 1956, Box 19, Kennan Papers.

15. See the discussion in chapter 4 of Pells, *Liberal Mind in a Conservative Age,* quotation from page 221.

16. Kennan, "Commencement, 1955," p. 136.

17. Kennan, "Notes on Diplomacy, Scholarship and Politics"; Kennan, "Alternate Strategic Concepts and Policies for the U.S.," Nov. 26, 1958, NWC lecture, Box 20, Kennan Papers.

18. Kennan, "Notes on Diplomacy, Scholarship and Politics"; Kennan, "Industrial Society and Western Political Dialogue," August 1959, Box 26, Kennan Papers.

19. Kennan comments, June 1963 Summer conference, M. Kisco, Box 21, Kennan Papers; Kennan, International Association for Cultural Freedom address.

20. On the linkage between the intellectual critics of the 1950s and the New Left, see Pells, *Liberal Mind in a Conservative Age,* pp. 346–409.

21. Rozek, *The Counter-Culture;* Hodgson, *America in Our Time;* O'Neill, *Coming Apart.*

22. Kennan interview by George Urban, in Herz, ed., *Decline of the West?,* pp. 14–15.

23. Kennan, Tavern Club speech (Boston), Feb. 26, 1968, Box 22, Kennan Papers; Kennan, *Democracy and the Student Left,* p. 153.

24. Kennan, *Democracy and the Student Left,* p. 6, 137; Kennan, "Rebels Without a Program", *New York Times Magazine,* Jan. 21, 1968.

25. Kennan, *Democracy and the Student Left,* pp. 216, 219; see also Kennan, "Address to members Finnish-American Society", Aug. 25, 1968, Tampere, Finland, Box 22, Kennan Papers.

26. Kennan, *Democracy and the Student Left,* pp. 219–24, 167; Kennan,

"After Vietnam," Prelude to Independence Celebration, Williamsburg, Va., June 1, 1968, Box , Kennan Papers.

27. *New York Times Book Review*, Sept. 29, 1968, p. 10; *Newsweek*, Sept. 23, 1968, p. 104.

28. *Newsweek*, Dec. 23, 1968, p. 33 and Dec. 16, 1968, p. 32; *New York Times Magazine*, Dec. 29, 1968; also see Kennan, "The Future of Communism," Feb. 27, 1969, St. Anthony's College notes, Box 22, Kennan Papers.

29. *New York Times*, May 29, 1968.

30. *New York Times*, March 7, 1968.

31. Kennan, "After Vietnam;" Kennan, International Association for Cultural Freedom Seminar, Dec. 2, 1968, Box , Kennan Papers.

32. *Report of the National Advisory Commission on Civil Disorders* (Kerner Commission), as published by the *New York Times* (1968), p. 1.

33. Kennan to Dr. Marion Grafin Donhoff, March 15, 1965, Box 31, Kennan Papers.

34. Kennan to Waldemar A. Nielsen, Oct. 19, 1967, Box 31, Kennan Papers.

35. *New York Times*, May 2, 1976; see also Kennan, "Hazardous Courses in Southern Africa."

36. *Philadelphia Evening Bulletin*, Jan 27, 1971, Kennan Clip file, Box 35, Kennan Papers; *New York Times*, Dec. 30, 1970.

37. Kennan, *Realities of American Foreign Policy*, p. 114.

38. Kennan, "United States External Relations Project, 1951–52," Box 26, Kennan Papers; Kennan, "The World Position and Problems of the United States," Aug. 30, 1949, NWC lecture, Box 17, Kennan Papers.

39. On the prewar isolationists, see Wayne S. Cole, *Roosevelt and the Isolationists;* Kennan, "Background of the Present World Situation," April 19, 1955, Haverford College address, Box 19, Kennan Papers; Mayer, ed., Tocqueville, *Democracy in America*, pp. 226–30.

40. Kennan, "Unused Material Written for Possible Use in Memoirs, vol. 2," Box 27, Kennan Papers.

41. Kennan, "Meet the Press" transcript, Nov. 5, 1967. Box 13, Kennan Papers; Kennan quoted in Berger, "Can Carter Handle Him?" p. 126.

42. Kennan, "Background of Present World Situation."

43. Quoted in Morgan, *The Puritan Dilemma*, p. 70.

44. Quoted in Kennan's testimony, U.S. Congress, Senate Committee on Foreign Relations, *To Amend Further the Foreign Assistance Act of 1961: Hearings on S. 2793*, 2 pts. 89th Cong. 2d sess., Feb. 10, 1966, p. 336.

45. Kennan, "Background of the Present World Situation"; Kennan, March 6, 1958 Aberus Society address (Oxford), Box 19, Kennan Papers.

46. Kennan to J. A. Lukacs, Oct. 31, 1955, Box 31, Kennan Papers.

47. Kennan, "Background of the Present World Situation."

48. Kennan to J. A. Lukacs, Oct. 31, 1955, and Kennan to Robert Pincus, Jan. 4, 1956, both in Box 31, Kennan Papers.

49. Kennan, *The Cloud of Danger*, pp. ix, 80–113, 27–51, 19–25; see Steel's review in *New York Review of Books*, July 14, 1977, p. 19.

50. Kennan interview by Urban quoted in Herz, ed., *Decline of the West?*, pp. 32, 18.

13. An Ephemeral Thaw

1. Kennan, "The Legacy of Stalinism," April 21, 1967, lecture, Massachusetts Historical Society, Box 13, Kennan Papers; Kennan testimony, "Communist World in 1967," p. 64.

2. See Seaborg, *Kennedy Khrushchev, and the Test Ban;* Kennan, "Can We Deal with Moscow?" p. 27; Kennan to Gen. Earle Wheeler, Nov. 16, 1965, Box 31, Kennan Papers.

3. Kennan testimony, "U.S. Relations with Communist Countries," Hearings Before the Committee on Foreign Relations, United States Senate, 93rd Cong., 2nd sess., Aug. 20, 1974, pp. 59–89; Kennan notes on Khrushchev's ouster, Council on Foreign Relations, November 1964, Box 21, Kennan Papers.

4. Kennan to Dr. Marion Grafin Donhoff, *Die Zeit*, March 15, 1965, Box 31, Kennan Papers.

5. Newhouse, *DeGaulle and the Anglo-Saxons*, pp. 277–304; Kennan to Dr. Marion G. Donhoff, March 15, 1965; Kennan, "Our Foreign Policy Is Paralyzed," p. 27.

6. Kennan to McGeorge Bundy, Nov. 18, 1964, Box 31, Kennan Papers; Barnet, *The Alliance*, pp. 219–21, 242.

7. Kennan to Henry Kissinger, May 21, 1965, Box 31, Kennan Papers; Kissinger, *The Troubled Partnership*, pp. 189–224.

8. Kennan to Hans Morgenthau, Dec. 6, 1966, Box 31, Kennan Papers.

9. Kennan to Adam Watson, Oct. 30, 1967, Box 31, Kennan Papers; *Daily Princetonian*, Oct. 21, 1964; Transcript, "Meet the Press," Nov. 5, 1967, Box 13, Kennan Papers.

10. Transcript, "Meet the Press"; Kennan to Adam Watson, Dec. 7, 1967.

11. *New York Times*, June 26, 1965.

12. Kovrig, *The Myth of Liberation*, pp. 268–85.

13. *New York Times*, Sept 22, 1968; *Akron Beacon-Journal*, Sept. 22, 1968, Kennan Clip File, Box 37, Kennan Papers.

14. *Akron Beacon-Journal*, Sept. 22, 1968, Kennan Clip File, Box 37, Kennan Papers.

15. "Draft of possible reply to James Reston on 'Spheres of Influence,' " Oct. 30, 1968, Box 27, Kennan Papers.

16. *Kansas City Star*, Sept. 22, 1968, Kennan Clip File, Box 37, Kennan Papers; "The Return of Mr. X," *National Review*, Oct. 8, 1968, p. 994.

17. Kennan, "Brezhnev-Kosygin in Historical Perspective," undated [1969], Box 22, Kennan Papers; Kennan testimony, March 11, 1970, "U.S. Relations with Europe in the Decade of the 1970s," Subcommittee on Europe Hearings, House Foreign Affairs Committee, 91st Cong., 2nd sess., p. 170.

18. Whetten, *Germany's Ostpolitik; Akron Beacon-Journal*, Sept. 22, 1968,

Kennan Clip File, Box 37, Kennan Papers; Garthoff, *Détente and Confrontation,* pp. 117–20.

19. Kennan testimony, "U.S. Relations with Europe in the 1970s," p. 165; Garthoff, *Detente and Confrontation,* pp. 115–17.

20. Garthoff, *Detente and Confrontation,* pp. 199–247.

21. Kennan testimony (Aug. 20, 1974), "U.S. Relations with Communist Countries," Hearings Before the Committee on Foreign Relations, United States Senate, 93rd Cong., 2nd sess., p. 65, 58–89; Kennan, "After the Cold War," p. 221.

22. Garthoff, *Detente and Confrontation,* pp. 127–29; 31–36.

23. Kennan testimony, "U.S. Relations With Europe in the Decade of the 1970s," p. 177.

24. Newhouse, *Cold Dawn: The Story of SALT:* Garthoff, *Detente and Confrontation,* p. 127–98.

25. Kennan testimony, "US Security Requirements in the Near East and South Asia," Senate Foreign Relations Committee, Subcommittee on Near Eastern and South Asian Affairs, Feb. 27, 1980, 96th Cong., 2d sess., p. 116.

26. Kissinger, *White House Years,* p. 840.

27. Kennan testimony, "U.S. Relations with Communist Countries," pp. 59–89; Kennan *The Nuclear Delusion,* p. 120.

28. *New York Times,* Feb. 11, 1977.

29. Kennan testimony, Hearings Before the Subcommittee on Europe and the Middle East of the Committee on Internal Relations of the House, 95th Cong. 1st sess., Sept. 27, 1977, p. 57.

30. *Washington Post,* Oct. 8, 1973.

31. Garthoff, *Detente and Confrontation,* pp. 412, 453–63.

32. Kennan testimony, Hearings Before the Subcommittee on Europe and the Middle East of the Committee on Internal Relations of the House, 95th Cong., 1st sess., Sept. 27, 1977, p. 62–63.

33. Ulam, *Dangerous Relations;* Kennan, *Nuclear Delusion,* p. 70.

34. Garthoff, *Detente and Confrontation,* pp. 409–13; 435–37.

35. Kennan, *Nuclear Delusion,* pp. 65–68.

36. Garthoff, *Detente and Confrontation,* pp. 502–15; Alexander L. George, "Missed Opportunities for Crisis Prevention," in George, ed., *Managing U.S.-Soviet Rivalry.*

37. *Washington Post,* Oct. 8, 1973, Feb. 16, 1976.

38. Ibid; Kennan testimony (Feb. 26, 1980), Hearings Before the Budget Committee, US Senate, 96th Cong., 2d sess., p. 49.

39. Ulam, *Dangerous Relations,* pp. 177–80; Berger, "Can Carter Handle Him?" p. 122.

40. "What Is the Soviet Union Up To?" Committee on the Present Danger pamphlet, in author's possession.

41. Kennan testimony (Sept. 27, 1977), Hearings Before the Subcommittee on Europe and the Middle East of the Committee on Internal Relations of the

House, 95th Cong, 1st sess., pp. 76–78; *Nuclear Delusion*, pp. 70–71; *New York Times*, Feb. 18, 1981.

42. *New York Times*, Jan. 11, 1977.

43. Ibid, Feb. 11, 1977.

44. Garthoff, *Detente and Confrontation*, p. 573; Kennan, *Nuclear Delusion*, pp. 112–18; see also Smith, *Morality, Reason, and Power*.

45. Brzenski, *Power and Principle*; Garthoff, *Detente and Confrontation*, pp. 563–630, 721–22; Smith, *Morality, Reason and Power*, pp. 208–40.

46. Garthoff, *Detente and Confrontation*, pp. 801–27; 849–86; Kennan testimony, "US Security Requirements in the Near East and South Asia," p. 116.

47. Newsom, *The Soviet Brigade in Cuba;* Kennan testimony, Hearings Before the Budget Committee, Feb. 26, 1980, p. 63.

48. For background on this subject, see Rubin, *Paved with Good Intentions*.

49. Garthoff, *Detente and Confrontation*, pp. 661–62.

50. Kennan testimony, "U.S. Security Requirements in the Near East and South Asia," p. 27.

51. Kennan testimony, Hearings Before the Budget Committee, pp. 27–28.

52. *National Review*, April 4, 1980, p. 32.

53. See Garthoff, *Detente and Confrontation*, pp. 887–915, 966–77; *New York Times*, Feb. 1, 1980.

54. Kennan testimony, Subcommittee on Near Eastern and South Asian Affairs, 96th Cong., 2d sess., p. 108; Kennan, Council on Foreign Relations, Discussion Group on Soviet Foreign Policy, Jan. 7, 1947, Records of Groups, Vol. 22, 1946–47, Council of Rofeign Relations, Pratt House, New York, p. 7.

55. Kennan testimony, Subcommittee on Near Eastern and South Asian Affairs, 96th Cong., 2d sess., p. 108.

56. *New York Times*, Feb. 1, 1980; Kennan testimony, Subcommittee on Near Eastern and South Asian Affairs, 96th Cong., 2d sess., p. 111–120.

57. Ibid., pp. 109, 122; Kennan, *Nuclear Delusion*, pp. 161–72.

58. Kennan testimony, "U.S. Relations with Communist Countries," p. 71.

59. Kennan testimony (Feb. 6, 1970), "To Provide for the Exchange of Governmental Officials, Senate Foreign Relations Committee, 91st, 2nd sess., pp. 33–34.

60. Kennan interview by Dan Rather on "60 Minutes," Feb. 9, 1980, reprinted pp. 93–95 of Feb. 27, 1980, Senate testimony.

61. Kennan testimony, Hearings Before the Budget Committee, p. 63; *New York Times*, Feb. 18, 1981.

62. Garthoff, *Detente and Confrontation*, pp. 1007–08, 1033–34.

63. *New York Times*, Jan. 5, 6, 1982; reprinted in Kennan, *The Nuclear Delusion*, pp. 167–72.

64. Wieseltier, "Liberals Against Liberty," p. 20; Herz, ed. *Decline of the West*, quotes from pages 74, 47, 115; see also Luttwak, "The Strange Case of George F. Kennan"; Henry Fairlie, The Special Senility of the Diplomat," *New Republic*, Dec. 24, 1977, p. 9–11.

65. Kennan testimony, "U.S. Relations with Communist Countries," p. 68.

66. Garthoff, *Detente and Confrontation*, pp. 31–33, 1109–10.

14. The Diplomacy of Survival

1. Garthoff, *Detente and Confrontation*, pp. 1009–67.

2. Quoted in Ibid., p. 1010.

3. *Washington Post*, May 24, 1981

4. Kennan, "On Nuclear War," p. 10.

5. *New York Times*, Nov. 18, 1981.

6. Kennan, "Two Views of the Soviet Problem," pp. 55–56.

7. Hollander, "The Two Faces of George Kennan," p. 30; Seabury, "George Kennan Vs. Mr. 'X'," pp. 17–20.

8. Kennan, "On Nuclear War," p. 10.

9. Kennan, "Two Letters," Sept. 24, 1984, *New Yorker*, pp. 60, 65, 70.

10. Kennan, "On Nuclear War," p. 10; Kennan, "Two Views of the Soviet Problem," pp. 55–56.

11. *Washington Post*, May 24, 1981; Kennan, "Breaking the Spell," *New Yorker*, Oct. 3, 1983, p. 53.

12. *New York Times*, May 18, 1983.

13. Kennan, "Cease This Madness," p. 128.

14. Garthoff, *Detente and Confrontation*, p. 1022.

15. *Washington Post*, May 20, 1981.

16. *New York Times*, May 19, 1981; *Washington Post*, May 20, 1981; Kennan, "Two Views of Soviet Problem," p. 62.

17. On this latter point, see Kennan, "A New Philosophy of Defense," review of Gene Sharp, *Making Europe Unconquerable*, Feb. 13, 1986, *New York Times Book Review*, pp. 3, 6.

18. *FRUS 1950*, 1:39.

19. The anticipated third volume of Kennan's study had not been completed by the end of 1988.

20. Kennan, "History, Literature and the Road to Peterhof" *New York Times Book Review*, June 2, 1986, p. 42; *New York Times*, Nov. 11, 1984.

21. Kennan, *The Decline of Bismarck's European Order*, p. 3, 4.

22. Ibid., p. 423.

23. Kennan, *The Fateful Alliance*, pp. xiv, 257–58.

24. *New York Times Book Review*, Dec. 16, 1979, p. 11; *New Yorker*, Jan. 21, 1980, p. 130; *Nation*, Dec. 15, 1984, p. 239; *Choice*, April 1985, p. 1212; *New York Times Book Review*, Oct. 21, 1984.

25. Kennan, *The Nuclear Delusion*, pp. 245–46, 250; see also Klare, *American Arms Supermarket*.

26. Kennan, *Nuclear Delusion*, pp. 201–207.

27. Ibid., p. 204; Schell, *The Fate of the Earth*.

28. *New York Times Book Review*, Nov. 7, 1982, p. 7; *Time*, Dec. 27, 1982, p. 75.

29. Garthoff, *Detente and Confrontation,* p. 1030.
30. Kennan, "On Nuclear War," p. 8.
31. Kennan, "On Nuclear War," p. 8; Talbott, *Deadly Gambits* provides a detailed account of the failure to achieve a consensus position on arms control in the first Reagan administration.
32. Kennan, "On Nuclear War," p. 8; Garthoff, *Detente and Confrontation,* pp. 780–81.
33. *New York Times,* April 8, 9, 1982.
34. Kennan, McNamara, Smith and Bundy, "Nuclear Weapons and the Atlantic Alliance" *Foreign Affairs* (Spring 1982):760.
35. Ibid., pp. 759, 761.
36. Ibid., pp. 764, 767.
37. Ibid., p. 766.
38. Haig news conference, *Department of State Bulletin* 82, April 6, 1982, pp. 31–34.
39. *New York Times,* April 8, 1982.
40. Kaiser, et al., "Nuclear Weapons and the Preservation of Peace."
41. Kennan interview, *U.S. News and World Report,* April 26, 1982, pp. 17–18.
42. Garthoff, *Detente and Confrontation,* p. 1026.
43. Kennan, "Zero Options," p. 3.
44. *New York Times,* Nov. 27, 1984.
45. Kennan, et al, "Back from the Brink," pp. 37–40.
46. For trenchant critiques of the Strategic Defense Initiative, see "Star Wars; Vision and Reality," *The Defense Monitor* 15 (1986) and The Union of Concerned Scientists, *The Fallacy of Star Wars.*
47. Kennan, McNamara, Smith and Bundy, "The President's Choice: Star Wars or Arms Control."
48. Kennan, "Two Letters," p. 78; Kennan, "On Nuclear War," p. 10.
49. *Rocky Mountain News,* May 22, 1983; *New York Times,* May 18, 1983.
50. Cohen, *Sovieticus,* pp. 56–64.
51. Kennan testimony, Subcommittee on Postsecondary Education, House Committee on Education and Labor, 98th. cong., 1st sess., March 22, 1983, p. 52.
52. Hersh, *The Target Is Destroyed.*
53. *New York Times,* Feb. 11, 1984, March 12, 1985.
54. *New York Times,* Nov. 3, 1985; Gorbachev, *Perestroika;* Kennan's review of *Perestroika* appeared in *The New York Review of Books,* Jan. 21, 1988, pp. 3, 6.
55. Kennan review of *Perestroika,* pp. 6, 7.
56. *New York Times,* Nov. 3, 1985.
57. Kennan, "Containment: Then and Now," p. 889.
58. *New York Times,* Dec. 8, 1985.
59. Kennan, "Morality and Foreign Policy," p. 216; Kennan, "Breaking the Spell," p. 49.

60. Kennan, *Atlantic* 247 (January 1981), p. 25; Kennan, "Morality and Foreign Policy," p. 218.

15. Kennan and Postwar Internationalism

1. Kennan to J. A. Lukacs, Oct. 31, 1955, Box 31, Kennan Papers.

2. Kennan, *Memoirs, 1925–1950*, p. 67.

3. The literature on the origins of the Cold War is extensive and controversial. I have drawn on orthodox, revisionist and post-revisionist scholarship in the course of this study (see the notes, especially in chapters two, three and four, and the bibliography). Gaddis, "The Emerging Post-Revisionist Synthesis," and the responses by Gardner, Kaplan, Kimball, and Kuniholm provide an excellent guide to the literature and to the interpretive debate.

4. See the discussion of realism at the beginning of Chapter 3.

5. Gardner, *Architects of Illusion*, p. 285.

6. Kennan, "Containment," All Soul's College seminar notes, April 29, 1969, Box 22, Kennan Papers; Kennan, *Russia, the Atom and the West*, p. 56.

7. Kennan, Russia, the Atom, and the West; Gaddis, *The Long Peace*.

8. Kennan, "Assessment of Foreign Policy," June 23, 1950, Box 24, Kennan Papers; Kennan, "The Soviet Union and the Atlantic Pact," Sept. 8, 1952, reprinted in *Memoirs, 1950–1963*, quote on p. 336; Kennan interview by Hixson.

9. Kennan, "Containment: Then and Now," pp. 889–90.

10. Hunt, *Ideology and U.S. Foreign Policy*.

11. See Kennedy's magisterial *Rise and Fall of the Great Powers*, especially pp. 514–40; Schmeisser, "Is America in Decline?"

BIBLIOGRAPHY

Manuscript Collections

Library of Congress
J. Robert Oppenheimer Papers

George C. Marshall Library, Lexington, Virginia
C. Ben Wright "Kennan Biography Project"

Seeley G. Mudd Manuscript Library, Princeton, N.J.
Hamilton Fish Armstrong Papers
Allen W. Dulles Papers
Albert Einstein Papers
James V. Forrestal Papers
Arthur M. Krock Papers
George F. Kennan Papers
Robert Lansing Papers
J. V. A. MacMurray Papers
Adlai E. Stevenson Papers

National Archives, Washington, D.C.
Record Group 59: Charles Bohlen Papers
Charles Bohlen 123 Personnel File

Bibliography

Decimal File
George F. Kennan 123 Personnel File
Records of the Policy Planning Staff

Harry S. Truman Library Institute, Independence, Missouri

Dean G. Acheson Papers
George M. Elsey Papers
President's Secretary's Files
Charles W. Thayer Papers
Harry S. Truman Papers

Yale University Manuscript Library

Chester W. Bowles Papers
Walter Lippman Papers

Oral Histories

George F. Kennan by Walter L. Hixson, Oct. 18, 1984, Princeton, N.J.

Columbia University

Richard T. Davies by Peter Jessup, Nov. 9, 1979.
Harry Hill by John T. Mason, Jr., Dec. 16, 1968.
Walter Lippmann by Allan Nevins and Dean Albertson, April 6, 1950.
Frank Rounds by Bluma Swerdloff, Sept. 21, 1962.
William T. Stone by John T. Mason, Aug. 6, 1980.

John Foster Dulles Oral History Project, Mudd Library, Princeton, N.J.

George V. Allen by Ed Edwin, March 7, 1967.
George F. Kennan by Richard Challener, March 3, 1967.

John F. Kennedy Oral History Project, John F. Kennedy Library, Boston

George F. Kennan by Louis Fischer, March 23, 1965.

Harry S. Truman Library Institute, Independence, Missouri

Admiral Robert L. Dennison by Jerry Hess, Oct. 6, 1971.
Perry Laukhuff by Richard D. McKinzie, July 3, 1974.
H. Freeman "Doc" Matthews by McKinzie, July 7, 1973.

Bibliography

C. Ben Wright Biography Project, George C. Marshall Library, Lexington, VA

Charles Bohlen by C. Ben Wright, Sept. 28, 1970.
Benjamin V. Cohen by Wright, Sept. 18, 1970.
William A. Crawford by Wright, Sept. 29, 1970.
Loy W. Henderson by Wright, Oct. 3, 1970.
Jeanette Hotchkiss by Wright, Sept. 26, 1960.
Paul Nitze by Wright, Oct. 2, 1970.

Memoirs and Diaries

Acheson, Dean G. *Present at the Creation: My Years in the State Department.*
New York, Norton, 1969.
Bohlen, Charles. *The Transformation of American Foreign Policy.* New York:
Norton, 1969.
—— *Witness to History, 1929–1969* New York, 1973.
Jones, Joseph. *The Fifteen Weeks.* New York, Viking, 1955.
Kennan, George F. *Memoirs, 1925–1950.* Boston: Little, Brown, 1967.
—— *From Prague After Munich: Diplomatic Papers, 1938–1940.* Princeton:
Princeton University Press, 1968.
—— *Memoirs, 1950–1963.* Boston: Little, Brown, 1972.
Murphy, Robert *Diplomat Among Warriors.* New York: Doubleday, 1964.
Talbott, Strobe, ed. *Khrushchev Remembers.* Boston: Little, Brown, 1970.

Government Documents and Congressional Testimony

United States Atomic Energy Commission, "In the Matter of J. Robert Oppenheimer," Transcript of a Hearing Before the Personnel Security Board, April
12–May 6, 1954.
Foreign Relations Series of the United States (FRUS): Diplomatic Papers: (Wash-
ington, D.C.: U.S. Government Printing Office, various years 1952–1987).
Anna K. Nelson, ed., (with a foreword by George F. Kennan), *The State Depart-
ment Policy Planning Staff Papers, 1947–1949,* 3 vols. (New York: Garland
Publishing, Inc., 1983).
U.S. Congress, "Hearings Into Military Assistance in Korea," Selected Executive
Sessions of the House Committee on International Relations, 1943–1950,
Vol. 8, United States Policy in the Far East, Par II, June 16, 17 and 20, 1949.
U.S. Congress, "Loyalty Security Board meeting on John S. Service," Hearings
Before a Subcommittee of the Committee on Foreign Relations, U.S. Senate,
81st Cong., 2nd Sess., pursuant to SR 231, Part 2, Appendix, May 29, 1950.
U.S. Congress, "Nomination of George F. Kennan as ambassador to the Soviet
Union," Executive Sessions of the Senate Foreign Relations Committee: 82nd
Cong., 2nd Sess., 1952, Vol. 4, April 1, 1952.
U.S. Congress, "Hearings Before a Subcommittee of the Committee on Foreign
Relations," U.S. Senate, 85th Cong., 1st Sess., Part 2, Jan. 9 and 10, 1957.

Bibliography

U.S. Congress, "Hearing Before the Subcommittee on National Security Staffing and Operations," House Committee on Foreign Affairs, 86th Cong., 1st sess., Part V, Dec. 11, 1963.

U.S. Congress, "Report on the Sino-Soviet Conflict and Its Implications," U.S. Congress, House Subcommittee on the Far East and the Pacific of the Committee of the Foreign Affairs Committee, 89th Cong., 1st sess., Mar. 11, 1965.

U.S. Congress, "To Amend Further the Foreign Assistance Act of 1961," Hearings on S. 2793 (2 parts), Senate Committee on Foreign Relations, 89th Cong., 2d sess., Feb. 10, 1966.

U.S. Congress, "The Communist World in 1967," Senate Committee on Foreign Relations, 90th Cong., 1st sess., Jan. 30, 1967.

U.S. Congress, "To Provide for the Exchange of Governmental Officials," Senate Foreign Relations Committee, 91st, 2nd sess., Feb. 6, 1970.

U.S. Congress, "U.S. Relations with Europe in the Decade of the 1970s," Subcommittee on Europe Hearings, House Foreign Affairs Committee, 91st Cong., 2nd sess., March 11, 1970.

U.S. Congress, "U.S. Relations with Communist Countries," Hearings Before the Committee on Foreign Relations, United States Senate, 93rd Cong., 2nd sess., Aug. 20, 1974.

U.S. Congress, "Supplementary Detailed Staff Reports on Foreign and Military Intelligence," Church Committee (U.S. Senate) Final Report, Book 4, 1975.

U.S. Congress, Hearings Before the Subcommittee on Europe and the Middle East of the Committee on Internal Relations of the House, 95th Cong., 1st sess., Sept. 27, 1977.

U.S. Congress, Hearings Before the Budget Committee, U.S. Senate, 96th Cong., 2d sess., Feb. 26, 1980.

U.S. Congress, "US Security Requirements in the Near East and South Asia," Senate Foreign Relations Committee, Subcommittee on Near Eastern and South Asian Affairs, 96th Cong., 2d sess., Feb. 27, 1980.

U.S. Congress, "The Soviet-East European Education and Training Act of 1983," Subcommittee on Postsecondary Education, House Committee on Education and Labor, 98th Cong., 1st sess., March 22, 1983.

Books and Articles

Acheson, Dean G. "The Illusion of Disengagement." *Foreign Affairs* (April 1958) 36: 371–82.

Adler, Les K. and Thomas G. Paterson. "Red Fascism: The Merger of Nazi Germany and Soviet Russia in the American Image of Totalitarianism, 1930s–1950s" *American Historical Review* (April 1970) 75: 1046–64.

Allison, Graham T. *The Essence of Decision: Explaining the Cuban Missile Crisis.* Boston: Little, Brown, 1971.

Ambrose, Stephen E. *Eisenhower the President.* New York: Simon and Schuster, 1983.

Bibliography

Ambrose, Stephen E. and Richard H. Immerman. *Ike's Spies: Eisenhower and the Espionage Establishment.* New York: Doubleday, 1981.

Arendt, Hannah. *Origins of Totalitarianism* New York: Harcourt, 1966—originally published in 1951.

Baldwin, Hanson. *Great Mistakes of the War.* New York: Harber and Row, 1950.

Barnet, Richard J. *The Alliance: America, Europe, Japan. Makers of the Postwar World.* New York: Simon and Schuster, 1983.

Berman, Larry. *Planning A Tragedy: The Americanization of the War in Vietnam.* New York: Norton, 1982.

Berger, Marilyn. "Can Carter Handle Him?" *New York Times Magazine,* May 7, 1978.

Beschloss, Michael R. *MAYDAY: Eisenhower, Khrushchev, and the U-2 Affair.* New York: Harper and Row, 1986.

Blum, Robert M. *Drawing the Line: The Origin of the American Containment Policy in East Asia.* New York: Norton, 1982.

Brands, Henry W. Jr. "Redefining the Cold War: American Policy Toward Yugoslavia, 1948–60," *Diplomatic History* 11 (Winter 1987): 41–53.

Brzenski, Zbigniew. *Power and Principle: Memoirs of the National Security Adviser, 1977–81.* New York: Farrar, Straus, Giroux, 1983.

Brown, Eugene. *J. William Fulbright, Advice and Dissent.* Iowa City, 1975.

Burnham, James. *Containment or Liberation? An Inquiry Into the Aims of United States Foreign Policy.* New York: John Day, 1952.

Churchill, Winston S. *The Second World War: Triumph and Tragedy.* Boston: Houghton Mifflin, 1953.

Coffey, John W. *Political Realism in American Thought.* Lewisburg, Maine: Bucknell University Press, 1977.

Cohen, Michael J. *Palestine and the Great Powers, 1945–1948.* Princeton, N.J.: Princeton University Press, 1982.

Cohen, Stephen F. *Rethinking the Soviet Experience.* New York: Norton, 1985.

—— *Sovieticus: American Perceptions and Soviet Realities.* Norton, 1985.

Cole, Wayne S. *Roosevelt and the Isolationists, 1932–1945.* Lincoln, Neb.: University of Nebraska Press, 1983.

Conquest, Robert. *The Great Terror: Stalin's Purge of the Thirties.* New York: Macmillan, 1973.

Cronin, Audrey Kurth. *Great Power Politics and the Struggle over Austria, 1945–1955.* Ithaca, N.Y.: Cornell University Press, 1986.

Cumings, Bruce. *The Origins of the Korean War: Liberation and the Emergence of Separate Regimes, 1945–1947.* Princeton: Princeton University Press, 1981.

——, *Child of Conflict: The Korean-American Relationship, 1943–1953.* Seattle: University of Washington Press, 1983.

Dallek, Robert. *Franklin D. Roosevelt and American Foreign Policy, 1932–1945.* New York: Oxford University Press, 1979.

Deane, John R. *The Strange Alliance: The Story of Our Efforts at Wartime Cooperation with Russia.* New York: Viking Press, 1946.

355

Bibliography

De Santis, Hugh. *The Diplomacy of Silence: The American Foreign Service, the Soviet Union, and the Cold War, 1933–1947*. Chicago, University of Chicago Press, 1979.

Divine, Robert A. *Blowing on the Wind: The Nuclear Test Ban Debate, 1954–1960*. New York: Oxford University Press, 1978.

Dobbs, Charles M. *The Unwanted Symbol: American Foreign Policy, the Cold War, and Korea, 1945–1950*. Kent, Ohio: Kent State University Press, 1981.

Donovan, Robert J. *Conflict and Crisis: The Presidency of Harry S. Truman, 1945–1948*. New York: Norton, 1977.

—— *Tumultuous Years: The Presidency of Harry S Truman, 1949–1953*. New York: Norton, 1982.

Dower, John W. "Occupied Japan and the American Lake, 1945–1950." In Edward Friedman and Mark Selden, eds. *America's Asia: Dissenting Essays on Asian-American Relations*. New York: Random House, 1969, pp. 186–206.

Etzold, Thomas and John L. Gaddis. *Containment: Documents on American Foreign Policy and Strategy*. New York: Columbia University Press, 1978.

Fairlie, Henry. "The Special Senility of the Diplomat." *New Republic,* December 24, 1977, pp. 9–11.

Freeland, Richard M. *The Truman Doctrine and the Origins of McCarthyism: Foreign Policy, Domestic Politics, and Internal Security, 1946–1948*. New York: Knopf, 1972.

Fitzpatrick, Peter Bryan. "George F. Kennan and the National War College." Unpublished MS, Princeton University, 1968.

Foot, Rosemary. *The Wrong War: American Policy and the Divisions of the Korean Conflict, 1950–1953*. Ithaca, N.Y.: Cornell University Press, 1985.

Friedrich, Carl J. *Totalitarianism: Proceedings of a Conference Held at the Academy of Arts and Sciences, March 1953*. Cambridge, Mass: Harvard University Press, 1954.

Fulbright, J. William. *The Arrogance of Power*. New York: Vintage Books, 1966.

Gaddis, John L. "Containment: A Reassessment." *Foreign Affairs* (July 1977) 55: 873–887, and a reply by Eduard Mark in *Foreign Affairs* (January 1978) 56: 430–441.

—— "The Corporatist Synthesis: A Skeptical View." *Diplomatic History* (Fall 1986) 10: 357–62.

—— "The Emerging Post-Revisionist Synthesis on the Origins of the Cold War" and responses by Lloyd C. Gardner, Lawrence S. Kaplan, Warren F. Kimball and Bruce R. Kuniholm. In *Diplomatic History* (Summer 1983) 7: 191–204.

—— *The Long Peace: Inquiries Into the History of the Cold War*. New York: Oxford University Press, 1987.

—— *Strategies of Containment: A Critical Appraisal of Postwar American National Security Policy*. New York: Oxford University Press, 1982.

Galbraith, John Kenneth. *The Affluent Society*. Boston: Houghton-Mifflin, 1958.

Gardner, Lloyd C. *Architects of Illusion: Men and Ideas in American Foreign Policy, 1941–1949*. Chicago: Quadrangle Books, 1970.

—— *Safe for Democracy: The Anglo-American Response to Revolution, 1913–1923*. New York: Oxford University Press, 1987.

Garthoff, Raymond L. *Detente and Confrontation: American-Soviet Relations From Nixon to Reagan*. Washington D.C.: The Brookings Institution, 1985.

Gati, Charles. "What Containment Meant." *Foreign Policy* (Summer 1972) 7: 22–40.

Gelb, Leslie with Richard K. Betts. *The Irony of Vietnam: The System Worked*. Washington: Brookings Institution, 1979.

Gellman, Barton. *Contending With Kennan: Toward a Philosophy of American Power*. New York: Praeger Publishers, 1984.

Gerber, Larry G. "The Baruch Plan and the Origins of the Cold War." *Diplomatic History* 6 (Winter 1982): 69–95.

Getty, J. Arch. *Origins of the Great Purges: The Soviet Communist Party Reconsidered, 1933–1938*. London: Cambridge University Press, 1985.

Gorbachev, Mikhail. *Perestroika*. New York: Harper, 1985.

Grant, Michael. *The Fall of the Roman Empire: A Reappraisal*. Radnor, Pa.: The Annenberg School of Communications, 1976.

Griffith, Robert. *The Politics of Fear: Joseph R. McCarthy and the Senate*. Lexington, Ky.: University of Kentucky Press, 1970.

Halle, Louis. *The Cold War As History*. New York: Harper and Row, 1967.

Harbutt, Fraser. *The Iron Curtain: Churchill, America, and the Origins of the Cold War*. New York: Oxford University Press, 1986.

Harriman, Averell and Elie Abel. *Special Envoy to Churchill and Stalin, 1941–1946*. New York: Random House, 1975.

Harrington, Michael. *The Other America: Poverty in the United States*. New York: Macmillan, 1962.

Herken, Gregg. *The Winning Weapon: The Atomic Bomb in the Cold War, 1945–1950*. New York: Vintage, 1982.

Herring, George C. *Aid to Russia, 1941–1946: Strategy, Diplomacy, and the Origins of the Cold War*. New York: Columbia University Press, 1973.

—— *America's Longest War: The United States in Vietnam, 1950–1975*. New York: Knopf, 1979.

Hersh, Seymour. *The Target Is Destroyed*. New York: Random House, 1986.

Herz, Martin F., ed. *Decline of the West? George Kennan and His Critics*. Washington D.C: Ethics and Public Policy Center, Georgetown University, 1978.

Hess, Gary R. *The United States' Emergence as a Southeast Asian Power, 1940–1950*. New York: Columbia University Press, 1987.

Hofstadter, Richard. *The Paranoid Style in American Politics*. New York: Knopf, 1965.

Hodgson, Godfrey. *America in Our Time*. New York: Vintage, 1976.

Hogan, Michael J. "Corporatism: A Positive Appraisal." *Diplomatic History* (Fall 1986) 10: 363–72.

Bibliography

—— *The Marshall Plan: America, Britain, and the Reconstruction of Western Europe, 1947–1952*. Cambridge: Cambridge University Press, 1987.

Hollander, Paul. "The Two Faces of George Kennan." *Policy Review* (Summer 1985): 30.

Holloway, David. *The Soviet Union and the Arms Race*. New Haven, Conn.: Yale University Press, 1983.

Hunt, Michael. *Ideology and U.S. Foreign Policy*. New Haven, Conn.: Yale University Press, 1987.

Iatrides, John O. *Revolt in Athens*. Princeton: Princeton University Press, 1972.

Isaacson, Walter and Evan Thomas. *The Wise Men. Six Friends and the World They Made: Acheson, Bohlen, Harriman, Kennan, Lovett, McCloy*. New York: Simon and Schuster, 1986.

Jordan, David P. *Gibbon and His Roman Empire*. Urbana, Ill.: University of Illinois Press, 1971.

Kahin, George McT. *Intervention: How America Became Involved in Vietnam*. New York: Knopf, 1986.

Kahn, Ely Jacques. *The China Hands: America's Foreign Service Officers and What Befell Them*. New York: Viking Press, 1975.

Kaiser, Karl, George Leber, Alois Mertes, and Franz-Josef Schulze. "Nuclear Weapons and the Preservation of Peace." *Foreign Affairs* (Summer 1982) 60: 1157–80.

Kalb, Marvin. "The Vital Interests of Mr. Kennan." *New York Times Magazine*, Mar. 27, 1966.

Kaplan, Lawrence S. *NATO and the United States: The Enduring Alliance* Boston: Twayne Publishers, 1988.

Karnow, Stanley. *Vietnam: A History* New York: Viking, 1983.

Kaufman, Burton. *The Korean War: Challenges in Crisis, Credibility, and Command*. New York: Knopf, 1986.

Kennan, George Frost. *Siberia and the Exile System* Chicago: University of Chicago Press, 1958—originally published in 1891.

Kennan, George F. "After the Cold War: American Foreign Policy in the 1970s." *Foreign Affairs*. (October 1972) 51: 210–27.

—— *American Diplomacy. 1900–1950*. Chicago: University of Chicago Press, 1970—originally published in 1951.

—— "Back from the Brink." *Atlantic* (August 1986) 258: 37–40.

—— "Breaking the Spell." *New Yorker*, October 3, 1983, p. 53.

—— "Can We Deal with Moscow?" *Saturday Evening Post*, October 14, 1963, p. 27.

—— "Cease This Madness." *Atlantic* 247 (January 1981): 128.

—— *The Cloud of Danger: Current Realities of American Foreign Policy*. Boston: Little, Brown, 1977.

—— "Concept in Foreign Policy." *Harvard Today* (Autumn 1967): 14.

—— "Containment Then and Now." *Foreign Affairs*. (Spring 1987) 65: 885–90.

—— *The Decline of Bismarck's European Order: Franco-Russian Relations, 1875–1890.* Princeton: Princeton University Press, 1979.

—— *Democracy and the Student Left.* Boston: Little, Brown, 1968.

—— *The Fateful Alliance: France, Russia, and the Coming of the First World War.* New York: Pantheon, 1984.

—— "Flashbacks." *The New Yorker,* February 25, 1985, p. 18.

—— "For the Defense of Europe: A New Approach." *New York Times Magazine,* September 12, 1954, p. 7.

—— "A Fresh Look at Our China Policy," *New York Times Magazine,* November 22, 1964, p. 10.

—— "Hazardous Courses in Southern Africa. *Foreign Affairs* (January 1971) 49: 218–37.

—— "Is War With Russia Inevitable." *Reader's Digest* (March 1950) 56: 1–9.

—— *The Marquis de Custine and His Russia in 1839.* Princeton: Princeton University Press, 1971.

—— "Morality and Foreign Policy." *Foreign Affairs.* (Winter 1985–86) 64: 205–18.

—— "A New Philosophy of Defense." Review of Gene Sharp, *Making Europe Unconquerable. New York Times Book Review,* February 13, 1986, p. 1.

—— *The Nuclear Delusion: Soviet-American Relations in the Atomic Age.* (New York: Pantheon, 1983.

—— Robert McNamara, Gerard Smith, and McGeorge Bundy. "Nuclear Weapons and the Atlantic Alliance." *Foreign Affairs* (Spring 1982) 60: 753–68.

—— "On Nuclear War." *New York Review of Books,* Jan. 21, 1982. p. 10.

—— "Our Foreign Policy Is Paralyzed." *Look,* Nov. 19, 1963, p. 14.

—— "Overdue Changes in Our Foreign Policy." *Harper's* (August 1956) 213: 27–33.

—— "Peaceful Coexistence: A Western View." *Foreign Affairs* (January 1960) 38: 171–90.

—— Robert McNamara, Gerard Smith, and McGeorge Bundy. "The President's Choice: Star Wars or Arms Control" *Foreign Affairs* (Winter 1984–85) 63: 264–78.

—— *Realities of American Foreign Policy.* Princeton: Princeton University Press, 1954.

—— Review of Mikhail Gorbachev's *Perestroika. The New York Review of Books,* Jan. 21, 1988, p. 3.

—— *Russia, the Atom and the West.* New York: Harper, 1958.

—— "Sources of Soviet Conduct." *Foreign Affairs* (July 1947) 25: 566–582.

—— "Training for Statesmanship." *Atlantic* (May 1963) 211:40–43.

—— "Two Views of the Soviet Problem," *New Yorker* November 2, 1981, pp. 55–56.

—— *U.S.-Soviet Relations 1917–1920: Russia Leaves the War,* 2 vols. Princeton, N.J.: Princeton University Press, 1956.

—— *U.S.-Soviet Relations 1917–1920: The Decision to Intervene,* 2 vols. Princeton: Princeton University Press, 1958.

Bibliography

—— "Where Do You Stand on Communism?" *New York Times Magazine,* May 27, 1951, p. 7.

—— "Zero Options." *New York Review of Books,* May 12, 1983, p. 3

Kennedy, David M. *Over Here: The First World War and American Society.* New York: Oxford University Press, 1980.

Kennedy, Paul. *The Rise and Fall of the Great Powers: Economic Change and Military Conflict From 1500 to 2000.* New York: Random House, 1987.

Kerner, Otto, chairman. *Report of the National Advisory Commission of Civil Disorders.* New York Times, 1968.

Khrushchev, Nikita S. *Khrushchev Remembers,* Strobe Talbott, ed. Boston: Little, Brown, 1970.

—— "Peaceful Coexistence," *Foreign Affairs* (October 1959) 38:1 –19.

Kirkpatrick, Jeane "Dictatorships and Double Standards." *Commentary* (November 1979) 68: 34–45.

Kissinger, Henry A. *The Troubled Partnership: A Reappraisal of the Atlantic Alliance.* New York: McGraw-Hill, 1965.

—— *White House Years.* Boston: Little, Brown, 1979.

Kovrig, Bennett *The Myth of Liberation: East-Central Europe in U.S. Diplomacy and Politics Since 1941.* Baltimore: The Johns Hopkins University Press, 1973.

Kubricht, A Paul. "Politics and Foreign Policy: a Brief Look at the Kennedy Administration's Eastern European Diplomacy." *Diplomatic History* (Winter 1987) 11: 41–53.

Kuklick, Bruce. *American Policy and the Division of Germany: The Clash With Russia Over Reparations.* Ithaca, N.Y.: Cornell University Press, 1972.

Kunilholm, Bruce R. *The Origins of the Cold War in the Near East: Great Power Conflict and Diplomacy in Iran, Turkey and Greece.* Princeton: Princeton University Press, 1980.

LaFeber, Walter, ed. *The Origins of the Cold War: A Historical Problem with Interpretations and Documents.* New York: Wiley, 1971.

Larson, Deborah Welch. *Origins of Containment: A Psychological Explanation.* Princeton: Princeton University Press, 1985.

Leffler, Melvyn P. *The Elusive Quest: America's Pursuit of European Stability and French Security, 1919–1933.* Chapel Hill, N.C.: University of North Carolina Press, 1979.

—— "Strategy, Diplomacy, and the Cold War: The United States, Turkey, and NATO, 1945–1952." *Journal of American History* (March 1985) 71: 807–25.

Levering, Ralph *American Opinion and the Russian Alliance.* Chapel Hill, N.C.: University of North Carolina Press, 1976.

Levin, N. Gordon. *Woodrow Wilson and World Politics.* New York: Oxford University Press, 1968.

Lippmann, Walter. *The Cold War: A Study in U.S. Foreign Policy.* New York: Harper, 1947.

—— "Mr. Kennan and Reappraisal in Europe." *The Atlantic* (April 1958) 201: 33–35.

Luttwak, Edward N. "The Strange Case of GFK: From Containment to Isolation." *Commentary* (November 1977) 64: 30–35.

McCormick, Thomas J. "Drift or Mastery: A Corporatist Synthesis for American Diplomatic History." *Reviews in American History* (December 1982) 10: 318–30.

McLellan, David S. *Dean Acheson: The State Department Years.* New York: Dodd, Mead, 1976.

McMahon, Robert J. *Colonialism and Cold War: The United States and the Struggle for Indonesian Independence, 1945–1949.* Ithaca, N.Y.: Cornell University Press, 1981.

Maddox, Robert James. *The New Left and the Origins of the Cold War.* Princeton: Princeton University Press, 1973.

Major, John. *The Oppenheimer Hearing.* New York: Stein and Day, 1971.

Martin, John Bartlow. *Adlai Stevenson and the World.* New York: Doubleday, 1977.

Mastny, Vojtech. *Russia's Road to the Cold War: Diplomacy, Warfare, and the Politics of Communism, 1941–1945.* New York: Columbia University Press, 1979.

Matray, James I. *The Reluctant Crusade: American Foreign Policy in Korea, 1941–1950.* Honolulu: University of Hawaii Press, 1985.

May, Gary. *China Scapegoat: The Diplomatic Ordeal of John Carter Vincent.* Washington, D.C.: New Republic Books, 1979).

Mayers, David. "Containment and the Primacy of Diplomacy: George Kennan's Views, 1947–1948." *International Security* (Summer 1986) 11: 124–162.

—— *George Kennan and the Dilemmas of U.S. Foreign Policy.* New York: Oxford University Press, 1988.

—— "Nazi Germany and the Future of Europe: George Kennan's Views, 1939–1945." *International History Review* (November 1986) 8: 550–72.

Medvedev, Roy A. *Let History Judge: The Origins and Consequences of Stalinism.* New York: Knopf, 1968—revised and enlarged edition, New York: Columbia University Press, 1989.

Messer, Robert L. *The End of Alliance: James F. Byrnes, Roosevelt, Truman, and the Origins of the Cold War.* Chapel Hill, N.C.: The University of North Carolina Press, 1982.

Millis, Walter, ed. *The Forrestal Diaries.* New York: Viking Press, 1951.

Miscamble, Wilson D. "George F. Kennan, the Policy Planning Staff, and American Foreign Policy, 1947–1949." Ph.D. dissertation, University of Notre Dame, 1979.

Morgan, Edmund S. *The Puritan Dilemma: The Story of John Winthrop.* Boston: Little, Brown and Co., 1958.

Morgenthau, Hans J. *Politics Among Nations: The Struggle for Power and Peace.* New York: Knopf, 1965.

Bibliography

Moynihan, Daniel, ed. *Encounters With Kennan: The Great Debate*. London: Frank Cass and Co., 1979.

Murray, Robert K. *Red Scare: A Study in National Hysteria*. Minneapolis: University of Minnesota Press, 1955.

Navasky, Victor S. *Naming Names*. New York: Penguin Books, 1980.

Nelson, Anna K. "President Truman and the Evolution of the National Security Council. *Journal of American History* (September 1985) 72: 360–78.

Newhouse, John. *DeGaulle and the Anglo-Saxons*. New York: Viking, 1970.

Newsom, David. *The Soviet Brigade in Cuba: A Study in Political Diplomacy*. Bloomington: Ind.: Indiana University Press, 1987.

O'Connor, Raymond G. *Diplomacy for Victory: FDR and Unconditional Surrender*. New York: Norton, 1971.

O'Neill, William. *Coming Apart: An Informal History of America in the 1960s*. Chicago: Quadrangle, 1971.

Oshinsky, David M. *A Conspiracy So Immense: The World of Joe McCarthy*. New York: Free Press, 1983.

Packard, Vance. *The Hidden Persuaders*. New York: David McKay, 1957.

Parmet, Herbert S. *Jack: The Struggles of John F. Kennedy*. New York: Dial Press, 1980.

Paterson, Thomas G. *Soviet-American Confrontation: Postwar Reconstruction and the Origins of the Cold War*. Baltimore: Johns Hopkins University Press, 1973.

Paterson, Thomas G., ed. *Kennedy's Quest for Victory: American Foreign Policy, 1961–1963*. New York: Oxford University Press, 1989.

Pells, Richard H. *The Liberal Mind in a Conservative Age: American Intellectuals in the 1940s and 1950s*. New York: Harper, 1985.

Porter, Gareth. *A Peace Denied: The United States, Vietnam, and the Paris Agreements*. Bloomington, Ind.: Indiana University Press, 1975.

Propas, Frederic L. "Creating a Hard Line Toward Russia: The Training of State Department Soviet Experts, 1927–1937." *Diplomatic History* (Summer 1984) 8: 208–26.

Prittie, Terence. "Have the 'Kennan Plans' Come Too Late?" *New Republic*, December 30, 1957, p. 13.

Quester, George H. *Nuclear Diplomacy: The First Twenty-Five Years*. New York: Dunellen, 1970.

Rearden, Steven J. *The Evolution of American Strategic Doctrine: Paul H. Nitze and the Soviet Challenge*. Boulder, Co.: Westview Press, 1984.

Resis, Albert. "The Churchill-Stalin Agreement on the Balkans, Moscow, October, 1944." *American Historical Review* (April 1978) 83: 368–87.

Riesman, David. *The Lonely Crowd: A Study of the Changing American Character*. New Haven, Conn: Yale University Press, 1950.

Rostow, Eugene V. "Searching for Kennan's Grand Design." *Yale Law Journal* (June 1978), pp. 1527–48.

Rotter, Andrew J. *The Path to Vietnam: Origins of the American Commitment to Southeast Asia*. Ithaca, N.Y.: Cornell University Press, 1987.

Rounds, Frank. "Diary of a U.S. Embassy Man." *U.S. News and World Report,* Nov. 28, 1952, p. 106.

Roszak, Theodore. *The Making of a Counter-Culture.* Garden City, N.Y.: Doubleday, 1969.

Rubin, Barry. *Paved With Good Intentions: The American Experience and Iran.* New York: Oxford University Press, 1980.

Ruddy, T. Michael. *The Cautious Diplomat: Charles E. Bohlen and the Soviet Union, 1929–1969.* Kent, Ohio: Kent State University Press, 1986.

Salisbury, Harrison. "The View from Mokhovaya Street." *New York Times Magazine,* June 1, 1952, p. 33.

Schaller, Michael. *The American Occupation of Japan: The Origins of the Cold War in Asia.* New York: Oxford University Press, 1985.

Schell, Jonathan. *The Fate of the Earth.* New York: Avon Books, 1983.

Schlesinger, Arthur Jr. *A Thousand Days: John F. Kennedy in the White House.* Boston: Houghton Mifflin, 1965.

Schmeisser, Peter. "Taking Stock: Is America in Decline?" *New York Times Magazine,* April 17, 1988, p. 24.

Schrecker, Ellen W. *No Ivory Tower: McCarthyism and the Universities.* New York: Oxford University Press, 1986.

Schulzinger, Robert D. *The Making of the Diplomatic Mind: The Training, Outlook, and Style of the United States Foreign Service Officers, 1908–1931.* Middletown, Conn.: Wesleyan University Press, 1975.

Seaborg, Glenn T. *Kennedy, Khrushchev, and the Test Ban.* Berkeley: University of California Press, 1981.

Seabury, Paul. "Reinspecting Containment." In Aaron Wildavsky, ed. *Beyond Containment: Alternative Policies Toward the Soviet Union.* San Francisco: Institute for Contemporary Studies, 1983.

—— "George Kennan Vs. Mr. 'X'." *New Republic,* December 16, 1981, p. 17.

Sherry, Michael S. *Preparing for the Next War: American Plans for Postwar Defense, 1941–1945.* New Haven, Conn.: Yale University Press, 1977.

Shulman, Marshall. *Stalin's Foreign Policy Reappraised.* Cambridge: Harvard University Press, 1963.

De Silva, Peer. *Sub Rosa: The CIA and the Uses of Intelligence.* New York: Times Books, 1978.

Smith, Gaddis. *Morality, Reason, and Power: American Diplomacy in the Carter Years.* New York: Hill and Wang, 1986.

Smith, Michael Joseph. *Realist Thought from Weber to Kissinger.* Baton Rouge, La: Louisiana State University Press, 1986.

Steel, Ronald. "Man Without a Country." *New York Review of Books,* January 4, 1968, p. 8.

—— *Walter Lippmann and the American Century.* New York: Random House, 1980.

Stephanson, Anders. *Kennan and the Art of Foreign Policy.* Cambridge: Harvard University Press, 1989.

Bibliography

Stiller, Jesse H. *George S. Messersmith: Diplomat of Democracy*. Chapel Hill: University of North Carolina Press, 1987.

Stueck, William. *The Road to Confrontation: American Policy Toward China and Korea, 1947–1950*. Chapel Hill, N.C.: University of North Carolina Press, 1981.

Sulzberger, Cyrus L. *A Long Row of Candles: Memoirs and Diaries*. New York: Macmillan, 1969.

Talbott, Strobe. *Deadly Gambits: The Reagan Administration and the Stalemate in Nuclear Arms Control*. New York: Knopf, 1984.

Taubman, William. *Stalin's American Policy: From Entente to Detente to Cold War*. New York: Norton, 1982.

Theoharis, Athan. *Seeds of Repression: Harry S. Truman and the Origins of McCarthyism*. Chicago: Quadrangle, 1971.

Thompson, Kenneth W. *Political Realism and the Crisis of World Politics: An American Approach to Foreign Policy*. Princeton, N.J.: Princeton University Press, 1960.

De Tocqueville, Alexis. *Democracy in America*. J. P. Mayer, ed. New York: Harper and Row, 1969.

Tucker, Nancy B. *Patterns in the Dust: Chinese-American Relations*. New York: Columbia University Press, 1983.

Tucker, Robert C. *Stalin As A Revolutionary, 1879–1929: A Study in History and Personality*. New York: Norton, 1973.

—— *Stalinism: Essays in Historical Interpretation*. New York: Norton, 1977.

Ulam, Adam. *Dangerous Relations: The Soviet Union in World Politics, 1970–82*. New York: Oxford University Press, 1983.

—— *Expansion and Coexistence: Soviet Foreign Policy, 1917–1973*. New York: Praeger, 1973.

—— *The Rivals: America and Russia Since World War II*. New York: Viking, 1971.

Union of Concerned Scientists. *The Fallacy of Star Wars*. New York: Vintage, 1983.

Walker, J. Samuel. *Henry Wallace and American Foreign Policy*. Westport, Conn.: Greenwood Press, 1976.

Walt, Stephen M. *The Origins of Alliances*. Ithaca, N.Y.: Cornell University Press, 1987.

Walton, Richard J. *Cold War and Counterrevolution: The Foreign Policy of John F. Kennedy*. New York: Viking, 1972.

Weil, Martin. *A Pretty Good Club, The Founding Fathers of the U.S. Foreign Service*. New York: Norton, 1978.

Whetten, Lawrence L. *Germany's Ostpolitik*. New York: Oxford University Press, 1971.

Whyte, William. *The Organization Man*. New York: Doubleday, 1956.

Wieseltier, Leon. "Liberals Against Liberty." *New Republic*, February 10, 1982, p. 20.

Williams, William A. *The Tragedy of American Diplomacy*. New York: Dell, 1972—originally published, 1959.

Wilson, Duncan. *Tito's Yugoslavia*. Cambridge: Cambridge University Press, 1979.

Wittner, Lawrence S. *American Intervention in Greece, 1943–1949*. New York: Columbia University Press, 1982.

Wright, C. Ben. "George F. Kennan: Scholar-Diplomat." Ph.D. dissertation, University of Wisconsin, 1972.

—— "Mr. 'X' and Containment." *Slavic Review* (March 1976) 35: 1–36.

Yergin, Daniel. *Shattered Peace: The Origins of the Cold War and the National Security State*. Boston: Houghton Mifflin Co., 1977.

INDEX

Acheson, Dean G., 59, 65, 82, 119, 134, 141, 156, 197-98, 201, 308; defends Kennan from Soviet criticism, 127-29; supports Kennan's containment policy, 34; Kennan advises on atomic weapons, 38-39; and Marshall Plan, 51, 52, 54; opposes Kennan on German reunification, 86-90; and military buildup, 90, 91, 96; and Korean conflict, 102, 103, 106, 107, 110, 112, 114; reinforces NATO, 120; and Soviet anti-American propaganda, 123, 124; and anti-communist hysteria, 159, 161, 166, 170; and Reith Lectures, 178, 180-83, 185-86, 188

Achilles, Theodore, 159

Adams, John Quincy, 254

Adams, Ware, 52

Adenauer, Konrad, 120-21, 140, 177, 178, 199, 264

Advertising, 10, 243-45, 248

Affluent Society, The (Galbraith), 242

Afghanistan, Soviet war in, 271-77, 279, 280, 281, 294

Africa, North, 254, 271; communist threat in, 60-61, 69, 71; and race, 251; Horn of, 269

Aiken, George, 236

Albania, 59, 205-8

Allen, George V., 136

Alsop, Joseph, 134, 144, 149-50, 178

Alsop, Stuart, 134, 144

Ambrose, Stephen, 140

Amerasia, 157-60, 163

American Academy of Arts and Letters, 250

American Broadcasting Company (ABC), 230

"American Century," 100, 240

American Committee on U.S.-Soviet Relations, 270

American Communist Party, 160, 161

American Council on Germany, 181

American Diplomacy, 1900–1950 (Kennan), 48, 118, 307

American Society of Newspaper Editors, 146

Andropov, Yuri, 293

Angola, civil war in, 268-69, 305

Anti-ballistic missiles (ABMs), 266, 292

Apartheid, 251

Arabs, 251, 256

Arms control. *See* Strategic Arms Limitation Talks (SALT)

Arms race. *See* Nuclear weapons

Armstrong, Hamilton Fish, 41, 82, 184, 207

Arneson, R. Gordon, 93-94

Index

Aron, Raymond, 178
Arts, 244-45, 250
Asia, 251, 254. *See also* China; Japan; Southeast Asia
Aspen Institute for Humanistic Studies, 291
Assembly of Captive European Nations, 148
Atlantic, 162-63, 283
Atlee, Clement, 27
Atomic bomb. *See* Nuclear weapons
Atomic Energy Commission (AEC), 39, 91-92, 146, 167-69
Austria, 25, 56, 139, 184, 186; social insurance in, 7-8; reconstruction of, 74, 81; neutralization of, 143-44, 154, 211
Automobile, 10, 242-43, 248
Azores, 17

Bad Nauheim, Germany, 17
Balance of power, 16, 141, 184, 191, 300; Kennan on, 47-50, 71, 118
Baldwin, Hanson, 118
Ball, George, 201, 232
Baltimore Sun, 127-28
Bao Dai, 224
Baruch, Bernard, 39
Bay of Pigs invasion, 205, 206
Beard, Charles A., 9, 252
Beard, Mary, 9
Belgrade, 202, 206-8. *See also* Yugoslavia
Benton, William, 32
Beria, Lavrenti, 139
Berlin, 15, 88, 105, 140, 304; Kennan studies in, 6; Kennan assigned to, 17; Blockade of, 78-80, 83, 84, 89, 111; Kennan condemns USSR in, 127-19, 134-35; East-West conflict in, 174, 184, 188, 189, 204-6, 208; Wall in, 192, 204, 206; Quadripartite Agreement on, 264
Bevan, Aneurin, 177
Bevin, Ernest, 75-76
Bismarck, Otto von, 6
Blacks, 8, 247-52, 254
Bly, Robert, 250
Bohlen, Charles ("Chip"), 17, 22, 28, 79, 119, 128, 136, 204; with Kennan in Moscow, 12; at Yalta summit, 25; Kennan replaces, 89-90; on Kennan, 97; and Korean War, 106, 108; named ambassa-

dor to USSR, 137; and Marshall Plan, 54, 55
Bolshevik Revolution. *See* Russian Revolution
Bombing, of North Vietnam, 226-27, 230, 232, 235-37
Boorstin, Daniel, 241
Borba, 207, 215
Boston Globe, 136-37
Bowles, Chester, 143, 151
Brandt, Willy, 260-61, 264-65
Brentano, Heinrich von, 177
Bretton Woods Conference, 27
Brezhnev, Leonid, 263, 264, 280, 287, 293
British Broadcasting Corporation (BBC), 171-76, 179, 180
Brodie, Bernard, 34
Brown, Sam, 249
Brownell, Herbert, 166
Brussels Pact, 75-77
Bryce, James, 240
Brzezinski, Zbigniew, 270
Buckley, William F., 272
Bulganin, Nikolai, 139, 143, 180
Bulgaria, 24, 25, 59
Bulletin of Atomic Scientists, 190
Bullitt, William C., 5, 11-13, 147-48
Bundy, McGeorge, 204, 210-11, 215, 261, 289, 287-91
Bundy, William, 289
Butler, George, 52
Byrnes, James F., 29, 32

Cabot, John Moors, 209
Cambodia, 236
Canada, 39, 61-62, 77, 87, 91, 167
Capitalism, 50, 54, 81
Captive Nations Week, 203-4, 217
Carnegie Foundation, 98
Carter, Jimmy, 270-74, 277
Carter Doctrine, 273
Case, Clifford, 232
Casey, Bob, 214
Castro, Fidel, 205
Central America, 291. *See also* Latin America
Central Intelligence Agency (CIA), 125, 126, 137, 139, 178, 224; creation of, 52, 57-58; Kennan offered position with, 136;

Index

Index

Greece, 76, 114, 256; liberation of, 24; Soviet threat to, 58-61; civil war in, 211; Greenberg, Clement, 244-45
Grew, Joseph C., 4
Gromyko, Andrei, 262
Gross, Ernest R., 251
Gross National Product, U.S., 241

Haig, Alexander, 286, 289
Halle, Louis, 31, 41
Hallstein Doctrine, 264
Hamburg, 6, 15
Hanoi, 235, 236
Hapsburg Empire, 16
Harper's, 144, 283
Harriman, W. Averell, 26, 27, 147, 204, 294; urges Kennan appointment in Moscow, 22; as influence on Kennan, 24
Harrington, Michael, 242
Hartz, Louis, 241
Harvard University, 98, 181, 197, 261
Helsinki Conference, 267-68, 270-72
Henderson, Loy, 5, 31
Herter, Christian, 210
Hickerson, John D., 77, 82, 94, 97
Hidden Persuaders, The (Packard), 244
Hill, Harry, 32
Hippies. *See* Counter-culture; Student protests
Hiss, Alger, 156, 166
Hitler, Adolf, 75, 78, 88, 118, 121, 184, 230-31, 248; Kennan's view of, 15; invades Soviet Union, 16. *See also* Germany; Nazis
Hobbes, Thomas, 48
Ho Chi Minh, 68, 104, 223, 232, 234, 237
Hofstadter, Richard, 169, 241
Hollander, Paul, 280
Honecker, Erich, 264
Hook, Sidney, 241
Horn of Africa, 269
House Committee on Un-American Activities, 156
House Ways and Means Committee, 208, 213
Hughes, Emmett John, 137
Humphrey, Hubert, 178, 182
Hungary, 25, 148; Soviet takeover of, 24;

uprising of 1956 in, 131, 148-51, 186, 203, 208, 262; and Reith proposals, 185, 186; Hunt, Michael, 306
Hurley, Patrick J., 159
Husak, Gustav, 262
Hydrogen bomb, 283, 292, 302; decision to build, 73, 91-94, 96, 97, 168. *See also* Nuclear weapons

India, 68, 222-23, 274
Indochina, French conflict in, 68-69, 104, 107, 138, 222-24, 227. *See also* Vietnam
Indonesia, 68
Industrialization, 10, 40
Institute for Advanced Study, 98, 108, 117-18, 142, 167-68, 197, 252
Intercontinental ballistic missiles (ICBMs), 173, 189-91
Internal Security Subcommittee, 164-66
International Association of Cultural Freedom, 249
International Monetary Fund (IMF), 27, 29, 55
Iran, 61-62, 104, 105, 280; Soviet threat to, 29, 32; U.S. hostages in, 271-72, 277, 279; U.S. and Shah of, 273; Iraq, 272
Israel, 69, 146, 151-52, 256
Italy, 76, 135-36, 211; reconstruction of, 51, 53, 56; communist threat in, 75, 58, 60

Jackson, Henry M., 267, 271
Japan, 87, 138, 153, 158, 237, 300; growing power of, 11; surrenders, 28; and containment policy, 43; reconstruction of, 47, 49, 50, 62-65, 71; and Korean conflict, 102, 107, 108, 114, 121; U.S. Treaty with, 107, 132; atomic bombing of, 190; threatened by communism in Southeast Asia, 222
Jaruzelski, Wojchiech, 275, 276
Jews, 8, 16, 69, 266-67, 271
Jiang Jieshi, 101, 102, 113; fall of, 66, 90-91; Kennan condemns, 153; charged with corruption, 157-59; Johnson, Joseph, 52
Johnson, Louis, 91, 94
Johnson, Lyndon B., 204, 305; and Viet-

nam War, 226-35, 238; Soviet policy under, 260-62; Joint Chiefs of Staff, U.S., 18, 65, 79, 112, 126, 290
Justice, U.S. Department of, 164

Kaiser, Karl, 290
Kalb, Marvin, 231
Kalinin, Mikhail, 12
Kaufman, Burton I., 103
Kelley, Robert F., 6, 14
Kellog-Briand Pact, 133, 285
Kennan, Annelise Sorensen, 8, 12, 15, 216
Kennan, George (cousin), 5-6, 12
Kennan, George Frost: birth and childhood of, 1-3, 5; studies at Princeton, 3; enters Foreign Service, 3-6; illnesses of, 7-8, 13, 18, 22, 29, 73, 75, 97, 181, 301; early authoritarian views of, 7-10; opposes U.S. recognition of USSR, 11-12; holds various Foreign Service posts, 12-18; opposes Grand Alliance, 18-19, 21-28; publishes "Russia—Seven Years Later," 23-24; reactions to Long Telegram of, 29-32; assigned to National War College, 32-33; writes and lectures on containment, 33-40; reactions to X-Article of, 40-45; becomes Policy Planning Staff director, 47, 51; as political realist, 48-50, 133, 196; and European Recovery Act, 52-56; supports CIA creation, 56-58; and Soviet threat in Mediterranean, 58-61; and reconstruction of Japan, 62-65; and fall of China, 65-67; and Third World containment, 67-72; Lippmann on X-Article of, 73-74; opposes NATO creation, 74-78, 80; and Berlin Blockade, 78-80; Program A of, 82-84; on Yugoslav-Soviet breach, 84-85; replaced on National Security Council, 86-87; proposes European federation, 87-89; opposes Truman military buildup, 90-94; and NSC-68, 94-97; at Institute for Advanced Study, 98, 117-18; and Korean War, 99, 101-15; on failure of U.S. diplomacy, 100-101; publishes *American Diplomacy*, 118; as ambassador to Moscow, 117, 119-30, 164-66, 170, 207-8; opposes West German rearmament, 120-21, 140-41; retires from State Depart-

ment, 130, 135-37, 162, 218, 303, 307-8; clashes with Dulles on containment, 131-37; advises Eisenhower administration, 137-39; becomes involved in Democratic politics, 141-42; advises Stevenson campaign, 142-48; on futility of liberation policy, 147-48; reacts to unrest in Eastern Europe, 148-51; and Suez crisis, 151-52; on Arab nationalism, 152-53; urges defense of Quemoy and Matsu, 153; defends China experts in State Department, 155, 157-67; targets domestic communists, 156-57; defends Oppenheimer, 155, 167-70; impact of Reith Lectures of, 171-94; publishes studies of U.S.-Soviet relations, 195-97; desires post in Kennedy administration, 197-201; as ambassador to Yugoslavia, 201-19, 221, 225, 230; publishes *Memoirs*, 221-22; and Vietnam War, 221-38; critical of U.S. internationalism, 239-40, 251-57; on U.S. society and culture, 240-46; and student protests, 246-51, 286-87; urges détente with USSR, 259-62, 265-70; and Soviet invasion of Czechoslovakia, 262-64; on normalization of relations with China, 265; and Iran hostage crisis, 271-72; and Soviet invasion of Afghanistan, 271-75; on unrest in Poland, 275-76; opposes Reagan policies, 279-96; publishes World War I study, 283-85; and "no first use" campaign, 287-91; on Gorbachev reforms, 297-309; and postwar internationalism, 297-309
Kennan, Kossuth ("Kent"), 2
Kennan Institute for Advanced Russian Studies, 283
Kennedy, John F., 247, 287; Kennan desires position under, 195, 198-200; Kennan's opinion of, 198, 218, 260; names Kennan ambassador to Yugoslavia, 201; and U.S. relations with Yugoslavia, 203, 209-11, 213-16; at Vienna summit, 203-4; and Cuban Missile Crisis, 205; death of, 218; and Vietnam, 225, 228-29
Kennedy, Joseph P., 198
Kennedy, Robert F., 235
Kerner Commission, 250
Khomeini, Ayatollah, 272

Index

Index

Index

Index

Ude-Ural, 203
Ukrainian Bulletin (journal), 178
Ulbricht, Walter, 148, 264
Union of Soviet Socialist Republics (USSR), 1, 10, 240, 245, 252; Kennan's early attitudes toward, 5-7; question of U.S. recognition of, 11-12; Kennan fills post in, 12-14; U.S. wartime alliance with, 15-19, 21-26; formulation of containment policy toward, 26-45; Kennan on balance of power and, 49-50, 71-72; stalls on German peace treaty, 51; reacts to Marshall Plan, 53-56; fears of European disruption by, 56-58; seen as threat in Mediterranean, 58-61; and reconstruction of Japan, 62-65; as influence in China, 65-66; and Third World nationalism, 66-69; Lippmann on power of, 73-74; and Truman policies, 73-98; and coup in Czechoslovakia, 74-75; reacts to NATO formation, 76-78, 80; and Berlin Blockade, 78-80; tests atom bomb, 90-91, 94; and Korean War, 99-114, 123-29; Kennan as ambassador to, 112, 117, 119-30, 164-66, 170, 207-8; and Eisenhower policies, 131-54; after Stalin's death, 138-39, 148; and Geneva summit, 143-44; and unrest in Eastern Europe, 148-51; and Suez crisis, 152; and anti-communist hysteria in U.S., 155, 160, 170; and Reith proposals, 171-93; launches *Sputnik,* 173, 174; mounts diplomatic offensive against West, 173-74, 179-80; signs treaty with East Germany, 189; Kennan's studies of U.S. relations with, 196-97; Kennan advises Kennedy on, 198-200; Tito's relations with, during Kennedy administration, 201-3, 205-12, 217; escalation of tensions with, 204-5; and Vietnam, 224-28, 232, 237; Kennan on Middle East role of, 256; efforts toward détente with, 259-62; invades Czechoslovakia, 262-65, 272, 277; and Nixon policies, 264-68; and Ford policies, 268-70; and Carter policies, 270-77; invades Afghanistan, 271-77; and Reagan policies, 279-96; *Nuclear Delusion* on, 285-86; and "no first use," 287-91; downs Korean airliner, 293; under Gorbachev, 293-95; and

U.S. postwar-internationalism, 297-308; United Nations (UN), 26, 27, 30, 32, 69, 75-76, 152, 201, 272; Kennan critical of, 49, 99; and European recovery, 54; and Korean War, 107-13; question of China's admission to, 132-33, 153, 206; Tito visits, 216; and Vietnam, 232. *See also* Atomic Energy Commission

United States: Kennan's early views on democracy in, 7-11, 14; recognizes USSR, 11-12; deterioration of Soviet relations with, 13-14; allied with USSR in World War II, 15-19, 21-25; consensus for containment in, 21-45; at wartime summits, 25-29; and globalization of containment, 21-45; *American Diplomacy* on foreign policy of, 48-50; and European Recovery Program, 51-57; creates CIA, 57-59; enunciates Truman Doctrine, 59; and militarization of containment, 73-98; and NATO creation, 75-78; Berlin airlift by, 78-79; in Kennan's European federation plan, 87-88; Truman military buildup in, 90-96; Kennan on failure of diplomacy by, 99-100; in Korean War, 99-115; Soviet propaganda campaign against, 123-24; Republicans attack containment policy of, 131-33; Eisenhower becomes president of, 132; and Geneva summit, 143-44; presidential race of 1956 in, 144-48; and Suez crisis, 151-52; anti-communist hysteria in, 155-70; media reactions to Reith proposals in, 178; Kennan's study of Soviet relations with, 196-97; presidential race of 1960 in, 197-200; increase in tensions between USSR and, 204-5; Tito visits, 215-16; in Vietnam War, 221-38; presidential race of 1968 in, 235; Kennan rejects international role for, 239-40, 251-54; Kennan on culture and society of, 240-46; political protests in, 246-51; Johnson becomes president of, 260; Nixon becomes president of, 264; moves toward normalized relations with China, 265; and SALT agreements, 265-66, 273, 282; Kennan argues against Angola intervention by, 268-69; presidential race of 1976 in, 270; Iran hostages of, 271-72; Reagan be-